AGAINST
FRAGMENTATION

AGAINST
FRAGMENTATION

THE ORIGINS OF MARXISM
AND THE SOCIOLOGY OF INTELLECTUALS

ALVIN W. GOULDNER

New York   Oxford
OXFORD UNIVERSITY PRESS
1985

Oxford University Press

Oxford   London   New York   Toronto
Delhi   Bombay   Calcutta   Madras   Karachi
Kuala Lumpur   Singapore   Hong Kong   Tokyo
Nairobi   Dar es Salaam   Cape Town
Melbourne   Auckland

and associated companies in
Beirut   Berlin   Ibadan   Mexico City   Nicosia

Published by Oxford University Press, Inc.,
200 Madison Avenue, New York, New York 10016

Library of Congress Cataloging in Publication Data
Gouldner, Alvin Ward, 1920–1981
Against fragmentation.
Includes index.
1. Communism and intellectuals—History—19th
century.   2. Communism and society—History—19th
century.   3. Communism—History—19th century.
4. Antisemitism—Germany—History—19th century.
5. Marx, Karl, 1818–1883.   I. Title.
HX528.G68   1983   335.4   82-22400
ISBN 0-19-503303-5

Printing (last digit):   9 8 7 6 5 4 3 2 1
Printed in the United States of America

*I walk among men as among the fragments of
the future—that future which I envisage.
And this is all my creating and striving,
that I create and carry together into
one what is fragment and riddle and
dreadful accident.*

> Nietzsche

Preface

In his preface to *The Two Marxisms*, Alvin Gouldner projected an additional three volumes to complete the sustained critique of Marxism he had promised in *The Coming Crisis of Western Sociology*. These volumes were to deal with, respectively, post-Marxist Marxists, the technical and sociohistorical origins of Marxism, and the rationality and limits of Marxism. Clearly, he had revised his intention to write separate volumes on the origins of Marxism and on its rationality and limits, because this book collapses the originally distinct treatments into one volume. It is a study of how the social, political, historical, theoretical, and cultural origins of Marxism shaped both its creative rationality and—simultaneously—the limits to that rationality.

Here Gouldner combines the close textual reading and social history characteristic of *The Two Marxisms* with the theory of discourse he had elaborated in *The Dialectic of Ideology and Technology* and the class analysis of *The Future of Intellectuals and the Rise of the New Class*. He is thereby able to grasp Marxism as a *totality*: as a politics, as an ideological discourse, as a culture, as an organization, and as a class project. At the same time he returns to themes from *The Dialectic* and *The Future of Intellectuals* within the context of a study of a specific politics and class ideology. *Against Fragmentation* applies resources developed by Gouldner over the last decade to the topic of Marxism. It also allows us to appraise those resources as effective means to understanding the sources of both Marxist rationality and irrationality, and reinserts the accomplishments of earlier work into the project on Marxism. The third and final volume of that project is currently in preparation and will comprise a study of post-Marxists, including Lenin, Stalin, Lukács, Gramsci, Sorel, Mao, and Althusser.

Something should also be said of Gouldner's longer-range project which this particular volume fits into but does not complete. This project inspired him all his days: Sociology, he said, was to reclaim society for man. He never lost faith in the importance of sociology as an enterprise despite its academic vicissitudes and trivializations, but it was not for the technicians, social or others, that social science was to be developed. It was to establish a liberative understanding of the social totality that could mitigate against the fragmentation of modern everyday life.

Gouldner saw Marxism as one such attempt: a project inspired in its analysis of reality by a vision of the larger context but ultimately flawed in its ability to return society to man. He felt that inherent in all "grand" systems—systems attempting a noble holism as Marxism did—is the ever-present danger of succumbing to discontinuity, to forgetting, to fragmentation. Whereas this present work is an account of how such fragmentation occurred in Marxism—keeping the whole beyond its reach—it is finally a call to social theory, personified in a community of critical theorists, to become the agent to develop a cognitive rationality capable at last of treading the delicate path between recovery and holism. Thus, it was Gouldner's belief, would society be reclaimed for man.

At the time of Gouldner's death, *Against Fragmentation* was substantially completed with the exception of final editing and a final organizational plan. We have limited our editorial involvement to improving syntax and grammar, deleting obviously repetitious passages, and providing a logical internal organization. The latter entailed both ordering the chapters and dividing the book into sections. The text is Gouldner's; its organization, to the extent he had left ambiguities, is ours.

Karen G. Lucas, aside from her substantive contribution, had assisted Gouldner with research for parts of the book and had discussed it with him at length. Her active editorial involvement, amplified by her knowledge of Gouldner's original intentions, have been invaluable in producing the present text. We wish especially to thank Mary Grove, Gouldner's long-time secretary and friend, who persevered in deciphering, typing, and retyping this text in the most trying of times.

St. Louis, Missouri   JANET GOULDNER
October 1984   CORNELIS DISCO

Contents

I

Marxism and the Intellectuals

1

The Social Origins
of Marxism

The historical and social origins of Marxism are tangled in a stubborn paradox, whose importance is not diminished by its obviousness: Marxism's proletarian communism begins in the theoretical work of two very advantaged sons of the well-to-do. It arises out of their privileged education, reading, leisure, and critical independence—another class privilege.[1]

Is it too harsh to characterize Marx and Engels as "bourgeois" and, in particular, Marx and his family who suffered so greatly from material want? If we use the term "bourgeois"—as nineteenth-century romantics had used it—to denote a mediocrity of taste and feeling (thus equating it with philistinism), such a judgment would be patently ridiculous. Yet there is no reason to degrade the meaning of bourgeois to a mere gesture of contempt. We may use "bourgeois" more exactingly to mean an historical social type who organizes a "private" life around personal achievement and the family: the father is expected to do disciplined and routine work and to live a family-centered existence devoted to the well-being of his family, especially the children; the bourgeois family itself is not a working but a consuming and socializing center under paternal domination and protection; consumption and proper education of the children aim to enable them to (at least) reproduce the parents' level of education and material comfort; the family's level of consumption and the children's education serve to give public evidence—to "keep up appearances"—of independence of character, family self-maintenance and respectability, and of the father's competence. Although the father routinely expends time in achievement efforts, the family's level of com-

3

fort, education, and well-being relies upon more than his current wages; it commonly depends also on a *reserve* of money—whether their own savings or unearned incomes from rents, interests, or profits, and (parental or family) inheritances, loans, gifts, and subsidies. This level of comfort is publicly taken as, and is meant to communicate, the family's claim to public respect. "Bourgeois," then, is partly a family and socializing thing; it is also partly a money thing defined by access to a surplus above what is earned through wages; and it is partly a moral and ideological thing. How do Marx and Engels qualify in terms of this "ideal type" bourgeois?

Certainly, no one has ever doubted that that beautiful man, Engels— son of a multinational cotton manufacturer and himself one—who generously supported Marx for much of his adult life, was a bourgeois. Or, at any rate, Engels was as much bourgeois as a bachelor can ever become in a bourgeois society. In effect, he had adopted Marx's family as his own and it was only "in 1896 that Engels threw off the servitude to commerce he had voluntarily entered upon 19 years before in order to support and further Marx's work."[2] Even after Marx's death in 1883, Engels continued to support the Marx family until his own death in 1895. The "ever-laughing Engels," as Paul Lafargue once called him, was "an enthusiastic rider to hounds, a mighty walker and deep drinker . . . of an equable temper, a man with a tender and chivalrous regard for women, turning a blind eye to the imperfections of those who successively held the reins of his household."[3] No petty-bourgeois, Engels's tastes were upper class.

For most of their life in England, the Marx family lived in an essentially petty-bourgeois manner, even though Marx refused routine employment, was reliant upon Engels's support, and often lived above his meager means. In 1856 the family moved to 9 Grafton Terrace, a small house in a then newly developed suburb of London; from that time on, this was about the poorest housing the family would have. It was a three-storied house with eight small rooms, balconies, stone coping and balastrade. It still stands today, now, however, "occupied by several families."[4]

One has but to consult Engels's own account of the condition of the English working class to see there is no question that the Marx family lived incomparably better than the masses of English workers. This may have also been the sour judgment of some of Marx's own acquaintances, to whom he responded: " 'Even if I were to reduce my expenses to the utmost, . . . by, for example, removing the children from school, going to live in a strictly working-class dwelling, dismissing the servants and living on potatoes,' the sale of the furniture would not realise enough to satisfy his creditors, while such drastic steps could have dangerous consequences for his wife in her nervous state and were hardly suitable for his growing girls," to whom he was the most devoted of fathers. Even as the family's water and gas supply was cut off for non-payment, Marx would write desperate letters about it "to the accompaniment of Laura and Jenny singing delightful duets at the piano, having made good progress with their music lessons . . . while there were now two servants to wait upon the family. . . ."[5]

Among the clearest expressions of the bourgeois character of revolutionary Marxists, and how these are adjusted to the special tastes of the well educated, are Rosa Luxemburg's poignant letters to her lover, Leo Jogiches. In a letter from Berlin, March 6, 1899, she writes:

> Soon I'll have such a strong moral position here that we'll be able to live quietly together, openly, as husband and wife! . . . I felt happiest about the part of your letter in which you wrote that we are both still young and able to arrange our personal life. Oh, Dyodyo, my golden one, if only you kept your promise! . . . Our own small apartment, our own nice furniture, our own library; quiet and regular work, walks together, an opera from time to time, a small, *very* small, circle of friends, who can sometimes be invited for dinner; every year a summer vacation in the country, one month with absolutely no work! . . . And perhaps even a little, a very little baby? . . . And we will never fight at home, will we? Our home must be quiet and peaceful, like everyone else's . . . Dyodyo if only you settled your citizenship, finished your doctorate, lived with me openly in our own home, and we *both* worked, our life would be *perfect!*[6]

In some respects, Luxemburg was more bourgeois than Marx, for earning her own income was important to her, and indeed one wonders whether the following letter of April 19, 1899, was not a silent reprimand of Marx himself:

> You think my plans to earn money threaten my scholarly and political future. You're wrong. I'd need more time to explain; anyhow it isn't all that bad. I, for one, follow the principle: people's *primary* concern is to support themselves and their children or their parents, *and next* to think of becoming great scholars. Besides—*sind's Rosen, nun sie werden bluhen* [if these are real roses, they'll bloom]. No genuine talent ever flourished just because it devoted *all* its time to self-development.[7]

The above was written just one day after Luxemburg had finished the introduction to her famous polemic against Eduard Bernstein's revisionism, *Reform or Revolution?*, in which she maintains that "the theory formulated by Bernstein, is nothing else than an unconscious attempt to assure the predominance to the petty-bourgeois elements that have entered our Party. . . ."[8] The underside of an "intransigent" and revolutionary public politics was thus, often enough, a private life dominated by the most temperate bourgeois aspirations and tastes.

In noting this, I do not intend to unmask the "hypocrisy" of revolutionary intellectuals, who are surely no more hypocritical than any other social stratum. My object, rather, is to make a sociological point concerning the nature of the social group that conceived and shaped Marxism. It tells us—quite apart from their public pronouncements and self-understandings—what they wanted and who they were; it alerts us to limits in their social theory that might otherwise be invisible; it helps us to understand Marxism itself.

From the standpoint of Marx's and Engels's own Marxism, which insisted that social consciousness is determined by social being, their own accomplishment must seem a sociological miracle. To decipher this eerie transformation of elites into elite-devouring revolutionaries will require us to essay the rudiments of a sociology of intellectuals and intelligentsia, i.e., of the *New Class*. It is only in this social stratum, seen in its historical specificity, that we may adequately comprehend the class sources of Marxism. Only in this comprehension may we construct a critique of Marxism which escapes the limits of that class's self-understanding and goes beyond Marxism's origins. Only by such a critique can we identify the ultimate curbs on Marxism's reflexivity and its vulnerability to false consciousness.

There is little reason to expect Marx and Engels to say much about the origins of their own theory beyond acknowledging their intellectual debts. Yet there is more to this silence than the healthy unselfconsciousness of two active men. For not only do they manifest a "normal" reticence to dwell on themselves, but they also have surprisingly little to say about the radicalization of intellectuals in general, about the entire social stratum of which they are a part, about how that social stratum becomes involved with the proletariat, socialism, revolution, and what this might mean. They do speak to this question but only hurriedly, *en passant,* as a kind of obligation to cover the topic; and the little they have to say is sharply anomalous with the main thrust of their own argument.

The Anomaly of Revolutionary Intellectuals

The intellectuals who enter Marx's and Engels's commentary are, for the most part, seen as members of the ruling class, or as the learned but all too pliable ideologues of the bourgeoisie. That intellectuals could plausibly be taken for members of the *ruling* class reminds us that the expansion and modernization of higher education had then only begun and was indeed still the privileged province of a very few. Even the rich in this period might forgo the university education of their sons (not to mention their daughters!), fearing that advanced education might unsuit them for business. For the most part, however, Marx and Engels correctly saw intellectuals as uniquely privileged persons who, if not actually outright members of the ruling class, were often their companions, allies, or kin.

Yet their very emphasis on the upper-class character of intellectuals must have created dissonance. For however much Marx and Engels emphasized that the emancipation of the proletariat was to be a *self-emancipation*, they surely glimpsed that it was incongruous that this should be heralded by sons of the well-to-do. The incongruity between Marx's and Engels's own class background and of those they claimed to represent, was real and painful and it helps us understand why they said so little about intellectuals in general and revolutionary intellectuals in particular. The communists have nothing to hide, said the *Communist Manifesto*. Nothing but the fact that they were bourgeois intellectuals.

The *Manifesto* contains a few familiar formulations about this matter that are typically oblique and fugitive: "Entire sections of the ruling classes are, by the advance of industry, precipitated into the proletariat, or are at least threatened in their conditions of existence. These also supply the proletariat with fresh elements of enlightenment and progress."[9] The logic seemed to be: when declassed, the bourgeoisie bring their greater education with them and can thus contribute to the enlightenment of the proletariat. The implication is that *education* is (somehow) *per se* a force for enlightenment and progress, at least when no longer compromised by privilege. If this sector of the bourgeoisie does not do what others might when threatened (that is, become the workers' enemy), the assumption seems to be that education can be separated from conditions that limit its capacity to emancipate. This would imply a certain capacity for higher education to serve class interests *opposed* to those of the bourgeoisie.

The importance of education and of theory in facilitating this transition of the bourgeoisie is also plainly indicated in the *Manifesto*: "when the class struggle nears the decisive hour, the process of dissolution going on within the ruling class, in fact, within the whole range of old society, assumes such a violent, glaring character that a small section of the ruling class cuts itself adrift, and joins the revolutionary class, the class that holds the future in its hands."

Why do they become class renegades? So that they can be identified with the historical future? But why doesn't the *entire* ruling class—allegedly doomed—go over to the revolutionary class? Why only a "small section" of it? What distinguishes this small section from the main body of the ruling class?

The answer to this last, at any rate, is stated clearly in the *Manifesto*: "a portion of the bourgeoisie goes over to the proletariat, and in particular, a portion of the bourgeois ideologists, who have raised themselves to the level of comprehending theoretically the historical movements as a whole." One difference, then, between those members of the ruling class who become radicalized—and those who do not—*is related to their education in general and to their theoretical comprehension of history in particular*: they can better foresee the end of their class, and thus where their future interests lie.

Much the same observation is made in *The German Ideology* which observes that "in the development of productive forces there comes a stage at which . . . a class is called forth . . . which forms the majority of all members of society and from which emanates the consciousness of the necessity of a fundamental revolution, the communist consciousness, which may, of course, arise among other classes too through the contemplation of the situation of this class."[10] Those possessing the ability or education for this theoretical contemplation, intellectuals, may thus become radicalized simply by "contemplating" the condition of the proletariat.

Several preliminary comments may be made about these essentially "idealistic" views: (1) They are brief and fugitive glosses, especially considering the importance of the issue. (2) Surprisingly, they are also at variance with the central and materialist theme usually argued, in both *The German Ideology* and the *Manifesto,* namely, that consciousness is determined by class being. From this standpoint, the bourgeoisie should be uniformly *opposed* to, rather than going over to, the proletariat, and intellectuals, being upper class, should share this bourgeois consciousness rather than one sympathetic to the proletariat. (3) It is unclear, however, exactly why theoretical contemplation leads the bourgeoisie to go over to the proletariat. Though cryptic, the image suggests that theoretical contemplation enables intellectuals to foresee who is destined to win and, being self-interested, they choose to be on the winning side. (Largely seen as a cerebral process, it is much akin to August Comte's view of how his own new sociology would facilitate social evolution: i.e., a reasonable man does not attempt to oppose what is foreordained by social evolution, as foreseen by scientific theory.) Thus when Marx speaks of the radicalization of intellectuals as produced by contemplating the condition of the proletariat, he is not alluding to the compassion evoked by the sight of their suffering, but to the prevision provided by theory that leads the intelligentsia to a calculating strategic decision rather than a moral obligation.

Marx correctly noted that some intellectuals went over to the proletariat, but mistakenly assumed that they did this only in the *final* hours of the class struggle. He saw them only as responding to a prior dissolution of the class system, rather than as contributing importantly to it. He glimpsed that the possession of education and theory distinguished those in the upper class who went over from those who did not, but he never systematically asked how education produced that difference. He realized that higher education might transform consciousness in ways at variance with upper-class interests and he noted that advanced education and the bourgeoisie were at odds under certain conditions. These observations, however, were anomalous and contradicted his own dominant theoretical commitments; he could not therefore take his observations as seriously as they deserved and they were left undeveloped.

Marx's social theory had normally held that "the ideas of the ruling class are in every epoch the ruling ideas: i.e., the class, which is the ruling material force in society, is at the same time its ruling intellectual force." But if "the class which has the means of material production at its disposal, has control at the same time over the means of mental production,"[11] the system of higher education *cannot* produce a consciousness hostile to the ruling class and its social order.

Intellectuals and the English Paradigm

Marx's neglect of intellectuals also rests on another sociological assumption, namely, that of all the classes that "stand face to face with the bourgeoisie today, the proletariat alone is a really revolutionary class. The other classes decay finally and disappear in the face of modern industry; the proletariat is its special and essential product."[12] In this framework intellectuals could either be a pliable part of the ruling bourgeoisie or a declining class without a future. Marx systematically ignored a third possibility: that far from being a declining class, intellectuals were a growing one, growing by reason of an industrial rationalization intensified by economic competition; and that far from simply being a servant of the ruling class and spreading the latter's consciousness, intellectuals bore an education that under some conditions made their consciousness diverge from and even oppose the bourgeoisie. While Marx recognizes this as a possibility, this is only a peripheral part of his vision of intellectuals. For the most part, Marx ignores the adversary potential of the educated sector of the bourgeoisie. Rather than seeing them actively chal-

lenging the bourgeoisie, Marx sees them as deserting the bourgeoisie
only when the latter are on their last legs and doing so primarily out of
interested egoism, i.e., defending "not their present, but their future interests" in view of their own impending transfer into the proletariat.[13]

This is strange because it was perfectly evident to the young Engels
that the philosophical communism to which he was drawn in 1843 was
recruiting largely from the educated:

> It will appear very singular to Englishmen, that a party which aims at
> the destruction of private property, is chiefly made up by those who have
> property; and yet this is the case in Germany. We can recruit our ranks
> from those classes only which have enjoyed a pretty good education; that
> is, from the universities and from the commercial classes; and in either
> we have not hitherto met with any considerable difficulty.[14]

Clearly, such an experience should have sensitized Marx's and Engels's expectation of the rebel potential of the educated and of intellectuals. That it did not was partly a function of their own "materialist"
commitments that repressed such an anticipation. It was also partly due
to the shifting of their base of operations from Germany (and from the
Continent more generally)—which had revealed this adversary potential
of the educated—to England where the educated were under the hegemony of a still culturally influential aristocracy and successful middle
class and thus did not in fact manifest the same alienation as Continental intellectuals. When Engels was sent to work in England he was soon
struck by the difference between the educated classes there, in contrast
with those in Germany to whom he had been accustomed. He observed
that Chartism in England had no following among the educated but
only among the workers:

> England exhibits the noteworthy fact [declared Engels] that the lower a
> class stands in society and the more "uneducated," in the usual sense of
> the word, the closer is its relation to progress and the greater is its fu-
> ture . . . in England the educated and the learned elements have been
> deaf and blind to the signs of the times for three hundred years.[15]

It was the English experience of economic development that became
Engels's paradigm of industrial capitalism and on which he focused his
economic analyses, supposing that England foreshadowed the future of
other nations. It was partly because England had an advanced industrial
economy that its correspondingly powerful middle class was, during this
period, able to exert hegemony over intellectuals. Marx and Engels had
supposed that the socialist future would grow out of precisely such industrially advanced societies and, therefore, that socialism's future must
depend on the "backward" proletariat rather than on the "enlightened"

classes. Marx expected working-class action to be grounded, in part, in an enlightenment derived from their exploited condition rather than their own small formal education, all the more so as he wrote before the spread of universal public education.

There were serious difficulties in this view of intellectuals. First, it did not anticipate the subsequently great spread of education in the advanced economies. Far from remaining a mere sliver of the bourgeoisie, the "knowledge" classes were yet to burgeon. In that sense, Marx, too, had come "too early"—as he had said of Saint-Simon, Owen, and Fourier—and it may be that Marx and Engels were thus only the last of the "utopian socialists." Second, Marx underestimated the extent to which the development of an advanced industrial economy facilitated capitalism's hegemony over the *proletariat,* so that they would not manifest the expected enlightenment. Third, Marx and Engels had supposed that socialism would first emerge in advanced industrial societies when, in fact, Marxism's breakthrough to state power came precisely in economies with little industrialization, whose moneyed middle classes were politically immature, whose landlords and aristocracy were de-legitimated and where, therefore, the educated classes or intellectuals had largely escaped the hegemony of other classes and had a freer hand politically. Fourth and finally, Marx and Engels premised that the mature middle classes would have an unbroken hegemony over the intellectuals; at the same time they assumed an intensified class polarization in advanced capitalist economies, alienating the proletariat, freeing them of middle-class hegemony and preparing *them* for a socialist consciousness of their own historical mission. What, in fact, happened was the reverse: advanced industrial capitalism, as mentioned, exerted increasing hegemony over the consciousness of the *proletariat* itself, inhibiting its socialist consciousness. While the proletariat became pacified by consumerism in advanced capitalism, intellectuals grew in numbers and influence. The spread of advanced public education increased their independence of bourgeois consciousness and gave them a common, character-shaping experience.

Marx and Engels had correctly understood the limits of the eighteenth-century conception of Enlightenment, which accented the importance of formal education for "reason." They saw that the "enlightenment" of even those with the most education might be limited by their class privilege, while correspondingly, that even the working class without formal education might be enlightened because of the deprivations of their class position. Rationality was thus not simply a function of formal education, but was seen here as also affected—as curbed or liberated—by a group's class interests. Relative to the limits of Enlightenment thought, this was a powerful insight. Nonetheless, it too was profoundly limited. Intellectuals' radicalization was not always inhibited by their bourgeois privileges—which, however, does *not* mean they were class free—and the working class's enlightenment was not fostered by its class deprivations, as the theory had supposed.

In some appreciable part, then, Marx's and Engels's use of the English case as the paradigm of their political economy had misled them into an over-reliance on the proletariat as the historical agent destined to bring socialism forth, and into an underestimate of the autonomy of the educated and their rebel potential.

Marx's "materialist" assumptions, i.e., his assumption that a group's "social being" (not its education) would determine its consciousness, contributed greatly to his underestimation of the role of intellectuals and inhibited his analysis of their radicalization. This materialism had emerged from a polemic against the reigning academic philosophy of the time, Hegel's objective idealism, which took the unfolding of consciousness, the Spirit or *Geist,* as history's central process and this as *self-*unfolding. Marx's materialism was rooted in his rejection of the decontextualizing idea that consciousness is *autonomous;* his polemical focus aimed at revealing the social and especially the *class* forces that limit and shape consciousness and its bearers and thus did not recognize intellectuals as a distinct class. The materialist critique of the autonomy of consciousness was thus conducive to a neglect of intellectuals' historical role, and they came to be seen primarily as adjuncts to other, more substantial social groups, i.e., to "actual" classes (as Marx called them in the *18th Brumaire*), lacking a sociological reality and special needs of their own. Marxism's revolt against the dominant idealism, and its own economistic conception of "classes," had the effect of obscuring the role of theorists and intellectuals in Marxism, of making Socialist discussion of this an uneasy one, until these ambivalences were decisively cast off by Lenin.

The Marxist Critique of Worker Intellectuals

It was not only the materialist critique of idealism that produced uncomfortable silences about theorists; so, too, did the very doctrine of the "unity of theory and practice" to which Marxism gave special force. If Marxism affirmed the special role of the proletariat, the latter was clearly expected to fulfill its historical mission when freed from bondage to the *status quo,* and this required that the proletariat submit itself to the tutelage of theory. But how can the working class submit itself to the tutelage of theory without at the same time submitting itself to the authority of theorists and intellectuals, which is dissonant with Marxism's claim that *its* socialism involves the *self*-emancipation of the working class? It is because Marxism faces both ways—on the one side, stressing the importance of working-class self-emancipation; and, on the other, accenting the significance of theory for socialism—that it develops a double ambivalence: it is uneasy about the intellectual's role in a working-class movement, and it is also uncomfortable about the working class's intellectual adequacy for its historical task.

Indeed, Marx and Engels were greatly uneasy about workers' theoretical creativity (although not their receptivity). Writing to Sorge from London on October 19, 1877, Marx observed that workers who "give up work and become professional literary men, always set some theoretical mischief going and are always ready to attach themselves to some muddle-heads from the alleged 'learned' caste." It was in this vein, as will soon be shown, that one of the first to be purged from the young Marx's revolutionary circles for his theoretical ignorance was Wilhelm Weitling, one of the few having authentically working-class origins.

Marx's attitude toward the working-class auto-didact philosopher Eugene Dietzgen was also harsh and condescending. In a letter to Engels of October 4, 1868, Marx held that in his opinion "Dietzgen would do best to condense all his ideas into two printer's sheets and have them published under his own name as a tanner." While Engels's reply of November 6, 1868, seems more generous, he too expressed the suspicion that the best part of Dietzgen's work was not his own: "if one could be *sure* that he had discovered it for himself."

Marxism's impulse to gloss over the presence and importance of theorist-intellectuals in its own ranks is nonetheless based on certain very real difficulties. For on *which* theorists could they rely? Given their own assumptions, they could rely neither upon the auto-didacts among the workers—whom they chastise for their susceptibility to the "muddle-heads among the alleged 'learned' caste," in short, academicians—nor could Marxism rely on these academicians themselves. If theorists are working class in origin and training, Marxism fears they will have the crudity of auto-didacts, a provincial narrowness, and the vulgar susceptibilities of the *parvenu* to the merely fashionable. Yet if theorists are trained academicians, Marxism fears their accommodation to respectable careers in the University or Civil Service, their middle-class origins, and the seductions of the comfortable life to which they may be exposed.

The Distrust of Intellectuals

There is, then, this ineluctable contradiction in Marxism: for it, *theory* is absolutely necessary for social transformation, yet *theorists* may not be trusted. From Marx to Mao, that contradiction is exhibited in a continuing distrust of intellectuals and in a corresponding self-effacement among Marxist intellectuals. Given this distrust of intellectuals, however, upon whom may Marxism then rely for the cumulative development of Marxist theory itself, so necessary to enable it to adjust to changing historical circumstances? Marxism's relation to theorists, then, is profoundly ambivalent: it needs but cannot trust intellectuals and theorists.

Marxism begins to cope with these ambivalences by disguising its dependence upon theorist-intellectuals, and it does this in a specific way: by stressing the value of "theory" but saying little about the *theorists* who make the theory. Marxism's "unity of theory and practice" is objectivistic, saying nothing about the unity of *intellectuals* and *working class,* about the *social strata* through which theory and practice are to be unified. Why?

The young Marx had briefly let the cat out of the bag. He had observed, in his *Critique of the Hegelian Philosophy of Right,* that philosophy was to be the "head" of the revolution, while the proletariat was to be its "heart." This organismic metaphor premises the smooth integration, as if they were two organs of one body, of intellectuals and workers. At the same time, however, this particular organismic metaphor has the fatal flaw of intimating all too clearly the *hierarchical* relationship between them. For however much head and heart are mutually dependent, there is small doubt which Marx thought the proper ruler. Indeed organismic metaphors commonly serve to occlude the reality of domination, hiding blunt subjugation by redefining it as polite "interdependence." In sum, Marxism at first sought to muffle the jarring presence of middle-class intellectuals in rude working-class movements by speaking more of *theory* than of *theorists* or intellectuals, and by flirting with organismic metaphor.

Intellectuals and Vanguard Party

In vaunting theory while suspecting the theorist, Marxism plainly implied that a special sort of theorist would be needed to enact its version of socialism. Since neither workers nor academicians could be relied upon as theorists, a very special theorist would have to be created, along with the sociological infrastructure that could reproduce them. The instrument to accomplish this task was the "vanguard party," which achieved its fullest self-conscious formulation with Lenin's organization of the Bolshevik Party and in the organizational code he laid down for it in *What Is To Be Done?* It is a latent function of the Bolshevik vanguard to overcome the contradiction between Marxism's insistence on the necessity of theory and its critique of theorists. More than that, the vanguard party functions to resolve Marxism's double ambivalence, toward the proletariat no less than toward intellectuals who construct the needed theory, calling a halt to discussion for its own sake.

The function of the vanguard, then, cannot be understood (except mythically) simply as a response to the proletariat's needs. The vanguard is surely not expressive of the proletariat's "natural" consciousness which, as Lenin noted, was primarily that of a trade-union economism intent on improved living standards. In one part, the vanguard serves to transmit the socialist theory created by intellectuals to the proletariat, thus serving in effect as an organizational instrument through which the New Class of intellectuals exerts ideological influence over the proletariat. That, on the one side. On the other, however, the vanguard is also an instrument for controlling and transforming intellectuals themselves.

That the vanguard functions as a control system over radicalized intellectuals was apparent in Lenin's early drive to define Party members as consisting only of those who accepted the discipline of some party unit. The historically evolving "autonomy" of intellectuals ceased as they enter the country of the vanguard. If, in part, the vanguard is a way of extricating intellectuals from respectable institutions and bourgeois culture, it does not replace this influence with proletarian control but with a third force, that of the Party itself. The vanguard is the political instrument of a segment of alienated intellectuals. Like a kind of Alcoholics Anonymous, in which one member helps the other "kick the habit," the vanguard helps intellectuals surrender discourse *as an end in itself,* defining this as "mere talk" that needs to be subordinated to real "praxis."

Yet, however much the vanguard party expresses an effort to bring intellectuals under control, it also remains unmistakably clear that its criteria for leadership call for exceptional manifestation of intellectual competence and theoretical sophistication. The important leaders of Communist parties have diligently striven to present their intellectual credentials and given untold hours to systematic study and to writing. Communist leaders are expected to be learned men, at least to the extent of knowing the Marxist classics. And it is not only socialist intellectuals such as Plekhanov, Trotsky, Bukharin, or Gramsci who devote themselves to substantial intellectual efforts and work but also great organizers such as Mao Tse-tung and even Stalin himself—the arch foe of Bolshevik intellectualism—who meticulously presented himself as a communist scholar and arranged to have himself publicly celebrated as a great thinker. It is also notable, in this connection, that Lukács's devotional little book on Lenin was at great pains to deny that Lenin was a mere organizer; Lukács insisted repeatedly he had also been a superb theorist.

In effect, the vanguard party is the collective holding company, the organizer and integrator of the political interests of radicalized intellectuals. It is a political instrument that reduces intellectuals' political dependence on the urban masses. Rather than being like the Jacobin Club, with an *ad hoc* forum and irregular following, the vanguard provides intellectuals with an ongoing organizational base which it controls, thus mediating the influence of intellectuals on masses. Being, however, also a system of controls over the intellectuals themselves, the vanguard thus also alienates them from the very organizational instrument they created. The fullest development of this alienation of the New Class intelligentsia from their own vanguard instrument is *Stalinism*.

In its Leninist beginnings, however, the vanguard is unmistakably the instrument with which the radicalized intellectuals impress a version of socialist theory upon the proletariat. In *What Is To Be Done?* Lenin insisted that the working class did not by itself achieve a socialist consciousness but had to have this brought to it by the intelligentsia. Although discussed in a later chapter the matter is of such moment both theoretically and historically, that I shall quote here from Lenin's argument:

> Those who are in the least acquainted with the actual state of our movement cannot but see that the spread of Marxism was accompanied by a certain deterioration of theoretical standards. Quite a number of people, with very little, and even totally lacking in, theoretical training, joined the movement for the sake of its practical significance and its practical successes. . . .
>
> The history of all countries shows that the working class, exclusively by its own efforts, is able to develop only trade-union consciousness. . . . The theory of socialism, however, grew out of the philosophic, historical and economic theories that were elaborated by the educated representatives of the propertied classes, the intellectuals . . . Marx and Engels themselves belong to the bourgeois intelligentsia. . . .
>
> To supplement what has been said above, we shall quote the following profoundly true and important utterances by Karl Kautsky. . . . "Many of our revisionist critics believe that Marx asserted that economic development and the class struggle create, not only conditions for Socialist production, but also, and directly, the *consciousness* (K.K.'s italics) of its necessity. . . . But this is absolutely untrue. . . . Modern socialist consciousness can arise only on the basis of profound scientific knowledge. . . . the vehicles of science are not the proletariat, but the *bourgeois intelligentsia* (K.K.'s italics). . . . Socialist consciousness is something

introduced into the proletarian class struggle from without . . . and not something that arose spontaneously within it. . . ."[16]

It is sometimes held that Lenin later relented in his elitist subordination of the working class to the intelligentsia, but the evidence for this is slight and unconvincing. Most important, however, there is no evidence that Lenin ever sought to revise the organizational code of the Bolshevik Party in which these early elitist premises were embedded. While it is clear that the day-to-day operations by the early Bolshevik Party, especially during the brief and fluid revolutionary period in 1917, exhibited considerable openness to popular pressure, it is equally clear that this did not last long. Very shortly after the Revolution, the party began that increasing rigidification that ultimately laid the organizational groundwork for the emergence of Stalinism. It read the threatening events of the Civil War and post-revolutionary struggle through Leninist spectacles, and saw them as requiring new limitations on party democracy and increasing party centralization.

G. V. Plekhanov, the founder of the Russian Social Democratic Party and Lenin's political mentor, in time denounced *What Is To Be Done?*, accusing "Lenin and his followers of constituting themselves a *super-intelligentsia*." Plekhanov rejected *What Is To Be Done?* for excluding "socialism from the mass and the mass from socialism [and for having] . . . proclaimed the socialist intelligentsia the demiurge of the socialist revolution."[17]

It is notable, however, that Plekhanov's critique of Lenin's organizational model appeared only slowly, indeed, only after Plekhanov had earlier collaborated in efforts to implement it. This reluctance to separate himself from Lenin's views on the intelligentsia's leading role is understandable in the light of the fact that Plekhanov himself had earlier held similar views. As Samuel Baron notes, Lenin's organizational views "echoed his predecessor's much more faithfully than has generally been recognized."[18] Plekhanov's theories, too, had earlier placed great importance on the leading role of the intelligentsia, arguing that the socialist intelligentsia "must become the leader of the working class in the projected liberation movement. . . ."[19] In large part, these views were crystallized in the course of Plekhanov's resistance to Bernstein's "revisionism" and to the "economism" that Plekhanov took to be its Russian reflection. Bernstein's studies of the development of the European economy had led him to conclude that the "natural evolution" of the working class would no longer underwrite a socialist outcome. Rather than viewing revisionism and working-class accommodation as grounded in the im-

proving life of the working class itself, however, Plekhanov began to define this as evidencing the failure of certain socialist intelligentsia. Per-
ceiving "that the working class was less steadfast than he had supposed,
he enlarged the role of the intelligentsia, as it were, to redress the
balance. . . . He now gave relatively greater weight to the will of the
intelligentsia as a requisite for socialism than to the 'natural' development of socialist inclinations among the proletarians."[20]

Baron is correct in noting that the *historical* basis of Plekhanov's emphasis on the intelligentsia's revolutionary initiative was his rejection of
revisionism; yet it would be mistaken to assume that this emphasis had
first been brought into Marxism by Plekhanov or that it constituted a
subversion of true Marxism. On the contrary. As my own previous remarks demonstrate, Marx himself never saw the working class itself as
the source of the *theory* he regarded as indispensable for socialist emancipation. Lenin's fear that Marxism's spread among the working class is
"accompanied by a certain deterioration of theoretical standards" expresses the same denigrating view of the working class's theoretical in-
eptitude that we had noted Marx expressing in his 1877 letter to Sorge,
as well as in his "head" and "heart" metaphor of an earlier period.

There is, however, this basic difference: Marxism at that earlier period had repressed/suppressed its distrust of the working class's theoretical limits, and had hidden its reliance on the intelligentsia. Leninism
was a truly different epoch in the history of Marxism partly because this
once repressed material now surfaced under his leadership. The difference, then, was not in their premises about the intelligentsia but was,
rather, a difference between the earlier repression and the later open expression of that premise. In noting the continuity of premises concerning the importance of the intelligentsia in these periods, the point is not
that this later surfacing is to be understood simply as an automatic unfolding of the earlier presence. It required certain specific historical conditions to overcome the initial repression and to allow Marxism's actual
relationship to intellectuals to surface. What needs to be stressed, however, is that Marxism did not only lately develop a special reliance upon
intellectuals; this was inherent in it throughout. In short, the class character of Marxism has not varied since its beginnings; it owes at least as
much to the intellectuals' special interests and culture as to the proletariat to whom it pledged allegiance.

On the Origins of Revolutionary Intellectuals

A key intellectual problem remains. Why and how do these "representatives of the propertied classes, the intellectuals," produce a theory that

seeks the overthrow of the propertied class? There is little or nothing in Kautsky or Lenin to explain how they can escape the normal consciousness of the bourgeoisie and produce another radically opposing it. The whole idea flagrantly violates the key postulate of Marxist materialism, namely, that social being determines social consciousness. Indeed, in Lenin's comment above there is a visible tendency to *regress* to an Hegelian idealism in which *ideas produce their own unfolding,* for it describes social democratic theory as the "natural and inevitable outcome of the development of *ideas* among the revolutionary Socialist intelligentsia" (italics added).

This contradiction has been of growing concern to contemporary Marxists. The English Marxist Norman Geras, acknowledging that Marxism was produced by bourgeois intellectuals, holds, however, that "these were not just any bourgeois intellectuals [but] . . . those who linked their fate with that of the working class," and who elaborated their science on the basis of "the experience of exploitation and repression, the experience of the struggle against these realities. . . ."[21] Geras raises a legitimate issue in attempting to specify the exact relationship of Marxism to the working class, yet his solution remains unsatisfactory, raising more questions than it answers. If, for example, Marxism was indeed created in the interior of the working class, faithfully reflecting its experience, how does it come about that so much of the working class rejects it? Again, why do certain intellectuals who, then as now, are without such working-class linkages, accept Marxism? More important: if Marxism is the product of intellectuals' assimilation of proletarian experience, which particular doctrines of Marxism—e.g., the theory of class conflict, of the contradiction between the forces and relations of production, of alienation, of surplus value—were derived, and in what specific ways, from their experience with the proletariat?

Geras holds that "Marx learned from the initiatives of the communards, of the need of the proletariat to smash the bourgeois state. Lenin learned . . . of the significance of the soviets. Marx learned . . . and Trotsky learned . . . the necessity of permanent revolution." But in this sense, the oceanographer learns of the oceans from the ocean; the anthropologist learns of incest taboo from studying his tribe—or do they? Geras here drifts into a kind of mirror epistemology, an empiricism, in which the theorist passively reflects what he "sees."

But obviously, though many socialists studied the Paris Commune, not all concluded that what it taught was the need to smash the bourgeois state. And did Trotsky get the theory of permanent revolution from the experience of the working class, or from his onetime friend Parvus? And if Lenin had really learned the significance of the soviets from anyone, why did he smash them? What exactly made Marx's Marxism a "theoretical practice interior to the working class movement"? Marx and Engels were never leaders of working-class parties, nor even editors of socialist newspapers; they were basically respected "consultants" to various working-class movements and parties. They were never on a picket line; they were never factory workers. What, then, is the meaning of Geras's Wagnerian phrase, they "linked their fate" with the workers? Marx lived much of his adult life a scholar in libraries, and he died at his desk. As he said, he was "a machine condemned to devour books." Engels for his part, could afford living well.

What, then, does this linking of their "fate" come down to? To two things: first, Marx and Engels had made a commitment to and identified with the working class; second, they studied history from the standpoint of its implications for working-class emancipation. But this is a matter of their *consciousness,* of their theoretical reflection, or, if you will, of their "theoretical practice." We are then back to the question: if social being determines social consciousness, where did that consciousness come from; how was it that they could reject their own bourgeois origins, identify with the working class, and study history from its standpoint? Marxism remains without an accounting of its own paradoxical class origins.

Göran Therborn's effort to confront this problem also acknowledges that the formation of Marxism had depended on bourgeois intellectuals, particularly non-Bohemian, "radicalized intelligentsia, profoundly alienated from all the reigning powers of the time."[22] But why should bourgeois intellectuals be alienated from bourgeois society? Therborn concurs with Geras in emphasizing that the origins of Marxism are grounded in "the encounter and union between a part of this radicalized intelligentsia and the working class, which had just embarked on its long history of independent struggle."[23] Like Geras's, however, this formulation too is littered with difficulties. Therborn begs the very question that needs answering; he *begins* with a radicalized intelligentsia, rather than accounting for that radicalization. He simply notes that, hitherto, intellectuals and the working class were each going their own separate ways and that, for unexplained reasons, Marx and Engels suddenly chose to swerve toward the proletariat. This obscures the fact that it was not just intellectuals who had been going their own way apart from the proletariat, but so, too, had *socialists* and *socialism.* As Kautsky mentioned in the remark that Lenin had cited favorably, "socialism and class struggle arise side by side and not one out of the other." Antonio Carlo similarly notes that "at first . . . the workers struggled against the capitalists, they organized strikes and unions, while the socialists stood aside from the working class movement, formulated doctrines criticizing the contemporary capitalist bourgeois system of society and demanding its replacement by another system."[24]

Socialism had thus been rooted originally in a critique of society derived from intellectuals and their own distinct motives, *arising quite independently of their knowledge of or sympathy for the working-class struggle*. As Carlo remarks, "By directing socialism towards a fusion with the working class movement, Karl Marx and Friedrich Engels did their greatest service." But what were intellectuals' motives in fusing their socialism with the working-class movement? Lenin's remarks reveal these quite plainly: ". . . the theories of the socialists, infused with the workers' struggle, remained nothing more than utopias, good wishes that had no effect on real life. . . ."[25] The fusion between socialism and working class, then, was motivated by the *powerlessness* of intellectuals—noting that intellectuals in that period were still a very undeveloped, small stratum. Without the workers, socialist intellectuals had no social basis with which to implement their socialism. Intellectuals, then, needed workers to empower and enact the socialisms they had formulated previously, *not in the "interior" of the proletariat but quite apart from them*. But even this formulation is unsatisfactory for it is essentially idealistic, implying that all that was involved in their fusion with the working class was the intellectuals' quest to fulfill their *ideas;* nothing is yet said about the *"material" interests* of intellectuals that lead them to socialism and to the working class. I must return to this shortly.

Therborn also argues that young German intellectuals were pushed toward a fusion with the working class because of the "abortive bourgeois revolution."[26] But if it was their bourgeois origins that had at first disposed intellectuals to support the emerging bourgeois revolutions of 1848, how and why did this induce them to have sympathy for the proletariat? Why should the latter's "atrociously exploited" condition—as Therborn holds—have attracted bourgeois intellectuals? If these are bourgeois intellectuals, or, in Therborn's terms, non-Bohemian (i.e., "achievement" oriented) intellectuals, then why isn't their political ambition satisfied if the bourgeois revolution succeeds, or surrendered, if it fails? Why do some intellectuals go over to the proletariat when they lose faith in the commitment of the bourgeoisie to their own revolution? Why should bourgeois *intellectuals* be more militant than other members of the bourgeoisie? Why should such intellectuals renounce a betrayed, defeated, or stalemated bourgeois revolution and opt instead for a proletarian one? And if they do go over to the proletariat, why don't such intellectuals simply treat the proletariat as a useful ally in making the *bourgeois* revolution, rather than abandoning that revolution altogether? Finally: in going over to the working class, do intelligentsia—as Weitling

asked—do so to further proletarian goals or are they coopting the proletariat to further their own goals? Who is master here?

Therborn misses an important implication of the fact that intellectuals
may go over to the proletariat following an abortive bourgeois revolution,
for this shift implies that the intellectuals have an important measure of
independence and can take initiatives in seeking allies in pursuance of
their own goals. Intellectuals' ability to shift to the proletarian revolution, following failure of the bourgeois revolution, throws new light on
the meaning of their earlier commitment to it. If intellectuals' commitment to the proletariat revolution cannot be explained by their bourgeois
character, except in the most fanciful accounting, it may be that they
were not even committed to the bourgeois revolution for bourgeois reasons. Therborn obscures the fact that intellectuals have not simply been
"agents" but principals capable of "shopping" on their own account, of
exploring different social sectors for an historical agent to secure their
own goals, seeking this at first among the bourgeoisie and, later when
this fails, among the proletariat and, in each case, having their own class
ambitions.

Shopping for an Agent

In Marxism there is a class that is "summoned"—the proletariat. There
is also a "summons"—the mission to which the class is summoned—the
revolution in which capitalism will be smashed and the building of socialism will begin. Finally, in Marxism there is a *summoner* announcing
the mission of the proletariat and calling upon it to perform its historical
duty. The objectivistic character of Marxism, the fundamental limit on
its reflexivity, however, is that it fails to confront the issue of the *summoner*. It does not systematically confront the question: *who* speaks
Marxism, *who* originates it, *who* calls upon the proletariat to perform its
historical mission? The objectivism of Marxism is expressed in the myth
that the proletariat's mission is laid upon it by *history* itself rather than
by some social stratum, who present themselves as the confidants of history. The objectivism of Marxism is expressed in the conflation of these
three levels—the summoned, the summons, and the summoner. The
function of this conflation is to cloud the fact that the summoned and
the summoner are sociologically different—profoundly different.

Marxism speaks of the proletariat in an idiom at once sacred and instrumental, characterizing it as the "historical agent." In other words,
the proletariat is said to have a mission it performs on behalf of *history*.
The very notion of an "historical agency," and the designation of the

proletariat as such, offers an answer in advance to the question: *whose* agent is the proletariat? Given this formulation, the obvious reply is that it is the agent of *history,* thereby making it unnecessary even to ask whether the proletariat is the agent of the intelligentsia. The intelligentsia obscures its own role by projecting it objectivistically onto "history," placing itself behind the mask of history. To which we must reply with Goethe:

> What spirit of the time you call
> Is but the scholar's spirit after all.

To understand what is involved in assigning this remarkable historical identity to the proletariat, it must be seen from an historical perspective; here it is plain that the proletariat was just one in a long series of efforts by secularized intelligentsia to find an "historical" agent. An historical perspective reveals that intellectuals' quest for an historical agent began long before Marx and has in fact continued into the present period.

A renewed probe for a new historical agent was launched by some Marxists in various parts of the world, beginning with the failure of the German revolution after World War I which left the Bolsheviks beached in a backward country. Today, many Marxists are looking for a new historical agent to replace the proletariat, who they fear has been pacified by consumerism. Some believe this agent may be found in Blacks; some, among the migrant foreign workers throughout Europe; some, in the exploited nations of the third world; and some even believe that the new historical agent may be the students themselves. Some intelligentsia are thus actively in quest of a new historical agent to replace the proletariat. When Marx said that philosophy was the "head" and the proletariat the "heart" of the revolution, he did not anticipate that the time would come for a heart transplant.

When Marxism cast the proletariat as historical agent, this was simply the latest stage of a search for historical agents that the secularized intelligentsia had started much earlier. The choice of the proletariat as historical agent follows previous claims by the intelligentsia that the "nation" or the *Volk* would be the new historical agent. For example, at the end of Fichte's *Reden* (as in certain of Saint-Simon's work) there is an image of an united endeavor, of scholars acting together with the rulers of the "temporal sphere." But, as George Kelly observes, ". . . in essence it is the learned caste, deserting the 'sphere of pure thought' . . . who must teach and consumate the republic."[27] Machiavelli's search for a "Prince" seems to have been similar, and when Gramsci speaks of the proletariat vanguard as a "New Prince" he tacitly acknowledges a certain continuity between Marxist and earlier forms of a search for an historical agency.

During the Enlightenment the *philosophes* maintained a similar search for an "Enlightened Monarch," whose invitations they were not slow to accept. The search for an agent is also noticeable in the later development of the Saint-Simonians. Their new Positivist Society was to be based on the "industrial" classes who were to be the historical agents of the transformation that would precede the mature Positivist Society. For Saint-Simon and Saint-Simonians such as Bazard and Enfantin, the new intelligentsia's role was hardly limited to announcing the rule of *other* strata. The intelligentsia itself was, they believed, destined to become a new scientific priesthood, assuming power *openly*, at least in the spiritual part of the social realm.

Both the German and the French intelligentsia, then, manifested a series of trial-and-error attempts to identify an historical agent who could produce a societal transformation. The Marxian assignment of the proletariat to the role of historical agent was continuous with the Saint-Simonians' search for an historical agent and with the latter's reliance upon the *industriels*. Indeed, their search had earlier brought the Saint-Simonians to the proletariat, although they continued to see it as an object of philanthropy. Marx made the jump to the *self-groundedness* of the proletariat, but it was a leap he *could* make because the Saint-Simonians' search had already brought the intelligentsia, even before Marx, to the very brink of electing the proletariat.

One should also note, even if briefly, that the secular intelligentsia's search for an historical agent begins long before the French revolution. One can see it clearly enough even in the efforts of Plato and the young men of his Academy. Their problem was: who was to be the historical agent that united ancient Hellas; who could unify it to stop internecine warfare among the cities; and who could lead it eastward against the Persians? This problem induced the secular intelligentsia of Greece to search for an historical agent. Plato, of course, shopped for an historical agent in the direction of Syracuse and Sicily, hoping to win over the tyrant of Syracuse.* Plato and his Academy were not, however, the only members of the secular intelligentsia "shopping" for an historical agent

---

* In this vain hope, Plato had made three trips to Syracuse, two of them reluctantly and at the urging of his young men. In the end, these young men gave up efforts at persuasion; gathering around one of their own number, they set sail with an army of mercenaries to win Syracuse for themselves, with force rather than persuasion. They succeeded, but in the end they behaved no better than the tyrant they overthrew.

in ancient Hellas. Isocrates looked north to Macedonia's Philip to resolve Greece's problem. In the end, it was not Plato's candidate, but the pupil of his pupil Aristotle who helped provide Greece with her agent: this, of course, was Alexander.

The point then is: Marxism was the product of an historically evolving social stratum, a secular intelligentsia which had been committed to a longstanding search for an historical agent, for agents whom it wished to tutor, in whom it wished to develop a correct consciousness, and whom it hoped would transform the social world in desirable ways. Far from simply being passive recipients of ruling-class initiatives—though it is that, too, frequently enough—the intelligentsia, secular or clerical, has often defined its own politics around its own special interests and it has actively undertaken initiatives on their behalf.

Marx's designation of the proletariat as the agency of societal transformation is simply a special case of a larger historical pattern: "shopping" for an agent. This existed long before the modern proletariat and continues today among those searching for a functional substitute for the proletariat. This reformulation is important because it helps us understand that what is involved is not only the (real or imputed) behavior of the *agent,* the proletariat, but also, that of the intellectuals, for it is they who are doing the shopping.

Marx failed to see that the bourgeois "ideologues" whom he denounced were in *some* ways no different from himself. Those whom Marx denounced as ideologues had also been shopping for an agent. But they, like almost all other intellectuals before them, had chosen an agent from a group that was already politically powerful and socially integrated. Still, we need not assume that the motives of those who seek an historical agent among the underdogs, victims, and the suffering are identical with those who seek it among the high and mighty. For the latter have situated themselves among those with whom they share a common cultural background, where there is the smell of money and power, and where there can be the hope that some of it might rub off. There are, then, differences as well as similarities in the shopping patterns and in the motives of those choosing the weak and of those choosing the powerful. Which intellectuals choose which agents, whether high or low, depends in part on their values or ideals and, in part, on their structured opportunities. Well-sponsored intellectuals trained at prestigeful institutions have readier access to, and can shop at, the more "expensive stores"; poorer, less reputable intellectuals, however, must go to the sociological "supermarkets" seeking the best bargain for their ambitions and talents. Yet both are probably shopping with similar motives and with the same idea of what constitutes a desirable agent. Those whom Marx called "ideologues" are not always "selling out" but, like others, are often just looking for ways to produce a world in which they can truly believe, while revolutionary intellectuals are not simply sacrificing themselves selflessly for others.

"Shopping for an agent" is grounded in certain necessary assumptions. One of the most important of these is that *the shopper assumes he knows what needs to be done;* those shopping for an agent assume that their *knowledge* of the world is not problematic; what is problematic to them is only the *mobilization of power* to enact that knowledge. It is when the good is taken as already known, and thus as given, that the search for an agent becomes problematic. The search for an agent is a search for power by those who feel that they already have knowledge.

Another tacit assumption in Marxism's search for an agent is that the stipulations of reason alone do not suffice to motivate a social stratum to undertake a difficult historical mission; an historical agent is a group imputedly motivated to pursue the desired course by reason of its interests. It premises that the agent has sufficient *power,* but that he will not be persuaded by theory or reason alone to use it in the desired direction, and that this motivation must come from other sources. In short, Marxism's shopping for an agent premises a distinction between *theory*-guided-intellectuals and *interest*-prompted-agents. There are, of course, two classical conceptions of this problem. In one, assumptions are made concerning the "spontaneity" with which an agent's interests will dispose him to take the path desired by the intellectuals. In the other, and specifically in the theory of the vanguard, it is assumed that the agent's interests are necessary but by themselves will not suffice, and must be activated by political initiatives and theoretical stimulation undertaken by intellectuals.

When we note that some Marxists have recently sought to replace the proletariat as the historical agency, we are in effect noting that there is a difference between the role "historical agent" and the specific role-*occupant,* the "proletariat." That Marxists can have second thoughts about the effectiveness with which the proletariat has performed the role they assigned to it implies that there is a question of the fit between role and actor. It implies that a theory of the historical task of the proletariat rests on a separate and anterior set of assumptions about *historical agency.*

Although on the surface of it, it seems as if Marxism might be understood as an historical theory limited to a capitalist society with a proletariat and, indeed, with an advanced, well-developed proletariat, it now becomes possible to suspect that Marxism is not *about* what it, in its normal self-understanding, proposes. Exploration of the implications of the historical agency problem indicates the dispensability of the proletariat and therefore that Marxism is not *necessarily* about the proletariat and capitalism and, hence, that it is *not* just about socialism, as conventionally defined in Marxism. In short, we begin to glimpse that, in Marxism, the proletariat, capitalism, and socialism are quite possibly *metaphors*, concrete examples of certain inarticulate, more general, values and interests which are themselves more accurately indicative of Marxism's truest and deepest goals.

2

Marxism as Politics
of the New Class

A silence is the prudent sister of a gloss; a gloss is a silence that only pretends to talk. When Nicos Poulantzas writes a tedious study, *Political Power and Social Classes,* in which all varieties of elites, classes, and formations are paraded by in that rhetoric of mock rigor that some French Marxists now substitute for clarity, and when we have only two references to intellectuals in a book of more than 350 pages, then this is essentially the silence that characteristically surrounds intellectuals in the Marxist community.

When Göran Therborn appears to be confronting the role of intellectuals in the origins of Marxism, but when he only tells us that Marxism was not created by ordinary academics but by marginal, radicalized intellectuals, he is reciting little more than Lenin and Kautsky had long ago acknowledged; it is a discussion whose seeming candor conceals the fact that the essential questions have not been raised, let alone answered. It is, in short, a gloss. Let us read Therborn closely:

> . . . the left-wing German intelligentsia of 1843-45 contributed something positive to the formation of historical materialism. . . . Left Hegelianism was not borne by established academicians but by a radical, alienated intelligentsia of "free"—in other words, insecure and often harassed—publicists. The Young or Left Hegelians of the early 1840's had not compromised their ideas for the sake of their careers. On the contrary, Feuerbach's academic career had been stopped short in the mid 1830's because of an heretical theological text. Strauss was driven from

his chair in Zurich in 1839. In the same year, Bruno Bauer had to move from Berlin to Bonn, and at the beginning of 1842, he was thrown out of the university there, which led Marx to give up his own academic plans. Another of Marx's closest friends, Rutenberg, later editor of the *Reinische Zeitung*, had also been dismissed from his teaching job.[1]

A gloss is symptomatic of a conflict: Therborn is caught between having to acknowledge, as Kautsky and Lenin had long done, that Marxism was born of bourgeois intellectuals, yet wanting to avoid the dissonance that such an admission brings for a Marxism which presents itself as a theory of working class *self*-emancipation. Therborn seeks to resolve the conflict by stressing the unusual character of the intellectuals who created Marxism. Denying that they were ordinary establishment academicians, and holding that they were extraordinary "radicalized" intellectuals, he has no account of that very radicalization.

Note, too, how Therborn barely mentions Marx's own personal academic fate—i.e., the disappointment of his early hopes for an academic career—slipping that into the subsidiary clause of a sentence about some-one else, Bruno Bauer. Therborn does not wish to raise the possibility that Marxism may be as much grounded in a career disappointment—in Marx's own blocked ascendance (and indeed, in that of larger sections of the New Class of intellectuals and intelligentsia)—as in anguish for the proletariat's suffering.

Yet there is no doubt that *the Young Hegelians' radicalization began well before their careers were blocked.* Indeed, their careers were blocked because they had undergone a prior radicalization, not the other way around. Instead of accounting for the radicalization of intellectuals, Therborn thus begs the question, treating this as if it were a fact of nature needing no explanation. Yet the radicalization of intellectuals is made acutely problematic by the very basis of Marxism which, having all along argued that consciousness was determined by social being, thereby made the revolutionary communism of young *bourgeois* intellectuals totally perplexing.

That the alienation of young intellectuals can start well before they experience career blockages indicates that these are but one factor in the development of that alienation. What else is involved? How, in particular, can the alienation of young intellectuals begin even before they experience a career blockage? I shall comment here on only one inducement to the early alienation of young intellectuals, namely, the culture of critical discourse (CCD) they bear and by which they are characterized. Having analyzed this special culture at some length in both the first and second volumes of my trilogy,[2] I shall discuss it here only briefly.

The Culture of Critical Discourse
and Political Radicalization

The culture of critical discourse insists that any assertion—about anything, by anyone—is open to criticism and that, if challenged, no assertion can be defended by invoking someone's authority. It forbids a reference to a speaker's position in society (or reliance upon his personal
character) in order to justify or refute his claims. The CCD is the special ideology of intellectuals and intelligentsia, and it is essentially an
ideology about how discourse should be conducted.

Why, however, is the CCD *alienating?* Under the scrutiny of the
culture of critical discourse, all claims to truth are in principle now
equal, and traditional authorities are now stripped of their special right
to define social reality. The credit normally given to the claims of those
with worldly success, to the rich and powerful, now needs to be hidden
if not withdrawn, because it comes to be defined as illicit and unworthy.
The CCD is alienating and even radicalizing because it demands the
right to sit in judgment over all claims, regardless of who makes them.

As a distinct speech community, the highly educated in general, and
intellectuals in particular, manifest distinctive speech patterns: their
speech is more analytical and abstract, less concrete and specific; they
employ more references to books and use more book-derived words and
ideas. The speech of intellectuals also insists on hewing to the proprieties
of discourse rather than accommodating responsively to the reactions of
those to whom the speech is made. There is, therefore, less gathering up
of group support during the discourse and less sensitivity to the ways the
speech can offend and rupture the solidarity of the group.

Intellectuals also commonly use bigger, more difficult words, and
longer, more structurally complex sentences. They engage in more talk
about talk—i.e., in more metacommunication—and manifest more linguistic narcissism. Being relatively more context-independent and cosmopolitan, the language of intellectuals enables them more readily to communicate with distant others and to enter into solidarities with those
elsewhere; as it frees intellectuals from the local version of common
sense, it also frees them to give it offense. The CCD common to intellectuals allows them greater access to beliefs, ideas, values, and knowledge from distant places and times which may be at variance with, and
may be used to challenge, the claims of local notables. The culture of
critical discourse can thus be an alienating and even radicalizing grammar of communication, for its very epistemology tacitly embodies a politics critical of the local *status quo.*

CCD requires that all speakers must be treated as sociologically equal in evaluating their speech. Considerations of race, class, sex, creed, wealth, or power in society may not be taken into account in judging a speaker's contentions and a special effort is made to guard against their intrusion on critical judgment. The CCD, then, suspects that all traditional social differentiations may be subversive of reason and critical judgment and thus facilitates a critical examination of establishment claims. It distances intellectuals from them and prevents elite views from becoming an unchallenged, conventional wisdom. As with any moral code, however, there is a difference between beliefs about and conformance with the CCD; grammar and performances of grammar are not the same. Intellectuals oriented to the CCD may thus cut corners and even violate its requirements; CCD influences but does not enslave performances.

Fundamentally, the CCD requires that all groups' claims be evaluated in the same manner, thus concealing the epistemological *credit* normally given to the claims of elites. (As Nietzsche noted, ". . . with dialectics, the plebs come to the top.") Still, if a stratification system persists, in which some have more power, prestige, or wealth than others, this will indeed dispose persons to *credit* elite claims. Persons will reject elite claims more cautiously, or accept them more rapidly, than claims made by lower persons. There then develops a complex dialectic between this epistemological credit, the conventional pressure of any stratification system to credit elite definitions of social reality, and the counterpressure of the CCD to exclude such credit.

Under some conditions, the CCD is stronger and more alienative, while under others, it is less so. The alienation of the New Class of intellectuals is produced partly by the *interaction* between (1) its culture of critical discourse (CCD) and (2) its career blockages. Each of these may, of course, vary separately. Intellectuals differ in the degree that their careers are blocked (or are successful) and they differ also in the extent to which they have learned, internalized, and committed themselves to CCD. Latency or disuse of CCD is (in part) due to the compensatory gratifications of a successful career, which disposes persons to credit established authority and to blunt critical judgment. The CCD of the rich and powerful is thus greatly crippled.

While career experiences amplify or dampen the alienative potential of the CCD, career experience among the young has not yet had much chance to produce either result. The alienative potential of the CCD may, therefore, be seen with relative purity among students. This is particularly the case for university or college students in the liberal arts or sciences which are less apt to select those committed to competitive success in remunerative conventional careers. (The same profession or occupation can, of course, be pursued for different motives under different historical and social conditions. For example, doctors or engineers in underdeveloped countries may, for various reasons, be more committed to collective welfare than those in advanced industrial societies.)

University students, then, are more likely than the less educated to internalize the culture of critical discourse, particularly those pursuing non-vocationally centered educations in the liberal arts, insofar as they are still too young to have had career successes that would accommodate them to the *status quo* and lead them to suspend critical distance from it. Thus the value-hewing character of the Left Hegelians, which Therborn invokes—they "had not compromised their ideas for the sake of their careers"—is an age-related phenomenon; one is reminded that the synonym for the Left Hegelians is, of course, the "Young" Hegelians. If we do not simply take persons' value commitments (their "idealism") as a given, as vulgar idealists do, then we must ask, *under what conditions* are value commitments—such as the CCD—likely to be enacted by those holding them. One of these conditions is surely age-related, and "idealism" is thus age-generated. The "idealism" of the young, however, is as much shaped by their "social being" as the "cynicism" or "hypocrisy"' of the old, so that neither has a greater *prima facie* claim to rationality than the other.

Persons may also be readier to surrender a merely prospective career than one already accomplished, an expected rather than an experienced success, imagined rather than tasted pleasures. For the young, the pursuit of a career may at first be just another value so that "career" versus "revolution" may be a question of one value versus another, rather than being a choice between a spiritual value and a base "interest." For the young, revolution is not only a spiritual value but is also a career alternative; it is a prospective career. There is—as I mentioned earlier—an indication of this in Lenin's emphasis on the "professional" revolutionary which invites the New Class young to define revolution as a career; the Leninist "vanguard" was from the start the offer of revolution as a career. In these terms, the choice a young radical faces is one between careers; between a conventional career with its known and limited possibilities— which is called its "security"—but which also has him walk in the footsteps of his father, or a career on the larger scale and stage of history.

Faced with the fact that some intellectuals do not "sell out," Marxism is caught in a dilemma: either they did not sell out because conditions prevented this—for example, no one ever offered to buy them out—in which event there is nothing heroic about them; or, they did not sell out because they were indeed governed by their ideals (or ideas), thus undermining Marxism's original "materialist" premises.

This is one of the major reasons for Marxism's silence and confusion about the role of the revolutionary intellectual. It cannot deal with the question of their middle-class origins without contradicting itself: the revolutionary intellectual is either (1) just another interest-pursuing egoist, and his revolutionary commitment and theory are therefore a disguise for that interest, or (2) he is truly an idealist who can transcend his interests. In the first case, revolutionary theory and Marxism itself become another "false consciousness" that can make no superior claim to truth or loyalty; in the second case, the facts acknowledged contradict the materialism premised by Marxist theory.[3]

The Grounding of Marxist Theory in the New Class

Marxism is only about, but not *by*, the proletariat. Its theory and politics have, rather, been importantly stamped by the New Class of intellectuals and intelligentsia, and Marxism eludes firm understanding until it is understood in its complex relation to this class. The *theory* of Marxism and the kind of socialism it pursues reflect both the material and ideal interests of the New Class. In the discussion that follows, I examine the manner in which the interests and experiences of the New Class have influenced two distinctive features of Marxist theory, (1) its theory of alienation and (2) its conception of the role of the *state* in socialism.

1. Alienation and Intellectuals

Grounded in Strauss, Feuerbach, and Hegel, Marx's critique of alienation first emerged as a critique of religion which conceived God as the projection of alienated humanity; behind the imputed power of God was the suffering and need of men. The critique of religion and of all alienations was the rediscovery of man's own activity behind various fetishes—whether religion, metaphysics, or the commodity—which camouflage men's presence and actions.

The critique of alienation, however, was no simple "reflection" of the human condition but a selective response emerging from a specific grounding. It is mistaken to believe that the critique of alienation passively reflects "what is." In point of fact, alienation is *problematic* only because some social situation outrages some social value, even though this value may be so engrained as to be beyond noticing. What then are the values whose frustration is premised by the critique of alienation? Beyond this, *whose* values are they?

Essentially, the values were those implicated from the beginning in the most fundamental structure of German idealism, especially its elemental distinction between Subjects and Objects, in an interaction in which the Subjects constitute Objects just as the Objects shape the Subjects. In this view, there are no "Objects" without Subjects to whom they are Objects, and conversely, Subjects are constituted by their relationship to Objects. But it is the Subject that is here the repository and giver of value, and who alone properly has initiatives. Alienation, then, is a statement about the Subject's failure to have acquired the power and control over his world—including the means of production—*inherent in the very notion of a Subject*. It is a grievance about the "constraint" to which the Subject has been exposed. Alienation would not be problematic without the premise that man is and should be a Subject, that persons should control their own activity. Alienation is thus a grievance felt and felt only by those conceiving themselves Subjects, and who feel that the world of Objects still eludes their rightful control. The servitude of alienation is condemned because servitude outrages a Promethean expectation of man's power. What is from one perspective a complaint that the Object world has not yet been brought under persons' control is, from another, chagrin that the Object world still retains *autonomy* and has escaped domination by the Subject. The aim of such a Subject, then, is not simply *self*-control and *self*-development; he also seeks domination over the Object world.

The critique of alienation, then, premises the Subject's right to dominate the cosmos. It is a tacit claim for mankind's right to master the universe and to subject everything in it to the needs and interests of his own species. The critique of alienation premises a human "emancipation" that requires human domination; it is an ideology of *humanistic imperialism*. It understands the remaining autonomy of others as a *failure* of men, and indeed as an injustice in which they have not been given their due. The critique of alienation premises that the world is man's oyster.

Let us ask the sociological question, for which *groups* does such an ideology have an elective affinity. It might seem that a critique of alienation, with its condemnation of servitude, would obviously have an affinity for the weak, and for them alone. But that conclusion rests on the mistaken assumption that the weak necessarily *expect* autonomy, power, and freedom, and that because they lack *these*, they would find a critique of alienation appealing. How can "freedom" and "autonomy" become problematic for the powerless with barely adequate subsistence and shelter? Those long oppressed and living precariously on the edge of survival develop practical, "economistic" concerns for immediate subsistence, protection from violence, and maintenance of their health, family obligations, ritual status, and for some measure of security. The oppressed of the world are often offended less at their lack of autonomy and power than at the failure of their traditional subsistence system, localistic territorial arrangements, and at offence to their concept of the sacred.

The *critique* of alienation as ideology, then, is not first on the agenda of the very weak and oppressed. To put the matter otherwise, we can use the distinction that Robert Redfield made between the Great Traditions and the Little Traditions, which corresponds roughly with distinctions between, on the first side, the cosmopolitan, urban, literate, elite traditions utilizing relatively "elaborated" linguistic codes, and, on the second, the localistic, rural, oral, and folk traditions utilizing "restricted" linguistic codes. Within this framework, it is plain that the critique of alienation is situated in the Great Tradition.

The nineteenth-century critique of alienation expressed the experience of elites at the urban centers of Europe, rather than of oppressed peasants or uprooted workers in the new industrial slums of great cities such as Manchester. And since the critique of alienation was congenial to those for whom power was *problematic,* then it was not congenial to those securely in power, i.e., to established and prospering middle classes, or to the industrial and financial magnates. For while they did, indeed, expect to be invested with power, their expectations in this regard had already been fulfilled.

Whose ideology, then, was the critique of alienation? It was the ideology of an elite without power, yet of those who had control over parts of a Great Tradition, whose specialized symbolic skills gave them tradition-mastery, but who were subordinated to other elites, i.e., to the old aristocratic elite of birth, or to the new elite of industrial attainment and money, the bourgeoisie. It was an elite without riches, without privileged access to political or religious office and, for the most part, with little public recognition, and thus with little regular influence on public affairs. Yet for all that, it was an elite with great expectation. Being in control of a worth-bestowing Great Tradition which it believed of enormous, perhaps even sacred, value, it felt its deprivations keenly, as nothing less than an abuse of justice, or as the usurpation of its true inheritance. The critique of alienation was the nineteenth-century ideology of those intellectuals who were not privileged in the rapidly rising new world of business, industry, science, and technology and whose own origins were in *older* spheres of culture, who were writers, philosophers, theologians, or academicians, who did not conceive of science as the defining essence of modernity. The critique of alienation thus loses salience with the emergence of Scientific Marxism.

2. Intellectuals, Marxism, and the State

The link between intellectuals and Marxism is traceable also in terms of the specific *kind* of socialism that Marxism seeks. As the *Communist Manifesto* plainly indicates, Marxism's vision of socialism centers on the expropriation of private ownership of the means of production and its transference to the *state*: The proletariat will, once in power, "centralize all instruments of production in the hands of the state . . . and seek centralization of credit in the hands of the state, by means of a national bank with State capital and exclusive monopoly, [and] Centralization of the means of communication and transport in the hands of the state. . . ."[4]

Whatever relationship such a socialism has to the working class, it bears the most intimate connection to the history of the state, whose modern emergence and centralization began in the contest between the absolute monarchy and the feudality, where development and centralization of the state were instruments used by the monarchy to suppress the nobility; and where, subsequently, the state continues its growth under the bourgeoisie (for all their liberal pieties), and grows still further during the development of the "welfare state." Marxist socialism, then, is in substantial part a special case of the continuing extension of the modern state's apparatus and powers.

What connection is there between Marxism as an extension of the state, and intellectuals? The most relevant consideration is that "collectivizing" the means of production, credit, and communication has two facets: in one, the power of the old moneyed class of bourgeoisie is destroyed; in the second, the transfer of property to the state vastly enlarges its bureaucratic apparatus, extending opportunities for the special technical skills, advanced education, and new "human capital" of intellectuals. Even under capitalism, the educated have already begun to make the state apparatus their special property. Note the exceptionally high proportion of those with college educations in government bureaucracies. The extension of the modern state furthers still more the career interests and the power position of intellectuals; jobs in it are made specially accessible to the educated.

Much alienation of intellectuals, as discussed earlier, derives from the blockage of their upward mobility. For example, one of the first appearances of radicalized intellectuals in modern politics, the highest Jacobin leadership during the French Revolution, was in part prompted by the fact that their careers had at first often manifested upward mobility, but their continuing upward mobility was blocked by aristocratic preemptions. In short, the top Jacobin leaders were not *déclassés* but blocked ascendants.

A similar phenomenon has of course been noted in the Third World of developing countries. Here, in order to meet their manpower needs, foreign invaders set up public schools and begin training a select group among native intellectuals whose number, however, soon exceeds the careers open to them under foreign domination. A trained, articulate elite has then been created which is devoid of continuing prospects except those that might be opened by revolution, especially by successful wars of national liberation against imperialism. Foreign imperialisms are the crucial obstacle to Third World intellectuals in colonized countries. A nationalist movement against foreign imperialisms is thus, among other things, the expropriation of foreigners' property rights in the colonial state apparatus, making it the property of local intellectuals.

In the more developed and politically autonomous capitalist societies, however, it is moneyed property organized as corporate capital that sets the ultimate limit on the New Class's prospects. The new cultural bourgeoisie, the educated, is limited in the positions to which its members can rise in the private sector, where there is private ownership of the means of production.

It is this moneyed class that constitutes the implacable limit on the continued upward mobility of those with cultural capital in capitalism. One can, after all, join the party; one cannot "join" the bourgeoisie. A new state extending its control over the economy and building "socialism" is thus useful to the class interests of a cultural bourgeoisie: first, by eliminating the class and institutions that limit its autonomy and, second, by extending career opportunities by expanding the state bureaucracy.

Marxism and the Political Limits of the CCD

There is a further link between Marxist socialism and New Class intellectuals, arising from the New Class's political situation. The New Class is a minority class which could not, by its own efforts, hope to wrest power in the state in an open contest with the old moneyed class. It must seek a mass basis, particularly when it wants to extend its influence on the state. Insofar as its movement is directed against or is costly to the old moneyed class, the only other substantial political ally open to the New Class is, of course, the working class.

Marxist socialism, then, is partly a strategy for optimizing the life chances of the new cultural bourgeoisie—intellectuals—by removing the moneyed class and old institutions that limit its upward mobility, and is partly a political strategy through which the New Class can attract allies to accomplish this. Marxism thus encompasses both the ultimate political goals of the New Class and the means necessary to achieve them; both the removal of the ceiling that private corporate property imposes on the New Class's mobility, and the provision of a class alliance to achieve that.

The politics implicit in Marxism does not only overcome the structural limits encountered by the New Class but also serves as an antidote to the political limits inherent in the New Class's culture of critical discourse. The CCD of the New Class is drawn to a politics stressing the power of ideas and implying that correct ideas have a special political efficacy. Which is to say, intellectuals will be drawn to an *ideological* politics. Exalting theory over practice and talk over action, the New Class's CCD is often concerned less with the success of a practice than that the practice should be rationally interpretable and consistent. Marxism, however, serves to counterbalance this New Class's disposition toward theoreticism by a self-conscious stress on the *unity* of theory and practice which accents the practice side, insisting, as Marx did (in his eleventh *Thesis on Feuerbach*), that philosophers had only interpreted the world but that the point was to change it.

Intellectuals' CCD also stresses the importance of self-awareness, self-reflection, and self-editing, all of which tend to induce stilted, convoluted speech, the loss of warmth and spontaneity, and the appearance of an "inhuman" coldness. This impairs the New Class's capacity for easy communication or solidarity with others, especially those of lesser education, and limits its political appeal. Marxism's stress upon the working class, however, curbs the New Class's impulse toward an aloof elitism, making it plain that their political future depends on responses by "common" people.

The New Class's CCD also emphasizes adjusting action to some pattern of priority subsuming it to some identifiable rule. Continually interpreting varied situations in terms of some single rule, the CCD of intellectuals runs the risk of ignoring the special character of different cases. This tendency to dogmatism implies an insensitivity to persons' feelings which cripples the New Class's political alliances and appeal. But with its historicist critique of all universal moralities, rules, or laws, and with its emphasis on the contextual analysis of the concrete case, Marxism is as it were a specific corrective for the politically debilitating abstractness, formalism, and coldness inherent in the New Class's ideology of discourse. Marxism thus does not simply reflect passively the interests of the New Class but actively confronts its political problems and offers solutions to them.

Liberating the Technical Intelligentsia

We should remind ourselves here that, for Marx, the most basic contradiction of capitalism devolves from the conflict between its *relations* of production, embedded in the old property system, and its *forces* of production, centered in but not limited to the new technology. It was this new technology that would, by revolutionizing productivity, free mankind of the ancient scourge of scarcity and deliver it from the realm of necessity. But this liberation would at some point be blocked, said Marx, by the old property system, which would then have to be overthrown to allow continuing industrial development. Marx's socialism, then, is largely a promise to liberate the forces of production; it seeks to expropriate private ownership and invest this in the state because this is expected to further the development of the *forces of production*. Marxian socialism, then, focally promises a liberation of the forces of production from capitalist venality. With this, however, it carries a tacit promise of the liberation of the technical intelligentsia, the bearers of the new technology, from that same limit. In this respect, too, Marxism is the ideology of the technical intelligentsia.

Marxism is an ideology of the New Class, not merely as a philosophy of the liberation of productivity, and of those intelligentsia who are its functionaries, but far more broadly. Indeed, Marxism is a critique not just of capitalism, but also of the old cultures of intellectuals, specifically "Neo-Classicism," which had been interwoven with the class system and religious institutions of the *ancien régime* and of earlier European societies. The critique of neo-classicism that Marxism mounted, was accomplished from a standpoint that was a fusion of romanticism and scientism.

Marxism thus rejected neo-classical metaphysics which saw reality as inherently structured, boundaried, stable, and as inherently disposed toward order, and instead favored a metaphysics that focused on change, process, conflict, and inner contradiction. Rather than seeing men as the product of a shaping "culture" and a disciplining morality, Marxism's materialism emphasized the *derivative* character of culture and morality as a "consciousness" shaped by social being. Marxism pursued the rupture with neo-classical culture by expressing new assumptions that resonated and recovered altogether different structures of feeling.

Thus instead of viewing man as a creature of reason or morality, as classicism had, Marxism emphasized man as a creature of action and struggle. Instead of seeing man as spirit and mind, Marxism saw him as no less a being of flesh and blood, allying itself tacitly with the emancipation of the flesh. Instead of pessimistically viewing man as having to come to terms with inherent limits and as never winning—but only as transcending his spiritually inevitable defeat—Marxism saw man more optimistically, as capable of winning more happiness on earth than he has so far known. Marxism rejected classicism's sense of the tragic, crediting man's doing and making with Promethean effectiveness.

Classicism's sense of the importance of man's maintaining a limited, well-defined place was contradicted also by Marxism's project of ultimately overcoming the division of labor and making a world in which a man in his lifetime might have many careers. Instead of regarding the class system as the earthly expression of an eternal principle of hierarchy, as classicism had, Marx viewed such a principle as the expression of earthly hierarchy. Looking forward to a world in which the domination of man by man would cease, he sought a society in which the "free development of each will lead to the free development of all." Instead of prizing leisure, the diligent performance of duty, or the life of contemplation—all classical virtues—Marx saw free and willing work, on the one side, and courageous struggle, on the other, as the way men transform themselves and master their circumstances.

Much of Marxism, then, is more than a critique of capitalism; it is a smashing attack on the *old culture of intellectuals*—on classicism and neo-classicism—which had normally integrated intellectuals into the old society and class system. That attack was launched, as indicated, from the standpoint of newer ideologies—romanticism and scientism—assertive of intellectuals' newer independence and growing marginality. If the new romantic critique of old classical culture voluntaristically accented the importance of what men did and made, the new scientism insisted that men would not succeed in their struggle without a scientific theory. Marxism incorporated both elements. *Its synthesis expresses a cultural framework for the social unification of both wings of the New Class, its new scientific and technical intelligentsia, on the one side, and of its older humanistic elite, on the other, providing an ideological basis for overcoming their emerging division.*

The scientistic and the romantic elements both contained a critique of the new bourgeois elites. Romanticism regarded the bourgeoisie as philistines, while scientism regarded the technical intelligentsia as uniquely possessing the culture appropriate to industrial society. Indeed, in both cases—if for different reasons—the advocates of scientism and romanticism each looked upon themselves as the very incarnation of modernity. If the attack on intellectuals' old culture undermined their integration into society and the old class system, both scientism and romanticism fostered distance from even the new bourgeois elites, expressing intellectuals' sense of their superiority, and their conviction that the future belonged to them. Insofar as Marxism is a synthesis of romanticism and scientism, it is a *synthesis* of the vanguard ideologies of intellectuals and technical intelligentsia, facilitating their political unity.

Leninism, Stalinism, and the Intelligentsia

Whatever its intent and self-consciousness, Marxism's basic concrete aim—as distinct from any "emancipation" it promises—is the liberation of the forces of production from bourgeois social relationships. This means, first, Marxism has viewed the mode of production as a neutral system transferable from capitalism to socialism without injury to the latter. This means, second, the level of productivity was decisive for Marxist theory, whatever its other more tacit assumptions about the importance of other elements of "culture." This means, third, Marxism regarded this as the single, most decisive requisite of socialism, which, if not present within a revolutionary society, is available to it from more advanced friends elsewhere. This means, fourth, Marxism intended to do all it could to heighten productivity, and to continue doing so indefinitely, seeking a growth in productivity without end. And finally, this means, fifth, Marxism, whatever its solemn proclamations about the "self-emancipation of the working class," is dependent on those social strata—technical intelligentsia, specialists, experts, the New Class—on which that productivity and its increase necessarily depend.

Who Marxism and Marxists represent is not to be learned from their own public pledges of fealty to the working class. We learn more from the private rather than the careful public pronouncement. We learn much more from the passionate inadvertence wrenched from the outraged Marx, who, when a deputation of uncultured workers (*Knoten*) dared to ask him whom *he* represented, imperiously thundered back: ". . . nobody but ourselves." But who, sociologically speaking, are "ourselves?" What is "our" social character and position? If not the working class, then who?

"We," of course, are the radicalized intellectuals and intelligentsia who claim "we" are not here at all, except as the bearers of necessary "theory," or as the friends and confidants of History. We, the ventriloquists who put our own hopes and plans into the mouth of history; we, the bodiless voice of the Logos without Being; we who speak only for rationality and justice but want nothing for ourselves, and whose ambitions for the working class are in no way colored by what and who we are; we who make our offering to the proletariat as a cat offers his trophy.

Much of this remained cryptic in Marxism because Marxism itself never had much in the way of a developed, articulate politics. But once Lenin asked that question generative of all politics, What is to be done?, and answered it in part by designing the vanguard party as the instrument of the *teoretiki*, things became much clearer. Embarrassingly clear. That earth-shaking book begins by insisting that socialism and socialist consciousness require the scientific theory which can come from bourgeois intellectuals alone; but it then proceeds to paper over this by speaking of "us" only as "professional revolutionaries," thus defining an identity for revolutionary leaders that, on the one hand, masks their social origins as intellectuals, and on the other, allows intellectuals to merge with revolutionaries of various origins in a single unifying identity. Having begun by insisting on the importance of intellectuals for socialism, *What Is To Be Done?* then proceeds to mask their presence. Soon there is nobody here but us "professional revolutionaries," who, in any event, shortly draw a line between ourselves and those other pathologically garrulous intellectuals who want to talk, separating from we-who-have-suffered and we whose right to represent the working class is vouchsafed by "the exclusive and universal hatred consecrated to us by all the parties and fractions of the old world."

Who Leninism represents is made clear if we ask, what did Lenin want to *do* with his *Knoten*, with the backward "semi-Asiatic" workers of Russia? This answer is that first, he wanted to send them to school under the tutelage of the Bolshevik Party, and then, after the Revolution, under the tutelage of the intelligentsia, although this group can hardly be separated from the Party. Both before and after the revolution, Lenin saw the intellectuals and intelligentsia as schoolmasters of the proletariat. There is an interregnum between these plans and their achievement in Soviet society named Stalinism; but in time even that catastrophe subsides and the original design begins to reassert itself. As we will note in what follows, Leninism meant a society in which proletariat and socialism would at first be schooled under the tutelage of the technical intelligentsia, and in which the old working class itself would in time be re-educated into a technical intelligentsia. At that point there would in truth be no one here but us intelligentsia.

All this—the commitment to productivity and, therefore, the intelligentsia—is fully evident in Lenin's own policies: As Lenin remarked in 1918, "the only socialism we can imagine is one based on all the lessons learned through large-scale capitalist culture. Socialism without postal and telegraph services, without machines, is the emptiest of phrases."[5] To build socialism, insisted Lenin in 1919, "We must take the entire culture that capitalism left behind. . . . We must take all its science, technology, knowledge and art. Without these we shall be unable to build communist society."[6] Quite apart from capitalism's mode of production and its technology, which Lenin largely treats as neutral and transferable to socialism, he even regarded elements of the *state* apparatus itself in the same way. Lenin thus distinguished between the state's repressive arm—its police, jails, armies—and its administrative mechanism, "an apparatus which has extremely close connexions with the banks and syndicates . . . which performs an enormous amount of accounting and registration work. . . . This apparatus must *not* and should *not* be smashed . . ." even though capitalist influence on it must be removed.[7]

"While the revolution in Germany is still slow 'coming forth,' " observed Lenin in 1918 with chagrin, he adds, "our task is to study the state capitalism of the Germans, to spare no effort in copying it. Our task is to hasten this copying of the Western culture by barbarous methods in fighting barbarism."[8] (Is it really true, then, that there were no continuities between Stalin's terror and Leninism, and is Stalin's claim that he was a diligent student of Leninism so manifestly false?) We may also note that in 1917, Lenin had made no bones that "We shall not invent the organizational form of the work, but take it ready made from capitalism—we shall take over the banks, syndicates, the best factories, experimental stations, academies, and so forth; all that we shall have to do is borrow the best models furnished by the advanced countries."[9] This was to include, he added, "applying much of what is scientific and progressive in the Taylor system; we must make wages correspond to the total amount of goods turned out, or to the amount of work done. . . ."[10] Nor did Lenin hesitate in 1918 to draw the conclusion that this required "individual dictatorial powers," a strict unity ensured "by thousands subordinating their will to the will of one . . . iron discipline while at work . . . unquestioning obedience to the will of a single person, the Soviet leader, while at work."[11]

For Lenin, then, economic success—as distinct from political—"can be assured only when the Russian proletarian state effectively controls a huge industrial machine built on up-to-date technology . . . ," and it also requires "raising the productivity of labour . . . securing better organization of labour . . . the raising of the educational and cultural level of the mass of the population. . . ."[12] All this, then, makes it plain that Leninism's horizon concerning the economy was that of scientific Marxism, and was authentically continuous, as I have held, with the theory held by Marx and Engels themselves, who continuously stressed the decisive importance of the level of productivity for establishing socialism. Which is to say: there is no Leninist crudity here; there is no distortion of Marxism in this.

Lenin is at the same time perfectly clear what this construction of socialism requires: As Carmen Claudin-Urondo makes thoroughly evident in her jewel of a book,[13] this means that the accent was on acquiring, not transforming, bourgeois culture; on seeing it as useful knowledge rather than as dangerous ideology; and without conducting that critical examination of it which might have separated out the culture's "bourgeois" elements—without, in short, mounting a "cultural revolution."

Lenin's "socialism" rests in the end on the Promethean culture of capitalism, having cut away only its unworthy property relationships and the old proprietary class of moneyed capital. It therefore also rests on and requires, as Lenin plainly argued, experts and intelligentsia essentially similar in their social character and privilege to that in capitalist society, and who in themselves are no more to be changed by a cultural revolution than is their "neutral" knowledge itself. In the future, said Lenin in 1922, the bourgeois intellectuals—in whom this advanced and necessary culture is embodied—need to be guarded by Soviet society "as the apple of their eye."[14] "Capitalism had left us a valuable legacy," said Lenin, "in the shape of its biggest experts. We must be sure to utilise them, and utilise them on a broad and mass scale. . . ."[15] They are no longer to be "servitors of the bourgeoisie"; they are now a national resource which the new Soviet society dare not squander. The intelligentsia is gradually to be won over to the society, primarily by suasion and material privileges, and is not to be ignored or terrorized. Only pseudo-radicals, said Lenin in 1919, imagine that "the working people are capable of overcoming capitalism and the bourgeois social system, without learning from bourgeois specialists, without making use of their services, and without undergoing the training of a lengthy period of work side by side with them."[16]

This, of course, is of a piece with Lenin's *What Is To Be Done?* If the latter held that only bourgeois intellectuals could create and transmit a genuine socialist consciousness, and teach the working class how to think, here Lenin insists that only bourgeois intelligentsia can teach the working class how to work. In order to get the bourgeois experts to perform this function, added Lenin, "we have to resort to the old bourgeois method and agree to pay a very high price for the 'services' of the top bourgeois experts . . ." even though, as Lenin here acknowledged, this violated the anti-careerist principles of the Paris Commune.[17] The commitment to productivity meant jettisoning equality (and those communists committed to it) and it meant a commitment to the New Class. "We have many such Communists among us," said Lenin, speaking of those who could not work effectively with the intelligentsia, "and

I would gladly swap dozens of them for one conscientious qualified bourgeois specialist."[18] It appears that something very much like this did indeed happen, and the trend line of the proportion of the college-educated and intelligentsia in the leadership of the CPSU steadily increased over the years.

If the leadership of the Communist Party of the Soviet Union began, in clear conformity with Lenin's emphasis on the importance of the *teoretiki* (as discussed in my *The Future of Intellectuals and the Rise of the New Class*, 1979), by the early 1930s admission to the CPSU was formally made more difficult for intellectuals, of whom the rising Stalin then thought he had quite enough, identifying them with his political opposition. Yet after the 17th Congress of the CPSU, the murder of Kirov, and Stalin's clamp-down on the opposition, and as the Party opposition was destroyed, sometime between 1937 and 1940 there was then a return to a more friendly policy toward recruitment of the intelligentsia into the Party. By 1939, almost 29 percent of the secretaries of republic, oblast, and krai committees had completed university education, and another 30 percent had either a complete secondary education or some university education.[19]

By 1936, Stalin was proclaiming that the Soviet intelligentsia was a new group deserving of confidence and support: "Our Soviet intelligentsia is an entirely new intelligentsia, bound up by its very roots with the working class and peasantry." In 1939 Stalin denounced those Party members who held views hostile "to the Soviet intelligentsia and incompatible with the Party position. . . . This theory is out of date and does not fit our new Soviet intelligentsia."[20]

If at the 16th Party Congress in 1930, 4.4 percent of the delegates had completed their higher education, at the fateful 17th Congress in 1934, 15.7 percent had completed higher education, and even after the purges and the near total destruction of these 17th Congress delegates, the delegates to the next, the 18th, Congress of the CPSU in 1939 had among them 26.5 percent who had completed their higher education, another 5 percent with an incompleted higher education, and almost 23 percent who had finished their secondary education.[21] The purges of the thirties, then, were not as such aimed at the New Class or at blocking their special class privileges, as Louis Althusser fancies, but, rather at destroying their *political autonomy* and, especially, crushing their traditional impulse toward the critique of authority, thus preventing their link-up with the anti-Stalinist faction. Once that had been done, and his own political power entrenched, Stalin continued the Leninist policy of support for the intelligentsia and, indeed, of special privileges for them.

Marxism's ambivalent grounding in the status interests of intellectuals came into pointed conflict with Mao's cultural revolutions. Indeed, these cultural revolutions are to be understood as in part a confrontation with the New Class as it emerges under Marxist hegemony. Unlike any other Marxism in power, Maoism determined to bring intellectuals under control and subject them to a radical egalitarianism. In the process, however, the contradictions of rationality itself—which Marxism shares with Western culture—were also acutely intensified and fearfully exhibited. Maoism provided a weird glimpse of the potentialities if not the prospect of that rationality. In short, rather than being an altogether Asian eccentricity, we may think of Maoism as having explored the limits of our own rationality.

The rationality in which the permanent revolution of our time is grounded is a self-contradictory, self-confounding structure. Its voice is the voice of universal equality, but its hands are the hands of a new elitism. Insofar as a Marxist socialism embodies this rationality it also partakes of these contradictions. It is both constrained and obligated to affirm equality: constrained by the need for the political mobilization of masses and for its own legitimacy, obligated by reason of its own rationality. It is also constrained and obligated to affirm at least certain forms of rationality as not altogether identical with equality: constrained by the exigencies of creating a technologically productive and administratively efficient new society, obligated by its own commitment to rationality to recognize and reward intellectual worth, thus generating new social hierarchies.

It is precisely as this tension-filled ambivalence in Marxist socialism mounts that a socialist intelligentsia at last begins to become problematic to itself and becomes aware of its own social situation. The problem of socialist alternatives becomes sharply posed at the concrete level: either Scientific Marxism, a bureaucratized and prudent social system that acknowledges and differentially rewards differences in competence, thus undermining the promise of equality; or, Critical Marxism, an uncompromising commitment to a full equality of rewards, comforts, and daily life styles for all, thus threatening administrative efficiency, economic productivity, and political survival. At this point, there is a mounting temptation to sever the ancient Western fusion of power and knowledge—of a governance grounded in knowledge. Here, a limit is reached that cannot be transcended without contemplating the abolition of the very social stratum that has historically reproduced that norm, the Western intelligentsia, and the academic institutions and dialectic that reproduce them.

The Commitments of Marxism

To whom and what, finally, is Marxism committed? To hold that Marxism is an ideology of intellectuals is not to deny that it is truly committed to the working class, nor even to imply that the latter is "merely" a means with which the New Class pursues its own ends. For if there is anything that modern organizational analysis has taught us it is that human "instruments" are always recalcitrant, and readily become centers of interest in their own right. Once public commitments are made to any group, they are not easily set aside.

Besides, why would the intelligentsia *want* to ignore the interests of the working class? Given its own limited resources and numbers, the intelligentsia is constrained to collaborate with the working class and to attend to its interests, at least as it understands them.

Nor is there reason to suppose that the intelligentsia's sympathy for the working class is dissembled or that its expressions of populism are cynical. There is, indeed, an important kind of egalitarianism in its own culture of critical discourse, prescribing as it does that it is the speech and not the speaker—or his social position—that counts.

The New Class is an embryonic pre-figuring of the "universal" class, or is as nearly such as our own fluid epoch may expect to see. The position and training of the intelligentsia permit it a greater range of rationality—instrumental and substantive—than that of any other class today. Since its special status interests are invested in its educationally implanted culture—its "human capital"—the intelligentsia's fundamental precepts of distributive justice may dispose it to promote social equity within the framework of a wage system, rather than by protecting interest, rents, and profits.[22] That is, the New Class's principle of distributive justice is, "From each according to his ability, to each according to his work." The New Class, then, is not egalitarian, and is a flawed universal class. It insists that those who produce more and better work deserve superior rewards and privileges; and, believing that its own education, knowledge, and skill invest its work with superior value, the New Class also believes that *it* is especially entitled to advantage. This seems as true for intellectuals under capitalism as under socialism, and for bourgeois no less than socialist intellectuals. Yet we ought not conflate the two, since socialist intellectuals are tied to the working class primarily by bonds of ideology, and the proletariat has few effective sanctions it can impose on "its" intellectuals, while the bourgeoisie is capable of imposing powerful controls on its. As between proletariat and intellectual, who, then, is agent and who master?

Interpretations of Marxism are commonly caught between accepting Marxism's mythical self-understanding as "the consciousness of the proletariat," or rejecting this without clarifying the alternative. The choice is thus often between accepting Marxism's naïve self-understanding or rejecting it by denying the possibility for any rational interpretation of Marxism's *class* grounding. In a cynical version of the latter, Marxism is thought of as generated by power-hungry persons with no coherent class origin, with only random interests of their own, bent on capriciously manipulating society, while the "ignorant masses" are seen as vulnerable to their blandishments. Marxism is thus seen as irrational in inception and in reception. A focus on the role of intellectuals in the origins of Marxism, however, begins to recover its real class dimension and, surprisingly, with this, its rationality. Any conception of Marxism as the consciousness of the proletariat is mythification; acknowledging the special place of intellectuals in Marxism begins to lift the limits on Marxism's own self-understanding and to deepen its potential for rationality.

The Ambiguous Archaeology of Marxism

Yet simply to characterize Marxism as the ideology of the New Class of intellectuals and intelligentsia risks replacing the myth of the proletariat with a no less vulgar view of the New Class as a new exploitative master class, which implies an eternal "circulation of elites" without real historical change. A more serious answer, however, will note that the proletariat, whose interests Marxism claimed to represent, was never merely a lie to disguise the interests of the New Class. Rather, the proletariat is better understood as the radicalized intelligentsia's metaphor for a variety of goods and values it has sought, and for its *ideal* no less than its material interests.

The "essence" of the radical intelligentsia's political striving is the removal of any social obstacle to societal rationality. This intelligentsia can be the enemy of not only the contradictions of capitalist society but of *any* society, anywhere in the world, at any level of development. Their enemies may be moneylenders who exploit small peasants; the enemy may be rural landlords, local notables, or tribal chieftains whose vested interests lead them to betray the rules that every modern elite promises to follow: first, to act on behalf of the collectivity, and second, to live in conformity with such rules as it professes.

A Marxist "critique" is above all a critique that focuses on the societal elite's lack of rationality, here construed as their failure to live by rules, especially rules they themselves affirm. Marxist critique thus takes the special form, in Marx's words, of "making these petrified relations dance by singing before them their own tune."

Marxism, then, is a tacit promise of rationality. It is a promise that socialists will constitute a new and legitimate elite that will live by a set of rules, most especially the rule of every modern elite: Serve the People. Marxists aver that their new society will, in its maturity, have no internal contradictions preventing them from conforming to that rule, and that they will therefore actually give conformity to it and provide at least a rational governance.

At the deeper reaches of Marxism, what we unearth is the ancient commitment to govern rationally—the commitment to the "philosopher king." That is, it is a commitment to that rule calling for the unification of the good and the powerful. It is a promise to put governance in the hands of those who, having no institutional blockages to such obedience, will, in turn, put themselves under the governance of a rule of law and rationality. One of Marxism's deepest commitments, then, is to rationality and only then to whatever else is necessary for that.

It is at this level that Marxism has its deepest affinity for the New Class intellectuals and intelligentsia. Rationality and a "just" social order constitute their *ideal* interest, from whose Olympian perspective the working class's material interests appear shamelessly "economistic." For such intellectuals, the aim of socialist revolution is not to be reduced to a richer material life which, indeed, they may view as redolent of petty bourgeois consumerism. Their ultimate object is the enactment of supreme values alongside which other goods may appear banal and readily sacrificable. And yet, there remains the New Class's own elitism and insistence on privilege, legitimated under the principle, From each according to his ability, to each according to his work. Resting on a commitment to productivity, Marxism accommodates to the New Class's rejection of equality. More than other Marxisms, Maoism had an eye for the dangers to the revolution arising within Marxism itself, and recognized that these had a social infrastructure in Marxism's alliance with the New Class.

As we have seen, then, the successive waves of Mao's cultural revolutions were an offensive mounted less against the old bourgeoisie than against the Communist Party and its fusion with the New Class, against the traditional privileges of the intelligentsia, and against the educational institutions through which the New Class routinely reproduces itself. Much of the point of Mao's cultural revolutions, then, was directed against the *new cultural bourgeoisie* whose economic grounding was not in money but in human or cultural capital, education, involving the private enclosure of the culture commons, and whose emergence Mao sought to block. Although at this time the story is far from ended, it now seems that Mao has lost, that his cultural revolutions and their changes have been liquidated, and that Chinese Marxism, too, has allied itself with a resurgent New Class.

Marxism, then, lives on two levels: at one, it is a revolutionary materialism suspicious of theory and intellectuals, and opposed to the old capitalist order on behalf of the working class's self-emancipation. At another increasingly visible level, however, Marxism is committed both to the power of ideas to change the world and to the pursuit of productivity. *Both* these latter commitments open Marxism to intellectuals and intelligentsia, to a rationality that premises all speakers are equal, but which also demands that those who are intellectually superior—in their contributions to truth or to productivity—deserve superior rewards. In this, in all of it—in the goals and in the privileges offered those achieving them—Marxism converges with its sworn enemy and has secreted within itself part of its adversary's culture. Even "permanent revolution" was begun by the bourgeoisie. The ultimate meaning of the *revolution en permanence* was, however, interpreted by the Maoists as requiring a critique of the Communist Party itself and brought Maoism to the brink of transcending even Marxism. Maoism, then, was that Marxism on the verge of liquidating itself on behalf of an uncompromising equality.

Unlike the New Class, Maoism was eager to say with Gracchus Babeuf: "Let all the arts perish if need be, if only we have true equality." Yet only those who have not paid close attention will fail to notice that the surfacing of the near hysteria against culture on behalf of equality is today by no means a uniquely Chinese or even a Marxist peculiarity. The public defacements of great art in recent years in Amsterdam, Rome, and the Philippines tell their own story. The Bakuninist project of the liquidation of culture is currently reborn and legitimated by the quest for equality. Or perhaps our own involvement will be plain enough if we remember that it was, after all, Gracchus Babeuf, good Frenchman that he was, who spoke as he did.

In a rather remarkable document, Thomas Cottle describes how he spent the afternoon with a Black child, whose family he knows well. He and the child had visited university laboratories in Cambridge (Massachusetts) because the child was interested in science. This is what Cottle reports the mother as saying, upon their return home.

> So you took my boy to see all the famous scientists this afternoon. . . .
> That boy and his love of science. . . . Do you know how hard it is for
> me to keep my hatred of these folks away from his hearing? . . . Scien-
> tists . . . rich folks is what they are. . . . Making up problems where

problems don't really exist. Making things complicated when really what we need done is so simple a child could understand . . . what good are they doing for this country? What good are they doing for the Black folks? What do they find to do with all that money? Making their experiments and all, and just who do they experiment on? . . . they got better conditions for the dogs they do their experiments on than we've got for our children. . . . I blame them all, every one of them . . . you folks are responsible for making the whole community filled with bad cells, evil cells. . . .[23]

Signals grow clearer that a period of the *moyenne dureé* (which began with the industrial revolution) may be ending; that a new culture of material scarcities will require a redefinition of all previous conflicts, that strains will intensify irrationalities, and that the support for material welfare once joined with support of culture, may have been but a temporary alliance. The Marxist pursuit of socialism was never intended as the achievement of material welfare alone. Although it premised that the latter was necessary, Marxism was also ultimately grounded in the Enlightenment's project, and the human emancipation it sought fused *both* material welfare and enlightenment or culture. The signals now being received, however, may well forecast an end to the infinite economic progress Marxism more than tacitly premised; this then spurs the growth of irrational hostilities to culture, so that *both* pillars of the Marxist project of emancipation are in peril.

II

The Ecology of Marxism

3

Popular Materialism
and Historical Origins
of Marxism

Marxism emerged in part as a response to the development of industrialism in Western Europe and the resulting social disruption and human misery that Engels had studied in Manchester. Yet it was a response grounded in the everyday culture of a Christian Europe that was in some respects thousands of years old; more than that, and despite all of Marx's cosmopolitanizing travels, the Marxist response was partly a special product of the German society by which Marx and Engels had first been formed. As Marx liked to say, "I am by birth a German."[1] What he never said and hated to hear,[2] however, was that although baptized at age six, he had also been born a Jew, the descendant of a famous line of rabbis going back to the late Middle Ages. Despite this, or perhaps because of this, he had little or no sympathy for Jews, to say the least. As his favorite daughter, Eleanor, ruefully said, "I am the only one of my family who felt drawn to Jewish people. . . ."[3]

Marx would have been the first to agree that it was not only Marx the thinker that made Marxism, but the whole Marx, including the baptized German Jew who had been born into Europe at a very special moment in its history.

In this and the chapter following, I will assess the consequences of Marxism's emergence in this particular historical and cultural milieu. The thesis is that elements of popular culture structure theoretical culture via the mediation of the theorist's personal experience. The theory in some part expresses what the theorist, as a whole person, knows practically and pre-theoretically. Thus, I will argue that Marxism was originally shaped, *in part,* by an historically specific culture of popular materialism and, in particular, by its identification of one part of that materialism with Judaism and huckstering. This cultural ecology of Marxism, as I will show, both provided it with theoretical resources and resonances as well as limited its ultimate potential for rationality in important ways.

Preface to 1848

Marx and Engels were educated in the German society that emerged following the defeat of Napoleon, to which the German War of Liberation in 1813 contributed, and in an international setting that the 1815 peace settlement of Vienna sought to stabilize.[4] From 1815 until the revolutions in 1848, this was the era of Metternich. The European settlement he pursued sought to bottle up the bourgeois revolution, to restrict its spread throughout Central Europe, and, above all, to prevent the recurrence of Jacobinism and revolution. The *system* of governance to which it lent support on the European continent sought to steady the power of the elites and institutions of the old regimes, that were for the most part dominated by *non*-bourgeois groups and pre-bourgeois institutions.

At the same time, however, the economies and social structures underlying this system of governance continued to change and became increasingly middle class in character. There was thus a European-wide tension between the backward-looking systems of governance established after 1815 and the new economies and emerging social structures. The existing regimes could maintain themselves only by continuing efforts to control, to repress, and to manipulate the newly emerging social structures and groups. In 1848, however, they were brought to revolution.

The Germany into which Marx and Engels were born had seen the humiliating French conquest revenged and expunged, now making it easier for the young to adopt cosmopolitan views. It was a Germany whose further development was no longer subordinated to a foreign conqueror and in which, therefore, a politics was now possible; there was now less need to sublimate political ambition into cultural aspiration. The movement for a cultural revitalization that had been spearheaded previously by German Idealism and Romanticism might now launch a political and social reconstruction. German Romanticism was thus transcended (not superseded) by "The Young German Movement." Aesthetic criticism and metaphysics gave way to social criticism and political reorganization.

At the same time, however, significant continuities prevailed in German culture and social structure. One of the most important of these, which had emerged in Prussia even prior to German Romanticism, was the rationalistic drive of the German state itself and most especially of Prussia. The German *Aufklärung* had proceeded under state auspices and had served in effect as a philosophy of the state. Prussian politics and administration had proceeded with a high degree of instrumental rationalism and self-consciousness; it was a rationalism early subordinated to "reasons of state" and whose character became increasingly suffused with *Realpolitik*.

During the German subjection to Napoleonic power, the Prussian state had mobilized a "reform from above," strengthening itself in preparation for Napoleon's overthrow. Even prior to the French revolution there had been efforts at agrarian reform motivated by the king's desire to check his aristocracy, to prevent unrest, and to maintain the peasantry as a basis of military power, and these state initiatives were accelerated by the Napoleonic presence. Various strategies for eliminating serfdom were pursued which permitted the serfs to escape from feudal obligations, often, however, on the condition that they cede part of their land to their manorial lord who, in turn, no longer had the obligation to protect, lodge, or feed them. Agriculture became increasingly capitalistic and entrepreneurial, enabling the German aristocracy to adapt to the emerging market economy. However, while it became easier for them to buy or seize certain peasant properties, their own property was also increasingly enmeshed in market institutions; it could be marketed, or bought and sold, with the result that even before 1848 the middle classes themselves were getting a solid foothold in Junker estates.

The period after 1815 in Germany saw great economic and demographic change. In 1800, for example, there were only about five German joint stock companies; in 1825, however, there were some twenty-five of these in the Hohenzollern possessions alone; and by 1850, there were more than one hundred joint stock companies there. Between 1834 and 1848, the investment in heavy industry and railroads grew apace. During those fourteen years, some sixty million marks were invested in Prussian heavy industry and some 450 million marks in Prussian railroads. By 1850 German railroads had reduced the cost of shipping one ton of coal per kilometer from forty pfennigs to less than thirteen. Generally, in this period the growth of the industrial working classes in Germany was somewhat slower than in either France or England. Throughout all the Germanies, factory workers were then probably no more than about one-third the number of non-agricultural workers.

From about 1815 until the great depression of the mid-1840s, factory wages were increasing and factory workers had a higher standard of living than those working in agriculture or as artisans in shops. Still, their working day was between twelve to eighteen hours; they were frequently subject to various factory fines; their wages were sometimes paid in truck produce whose value was established by their employer; child and female labor was extensive. Indeed, as late as the middle of the nineteenth century, about 5 percent of all Prussian factory workers were children under fifteen years of age. In 1839, however, King Frederick Wilhelm III, in large part out of concern for military efficiency, passed the first child labor law, prohibiting the employment of children under nine as factory labor, and benevolently restricting those under sixteen to a mere ten hours a day.

From 1815 to 1845 the population of the Germanies grew about 38 percent, that is, from about 25,000,000 to about 34,500,000. With this, and particularly in the western and southern parts of Germany, there was a growing problem of relative overpopulation, an increasing labor supply, a growing land hunger, and a growing pressure for emigration from the countryside to the cities. Even in 1848, however, two-thirds of all Germans were still living on the land. Yet the growth of urban populations is also plainly visible if it is remembered that, at the time of the Congress of Vienna (at the beginning of this period), about 80 percent of all Germans then lived on the land.

The German agrarian problem intensified, partly because of growing land hunger, partly because of growing needs for economic efficiency, and partly because serfdom itself became increasingly regarded as immoral, while at the same time the actual rate of peasant emancipation was extremely slow. Indeed, between 1811 and 1848, only about 70,000 peasants in East Prussia had freed themselves, and in most cases this had required the cession of some part of their land, while another 170,000 had freed themselves through money payments. In contrast, and on the basis of the Law of 1850, some 640,000 peasants had freed themselves in East Prussia between that time and 1865, and in this case primarily by money payments rather than by ceding land.

The growth of capitalist institutions and industrialism, however, did not disturb merely the rural *countryside* and its institutions but also the *city* and its institutions. As a consequence of large intra-national migrations many city-dwellers were newcomers uncomfortable with urban life. Increasing industrialization meant the destruction of guilds and the old protections that these afforded artisans. Nonetheless, this change took place more gradually in Central than in Western Europe and it was, for the most part, only after the French revolution that the guilds lost their ancient prerogatives in Central Europe.

While the period of French domination had been a period of liberal reform by the German state, in the period after liberation reform gave way to conservatism and reaction by the state. After 1813 the German middle classes were poorly represented in the Diets of German provinces which were, to boot, relatively powerless. The middle classes experienced themselves as being taxed but underprivileged, as being subordinated to an aristocracy unjustly preferred by the Court and the Army, and as having to pursue economic development within the confines of a disunited Germany with its costly variety of legal and monetary systems. Resentment spread diffusely throughout the middle and, especially, lower middle classes in Germany, and they began to press for liberal reforms, for institutions facilitating economic development. They sought expansion of the Customs Union to all the Germanies; a unified system of transport and communication; greater freedom of enterprise and of occupational movement.

They began, also, to develop various programs for a liberal constitutionalism and extension of the franchise within which they, at least, could have more political influence, although they commonly did not press for *universal* manhood suffrage. Another form of emerging opposition to royal absolutism, however, was a more radical, democratic, or Jacobin-tinged opposition which did stress universal manhood suffrage, as well as increased welfare legislation; opting for a republican government, it sought reforms in a less compromising spirit.

The dissatisfactions of the emerging industrial proletariat, of the confined and relatively impotent middle classes, and of the peasantry or serfs, different though they were, came to be united against royal absolutism by the depression that began in the Germanies in the mid-1840s. The effects of this depression were coincident with a major European famine, the potato blight of 1845, that deprived the lower classes of one of their staple foods. As a result between 1844 and 1847 food prices rose about 50 percent concurrent with growing unemployment and destitution. It has been estimated that 10 percent of the Berlin population in 1846 were living by either crime or prostitution. Widespread and mass hunger riots began to occur in Germany in the years before 1848. There were peasant insurrections in the countryside, artisan riots in the city. When Louis Philippe was driven from his throne by the masses of Paris, the signal was given for European-wide revolution. It was plain that the old order was in desperate straits when the Habsburgs forced the resignation of Metternich. It was in this revolutionary historical setting that Marxism was conceived and developed.

Much of the experience of the forties had added up to this:

(1) That the economic and political orders were increasingly distinguishable and differentiated spheres; it was publicly manifest that it

was one thing to demand the *franchise* and quite another to seek *welfare* legislation; that it was one thing to be able to *vote* and another to be able to *eat*.

(2) Most particularly, with the depression and famine, it was evident that economic cycles had a certain autonomy and did not depend on (and might not be circumvented by) the political actions of parliaments or the decisions of constitutional conventions. It was seen that "objective" structures, as distinct from government policies, affected outcomes.

(3) It was also seen increasingly that political forces—e.g., the political interest of the middle class in opposing urban riots and peasant uprisings—were rooted in economic interests and motives. The political sphere was widely coming to be looked upon as a structure shaped by material forces and motives external to it. The common experience seemed to indicate the weakness of politics and the potency of economics. This, at any rate, was a definition of society congenial to a middle class whose own everyday life testified to the difference between their economic and political positions, to the weakness of their politics, and to the growing power of their economic position.

Revolution and Reaction

With the beginning of the German revolution of 1848, the liberals were swept into office. Once there, however, they almost immediately sought to repress the disorder and to control the urban masses and peasant *jacqueries*. The Jacobin impulses of the middle-class revolution were immediately smothered, and for much the same reasons that had brought Thermidor in France. The middle class feared the danger to their property, which was probably realistically greater than that existing when the French revolution had first taken place, given the greater development of the industrial working classes by 1848. The *Communist Manifesto* was undoubtedly correct in stating that many of the European middle classes were then haunted by the specter of communism.

It was very largely these fears of social revolution and of danger to property that disposed the new middle-class governments to crush the disorders: "From the destruction of ledgers and registers of landed holdings it is but one step to the destruction of mortgage records and promissory notes to the division of property or a common ownership of goods."[5] In short, "mob violence" was seen by some as leading to communism and as rooted in the economic and property interests—i.e., in the "material" interests—of urban masses. The urban "mob" was not seen (by the middle class) as motivated by *ideology, ethics,* or *moral outrage* but by the base "interests" of its "material" condition. This was a view congenial to a middle class that took it for granted that (its) property interests were the foundation of social order.

The very success of the new liberal governments in repressing mass militancy succeeded in destroying their *own* political position. In repressing the urban and rural masses, the liberal middle classes simultaneously lost them as allies, thus exposing themselves to the power of the monarchy. And it was not only their political repressiveness that isolated the middle classes, but their economic policies as well. The economic liberalism of the middle classes which sought to remove guild restrictions had the effect of thrusting the most militant wing of the revolution—namely, the artisans, who were commonly the streetfighters—back into the welcoming hands of the conservative-aristocratic faction. In this way, the middle-class revolution in Germany, having isolated itself from its own allies, was crushed.

With the defeat of the revolution of 1848, its leaders were swiftly disposed of: some were quickly dismissed from government, some tried and executed, others received long prison sentences, still others were expelled from their towns or bureaucratically harassed while remaining there, some lost their jobs, and some fled abroad. A cold wave of repression passed over German institutions: newspapers were intimidated; political meetings were subject to increased police surveillance; religious instruction was intensified in the schools.

The defeat of the German revolution of 1848 was one of the watersheds of modern German history. Out of it came a form of economic development which required the subordination of the German middle classes to a Prussian political framework based on the hegemony of an aristocratic elite and a rational bureaucracy united by a nationalistic ideology. The liberals remaining in Germany, at least immediately after the defeat, had little room for political maneuver, and whatever improvement they could foresee looked to the future. At this time, a period of economic recovery from the depression set in—a recovery that (according to some accounts) had already started shortly before the revolution itself and which was swiftly consolidated after its defeat. The period that followed was one of improved living standards and intensified economic growth.

Here, again, middle-class experience might be read as confirming the distinction between the political and economic orders, and the autonomy of the economic. Its defeat in politics was, in a way, compensated for by the improvement in business conditions and opportunities; *a kind of vulgar, economic materialism blanketed some sections of the middle classes* while the industrial working class continued, as before, to focus upon the improvement of its own economic conditions.

Popular Materialism:
The Economic Under the Political

One major consequence of the defeat of the German revolution was an accelerated effort to develop the German welfare state. Conservative and aristocratic factions began developing programs and policies that sought to forge an alliance between the Crown and the proletariat against the liberal middle class, and to justify autocratic power by developing a monarchy of social justice.

Not without reason, the conservative-aristocratic alliance conceived of the working class—and, indeed, of others—as capable of being placated by concessions to their *material* welfare and economic interests. They began to operate on the assumption that it was very largely these economic interests that were at the core of political ambitions. In short, the German "welfare state" began to emerge well prior to Bismarck's government as a deliberate stratagem of social control. Thus, one of King Frederick Wilhelm IV's advisers, General Joseph von Radowitz, advised the king as follows: "Any form of government which defends its interests boldly and wisely, which advocates the progressive income tax, the system of poor relief, the regulation of conflicts between capital and labor, will have the 'common man' on its side and thus a powerful force."[6]

This advice was seconded by the historian Leopold von Ranke, who wrote the king that

> . . . It is dangerous to train year after year the entire youthful population in the use of arms, and then alienate a large and physically perhaps the most vigorous part, leaving it exposed to the agitation of the enemies of all order. Either we must exempt the propertyless from the duty to serve the army, or we must place them under an obligation to the state by the prospect of gainful employment. Since the first course is out of the question because it would reduce our military strength, nothing remains but the second alternative.[7]

The Professor and the General thus agreed that what Germany needed was a "welfare" state; they also agreed tacitly that such a welfare state did not preclude a *warfare* state, but rather strengthened it.

To repeat: this political stratagem largely rested upon a tacit conception of the nature of political motivation and the sources of political unrest. It premised that political unrest can be obviated by economic and "material" concessions. It therefore premised that at the core of the political man there is an economic man. Such a "materialism" was consonant with the everyday life of the German (and Western) middle classes, convinced as they were that the foundation of order was property. What was happening was that the politically dominant aristocracy was in effect coopting the materialist discourse long current among the moneyed bourgeoisie. A newfound emphasis on and widespread respect for the "material" factor in politics and history thus emerged in Germany, an emphasis vital but by no means peculiar to Marxism. In a speech to the Association for the Protection of Property, Ernst von Bülow-Commerow insisted that: "material interests have a significance *outweighing all others,* and by pursuing them we will always be on firm grounds. Let us exert all our energies to advance these interests."[8]

In April of 1848, when Bismarck had asserted that ". . . we live in a time of material interests," he too acknowledged their potency even though complaining of it. By June of 1851, however, an orientation to material interests had become central to Bismarck's strategy of *Realpolitik.* "I would consider it most useful," he then remarked, "if we were to concern ourselves in good time with questions of German material welfare."[9] Again in 1862, in his famous address to the Budget Committee of the Prussian legislature, Bismarck stated, "The great questions of the time are decided not by speeches and majority resolutions. That was the mistake of 1848 and 1849. They are decided by blood and iron."

In short, the great questions of the time were to be dealt with, according to Bismarck, not by parliamentary politics but by the "hardest" of material concerns. These material factors are symbolized by the "blood and iron" which he counterposed to debate and discussion, implying that the latter are empty rhetoric. *Materialism, in short, became an aspect of the everyday ideology of German high politics and it emerged,* in some part at least, in the course of a polemic against the realm of rationality and rational discussion. Everyday "vulgar" materialism implied that rationalism was a "paper tiger." Popular materialism developed by counterposing itself to idealism: to be political meant to be realistic—i.e., not to confuse one's ideals with the "hard" realities—and to be realistic meant, for many, to acknowledge the force and legitimacy of materialistic interests.

This popular materialism entailed certain basic assumptions about man and society. There is, first, an assumption about *the distinction between the economy and polity* which converges with the widespread distinction between "civic society" and the "state," and, second, there is an assumption about the *priority* of the economy, that politics and ideology depend on material interests. This materialism was not a narrow technical doctrine of philosophers but background assumptions of everyday life widely shared among the European middle classes during their emergence in public life. As one observer remarked in 1847, "as long as there was an honest livelihood, none of the Silesian weavers paid any attention to Communist agitation."[10] Marx's own materialism was grounded in a popular materialism that was not then the monopoly of the left, of the radicals, or of revolutionary groups; indeed, at certain periods, it was no less attractive to conservative thinkers and to established or dominant social classes.

An interesting case in point of a conservative—indeed, of a monarchist —who was also attracted to the emerging "materialist" background assumptions was Lorenz von Stein. In manifest kinship with Marx's materialism, Stein's views postulated "the conflict of interests between social classes in the center . . . of history . . ."[11] and held that "the differentiation of wealth and status established a class pattern in any society. . . ." Stein's concept of class is based mainly on the distribution of property; ". . . he often speaks of the 'property-owning vs. the property-less classes. . . .' "[12] In his study of France, he regards property as the decisive factor in modern society.

He held that "state power becomes misused in the interest of the upper class."[13] "He considered changes in constitutional and civil law to be the result of economic factors rather than ideas. . . ."[14] "He developed the concept of the proletariat . . . [seeing it] as a class-conscious unit struggling for power in pursuit of their interests."[15] Unlike Marx, however, Stein did not see the destruction of capitalism as inevitable; Stein regarded the proletariat as potentially dangerous to society and as needing to be protected by social reforms that, he believed, the state might initiate to protect private property. Stein's materialism, then, was a conservative version of the popular materialism of everyday life. Marx's materialism was a radical revision of the popular materialism of everyday life and thus a product of bourgeois culture and its materialist discourse.

Interests and Popular Materialism[16]

Popular materialism was (and is) a tacit theory of human nature and of social action which is nucleated, in part, by assumptions concerning "interests" and "interest." As a first step, it is useful to notice that, in this everyday theory, interests = material; that is, "material" and "interests" have a metaphorical equivalence. According to the rules of popular materialism, one may speak of "material interests," but one is more likely to refer to spiritual "commitments" rather than interests. The idea of an "ideal interest" will later be formulated, but primarily on the basis of a post-Marxist analogy with "material interests." Interests thus invokes the material and the material invokes interests; the sense of each implicates the other.

As "material," interest has the sense of a hard, tangible thing—on a tacit analogy with "matter"—having substance and weight, limiting, shaping, and affecting outcomes, needing to be adapted to. An interest is an out-there thing existing apart from what anyone thinks of it, thus constraining persons and their plans. In popular materialism, an interest does not arise from a choice made by actors but resides outside of them, constituting the grounds to which their action must adapt. One does not choose one's interests as one might an ideology but rather these impose themselves as constraints. The idea of an interest, therefore, is implicated in the metaphysics of constraint. Constraint is the fetishistic structuralism of an impersonal interest; unlike the exercise of force and violence, it is not inflicted by persons but by things—structures or systems.

While *knowledge* about interests may require work, interests themselves are not conceived as worked-up and produced but, rather, as having a kind of presented "givenness." The givenness of interests has the character of a non-negotiable thing which, being linked to a gratification, resists appraisals that might inhibit or frustrate it. In popular materialism, an interest, then, is that which is experienced and presented as beyond discussion. It is the starting point and motor of discussion rather than a topic of discussion. What is in our interests is taken as already there and, indeed, as usually known intuitively to the normal actor; efforts to make it problematic are experienced as unrealistic or "double-talk." Common sense assumes that you cannot talk someone into accepting slavery or his own capital punishment.

Material interests are thus dissonant with rational discourse, for rational discourse never regards anything as permanently unproblematic and beyond discussion. Status groups whose ideology centers on discourse are, therefore, likely to experience the rhetoric of material interests as violating the norms of rationality. Here is an essential tension between the propertied section of the middle class and its educated sector, the New Class intellectuals. The latter, or radicalized sections of them, are willing to make the property interests of the middle class problematic and to discuss them critically.

If this tension is one source of the intellectuals' critique of bourgeois society and of their own alienation from it, it is also a basic source of the false consciousness of the New Class of intellectuals and intelligentsia insofar as they conceive themselves as "autonomous"—i.e., as free of limiting class (or material) interests. Apart from manifest social conflicts based on opposing material interests, there is, then, a hidden conflict in bourgeois society, the conflict between social strata governed by the rhetoric of "interests" and others who conceive themselves as controlled by commitments to "rationality." From this standpoint, a sector of the intelligentsia places itself in opposition to the bourgeoisie, not only because their "interests" are in opposition, but also because the very materialist logic of interest is offensive to the intelligentsia's ideology—i.e., its commitment to discursive rationality.

Marxism thus views the bourgeoisie—and not only them—as possessing a common interest which, in turn, is understood as an ultimate limit on their rationality. The proletariat is seen in like manner: as having interests that oppose those of the bourgeoisie. "Profit rises in the same degree in which wages fall," observed Marx, and "it falls in the same degree in which wages rise."[17] Yet even the proletariat's own immediate interests in "material" benefits are also seen as inhibiting pursuit of its own long-range interests. The proletariat's interest in higher wages and better working conditions may divert it from its historical mission of overthrowing the entire wage-labor system and replacing it with an emancipatory socialism. ". . . [T]he working class ought not to exaggerate to themselves the ultimate working of these everyday struggles," warned Marx; "they ought not to forget they are fighting with effects, but not with the causes of these effects."[18] In confusing surface appearances with reality, effects for causes, the working class is clearly manifesting a defective *rationality*.

A working class's exclusive focus on the immediate, on material interests, is thus seen as manifesting the limits of its everyday, common-sensical theory of action; revealing a tacit theory that needs to be transcended by a larger, more encompassing and articulate rationality, which incorporates but does not limit itself to the logic of interests. The working class's everyday, "natural" theory of action is in effect a popular materialism that it has not yet transcended. In Lenin's later term, this materialism will be characterized and condemned as "economism." Lenin and Kautsky will also both argue that the proletariat must, if it is to emancipate itself, be subjected to a higher rationality, to a theory that will free it from its bondage to immediate interests. This theory, both Kautsky and Lenin agree, can come only from bourgeois intellectuals outside the proletariat. This tacitly says that the working class must accept the governance of a theoretical rationality (and of status groups bearing it) that critically examines unexamined interest and which sublates the working class's popular materialism.

Marxism thus accepts popular materialism, and with this the working class's everyday theory of interests, but only to a limited extent, only as a starting mechanism to launch the proletariat in "spontaneous," i.e., interest spurred, struggle against the bourgeoisie. For interests of the working class are seen as limited. They permit what is at best a courageous but essentially blind guerrilla warfare and are unable to bring the working class's struggle to a successful emancipatory conclusion.

Marxism's "materialism" thus incorporates popular materialism but also transcends it. Marxism converges with popular materialism's critique of the weakness of rationality, discourse, and parliamentarianism and its effort to ground itself in something "stronger" than "mere talk,"—i.e., in power, in struggle (i.e., "blood and iron"), and in the hardening of the self. Marxism uses popular materialism as an antidote to the "sentimental" assumption that the world could be changed by rational persuasion alone, an assumption which pathetically premises that the ills of the world are grounded in wrong thinking. Yet Marxism also insists that popular materialism is vulgar, incapable of seeing beyond the immediate present, and has only a limited idea of what an interest is.

Marxism is thus an effort to incorporate, yet to transcend, popular materialism. It reinterprets it from the standpoint of a specific stratum, that of New Class intellectuals, and from a specific culture, the culture of critical discourse. Yet there is both transcendence of popular materialism and CCD, and the subversion of contradiction of each. Interest violates CCD politically. Here the CCD is used to help the proletariat escape the limits of its immediate interests; correspondingly, Marxism uses the standpoint of "interest" to develop a critique of the CCD itself. In effect, then, Marxism infuses the CCD and intellectuals with a strain of "realism," bringing them into closer contact with the everyday world, while enabling the working class to transcend and see alternatives to their everyday world.

Theorist in the Theory

Certainly, Marx's is a philosophical and historical materialism which was developed within the idiom of a technical intellectual tradition in Germany and, in that respect, differs from the everyday materialism then becoming pervasive in German culture. While the two are therefore by no means identical, they are nonetheless interconnected.

One kind of relationship that exists between everyday materialism and Marx's theorized materialism is the relationship of the articulate to the tacit, of the critically examined to the uncritically affirmed. In one part, popular materialism was an unreflective, taken-for-granted belief system anchored in a symbolism that was clarified in Marx's explicit theoretical system. Given the idealism of the dominant philosophical orientations that surrounded Marx in his early development and education, it is clear that his philosophical materialism cannot be accounted for merely as a simple extension and systematic refinement of this technical academic tradition. This is not to say, however, that Marx's materialism was not importantly influenced by earlier technical philosophical developments, perhaps most particularly by Ludwig Feuerbach and the Left Hegelians who, in their critique of religion, took a 180-degree turn toward materialism. Yet even these theoretical "anticipations" of Marx's materialism do not deny the importance of the everyday for philosophical materialism, for these anticipations themselves need an explanation. In short, while Marx's own emerging philosophical materialism was part of a larger technical development of intellectual materialism in the Germany of his period, this larger drift too must be seen in its relationship to popular German materialism. Indeed, one may say of *all* the German philosophical materialists of the period what I have said of Marx alone: they refined the emerging popular materialism; their technical materialism resonates and recovers popular materialism and finds in it an "intuitive" and verifying isomorphism. Everyday materialism provides technical materialism with a *déjà vu* sense of confirmation.

But the relationship between these two levels, between everyday culture and philosophical theory, is still more complex. For one thing, emerging everyday materialism expressed and inculcated a structure of sentiment dissonant with the prior philosophical idealism, still academically dominant. There was a tension between the emerging culture of everyday materalism and the mandarin tradition of technical philosophical idealism which, at first, only vaguely discomfited some theorists and initially disposed them to back away from idealism. Indeed, Marx had a sense of the craggy grotesqueness of Hegel from his very first, youthful reading. The cultural level, then, in effect generated an unnoticed dissonance with received idealism spurring a quest for other, less dissonant, intellectual positions.

Something of this dissonance can be seen in one of Marx's earliest known manuscripts (1835), "Reflections of a Youth on Choosing an Occupation," which he wrote just prior to graduating from the Trier Gymnasium. Here two very different impulses are expressed. In one, there is a strongly idealistic, even romantic emphasis on the significance of making a correct decision concerning vocational choice, experienced as a part of a lofty "striving beyond" and as infused with an articulate religious conception of vocation as divinely instilled: "Everyone has a goal which appears to be great, at least to himself, and is great when deepest conviction, the innermost voice of the heart, pronounces it great; for the Deity never leaves man entirely without a guide; the Deity speaks softly, but with certainty."[19] In short, an emphasis is placed upon "decision" as a crucial art of the self, and as entailing an obligation to make certain that the inward call is a genuine one and not a self-deception.

Yet counterposed to this idealistic stress, an emphasis is also placed upon materialistic factors whose legitimacy (not simply their potency) is clearly underlined. Marx remarks that "even our physical nature often threateningly opposes us, and no one dare mock its rights!" Here there is an echo of the Saint-Simonian resurrection of the flesh. In a similar vein, he worries that one's entire life can become "an unfortunate struggle between the intellectual and the physical principle." It is hard to believe that this "materialist" component, in the essay of this seventeen-year-old boy, is primarily attributable to the influence of other philosophical materialists and of his prior philosophical sophistication. Here, the deeper paleosymbolism of the later materialism is discernible with biographical specificity.

If popular materialism stimulated sentiments at variance with German philosophical idealism, tending thereby to withdraw credence from it, they conversely lent credence to the emerging *philosophical* materialism, even if only unexamined credence. This new popular ideology and paleosymbolism appeared as a two-edged development, on the one hand discomfiting old technical theories, and, on the other hand, generating a diffuse atmosphere that "fit" certain new technical theories. The new technical theory served to resolve the dissonance between the received, older intellectual tradition formally transmitted to the thinker and the new everyday ideology into which he had been socialized well before his formal training.

The question of the relationship of Marx's philosophic materialism to popular German materialism is of interest also because it is a case of a larger and more general problem in the sociology of social theory, namely, the conditions that generally lead theorists to reject older theories and to commit themselves to new ones.

The answer suggested here to this question is decidedly different from the conventionally rationalistic one, which tends to assume that social theorists make commitments only after they have acquired data relevant to the theory, and that if they do otherwise there is something wrong with them. Marx's own position on this matter was quite close to the contemporary scholarly self-understanding; i.e., he too stressed the empirical foundations and scholarly scruples of his theory. He tells us, for instance, that, "Science is only genuine science when it proceeds from sense experience, in the two forms of sense perception and sensuous need. . . ."[20] Similarly, he remarks in a positivistic vein, also in the *Economic and Philosophical Manuscripts*, "It is hardly necessary to assure the reader who is familiar with political economy that my conclusions are the fruit of an entirely empirical analysis, based upon a careful critical study of political economy."[21] (So much for Engels as the positivistic seducer of Marxism!) Some regard such statements by Marx as a self-deception, holding that they conceal the fact that Marx had formulated his position prior to his empirical economic studies. I do not disagree with the first observation, but only with the implication that this distinguishes Marx from other, more "truly scientific," contemporary social scientists. This false-consciousness was not peculiar to Marx and continues to be shared by most social scientists today. In contrast to conventional methodological moralism, my own view is that *one* fundamental reason social theorists commit themselves to a specific theory is precisely because this theory seems "intuitively" right to them, well in advance of any systematic empirical test given to it; and it seems right because it is consonant with their own "experience," which is to say because it recovers and congenially resonates the popular theories and deeper paleosymbolism into which they had been socialized.

The theory seems right because it recovers and is consonant with their experience; and because it enables them to live without contradicting what the theorists take to be their own personal experience. A theory that is felt to be right, however, also *transforms* the theorist's deeper paleosymbolism—hitherto residing only in his subsidiary awareness—by shifting it into focal awareness. In that sense, the new technical theory serves to validate and resituate fundamental aspects of the theorist's self. Social theory, then, is a recovery of self, however much it may be formulated with positivistic false consciousness as only a discovery about the *world*.

Articulate theory or ideology is a liberation of a structure of belief and symbolism alienated within the theorist; in short, theory-making is in part a recovery and a liberation of the theorist's suppressed self. Which may explain why so much of theory-making (and of science) is so often experienced by the theorist as a kind of "birth." He does not commonly regard his theory as a mere intellectual artifice which he himself has invented, but as something more nearly akin to a "delivery" or recovery of something that was already "there." The point of my remarks above is that, often enough, this is indeed correct. In embarking on his explorations of the world, what the theorist will in time inevitably encounter is—himself. Technical social theory is thus often nothing less than the theorist's self-consciousness disguised as rationality.

Paradoxically, however, the theorist almost immediately proceeds to alienate this self-awareness by casting it in terms of received technical traditions. He must, that is, deny that his knowledge is in part a recovery of some aspect of himself and is based upon his *personal* experience.

He proceeds with all speed to conceal his personal involvement; he denies that his theory is rooted in a personal knowledge, by socializing this knowledge in the grammar of a technical tradition, thereby objectifying it. Having given birth to this child, the theorist denies that it is his.

And in some part, he is right. For the popular theory and deeper symbolism the theorist recovers and reworks is not his own personal invention, but that of the culture into which he was born. It is not "his" in the further sense that "he" does not merely possess or use it but he is in part possessed, *constituted*, and *shaped* by it. Like the germ plasm borne by people, this anterior culture is only ambiguously "theirs"; they mediate it rather than invent it; are shaped by it, even before they actively and selectively transmit it. The theorist's work then is not simply that of research but also that of recovery.

4

The Binary Fission
of Popular Materialism

Marx's philosophical materialism was not only a recovery but a reworking of popular materialism that proceeded in a very specific way, by
splitting the latter into two parts—a positive or prized part and a negative or disvalued part. Marx tacitly divided everyday materialism—and
capitalism, itself—into the "sacred and the profane," the clean and the
dirty. For Marx, everyday materialism was grounded in a symbolism
that included egoism-venality-huckstering-money-materialism, the crass
or "vulgar" materialism which he sought to segregate and isolate, preventing it from polluting the valued side of materialism, which was realistic and demystifying.

What is the economic content of these two sides of materialism? The
valued component consists of the productive, or work side, the *forces* of
production (i.e., the *Produktivkrafte* or *produktive Fahigkraften*). In
short, Marx accepts the power of the *Produktivkrafte;* however, he finds
capitalist relations of production, its *verhalten*,[1] contemptible; he wishes
to split the two, extricating capitalism's powerful forces of production
from its crippling association with its relations of production, and re-
situating this power in a new system of socialist relationships that will
emancipate it.

Marx conceives of the valued side of materialism, then, as incorporating man's "species being," his capacity of *self*-creation through conscious
labor—"a condition of human existence . . . independent of all forms
of society." It is through labor that man makes nature his own, simultaneously transforming his consciousness, his self, and creating his very

world. For Marx, the unity of man and nature is an act achieved through work. The central component of the valued side of the materialistic is labor, through which man overcomes fragmentation, makes the world whole, unites himself with, but at the same time sets himself above, nature. Marx's materialism, then, is grounded in a symbolism of *a redemptive labor, the gospel of labor,* in which man will be transfigured and made worthy by work, in accord with Hegel's master-bondsman dialectic.

Marx's Binary Fission of Capitalism

Paleosymbols on the Positive Side (*Industrialism*)	Paleosymbols on the Negative Side (*Capitalism*)
Sacred	Profane
Rational	"Interest"
Healthy	Pathological
Work, labor, technology	Commerce, venality, acquisitiveness, money
Forces of production	Relations of production
Self-creation	Self-alienation
Gentile	Jewish
Honest	Dishonest
Need-satisfying	Profit-making
Masculine	Feminine

Marx's materialism entails a tacit fission of popular materialism's symbolism into two parts, a pathological or venal part and a healthy or productive part. If the first is the vulgar or crass side of popular materialism, the second—paradoxically—is the "spiritual" side of materialism, in the sense that, for Marx, it expresses the highest, truest, and most authentic character of the human species. In short, Marx's philosophical materialism refines popular materialism precisely by spiritualizing it; by idealizing work and romanticizing productivity. At the same time, Marx refines popular materialism by condemning and extruding *commerce* and *money.* Marx's own materialism, then, is produced by waging war against two great symbol systems: God/religion and commerce/money, the first being central to his critique of popular idealism (i.e., religion), the second, central to his critique of popular materialism.

Money, says the young Marx ironically in his *Economic and Philosophical Manuscripts,* overcomes and transforms every individual flaw and vice; it enables people to compensate for their own personal defects. The stupid man with money "can buy talented people for himself," complains the brilliant Marx; the ugly man with money "can buy the most beautiful woman,"[2] complains the vigorous young man without money. Money can achieve all that men seek, even if they lack the individual qualities that would merit such satisfactions. Without money, men's desires are unreal, imaginary; only with money do they achieve real being. Money, then, is what transforms desire into reality. At one and the same time, says Marx, money is the universal whore and the visible deity of bourgeois society. Capitalism, in effect, is a false worship of Mammon, involving a hidden metaphoricality in which god = money.[3]

Moreover, money is the fundamental source of the grotesque in the modern world, for it is that which brings about the "fraternization of incompatibles."[4] It is that which enables ugly men to possess beautiful women, stupid men to control talented men, and cowards to buy the protection of the brave. Money ". . . exchanges every quality and object for every other, even though they are contradictory. It is the fraternization of incompatibles; it forces contraries to embrace." It produces the "unnatural."[5] Money, in short, produces the sociological miscegenation central to the Romantic idea of the "grotesque."

It is evident from Marx's conception of money as the fount of the grotesque, that he holds this aspect of popular materialism in contempt. Similarly, in Marx's critique of "crude" Communism, he also condemns a society that entails "the domination of material property . . . [and seeks] immediate physical possession." Here Marx clearly rejects the part of popular materialism which equates welfare with consumerism.

Anti-Semitism and the Critique of Capitalism

There is at least one other distinctive site in which Marx's splicing of popular materialism is manifested forcefully and, in particular, where he rejects most violently its huckstering or venal side. This is in his discussion of the Jews, especially in his 1844 essays responding to Bruno Bauer on the Jewish question in the *Deutsch-Franzoische Jahrbucher*. The "secret of the Jew," says Marx here, is not in his religion; rather, he says, this religion itself must be understood in terms of its everyday, profane basis: "What is the profane basis of Judaism? Practical self-interest. What is the worldly cult of the Jew? Huckstering. What is his worldly god? Money."[6] Our age, he says, cannot emancipate itself except by emancipating itself from practical Judaism. Here, then, Marx fuses two powerful negative symbols: money and Jews.

The crux of the matter is, first, that Marx does split popular materialism into two parts—an industrial-productive part or the "forces of production" that he prizes—distinguishing it from the commercial huckstering side that he condemns—and, second, that *he links the latter to the symbolism of the Jew.* Marx specifically held that "the essence of the Jew was universally realized and secularized in civil society. . . ."[7] He maintained, moreover, that "we discern in Judaism, therefore, a universal anti-social element of the present time, whose historical development zealously aided in its harmful aspects by the Jews, has now attained its culminating point. . . ."[8] Marx, in short, equated the rejected, anti-social, commercial side of contemporary society with Jewishness and, conversely, he equated Jewishness with huckstering, an equation already built into the German term *Judentum.* The metaphoricality here is blatant: Capitalism = Jewishness = Huckstering. This suggests that an anti-Semitic symbolism was *one* of the crucial elements that led Marx to split popular materialism and capitalism precisely along the lines that he did; to conceive of the commercial market or "huckstering" relations of capitalism as the baneful, negative essence of capitalism, and to seek to "purify" and protect the forces of production, the industrial, honest "gentile" component, by extruding commercial huckstering. Our age, he says, cannot emancipate itself except by emancipating itself from "real and practical Judaism," which is huckstering and money. The Jew and his religious consciousness, Marx says, would "evaporate" in any society that would eliminate the need for the possibility of huckstering.

Marx quotes Bruno Bauer as stating that the Jew determines the fate of "the whole Austrian Empire by his financial power."[9] Far from contradicting Bauer, Marx adds, "this is not an isolated instance," and he continues by remarking that "it is through the Jew—and also apart from him—that money became a world power."

Moreover, Marx also maintains that the Jewish religion as such contains "in an abstract form . . . contempt for theory, for art, for history, and for man as an end in itself." In short, for Marx, the Jewish religion contained a contempt for almost every aspect of culture dear to German idealism. Moreover, the Jews' nationality, Marx held, is a "chimerical nationality,"[10] the nationality of a financier. Concerning the relative moral merits of Judaism as compared with Christianity, Marx maintains inviduously that "Christianity is the sublime thought of Judaism; Judaism is the vulgar practical application of Christianity."[11]

What needs to be noted is the distorted character of the judgment that Marx pronounced upon Judaism rather than simply assimilating his views, as does Hal Draper, to the anti-Semitism conventional to his time. Certain obvious internal discrepancies in Marx's commentary on Judaism may be briefly noted. For one, even as Marx was holding Jewry up to public contempt, as the universal worshipper of money and loathsome practitioner of huckstering, many of the Jews that Marx knew personally, and, indeed, from whom he learned intellectually, in short, Jews who might have been personally real to him—such as Eduard Gans, Moses Hess, Heinrich Heine, Ludwig Borne, Spinoza, and others—were altogether unlike his description of Jews in *The Jewish Question*. To write as he did, then, Marx literally had to defy the evidence of his own experience.

Indeed, even as Marx was stereotyping Jewry for its love of money, there was then emerging throughout Europe the phenomenon of the Jewish radical who, like Marx, hated rather than worshipped money but found no acknowledgment in Marx's *Jewish Question* or in his later writings. Indeed, Marx's analysis of the social nature of Judaism exhibits an almost willful ignorance of what he might have known personally or learned readily from his studies. Even an elementary knowledge of the then normal Jewish community plainly exhibited the exceptional importance Jews attributed to *learning*, not simply to money. Jewish communities at that time were internally governed by a social elite that was a unique combination of the moneyed and the scholarly; rich Jewish fathers traditionally sought eligible young scholars to marry their daughters. The desire of young Jews for a higher education was exceptional and, indeed, they often retreated into business, trade, or banking only— as for example, in the case of the Saint-Simonian, Olinde Rodriques— when religious discrimination excluded them from college. To have condemned Jewry for devotion to money when Jewish youth, as much or more than most, were frequently radical and were traditionally devoted to learning and scholarship, was willfully obtuse and a travesty of scholarship.

Indeed, what scholarship justified Marx's view that Judaism was an ahistorical essence which, under any and all social conditions, eternally expressed itself as huckstering? The learned Saul Padover chides Marx, observing that as an historian he "should have known that the founders and earliest practictioners of Judaism were not money-minded tradesmen but shepherds and simple country people who were moved by an overwhelming sense of a monotheistic Deity; and that insofar as later Jews, dispersed in Christian Europe, pursued money affairs, they did so out of desperate necessity, and not out of an inner faith, primarily in countries where virtually all other means of livelihood were closed to them, as, for example, in Czarist Russia."[12] Indeed, any perceptive social analysis of the Jewish trade would have at least considered the possibility that the Jews were not stigmatized by Christians because they pursued money but that they pursued money because they were stigmatized; i.e., because they were vulnerable in a world dominated by Christians, many of whom held that the Jews had "killed Christ" and accused them of the ritual murder of Gentile children. (Certainly any disinterested devotee of "transformative criticism," such as Marx, might be expected to consider *this* reversal of subject and predicate.)

If Marx lauds the bourgeoisie for revolutionizing production, one wonders why he knew (or said) nothing about those Jews who were "the moving spirits behind branches of new activities such as railroad building or the German textile industry . . . the non-ferrous metals trade, the creation of the electrical industry. . . ."[13] In short, Jews no less than their Gentile counterparts were then revolutionizing productivity. Why not, therefore, acknowledge the Jewish contribution to this then progressive phase of bourgeois development, as Marx extolled that of Christian entrepreneurs? Indeed, even the bitterly anti-Semitic utopian socialist Charles Fourier admitted that (at least in France) the populace welcomed the reduction in prices that Jewish businessmen brought. ". . . [T]he people exclaim in admiration," observed Fourier, " 'Long live competition! Long live the Jews, philosophy and fraternity! The price of all goods has fallen since Iscariot arrived'; and the public says to the rival firms: 'It is you gentlemen who are real Jews.' "[14] Marx makes no such acknowledgment of the public utility of Jewish businessmen.

In some part, the special vehemence of Marx's judgment on Jews derives from his submersion in German culture. The special character of German anti-Semitism was evidenced by the greater propensity of prominent German Jews to convert to Christianity than those of other nationalities.[15] Indeed, "the phenomenon of the cult of the Germanic race which surged up in Germany at the beginning of the nineteenth century has no analogy in any other country. None of the varieties of European nationalism which were beginning to compete with one another at the time assumed this biologically oriented form. Between 1790 and 1815, with practically no transition, writers moved on from the idea of a specifically German mission, to the glorification of the language, and from there to a glorification of German blood. . . ."[16] The vehemence of Marx's judgment on Judaism is as much grounded in this emerging peculiarity of German culture as in the imposed apostasy of this descendant of long generations of rabbis.

The obvious question that arises is whether Marx's feelings about Jews were the source of his critique of the commercial huckstering side of capitalism, or whether his hostility to a huckstering-market society was the source of his views about Jews. Doubtless the two tendencies interpenetrate and are difficult if not impossible to separate. Yet the fact remains that Marx's contempt for huckstering and commercialization was, in some part, given specifically anti-Jewish form and crystallization.

Nonetheless, it would be mistaken to regard this as the only source of

Marx's condemnation of commercialization. For behind the hostility to huckstering and behind the anti-Jewishness common among German university youth at that time—and indeed underlying them both—there were other powerful motives: the concern for the welfare of larger collectivities; for German society and "humanity" as a whole; for "man" in his universal character as a "species-being." Commercialization was condemned, then, as an expression of selfish "eogism"; as a social arrangement that incites a base egoism diverting men from their true nature and highest ideals. In other words, behind both anti-Jewishness and anti-commercialism—particularly among university youth—there was a German idealism whose particularistic expression was nationalism. For the most part, Marx shared these collectivity oriented sentiments—including the nationalism—except, however, that he focused them more universalistically upon the need for a human emancipation whose instrument would be the proletariat.

There were, then, at least two overlapping elements in Marx's condemnation of commercial huckstering: anti-Jewishness and anti-egoism. Yet the anti-Jewish element is important because it sharpens Marx's conception of capitalism as at bottom "commercial" and huckstering, while focusing his conception of socialism on the elimination of commodity production for private gain.

The Nuclear Metaphor of Marxism: Capitalism = Huckstering = Judaism

Marx held that the historical stimulus to (and continuing essence of) capitalism was huckstering, the buying and selling of products and labor power: "The circulation of commodities is the starting point of capital. Commodity production and that highly developed form of commodity circulation which is known as commerce constitute the historical groundwork upon which it rises. The modern history of capital begins in the sixteenth century with the establishment of a worldwide commercial system and the opening of the world market."[17] And again, Marx adds that "the starting point of capitalist production is where a large number of workers are aggregated at one time and in one place . . . under the command of one capitalist, for the production of one and the same kind of commodity. As regards the actual method of production, manufacture, for instance, can hardly be said to differ from the handicraft industry of the guilds. . . . Thus at first the difference is merely quantitative."[18] In short, the capitalist has really added nothing to the process; he has merely brought the process already existing under his own control, and the importance attributed to the technological changes Engels focused on in his study of the working class in Manchester is here downplayed.

Two points are noteworthy: one, that capitalism starts when the same process of production is subjected to the control of commercial capital, of money; second, rather less focal, is that the sheer difference in the social organization of the work group is not seen as an element of *rationality* contributed by the commercial capitalist, even though Marx recognizes that this reorganization does heighten productivity. Capitalism begins, then, in the original sin of huckstering and continues to carry this sociological taint within itself, stamped indelibly upon its most elemental structure, the commodity. Marx sees huckstering—the quest for private gain by buying and selling—as a central part of the infrastructure of capitalism, as the essence of modern capitalism. In *Capital*, Marx asserted that the core of capitalism was an economic system in which, on the one hand, men produce "commodities" to sell for a profit on an impersonal market, and in which, on the other hand, this production involves a relationship between capitalists owning the means of production and buying the labor power of the workers, while the propertyless workers themselves are forced to sell their labor power to capitalists. The objects produced are "commodities," born in sin because produced with the intention of selling them for a profit rather than to satisfy human needs. The capitalist is regarded as historically unique in that he has an *endless,* avaricious, insatiable thirst for profit.

Marx thus sees the worker-capitalist relationship as venal to the core, as characterized by the fact that the capitalist buys, and the worker sells, labor power. It is this buying and selling of human beings' capacity for work that he regards as the most disgusting essence of the historically distinctive system of capitalism. Marx thus locates the market, commercial, huckstering component directly within the *nucleus* of the productive arrangements of capitalism. He does not simply see commerce as distinct from or auxiliary to capitalism, or as separated from it in a specialized, "commercial" system of distribution or finance. The entire capitalist apparatus, in its most essential respects, is held to be shaped by the buying and selling of human lifetime and the manufacture of products intended to produce a profit through their sale. The commercial disease is thus located within the productive core of capitalism.

Although there is a substantial shift in focus from the Marx of 1844 to that of *Capital*—from his early focus on money and its corrupting grotesqueness to the later analysis of capitalist modes of reproduction—money does not disappear in the late Marx, or even become less salient in his developing conception of capitalism. One might be tempted to say that the early Marx focused on and condemned money as the false worship of Mammon, but that the older Marx of *Capital* focused on profit or gain, rather than money as such. Yet money and gain/profit are inseparable in Marx's mature analysis of capitalism.

As he notes in *Capital*, "Every new aggregate of capital enters upon the stage, comes into the market (the commodity market, the labour market, or the money market), in the form of money—of money which by a definite process, has to be transformed into capital."[19] Marx distinguishes a process (1) of simple commodity circulation, C-M-C, "the transformation of a commodity into money, and the retransformation of money into a commodity; selling in order to buy" from that other process (2) of mature commodity circulation, whose formula is M-C-M, "the transformation of money into commodities, and the retransformation of commodities into money. . . ." It is through this second process that money becomes capital: "Money that circulates in the latter way is thereby transformed into capital, is already potential capital."[20] In the first formula, says Marx, money is surrendered to produce "use values" but in the second, M-C-M formula, "the purchaser surrenders money in order that, as a seller, he may get money back."[21] Marx adds: "The circuit, M-C-M . . . sets out from money, and ultimately comes back to money again"; hopefully and necessarily, *more* money, M', or else the process will not continue. The circulation of money as capital, states Marx, "is an end in itself, for the expansion of value can only occur within this perpetually renewed movement. Consequently, the circulation of capital knows no limits."[22] (It is, in the words of Emile Durkheim, an insatiably *anomic* process, incapable of final satisfaction.)

And again:

> It is as the conscious representative of this movement that the owner of money becomes a capitalist. His person, or rather his pocket, is the point from which money sets out and the point to which it returns. The objective purpose of this circulation, the expansion of value, is his subjective aim; and only in so far as the increasing appropriation of abstract wealth is the sole motive of his operations does he function as a *capitalist*. . . . Thus use-value is never to be regarded as the direct aim of the capitalist. Nor is the profit on any single transaction his aim, for what he aims at is the never-ending process of profit making. This urge towards absolute enrichment, this passionate hunt for value, is shared by the capitalist with the miser; but whereas a miser is only a capitalist gone mad, a capitalist is a miser who has come to his senses. The unceasing increment of value at which the miser aims in his endeavor to save his money from circulation, is attained by the shrewder capitalist by again and again handing over his money to circulation.[23]

Marx observes that, at one level, the circulation of commodities for money can be summed up in two propositions, "Capital is money" and

"Capital is commodities," but adds that the active underlying force is really "value," which assumes the form of both money and commodities. But value requires "an independent form whereby its identity [sic] may at any time be established. Only in money does it possess such a form. Money, therefore, constitutes the starting point and goal of every process of the self-expansion of capital . . . the capitalist knows that all commodities, however paltry they may look or however evil they may smell, are in faith and in truth money, are inwardly circumcised Jews, and what is more, are a wonderful means whereby, out of money, more money can be made."[24]

Marx notes that if each merchant simply charged more than he paid, then he, in turn, would also be paying more for things he purchased, so that the surcharge he put on his product would be offset by that he paid to others, and hence no profit could ensue. Profit therefore does not simply come from adding to the cost of production but, rather, only from the workers' addition of a surplus value to the product during his work, a value only *appropriated* (not generated) by owners during the circulation process. And it is essentially through this that their M is transformed into M', their money increased, and M-C-M' "becomes the general formula of capital. . . ."[25]

Marx thus linked capitalism to a money-pursuing huckstering essence, a commercial lust. In this fusion of money, huckstering, and venality, Marx tended to treat money's *numerical* symbolism with only auxiliary awareness, although noting its more diffuse symbolic importance. It stands for value, he said. The viability of the entire process of M-C-M' depends, after all, not only upon the initial availability of money, but also upon the ability to assign an *amount* to the money at that time, as well as at some later time, thereby determining whether the money has grown and the process of commodity circulation may continue, or whether it has shrunk and will be stopped. The entire process of M-C-M' depends *entirely* upon the availability of money, not simply as a means of exchange, but also as a system for measuring the growth or decline in the original investment. Marx thus tended to defocalize the rational dimension in capitalist commerce as such, and underestimated how new money, banking, credit, and bookkeeping systems generated a major historical breakthrough in formal rationality which facilitated an historically new level in the effectiveness with which resources were used and products produced. Without this new system of formal rationality, grounded in the calculus made possible by money and by the development of double-entry bookkeeping, it would not have been possible to determine whether M' was larger or smaller than M. It is in that vein that Max Weber made the following observation.

> A rationalistic capitalistic establishment is one with capital accounting, that is, an establishment which determines its income-yielding power by calculation according to the methods of modern bookkeeping and the striking of a balance. The device of the balance was first insisted upon by the Dutch theorist Simon Stevin in the year 1698. . . . The most general presupposition for the existence of this present-day capitalism is that of rational capital accounting as the norm of all large industrial undertakings. . . .[26]

Marx conceived of the rationality of capitalism as centered in the forces of production, its *productive* side, and in its mobilization of science and technology to heighten efficiency. While such rationalization would not have sufficed to rationalize production unless it yielded a profit, Marx generally underestimated the extent to which the development of capitalism depended also on the rationalization provided by measurement, commerce, legal systems, and a rational state. Marx's underestimation of the rational dimension of commerce and of its importance for commodity circulation was simply the other side of his overemphasis on the pathology of commerce; and he dwelt on this pathology with passionate concentration in part because he had fused commerce with the highly charged symbolism of huckstering Judaism, defining commodities as "inwardly circumcised Jews."

If Marx tended to underestimate the rational side of capitalist commerce, he correspondingly overestimated the rationality of the purely *industrial* side of capitalism. While Marx's critique of capitalism hardly neglects this industrial and technological side, nonetheless he treats it as a subsidiary problem. For Marx, capitalism's "virus" is not lodged in its industrial intestines but in its commercial relations and system of private property. Marx focused primarily on the ills of an "acquisitive" society, not on those ills common to the logic of industrialism as such, and which may be common to any form of industrial society, including socialism.

It is thus the fundamental premise of Marx's socialism that it is possible to solve societal ills by eliminating the private capitalist (i.e., the purely commercial and property aspects), while retaining industrialism, transferring it more or less intact to the state. From this perspective, technology and industrialism as such were not at the root of the problem. It was, rather, commercial pursuit of private profit which corrupted men and exacerbated their greed and egoism. The problem of capitalism was thus its huckstering, "inwardly circumcised" Jewish essence, rather than its honest, gentile productive vigor.

In short, Marx did not systematically explore the possibility that bureaucratically rational industry *per se*—which focuses on heightening efficiency, including the efficiency with which it uses capital—generates its own distinctive discontents and human perils. Marx's violent rejection of the egoistic and commercial side of capitalism, his very conceptualization of capitalism in terms of its venal-commercial money-making side, led him to tolerate and extol the specifically industrial inheritance, to ignore the virus in the forces of production. He fails systematically to distinguish between the social pathologies peculiar to an acquisitive capitalism and those others it might share even with a bureaucratic socialism.

One reason for this limit in Marx's analysis is that it contains an irrational element: it is grounded in a violent animus toward commerce that is all the more intensified because commerce is defined as the special province of Judaism. In part, the fervent animus toward commerce generates an impulse to associate it with Jewry which, being historically excluded from "respectable" occupations, had been stigmatized for its association with commerce. That association of commerce with Jewry (*Judentum*) reciprocally intensified a hostility toward commerce engendered for other reasons, inflaming popular sentiments activated by the recent disruptive growth of capitalist commerce with two thousand years of incendiary religious bigotry.

Without putting too fine a point upon it, Marx's theoretical system was distorted by the anti-Semitic symbolism with which it had one interface. Suggesting that this anti-Semitism had theoretical consequences does not, however, necessarily imply that Marx was exceptional in his anti-Semitism, or, more exactly, in his anti-Jewishness; nor does it even require us to argue that the anti-Jewishness was "his." Plato's philosophy was limited by the slave society surrounding him, even though he may not have been anti-slave. Whether or not Marx was personally anti-Jewish, or whether he simply lived in a German culture in which anti-Semitism was a taken-for-granted feature of his everyday life, the pressures on Marx's theory would have much the same import: an intensified hostility toward commerce as such; a neglect of the rational dimension of commerce; a one-sided emphasis on the rationality of *industry* which neglects its distinctive societal pathologies; a neglect of the bureaucratic vulnerabilities of an industrial socialism.

One of Marx's great insights was to conceive of capitalism in a de-reified manner: "instead of being a thing, capital is a social relation among persons, which is established by the intermediary of things."[27] The problem, however, was that Marx selectively focused this de-reifying logic on only certain kinds of social relationships. He focused on property and commercial relations as being the essence of capitalism, but not on the social relations of *production* itself. He thus leaves dangling the issue of whether there is a distinctively *capitalist mode of production* apart from the domination of use value by exchange value, that is, apart from the hegemony of private profit via the buying and selling of labor power and other requisites of production. Does capitalism express itself in something more than the control of production by those who seek profit by buying and selling commodities? For if capitalism is nothing more than that, then it can be extirpated by forbidding the pursuit of private gain by commerce. Socialism thus simply becomes whatever is left of the remaining system of production as it is transferred intact to the State (on the assumption that the latter represents the collectivity).

If Marxism views capitalism as the exploitation of wage labor, by constraining workers to sell their labor time for a wage, we must ask, what exactly is wage labor, how is wage labor produced or achieved, and in conformity with what rules? One important factor that Marx stressed was that it is produced by way of "freeing" the worker from productive property of his own, so that he is constrained to sell his labor power to earn a living. This is based on the tacit metaphor that labor power is the same as any other commodity, which is why *Capital* proceeds at once to the analysis of the commodity. But what is one doing in transforming labor power into a commodity? In effect, there is an exchange, the offering and accepting of a "wage"—a certain sum of money—in return for a surrender of the worker's lifetime. But labor power and wage labor recognize limits on the control of the workers. A wage does not buy unlimited control over workers; the amount of control is limited in time, and only certain directives may be imposed on the worker during that limited time.

Fundamental to wage labor there is a tacit distinction between working and private spheres. In short, even during the working day the authority of the employer is limited to what is conceived as a legitimate sphere, which excludes things and activities considered "private." For instance, the employer cannot, even during the working day, legitimately instruct the worker to send his child to one school rather than another, to relate to his wife in one rather than another way. Wage labor does not buy unlimited control, for it implies a (bureaucratic) distinction between private and working time. Wage labor means that the worker is subject to the employer's authority only during certain times and in certain spheres. This is the tacit rule compliance[28] expected and which, when forthcoming, contributes to transforming the employer's power into authority, legitimating it. Because of its limited control over labor, capitalism constituted an historical advance; an advance that was threatened and undermined by the emergence of state socialism in which the state, as the only employer, moves to obliterate the distinction between

private and public spheres. State socialism is thus, in this respect, historical regression.

As capitalists have no obligation to buy labor power when they cannot
use it efficiently, their efficiency is greatly enhanced, even as they exhibit their heartlessness. Under capitalism, then, the employer's efficiency is enhanced precisely insofar as his powers and obligations are
limited. But the distinction between private and working spheres intrinsic to wage labor also means that capital has no direct power over the
reproduction of the very labor power it requires. In short, its limited control is a source of heightened efficiency but, at the same time, threatens
the supply of labor power. The system responds in several ways: one is
by technological development and intensive economies with respect to its
purchase and use of things; another is by developing its controls extensively, in a "totalitarian" direction, reaching into the "private" background in which workers live and in which their labor power is reproduced, in order to assure its availability in the quantities and forms
desired, as well as in terms of appropriate attitudes of obedience. The
very distinction between private and working time, to which capitalist
efficiency is linked, is then threatened with eventual extinction, as already manifested under Nazism and Fascism, as well as under the state
socialisms of Eastern Europe.

The culture of capitalist production maintains that, within the sphere
of the firm, the primary rule is that calling for the most efficient utiliza-
tion of resources, including labor power. But this is only the formal rule
of capitalism; the real rule is the rule of profitability. Efficiency is only a
means to the end of profitability, and Marx sees this clearly. The real
rule is not "maximum production of commodities" but "maximum production of profit." Basically, it is the latter and not the former, profitability and not efficiency, that Marx challenges. Marx wants the system to
hew to its own logic; to accept the logic of efficiency, it must rid itself
of the logic of profitability. Under the latter, each firm hides what it
does from the others because it is competing with them, seeking its own
profit rather than the collective welfare. Production, Marx says, is social
and collective, but the property system is private, and venal relations of
production produce ignorance, over-production, gluts, depressions; ultimately the property system limits the forces of production. Socialism is
the removal of that limit.

What Marx wants, then, is the removal of the logic, so that the forces
of production can live by the logic of efficiency alone, rather than being
subjected to an alien logic. Thus when Marx's capitalism is conceptualized as the subjection of production to huckstering, it allows the logic

of efficiency to remain intact. The efficiency logic of capitalism is retained in Marx's vision of a socialism that will remedy a huckstering capitalism. It is essentially in this way—where the encompassing logic of profit is eliminated but the logic of efficiency allowed to remain—that Marxism produces *itself* as a *Scientific Marxism*. (It is precisely because Scientific Marxism accepts the efficiency logic of capitalism that it is resisted by Maoism and by Critical Marxism, which radically reject the continuity of *production* methods between capitalism and Soviet Marxism, defining the latter as "revisionist" and worse.)

The Marxist critique of capitalism predicates that capitalism must be made to dance to its own music; making an "inner" critique of capitalism, it calls for the elimination of property and venal institutions which block the development of the very efficiency that capitalism purports to further. The unleashing and liberation of the forces of production thus become decisive for Marxism.[29] There is a complementary conception of socialism where, as Lenin put it, sheer "expropriation will facilitate an enormous development of productive forces . . . [and where] the expropriation of the capitalists will inevitably result in an enormous development of the productive forces of human society."[30]

Given a system of production in which the logic of efficiency remains central, however qualified by welfare concerns or political prudence, and in which technical competence becomes the grounding of authority in the sphere of production, those depending upon "ownership" or upon their political reliability come to find themselves in an ambiguous position. In both cases, they must buttress their tenuous authority with bureaucratic controls. In each case, the everyday life of the worker, the basic mode of production, and the allocation of the surplus are essentially governed by persons outside of the worker's group, who impose themselves. The worker's group is in either case colonized, and bureaucratic management of workers becomes the chief mechanism of an internal colonialism. Here the expertise of technicians undermines the control of those who are technically uninformed while at the same time it conceals the formal domination of owners and political authorities. Bureaucracy, then, becomes the mechanism of the internal colonization of production, bridging tensions among those whose cooperation is required, and controlling the input of their services.

In the view proposed here, then, the capitalist mode of production is characterized by a fusion of venality, on the one side—production for private profit—with, on the other, a drive for efficiency, *in so far as this is necessary for the former*. Venality and lust for gain have existed at many times and places, and scarcely distinguish capitalism; they become capitalism only when integrated with the logic of efficiency. Yet much of the alienation of work, born of a heightened division of labor, of remote centralized authority, of impersonal treatment of persons, derives no less from the logic of efficiency than from venality. Indeed, in *The Germany Ideology*, Marx and Engels cited the division of labor as the very source of alienation. This, surely, is not eliminated when private forms of property in production are expropriated and handed over to the State. Indeed, nationalization of production intensifies alienation still further, heightening centralization of control, increasing size, specialization, and remoteness, and strengthening depersonalization.

Marx assumed that the endless pursuit of capital growth, of M-C-M'— the anomic insatiable pursuit of capital accumulation—was constrained only by capitalism's quest for private gain. Yet the quest for *power*, the effort to strengthen the power of the industrial state internally and internationally, just as surely leads it to an insatiable quest for capital growth through the endless intensifications of an impersonal efficiency. There can then be other forms of capitalism, where the pursuit of capital accumulation is no less endless, but where the controlling impulse is power not profit. Efficiency motivated by a private animus was only one form of capitalism; in the quest for a state-governed socialism, it gave way to a new form of capitalism, one whose drive for efficiency is linked to its power drive.

But the analysis of this side of capitalism was subordinated by Marx, who dwelled instead on capitalism's venality, its lust for money, its huckstering, rather than seeing that cold-blooded huckstering need be no more deadly to a humane existence than cold-blooded efficiency in servitude to power. That Marx fastened onto huckstering, but neglected the pathologies of efficiency, bespoke an irrational element. That element was his nuclear metaphor which linked capitalism through huckstering and anchored it in strong and angry feelings toward Jewry. He could not seriously entertain the possibility that what he called capitalism might be only one species of capitalism, but that another, freed of its limits of private ownership, might then pursue the endless accumulation of capital with an impersonal efficiency even more deadly than private venality because it could do so in the name of a higher value, the Species Being, for which no sacrifice could be too great.

5

Artisans and Intellectuals: Socialism and the Revolution of 1848

Marxism developed through a double movement. In the forward phase it asserted a positive doctrine that it held to be correct and true. Yet no theory is born into unoccupied territory. Like an invading tribe that enters a land, it must deal with those who came before. Any new theory, then, enters a theoretical terrain, parts of which have already been claimed by other theories and (what is not identical) by other theorists.

In a second phase, Marxism thus develops through a process of selective rejections (antitheses), offering a critique of doctrines that came before it as well as of the theorists whose intellectual property they were. Marxism adapted to its theoretical terrain and sought to win a place for itself by responding selectively to earlier theories, allying itself with some, opposing others, and distinguishing itself from both adversaries and allies by claiming to make a contribution that is original. It claimed certain ideas as the intellectual property of its founders and adherents.

The ecology of a theoretical terrain is not just bipolar, but tripartite, consisting of those defined as adherents, adversaries, and competitors. Commonly, the first two will be acknowledged openly for what they are, while "competitors" are not always openly defined as such. Competitors' theories are those seeking to occupy the same social space, to perform a similar social or intellectual function, to win over the same social group; indeed, they may even be those opposing the same adversaries. Competitors are often allies who have had a falling out; allies are often competitors who (at least temporarily) resolved their differences.

By way of both its positive and negative movements, a theory such as

Marxism grows a cultural membrane separating itself from its adversaries and competitors, thus defining the boundaries that constitute its identity. Clearly, for example, Marxism was shaped by its contest in two directions, against bourgeois theory—e.g., "vulgar" political economy—and also against competing socialism. If the *Communist Manifesto* begins with a vivid critique of bourgeois society and its class culture, it ends with a critique—no less biting—of "utopian" socialism and others: feudal socialism, reactionary socialism, and "true" socialism. Thus the enemies of a theory's enemies are not always its friends, precisely because they are sometimes its competitors.

Like other theories, Marxism established itself by accentuating those of its doctrines that separate and distinguish it from its adversaries *and* from its competitors, while at the same time glossing over or remaining silent about doctrines it may *share* with them. It thereby established distinguishable identity for itself, enabling it to make claims, and seek resources and commitments in its own name. It is neither just research nor facts and logic, then, that shape the character of a theory; the identity of a theory is shaped *also* by the politics and the political economy of the intellectual life.

Believing in the validity of its own view of the social world and believing that much hangs on the possession of correct ideas, Marxists (like others) work to place themselves in strategic positions where their theory can shape events; at the same time, they seek to prevent others, bearing theories they deem wrong, from capturing influential positions. The contest between theories is thus accompanied by a more or less visible struggle among different theorists to control social positions, to co-opt resources, or to influence social movements.

Theorists in "scientific" communities insist that a theory's survival should depend only on the indications of research; the influence of the politics and political economy of the intellectual life, being taken as deviant from prescription, is commonly glossed or denied. In more openly political communities, however, the struggle for control of resources and positions is less disguised. Attempting to live in both worlds, seeing itself as both science and as politics, Marxism does not acknowledge openly that its struggle for advantageous positions has a certain autonomy; it tends, instead, to define this struggle only as a means of blocking erroneous—e.g., "bourgeois reformist"—theories, rather than seeking positions for the advantages accruing to their incumbents.

Every theory, then, has a palpable everyday practice and, indeed, a political practice however fogged over by intellectual pieties. This practice aims at the creation or capture of organizational instruments—and of their control centers—whether these are in universities, political parties, or social movements. If socialism is more than a theory but an historical movement, as Marx insisted, this means in part that it has an *organizational* infrastructure which serves as an arena for the struggle of competing theories, which generates desired offices and benefits, and in part serves as an instrument of the theory. While it was always of great importance for Marxism, the organizational infrastructure was not systematically theorized by Marxists until Lenin's *What Is To Be Done?* (1902). Yet Marxism's organizational life, even during Marx's lifetime, is no less consequential for its history than the theoretical ancestors from whom it learned or with whom it struggled. We shall see then that Marxism begins on a terrain already occupied not only by other theories but also by a set of social *organizations* associated with them. Marxism develops its theories while it also searches for or creates an organizational apparatus. Its theorists make a deliberate and active search for organizations that can be their instrument, sometimes creating new organizations of their own (the Communist League), and sometimes joining and influencing organizations at first largely launched by others (the International Workingmen's Association).

Yet any formulation that predicates that an organization is simply the instrument of a theory or theorists is also too simplified by far. Marxism's doctrines are not to be construed as the only source of its *goals*, nor are its organizations simply the *means* used to pursue these previously formulated objectives. If theory and organization each has a life of its own, each also depends on the other. I shall suggest that a theory is in part produced not just by theorizing, but by the entire way of life it leads within its organizational milieu. For its part, the organization is not just an instrument that submits to a theory, but is also a political community in which persons may spend much of their lives and satisfy many of their needs. It can thus become an end in itself that strives to survive quite apart from its serviceability for achieving socialism or other goals. Any idea, then, that an organization is a mere instrument obediently serving a theory is devoid of sociological realism; no historiography or ethnography supports this rationalist illusion. Both theory and organization influence each other; each is an environment for the other.

A theory such as Marxism is thus not just the "mind," "eyes," or "steering" organ of an organization precisely because it is also greatly *dependent* on the organizational "body." (Indeed, this is consistent with Marxism itself, when it asserts that consciousness is not independent of "social being.") An organismic metaphor is deceptive here if, as is commonly the case, it is taken to imply an hierarchical ordering in which one "organ"—mind, philosophy, theory, or any other—"steers" the entire organism, while the latter genially submits to this without resistance,

and as if all the "organs" were brought together by the steering mechanism into an harmonious integration. Yet much of what is called "systems theory" today is distorted by just such a rationalistic and organismic
perspective.

A better model (better, ethnographically and historiographically) takes
an ecological view of organizations and of their component structures,
including their "steering" mechanism. Implicit in the usual systems theory is a tacit subject-object distinction, in which the "object" is seen
primarily from the standpoint of the "subject"; i.e., in which the steering organ has powers, knowledge, and interests that presumably *differ-
entiate* it radically from other organizational structures or "organs." In
an ecological view of organizations, however, the steering structure is
seen as having many similarities to the others, sharing with them qualita-
tively similar powers, knowledge, and interests, as well as limits on these.
An ecological view, then, sees steering structures as fundamentally akin
to, part of, and dependent on, the other structures it steers.

In this view, *all* sub-structures seek steering powers, and *all* seek to
reproduce or enhance their steering powers, as well as advantages deemed
necessary for effective steering or as appropriate rewards for it. And all
structures, whether nominally in charge of steering or not, seek to separate their incoming resources and gratifications from too close a dependence on their steering performances, thus enabling them to receive continued rewards even if failing to achieve their goals. The ecological view,
then, sees even planned organization as consisting of conflicting, competing, or contending parts—rather than as an harmoniously integrated
organism—each part alike in pursuing its own advantage, and each al-
leging that it seeks the collective good (and is therefore deserving of
greater influence on steering).

This is not to say that all structures contribute *equally* to the collective good of the organization as a whole, at any particular time. Nor is it
to say that certain structures do not sometimes actually make "altruistic"
contributions. Yet a structure may be *constrained* to contribute to the
welfare of the whole rather than doing so gladly and willingly. If a structure has succeeded in capturing the steering function, if it gets itself defined as "steerer" of sorts, it is then often constrained (by that very identity and by the substantial advantages associated with it) to concern
itself with the welfare of its collectivity, if only to preserve its own privileges. The egoism of a steering organ, then, is not unlimited precisely
because its private advantage depends in part on how it performs its
public function.

In an ecological view, all organization parts—including the steering
organs—are alike in competing for scarce resources, although those who

succeed in capturing the steering function have a great competitive advantage. None, therefore, is ever the entirely selfless "representative" or obedient servant of another. In order to ensure secure access, each seeks a measure of control over resources on which its own future depends. Thus even a steering structure supposedly serving the collectivity competes with that very collectivity or parts of it. In this view, all functions are performed by structures which can become Calibans.

Those successful in securing or capturing "steering" structures, commonly legitimate these powers by a universalistic rhetoric; they *present themselves* as significantly different from other organization structures by reason of their supposed non-partisan, above-the-struggle neutrality, a universalistic rhetoric through which the steering structure protects its particularistic interests. Yet all structures use much the same rhetoric to justify their claims on group resources. An organizational analysis grounded in a systems theory that fails to see the partisan, self-interested character of any steering structure is a regression to a utopianism that returns behind Marx to Hegel.

The organizational context of Marxism has a specifically historical character; it is part of a larger, more diffuse proliferation of organizations in the nineteenth century. "The nineteenth century was *par excellence* a century of organization," writes P. H. Noyes, "hosts of associations sprang up, from secret revolutionary conspiracies and public political parties to trade unions, singing and gymnastic clubs, *temperance and ladies' political societies.*"[1] Noyes sees the rapid development of such associations as a response to the decline of the old hierarchical society and the need for new group memberships to compensate for a new anonymity. To this it may be added that many Western Europeans, both rural and urban, had long acquired considerable organizational experience and competence, one of the most important groups of this sort being the artisans with their long tradition of guild experience. Thus when the old arrangements began to deteriorate in Europe, there were many with ample organizational competence to begin a rebuilding which might provide them with special-purpose organizations to protect their threatened interests and to serve as new rudimentary communities.

As a "real historical movement," Marxism was a fusion of ideology with organization, each bleeding into and defining the other. To view theory only as organization's steering mechanism, however, is an anthropomorphic reification. It conceals the fact that theory is not self-maintaining, but is strategically situated in a relatively few privileged *persons* who steer or, more precisely, who attempt to steer. Their interpretations and applications of theory are selectively structured by the privileged positions they occupy and seek to retain. The content of the theory itself only provides a provisional grammar—part cause and part post-factum ideology—allowing or disallowing a large variety of interpretations and steering maneuvers, and often merely serving to justify strategies grounded in interests, expedience, and prudence.

In what follows, these very general considerations are used to alert us to selected aspects of Marxism's early history. Out of this interplay between the theoretical sketch above,[2] and the historical sketch to follow, there will emerge an account of Marxism's group and class origins.

Critical Episode 1: The Weitling Paradigm

"After the Congress of Vienna," wrote Boris Nicolaievsky and Otto Maenchen-Helfen in their classic biography of Marx, "Europe was full of secret societies."[3] *The Communist Manifesto* was of course written for the Communist League, as the organization founded by Marx and Engels in 1845 came to be known. While differing from earlier groups, the Communist League was nonetheless their lineal descendant: In particular, the League was successor to the League of the Just which, in turn, had emerged from the League of Exiles.

> For a long time secret societies in Germany continued to be almost exclusively composed of students and professional men. . . . The "League of Exiles" had arisen originally of *émigré* intellectuals and it had increased its members by admitting workers to its ranks. . . . The workers in the League of Exiles cut themselves adrift from the intellectuals and formed a new society of their own—the League of the Just. Hardly any educated men belonged to it. The League of the Just entirely dissociated themselves from the radical literary groups, with whom they wished to have nothing whatsoever to do.[4]

One of the important persons linking the earlier secret societies and the Communist League was Wilhelm Weitling, who was the leading founder of the League of the Just, as well as one of the eighteen members founding the Communist League. Born in 1818 in Magdeburg, Weitling "was the illegitimate son of a French officer and a German laundress . . . often subjected to humiliation, the young, brooding, talented and gifted tailor's apprentice became a rebel early."[5] In time, Weitling became "a very talented writer and a successful political organizer. His eloquence was often spellbinding and he even wrote poems in prison."[6]

Arrested and imprisoned by the Swiss in 1843 for blasphemy and attacking private property, his trial had attracted attention throughout Europe and "caused many people to hear of Communism for the first time."[7] For some, Weitling and communism were then almost one.

After his release from prison, Weitling went to Hamburg and then on to London where he was feted by the Chartists, and rejoined the Germans who had fled there after the Blanquist rising in Paris of May 12, 1839. After the failure of that rising, the League of the Just had separated into two groups. One had developed under Weitling's tutelage in Switzerland, the other had gone to London where it came under the leadership of Karl Schapper, Heinrich Bauer, and Joseph Moll.

The two groups soon developed different perspectives and policies, Weitling's Swiss faction stressing an egalitarian communism concerned with justice and grounded in moral principles. During 1848, for example, he called for equal pay for all.[8] He also began to develop ideas about launching guerrilla warfare with an army made up of those Marx would deride as *"lumpenproletarians."* Believing that property was theft, he called upon the proletariat to get what was rightfully theirs by stealing it back. Less militant by far, the London faction developed connections with the Chartist movement, seeking social and parliamentary reform, and conducted an intensive educational program. Schapper and his London group were gradualists contemptuous of conspiracy. "We have given up such stupidities long ago," he wrote Marx on June 6, 1846, "and we have seen with joy that you hold the same view. Naturally, we are convinced that one will not and cannot dispense with a thorough revolution, but to want to bring it about by conspiracies and stupid proclamations à la Weitling is ridiculous."[9]

Weitling, however, insisted that "the people were long since ripe for the new social order . . . for which all that was required was the determined initiative of a revolutionary organisation [and that] . . . the obsolete old world must be crushed at a blow by the dictatorship of a revolutionary minority."[10] Nicolaievsky and Maenchen-Helfen, who champion Marx against Weitling, add that this was a theme to be sounded again: "One almost seems to hear the voice of Bakunin, with whom Marx was to repeat the same struggle twenty years later." Weitling's message was "revolution now"; ". . . everybody is ripe for Communism, even the criminals. . . . Humanity is of necessity always ripe for revolution, or it never will be. The latter is nothing but the phraseology of our opponents. If we follow them [said Weitling] we shall have no choice but to lay our hands on our knees and wait until the roasted pigeons fly into our mouths."[11] Weitling held that "Democracy and military rule amount to the same thing: only in the immediate setting up of a communist state is there any sense."[12]

Weitling, then, was a revolutionary voluntarist who stressed justice, equality, morality, passion, feeling and choice; Schapper's faction was (at least for a while) guided by a more prudent "reason"—in the slanted account of Nicolaievsky and Maenchen-Helfen. Schapper's faction insisted that people were not yet ready for revolution, and that "truth could not be knocked into people's heads with rifle butts," hence a long-range program of education and propaganda was needed. Their group's London meetings "were orderly and followed a fixed routine of instruction. One evening each week was devoted to studying the English language, another to geography, another to history, another to drawing and physics, another to singing, another to dancing, another to the dissemination of Communist ideas. Each half-year the subjects of instruction changed. The atmosphere was thoroughly Germanic; there were regulations to be obeyed, and everyone took his pipe from his mouth when the speakers delivered their speeches."[13] For his part, however, Weitling suspected and disliked the intellectuals and "humanists" to whom he felt such an educational program was congenial.

In his *Guaranties of Harmony and Freedom* of 1842, Weitling made a decisive break with earlier Saint-Simonian "philanthropism" and proposed the principle of working-class "self-emancipation," aiming this in particular *against intellectuals:* "We want to have the right to voice our opinion in the public discussions concerning the good and suffering of humanity, for we, the people with the blouses, the jackets, the work-coats, are the most numerous and the most powerful and yet the least esteemed on God's earth. Since time immemorial the others are always the ones who fight for our interests, or better, for theirs, and it is really time that we became at last adults and liberate ourselves from that annoying and hateful tutelage. How could one who participates neither in our joy nor our sorrow, develop an idea about them. . . . Even if he wanted to, he could not do it, for only experience makes [people] enlightened and wise."[14] Intellectuals were thus being stigmatized as "outsiders," disqualified from working-class leadership by reason of their outsider's ignorance. Schapper's accent on education, by contrast, disposed the London group to an alliance with educated intellectuals and, indeed, found favor with another recent German *émigré,* Karl Marx.

Marx and Engels had earlier viewed Weitling as one of the main leaders of European communism. In September 1843, for example, Marx had lauded the "real existing communism, as Cabet, Dézamy, Weitling, etc., teach and conceive it. This communism is itself separate from the humanist principle."[15] (The "humanism" of intellectuals, mocked Weitling, derived not from *homo,* man, "but from Humaine . . . one of the leading Paris Tailors. All humanists had to have a suit from Humaine, Weitling maintained."[16]) In an article in *Vorwärts,* Marx had also earlier celebrated Weitling's *Guaranties of Harmony and Freedom* as the "unbounded brilliance of the literary début of the German worker. . . ."[17]

Now, however, as Marx was developing his own position, and as the split between Weitling and Schapper widened, Marx increasingly separated himself from views such as Weitling's, defining them as expressions of primitivism or utopianism, as tainted with religious sentimentality, and above all, as substituting sheer will for true knowledge of the social requisites of a successful communist revolution.

Nonetheless, in 1844, Marx still had little connection with workers. "Marx had no easy task in gaining the ear of the Communist workers. Most of those who had ever made contact with bourgeois revolutionary writers had regretted the experience."[18] Unaffiliated with any of the older secret societies, in 1845-46, Marx gathered around himself a new grouping that became the Communist League. Its eighteen founders included Engels, Marx's wife, Jenny, her brother, Edgar von Westphalen, the poet Ferdinand Freiligrath, Moses Hess, and Weitling. At that time, Marx was twenty-eight, the average age of the group, while Weitling was thirty-seven, the oldest man in the group. He was clearly odd-man-out.

Unlike the League of the Just, which had been influenced by the "professor eater" Weitling and his artisan following, Marx's new group was under the hegemony of intellectuals, the foremost of course being Marx himself. Under his leadership, the new group concerned itself with the ideological correctness of its members and, rather than being a loose coalition, exerted ideological discipline over its membership, seeking to commit it to a single theory—Marx's.

The basic structure of the new League augured a split between Marx and Weitling which was not long in coming. Given that Weitling's group and Schapper's group were moving apart; given Marx's growing theoretical differences with Weitling's form of "primitive" communism and his growing (if temporary) convergence with Schapper's faction; given Weitling's established prominence in the international communist movement, while Marx was then a "brand new convert to socialism" (in Hal Draper's words); given that Weitling was ten years older than the League's average member, addressing them as *Lieben Jungen*, while Marx's age was exactly that of the average; and given that the group contained Marx's wife, Jenny, her brother, and Marx's close friend Engels, Weitling clearly had little future in what was from the beginning *Marx's* group.

What subsequently happened between Marx and Weitling has been recounted many times and my intention here is not, therefore, to add to the supposed "facts" of the case but to illuminate their meaning, establishing their relevance for our theoretical perspective. I want to stress that what "actually happened" between Marx and Weitling should be regarded as more problematic than is the case in the usual accounts of the episode. There are in fact only two first-hand accounts of what took place, each written by a partisan of one of the two adversaries, Weitling and Marx. One account was rendered by the Russian writer, Paul Annenkov, "who was very close to Marx at the time . . . ,"[19] while the other was written by Weitling, himself, in a letter to another of the Communist League's founding members, Moses Hess. Weitling's letter was written while events were still fresh in his mind, as were the feelings they had aroused, the day after they occurred. Annenkov's account, however, was published some thirty-five years later in *Vyestnik Yevropy*, April 1880 (pp. 497-99), while a German translation of this appeared in the Stuttgart *Die Neue Zeit* in 1883 (pp. 236-41).[20] While not necessarily contradictory, the two accounts differ substantially in emphasis. Any discussion of the matter based on these sources should not, therefore, foster the impression that we are actually recounting an "event"; we are, rather, sifting and appraising two *texts* which are grounded in diametrically opposed loyalties.

As for the "events": On his way back from London to the Continent in 1846, Weitling stopped in at Brussels where Marx's new Communist committee of correspondence had recently been organized and which Marx had invited him to join, and a bitter confrontation occurred between the two, at a meeting on March 30. Annenkov, invited to the meeting by Marx, was greatly impressed with the latter's "energy, force of will, and unshakable conviction . . . ," but Marx was also portrayed as "proud, with a touch of disdain, and his voice sharp. . . . He spoke only in the imperative, brooking no contradiction." Greatly attracted, Annenkov favorably characterized Marx as a "democratic dictator." In contrast, Annenkov describes Weitling as surprisingly well turned out in a foppishly cut coat,[21] with a foppishly trimmed beard, looking more like a smooth traveling salesman than a solid proletarian, according to Annenkov.

What followed between the two has been described by Robert Payne as the "first purge"; I, for my part, see the event as a ceremony of status degradation. Marx publicly humiliated Weitling at a meeting which Marx chaired, on a topic of Marx's own choosing, debated before Marx's own entourage including his friend Engels, and his brother-in-law, Edgar von Westphalen. Marx used the meeting to crush Weitling's self-confidence and public repute as a communist leader, exhibiting before his troupe of admirers that it was he, the unknown Marx, rather than the prominent Weitling, who was now communism's "fastest gun."

Marx and his troupe launched a verbal *Blitzkrieg* that Weitling had no reason to expect, considering Marx's previous hospitality, his public appreciation of Weitling's book, and his recent invitation to collaborate

politically. The social function of that ceremony of status degradation
was, in effect, to appropriate Weitling's charisma for Marx and validate
Marx's claim to lead the Communist League while serving to de-legiti-
mate his competitor.

There Marx sat that day, "pencil in hand and leonine head bent over
a sheet of paper," ensconced at the head of the table, surrounded by
admiring friends and kin, controlling the meeting's agenda, recognizing
who might speak, deciding who was to ask questions and who answer
them. Called upon, Engels began the discussion by asking for clarification of the theoretical grounds that could serve as the intellectual under-
girding of communism and as the basis for communism's political unity.
Barely able to contain himself, Marx, however, interjected with a question whose form Annenkov insists he remembered exactly:

"But tell us, Weitling," demanded Marx, "what are the arguments
with which you defend your social-revolutionary agitation and on what
do you intend to base it in the future?"

The tacit premise of Marx's belligerent query is worth noting. Most
fundamentally, he speaks here within the framework of the culture of
critical discourse—that is, of the grammar of theoreticity commonly congenial to Western intellectuals, an ideology of discourse for which they
(we) have an elective affinity. This culture of speech premises that one
must given reasons (arguments) in favor of one's claims, that these and
the principles on which they rest must be stated articulately, and that
those who fail to do so are intellectually deficient and deviant. As I have
discussed elsewhere, "the culture of critical discourse requires that the
validity of claims be justified without reference to the speaker's societal
position or authority . . ."[22] and therefore without reference to his
achievements.

The culture of critical discourse is thus a rhetorical strategy that appeals to *younger* persons who are commonly the *less prominent* and *less
accomplished*. It is useful against those who are older and more prestigious, by in effect declaring that the latter's claims—even when grounded
in their achievements—are irrelevant to the discussion. Younger men
prefer to compare their arguments, and those alone, with the arguments
of their older competitors. Being at a disadvantage should the issue be
made to rest on their relative accomplishments, the younger men declare
these to be irrelevant. Weitling's accomplishments in the communist
world were, of course, far more substantial than Marx's, and the latter,
therefore, chose a different battleground: the relative merits of their
views. "Practical" men of some accomplishment further their claims by
exhibiting their deeds; "intellectuals," however, prefer to exhibit their
reasons. Each offers what serves him best.

Shocked by Marx's sudden belligerence, Weitling (according to Annenkov) fumbled for a reply, committing a sin intolerable to intellectuals: he spoke poorly, haltingly, with evident confusion.[23] He held that it was not incumbent on him to concoct new theories to justify revolution; workers' conditions spoke for this more eloquently and they had but to open their eyes to their plight. Moreover, workers need not look to outsiders to deliver them but could emancipate themselves; they were tired of being patronized by those who, though not sharing their lives, presumed to speak on their behalf.

Once again Marx interrupted, sarcastically declaring that those, like Weitling, whose agitation mobilized people without having a proper theoretical foundation were frauds who would lead their followers to ruin: "If you attempt to influence the workers—especially the German workers—without a body of doctrine and clear scientific ideas, then you are merely playing an unscrupulous game . . . in a civilized country like Germany [unlike an uncivilized one like Russia, said Marx] . . . nothing can be achieved without a doctrine."

Weitling quite naturally replied that he was not interested in the doctrines of impractical pedants, but was guided by his ample experience and indeed workers all over Germany recognized him as their leader. While Marx, said Weitling, had only theories about revolution, he had participated in it and, though modest, his contribution made a better start than Marx's ivory-tower theories. At this, Marx lost control of himself. ". . . [J]umping to his feet, he shouted: Ignorance has never helped anybody yet." We followed Marx's example, says Annenkov, ". . . rose to our feet, and the conference was over."

The next day Weitling wrote Hess a letter containing his own account, which Hal Draper characterizes as "full of distortions" (as if Annenkov's account could safely be taken as the standard against which to measure it) although Engels, in a letter to August Bebel of October 25, 1888, acknowledges that Marx's main thesis had been rendered clearly enough by Weitling, even if his wording might be inexact.

According to Weitling's letter, Marx had argued that, "as for the realization of communism, there can be no talk of it to begin with; the bourgeoisie must first come to the helm." Thus a difference between them was whether it was (in Mao's words) "always right to rebel" or whether, as Marx argued against the utopians (and according to Weitling, that night, too) that a revolution without an industrial foundation created by the bourgeoisie would be premature and doomed to fail. Weitling's distressed letter to Hess expressed the fear that Marx meant to destroy him in the press which, Weitling stressed, was available to Marx because of sponsorship by the rich: "Rich people have made him an editor, *voilà tout*." Outraged at Weitling's account, and clearly believing it, Hess wrote Marx on May 20, 1846, that Weitling's "Mistrust of you two [i.e., of Marx and Engels] has reached a peak. You two have driven him crazy and now you wonder that he is mad. I do not wish to have anything more to do with this whole affair; it makes me want to vomit."[24]

Marx then "insisted on the sifting [purging?] of the party and the first blow fell on Hermann Kriege, a close friend of Weitling's and a man of the same way of thinking as he."[25] Although Kriege had by then migrated to the United States, Marx insisted on proceeding against him; Kriege was formally condemned, a resolution denouncing him being adopted by vote. This subsequently led Schapper to accuse Marx of overkill, while the disgusted Hess took the occasion to remove himself from the new party.

I have earlier suggested that the break between Weitling and Marx was foreseeable; yet if this is hindsight, others saw such outcomes with true foresight. In its basic lineaments it (or the conditions inducing it) was clearly foreseen by one of Marx's contemporaries and another of his chief adversaries, or, more accurately, polemical targets. This was the compositor and writer, the anarchist, Pierre Joseph Proudhon, who, like Weitling, was also asked to join the Communist League but who, unlike him, refused. "With all my heart I applaud your idea of bringing all opinions out into the open," declared Proudhon in his May 17 response to Marx's invitation of May 5, 1846. Proudhon adds, however,

> Let us have decent and sincere polemics. Let us give the world an example of learned and farsighted tolerance. But simply because we are at the head of the movement, let us not make ourselves the leaders of a new intolerance, let us not pose as the apostles of a new religion—even though this religion be the religion of logic, the religion of reason. Let us welcome, let us encourage all the protests. Let us condemn all exclusiveness, all mysticism. Let us never regard a question as exhausted, and even when we have used up our last argument, let us begin again, if necessary.

Such, however, was not Marx's way.

*Notes on the Relation Between Artisans and Intellectuals in 1848: A Brief Overview**

What is often referred to, by Marxists such as Louis Althusser and Göran Therborn, as Marx's "history-making encounter with the working

* This section written by Karen G. Lucas.

class" is wrongly described by that phrase on several counts. For this encounter was, first, neither with a "class"—if one can ever be said to encounter a class as such—nor, second, was it primarily with "workers" in any Marxist sense of factory proletarians.

Marx's early encounter was with men such as Weitling (a tailor) and other artisans, not the industrial proletariat. As modern social historians have documented, it was artisans, not the proletariat, that had exhibited the greatest militancy during the 1848 revolutions and, indeed, before then. Marx's relationship to these radical artisans was, moreover, primarily a relationship with their *organizations,* particularly secret societies such as the League of the Just, and with the militants and activists in them. Standing between Marx and the working class, then, were the proliferating new organizations. While often radical or revolutionary, their members and still more, their *leaders* were not factory hands, whatever their professions of devotion to the "proletariat"—a term then increasingly current. Thus, one of these early organizations, The Society of Seasons, had as its four chief revolutionary agents a cabinet-maker, a copper-turner, a gilder, and a journalist. It is notable that artisans were then connected with intellectuals, or near intellectuals such as journalists. Journalism was, then, an occupation to which artisans and professionals who had failed often turned. Indeed, the differentiation between plainly artisanal occupations and more intellectual ones was then considerably less developed than now. For formal tertiary education was then less universally requisite for entrance to some of the intellectual or professional occupations. Both intellectuals and artisans played dominant roles in radical groups. In that vein, Eric Hobsbawm also relates that among the leaders of the Societé Communiste Revolutionnaire were a doctor, two tailors, a former soldier, a maker of straw covers, and a wine merchant.[26]

At least since Rudolf Stadelmann's path-breaking work, *Soziale und politische Geschichte der Revolution von 1848* (Munich, 1948), it has been clear that artisans played a major role in organizing rebellion in Europe. Stadelmann argued that it was not sheer economic deprivation that generated revolution. ". . . [O]ppression creates discontent and opposition [he held] only where it is perceived as injustice."[27] a theme to which Barrington Moore would return. Stadelmann found that the artisans uprooted by the rising factory system were the most militant revolutionaries in the German revolution of 1848. Fragmented and without uniform trade regulations, Germany was late to join the movement toward industrialization: but as factories developed there, as free trade regulations were promulgated, as the *Zollverein* increased its market area, and as railroads grew and brought goods from Russia and England to distant German markets, competition among the artisans increased and their socioeconomic position deteriorated.

The factory system rose alongside the artisan guild system, slowly destroying the latter as it did so. Artisans at all levels—masters, journeymen, and apprentices—feared and suffered the resulting damage. Yet while commonly injured by the rising factory system, lines of cleavage appeared soon enough between journeymen and those masters who could hire larger numbers of unemployed workers; some of the masters began to set up what were in effect small factories. By the time of the depression of the late 1840s, journeymen were increasingly desperate and alienated, and they became increasingly involved in many political projects and secret societies, as they had earlier been active in the *Gesellenbruderschaften* (*compagnonnage* in France). At that time, moreover, the largest part of the working class consisted of artisans and guild members. According to Hamerow there were still about 2,800,000 artisans in Prussia, but there were only about 571,000 workers in factories.[28] Indeed, in some analyses, the artisans have been pictured as an expanding group whose numbers were growing more rapidly than that of the population at large.[29]

Members at all levels of the artisan hierarchy had defined their personal identity in relation to their craft and guild. They had once seen their future in terms of a predictable movement up this traditional hierarchy. In large part, social differences between masters and journeymen had been accepted because the latter might hope to become masters themselves, gaining social prestige and its privileges, such as being able to marry daughters of masters.

Status differences within the guilds coincided with age differences; the age hierarchy thus reinforced the occupational. Masters had normally taken one or two apprentices or journeymen, who often lived in their homes. This living arrangement provided opportunity for the master and his wife to educate these workers not only in the craft, but more broadly as well, in matters of social behavior and political thought. Regardless of their position in the hierarchy, artisans usually considered themselves as substantial members of their community and as members of an honorable corporate group with proud traditions. This self-view, which was also held by the general public, was often retained even after journeymen's incomes fell below those of factory workers.

As the decline of the guilds and artisanship continued, masters severely restricted the numbers of journeymen who might rise to mastership: those masters who could afford to took on more journeymen than before, with the result that the latter were now less likely to be able to live with the masters. Having little money, they often roomed with other journeymen and kept each other company after working hours, so that the master's influence on their ideological and political views was replaced by peer group influences which might support more unconventional views.

Soon masters ceased to welcome journeymen as husbands for their daughters, because the journeymen were not, and were not going to become, their social equals.[30] The two artisan groups were increasingly cut off from one another. With their prospects of moving upward sharply curtailed, artisans' hopes for the future became less optimistic; their life styles were diminished; their social status undermined. An old feature of the guild structure took on new importance: the *Wanderjahren*, the required years of "wandering." Each journeyman was required to travel to other cities and countries to develop his knowledge of the trade by observing the techniques and products of other places. These travels often were to Paris and Switzerland, where the journeymen were increasingly open to the new and even radical ideas which they would encounter frequently in meetings of political groups such as the League of the Just.[31]

New cosmopolitan ideologies began to circulate rapidly among the well-traveled artisans, and, as they began to be viewed as suspect, they were subjected to harassment by Prussian customs officials and border guards. Indeed, in 1835, the German Federal Diet outlawed travel by journeymen to places where there were groups and meetings "openly aiming at endangering and destroying public order." Students were also victims of bureaucratic harassment when traveling, which provided one of the common grounds for the discontent of artisans and intellectuals.[32]

Although artisans were of crucial importance to the 1848 revolution, by no means all were actually radicalized, though there was widespread disaffection among them and some turned to socialist views. Many simply wanted restoration of the guild system, limitations on factories, tariffs on imported manufactured goods. Many others among the journeymen, however, also plainly saw that there could be no returning to the old days of the guild's glory. Journeymen in particular wanted the guilds changed in various ways, especially the removal of hereditary privileges bestowed upon masters. It would clearly be an error to view all artisan demands as either reactionary or as narrowly economistic. They often supported freedom of the press, free education, and they wished to expand the powers of parliaments and to protect religious liberties. Even the Artisan Congress, which was composed of masters rather than less conservative journeymen, urged the Frankfurt Parliament in 1848 to support a progressive income tax, a property tax, and to substitute deportation for capital punishment—demands that the Parliament found "radical."[33] That artisans' demands were not narrowly economistic was nothing new in 1848. The French artisan-led Conspiracy of the Equals, of 1797, whose main object is evident in their name and from their *Manifeste des Egaux*, is another and important indication of this. Yet whether the artisans wanted to return to the past and restore the guilds, or whether they wanted to move forward toward a new more egalitarian future, the middle-class liberals dominant at the Frankfurt Parliament rejected the artisans' demands. The liberals thereby lost their most militant supporters and were then vulnerable to the monarchy's counterattack.

As Hamerow remarks, a picture of the artisans was, at that point, ". . . the portrait of a social class on the brink of disaster."[34] It was an uprooted class caught in the middle, as Stadelmann had seen. Artisans increasingly found themselves deprived of their privileged legal and social position, which had formerly made them respected community members and protected them from competition. It was thus not just economic injury but also status threat that led the artisans into opposition: "the man who gave up his own shop and offered himself for hire lost social status, and surrendered his claim to independence."[35]

All over Europe, therefore, it was the artisans, not the factory workers, who became the street fighters of the revolution in the mid-nineteenth century. "Masses of impoverished handicraftsmen roamed through the streets of central Europe, demonstrating, rioting, demanding bread, threatening millowners, stoning factories. . . . They were the shock troops of the spring uprising" in 1848.[36]

"In Paris the revolutionary crowds consisted of many crafts that had been prominent in earlier agitation, from the riots of 1789-93 through abortive risings early during the 1830s and early 1840s. . . . Traditional leaders of street fighting included construction workers and butchers. Weavers played a major role in the Berlin revolution, which began in a weaving district. Artisans of various sorts spearheaded the rising in Vienna . . . craftsmen were prominent in revolutionary agitation in cities like Marseilles and Lyons, while artisan congresses during the German revolution drew support from a wide range of cities."[37]

In France and Germany, guilds had deteriorated as early as 1789, but they remained stronger in economically backward Central Europe. In 1810, however, the Prussian government limited guilds, while in 1819 the Duchy of Nassau abolished the rights of guilds, opening occupations to all comers, and Hanover completed the process in the Germanies in 1846-47.

> . . . news of the successful revolution in Paris became for Central Europe the signal for widespread attacks on factories and business establishments . . . [there was] extensive destruction of property by impoverished handicraftsmen, as unruly mobs in the Rhineland and Westphalia paraded through the streets, stoned the residences of the rich, and set fire to mills.[38]

With the entrance of Hesse-Hassel to the *Zollverein* in 1831, there were riots in Hanover that, some months later, were repeated in the Palatinate. In 1844, five thousand starving Silesian weavers rioted and were crushed—after the riot had spent itself—with bloody vengeance. Thuringen artisans wrecked the nail factory in Schmalkaden; the Rhine cutlers rampaged against the iron foundries; the craftsmen of Solingen rioted; teamsters and freightmen rose against the railroads near Kastel in Nassau; Rhine sailors warred on the steamships.

When Karl Marx met those he thought of as real workers, they were actually, for the most part, artisans seething with unrest and bitter about injustice no less than deprivation, artisans who, with their guild traditions, had considerable organizational competence. Yet it was precisely because these artisans were the most politically vocal and radicalized workers that Marx acquired an exaggerated view of the radical potential of the proletariat which, in the common parlance of his time, usually included various impoverished groups. In short, when the ordinary language of Marx's time spoke of the "proletariat" and "proletarianization," it did not neatly distinguish between uprooted artisans and poor factory workers. As a result, the obvious radicalism of the artisans might metonymically, but mistakenly, be seen as standing for the radicalism of the whole, including the factory workers.

Marx stigmatized artisans as conservative or even as reactionary petty bourgeoisie, and yet Marx's view of the revolutionary potential of the proletariat seems to have been grounded in his encounter with radical *artisans*, a judgment which he then dubiously applied to factory workers instead. "Dubiously" because the German factory workers had been passive onlookers at the 1848 revolution, and although "their standard of living was scarcely high and their working conditions punishing, they were often better off than the artisans."[39] The demand for trained factory labor remained relatively stable during the depression and industrial wages were consistently higher than those of the guild shops. The failure of Marx's prediction of the radicalization of factory workers in the technologically advanced industrial system of Western Europe derived from his mistaken view of the actual locus of militancy in the working class, and from his failure to see that at the center of the revolution were the very artisans whose revolutionary potential he had denied. It was only as the artisans were diminished and defeated by the rising industrial system, and only as a factory proletariat became more important, that the European working class *accommodated* itself increasingly to the *status quo*,[40] ignoring the historical destiny Marx had laid upon them.

Socialism had little influence on German artisans up to this point; "far more middle class intellectuals than actual workers were converted."[41] Marx and Engels's own movement into communism was part of just that shift among middle-class intellectuals. Veit Valentin's classical study of the revolution of 1848 emphasized that it was precisely the educated, often sons of the rich, teachers, doctors, journalists, lawyers, intellectuals, who went over to the 1848 revolution.[42] The *radicals* among the 1848 revolutionaries were more likely to include independent professions such as the lawyers, doctors, or journalists, as well as some teachers. The center was more likely to be represented by prestigious college professors and judicial officials. While one reason for the presence of teachers among the Left parties was that they and "writers are required to cultivate a critical disposition,"[43] there were, also, straightforward *market* motives.

Just as the disaffection of artisans had been partly fostered by their oversupply relative to market opportunities, a similar excess of educated manpower had also occurred at that time. W. H. Riehl had remarked that "Germany produces a greater intellectual product than she can use and pay."[44] Friedrich Paulsen also spoke of the "chronic overcrowding of the learned professions and their greatly depressed economic conditions" in the nineteenth century, an overcrowding fostered by reform of the university system in Germany and by the state's encouragement of training in professions useful in its bureaucracy. Lenore O'Boyle has contributed important support to the hypothesis that certain professions were overcrowded, perhaps particularly writers. Indeed, one English wit had observed that they might soon exceed their readers in numbers. At the same time, O'Boyle makes clear that the discontent among certain of the professions—lawyers, journalists, teachers—was much like that found among the artisans in being due "more to lack of status than to poverty," a status threat occasioned by the blockage of their upward mobility.[45]

The overproduction of educated labor power helps explain why intellectuals played a leading role in the revolutions of 1848, particularly in Germany, to the point where these have been characterized by L. B. Namier and others as the "revolution of the intellectuals." Thus the 586 members of the Frankfurt Parliament of 1848, the first substantial victory of that revolution in Germany, were drawn mostly from the ranks of the highly educated. They included 124 bureaucrats, 104 professors,

100 judicial officials, 95 lawyers, and only 34 landowners and 13 businessmen.[46]

The important part played by intellectuals in 1830 and 1848, both in Germany and France, was attributable in significant measure to the emergence of something like an intellectual "proletariat." From 1800 to 1830, the absolute and *per capita* numbers of college and university students accelerated in both Germany at large and Prussia in particular. Absolute numbers of students increased threefold from 5,000 to 15,000, and from 20 to 52.5 per 100,000 inhabitants. Thus the *per capita* increase of the educated indicates that their growth substantially exceeded what might have been expected to be caused by the growth in population alone.[47] Characterized by a significant status disparity between their public prestige and their incomes, many of these intellectuals were unable to live in a manner traditionally held to be appropriate for them. Lenore O'Boyle's later work[48] has moved toward a systematic comparison between intellectuals in Germany, France, and England, in an impressive attempt to understand why overproduction of educated manpower was greater in some countries, and why it was a locus of political instability in some, yet not in all places. Western Europe was then living through a period of rising expectations, especially among the educated and middle classes, which had begun with the French revolution. Education was seen as a major means of acquiring position and wealth, encouraging increased entrance into law, medicine, church, the military, the state bureaucracy and to the education systems preparing for them. Konrad Jarausch states, however, that "after a period of rising expectations in the 1820s and 1830s opportunities for upward mobility into the educated elite were drastically contracting in the 1840s."[49] As a result, in Prussia of 1835, "there were 262 candidates for every 100 livings in the church, 265 candidates for every 100 judicial offices and 194 candidates for every 100 medical appointments."[50] Partly due to the reform of the German university system, the increase in university students during the 1820s was so large as to cause concern for the governments. The very reform of the university system and the emergence of a distinct mandarin subculture among academicians nucleated by a common commitment to the idealism of Fichte, Schleiermacher, and Schelling, endowed intellectuals with a sense of social and national obligation.[51] This often made them a center for reform programs, even among the bureaucracy. The Romantic movement to which the youth were especially susceptible encouraged many young intellectuals to resist paternal expectations of business careers, their resistance often finding support among sympathetic, increasingly educated mothers. Thus the ranks of the educated seeking professional and intellectual careers were burgeoning. Career blockage among educated youth was also furthered insofar as modernization and the expectation of progress, personal and societal, outstripped industrial development, reducing the number of careers possible for young people in the private sector. This appears to have been most strongly the case in Germany.

In England, however, the possibility of emigration and of careers in the colonial services of an expanding empire served as a kind of "safety valve" for educated manpower. Indeed, ideologists of colonialization such as Edward Wakefield, Charles Buller, and Sir William Molesworth used the growing competition in the professions in England to justify the expansion of English colonialization. In England, too, the growth and perquisites of the newly developing civil service were also carefully limited—so as not to encourage the educated to place too great a reliance on employment with the state—thereby encouraging careers in the independent professions.

Thus while England did exhibit some overproduction of the educated, it was not as severe as in Germany and France, and such overproduction as developed was attenuated by the growth of the colonial and civil services. Moreover, the educated in England were situated in a class system whose aristocracy still retained widespread influence and into whose ranks the rising middle class often hoped to enter. The growing group of the educated therefore continued to accept the cultural hegemony of the aristocracy, as did the middle class itself, so that English intellectuals were less likely than their Continental counterparts to serve as a locus of political instability.

The situation of educated manpower in France was affected by the widespread prestige of the colleges, universities, and the *grandes écoles,* while business and commerce were often viewed, as in Germany, as unworthy outlets for educated young men. At the same time, French industrial and commercial development lagged behind England's. France also lacked a colonial expansion that could serve as a safety valve for the ambitions of the educated. The educated in France tended to be concentrated in Paris, thus creating an unstabilizing excess of intellectuals at the nation's political and cultural center, more so than in the provinces.

It is important to note that industrialization and modernization meant that the overproduction of educated manpower did not equally affect all intellectuals but centered on those humanistically educated and in certain professions; overcrowding was rather less evident or even nonexistent in the newer technological and scientific occupations. Thus, it is not to be expected that the political alienation attendant on career blockage would be manifested equally among all the educated but would be most especially exhibited by those in occupations either marginal to the growth of the industrial private sector or excluded from the expanding state bureaucracies.

The *ability* of intellectuals, as distinct from their *willingness,* to play a decisive role in the German revolution of 1848 derived from several factors. One of the most important of these was the development of new mass media, the newspapers, and the corresponding development of a new "profession," journalism. The development of newspapers and journalism provided intellectuals with a medium for disseminating their views, for mobilizing publics that they could lead, and for exerting pressure upon political authority, as well as with occupational outlets consistent with their intellectual aspirations. Acquiring newspapers required relatively little capital and entering journalism needed no long specialized preparation. Often enough, and especially in Germany, journalism was an occupation which was widely claimed to be the last refuge of those who had failed in other middle-class or professional careers.[52]

Journalism provided not only a possible source of income, however, but also a high degree of visibility and thus prepared writers and editors for political leadership. While this use of journalism as a springboard for political careers was much more institutionalized in France, where young men who sought political futures might often begin as writers and editors, the access of intellectuals to the newspapers, and the newspapers' corresponding need for writers, meant that even in the Germanies intellectuals had more access to publics than they would otherwise have had. The appearance of the intelligentsia on the revolutionary stage in 1848, then, was in part based on the prior development of newspapers which intellectuals could use to reach mass audiences, and which could be launched with relatively modest investments. Thus Marx and Engels very largely started the *Neue Rheinische Zeitung* in Cologne with their own out-of-pocket monies.

In the light of contemporary discussion of the adversary impulse of journalism, it is noteworthy that much the same complaints were voiced about this even in these earlier periods. O'Boyle thus remarks that "the press was almost the sole instrument for the intellectuals in opposition during the Restoration"[53] in post-revolutionary France. In like vein, "the Tory *Quarterly Review* described the 1848 revolution as arising from 'the accidental audacity of a dozen obscure agitators, the spawn of two printing offices . . .' and . . . Lamartine nor anyone else seemed to have thought it odd that a handful of journalists should dethrone a king and themselves decide on a new form of government."[54] As for Germany,

Metternich himself remarked in 1819 that "All the German Governments have arrived at the conviction that . . . the press serves a party
antagonistic to all existing governments."[55]

Although any view of the revolution of 1848 as the "revolution of the
intellectuals" is exaggerated, especially if it obscures the local initiative
of merchants and industrialists, the influence achieved by intellectuals
at the national level in Germany was important and this was partly
grounded in the prior development of newspapers and in intellectuals'
access to them, either through contributing to them as journalists or
through modest ownership investments.

Intellectuals' leadership roles in the German revolution (as in others)
was most important at the parliamentary and other national levels of
political action. If the leadership cadres of the German revolution are
studied only through the occupational backgrounds of the Frankfurt
Parliament, the role of intellectuals tends to be overestimated while that
of businessmen is underestimated. The latter, while unable to leave their
business for any length of time to pursue political leadership, could more
readily participate in local government in their own towns, where they
could play leading roles. There were, therefore, "important discrepancies
between national and local leadership groups."[56] Nonetheless, sustained
participation in national parliaments and in the leadership of national
political parties did require businessmen to absent themselves from their
businesses. This could be hazardous to new enterprises, and might thus
deter businessmen, merchants, shopkeepers, and tradesmen from seeking
the national leadership of political movements. This same impediment,
however, did not apply equally to the educated elite. In Germany, "state
employees could apply for leave to participate in parliamentary life,
lawyers could seek to combine a practice with political activity, and
journalists could try to make a living writing about the events in which
they took part,"[57] allowing them influence on *national* politics far in
excess of their economic power and wealth. Thus the very kind of occupations in which the educated elite were involved often gave them a
motive for dissident participation, while allowing them more time in
which they could achieve leadership visibility and effectiveness with
national publics. Coupled with their access to the new media and with
their longstanding prestige in Germany, this made the educated elite
there formidable competitors for national political leadership.

The 1848 revolutions throughout Europe and especially Germany
were the decisive political environment within which Marxism was crystallized as a social movement. These revolutions were characterized by a
confluence of collective unrest in two critical social strata, artisans and
intellectuals, respectively the fighting militants and national leaders of

the revolution. Often enough, however, artisans saw the educated as class enemies and as hired ideologues for the free trade movement that, together with the factory system, was ruining them. "Handicraftsmen regarded higher education with the same suspicion which they felt toward great wealth,"[58] reports Theodore Hamerow. It was just this widespread tradition of suspicion of the educated that Marx and Engels encountered from sections of the League of the Just, and indeed, from their own Communist League, as well as later in the International Workingmen's Association. Nonetheless, intellectuals' own critical traditions and impaired market situation led some of them to become radicalized and to seek alliance with artisans and their organizations.

Both artisans and intellectuals had in part been brought to oppose the *status quo* by a similar increase in their numbers and by the consequent threat to status and career. The similarities between artisans and intellectuals, however, went well beyond this common impairment of their market situation. The two occupations were alike in other ways that made both resentful of threats to their traditional status. They were alike in having important traditions of craftsmanship, even if, in the one case, manual and, in the other, intellectual. They were alike, too, in their common desire to produce objects or services of high quality, and not just those that would sell on the market. Neither worked simply to procure livelihoods.

When William Sewall, Jr., describes the artisan ethos, he is in effect also describing that of university academicians: "a consistent moral collectivism, an assertion of their own capacity to preserve order and pursue the common good, an insistence on the distinct value and identity of the various trades, and a pride in their work as a contribution to the public welfare." The mechanical and manual trades were also often viewed as "arts" requiring discipline and intelligence, not just physical labor or dexterity and were thus not radically split from the "mental" labor of intellectuals and professionals. Indeed, the term "arts" spread from poetry or architecture to the military and government arts, again serving to bridge both mental and manual labor and to note their common subordination to a system of disciplined production according to rules. There was, then, an emphasis on certain *continuities* between artisan and artist, and certain trades and arts.

In France, the "liberal arts" were also long organized in a manner similar to the corporatively organized *gens de métier* and the *mechanical arts*. As Sewall writes,

> The universities, the legal and medical professions and the royal officers all had organizations juridically similar to the *corp d'arts et métiers*— with their privileges, their internal regulations and their recognized

standing in the state. In the Middle Ages, the similarities between universities and trade corporations were clearly signaled in language: not
only were both headed by "masters," but apprentices in the manual arts
were frequently called *escolons* and journeymen, *bacheliers*. And as late
as the sixteenth century, a royal decree banning disorderly banquets
could include in a single sentence "all banquets whether for doctorates
or other degrees in any faculty, or for masterships of sciences, arts and
trades."[59]

Artisans and intellectuals alike had conceptions of themselves as possessing skills that required long and specialized training. Their skills
were a center of their selfhood on which they based claims to personal
worthiness and community honor. Artisans and educated elites were
alike, too, in their membership in ancient and honorable institutions
that monitored their work and protected their careers—the guilds and
universities. Both these pre-modern institutions upheld traditions that
did not endorse a merely competitive egoism or possessive individualism
but encouraged a measure of responsibility to the larger community and
a concern for the latter's needs. By reason of their collectivity-responsive-
ness and their skill commitments, both artisans and intellectuals made
claims to independence in the conduct of their work and in the management of their corporate groups and these expectations, when violated,
would further alienate both groups.

Artisans and intellectuals, then, were alike in significant ways. They
were both threatened elites during the pre-revolutionary era when Marxism was formed. Both felt an alienation from the growing industrial
capitalism. Fritz Ringer remarks that higher officials, secondary school
teachers, judges, lawyers, doctors, and university professors were an elite
of the cultivated who "had no more in common with the new commercial and industrial class than they had with the Junkers."[60] Much the
same could, however, also be said of the many journeymen who despised
the new factories and factory owners, as well as the merchants who sold
their cheaper goods to the ruin of the artisans. That many artisans and
intellectuals were commonly disaffected was due in large part because
their occupations were then more similar than they subsequently became. Even their training was then more alike, as certain of the learned
professions still trained new recruits by apprenticeships not much different than those used to train artisans.

The revolutionary militancy that Marx had predicted for the proletariat waned in Western Europe precisely with the decline of the artisans, as the factory system spread, for it was the artisans who had been
the most militant wing of the working class. If intellectuals, or sections of
intellectuals among the humanistically trained, continued to evidence

discontent with the *status quo* this was in part because their market and social position was increasingly threatened in the technological and scientific world of advanced industrial capitalism. Humanistic intellectuals continued to be alienated, in short, for much the same reasons that artisans in the first half of the nineteenth century were, for the intellectuals were in part artisans protecting their elite positions from threatening encroachments. Intellectuals, especially humanistic intellectuals and academicians, are the last of the artisans; their disaffection remains grounded in much the same social forces that led the more horny-handed artisans to their earlier rebellion.

The Exclusionary Politics of Artisan Organizations

One way artisans sought to cushion themselves from the costs of the rising factory system and to express their resistance to the new industrialism was to develop new organizations, among them the proliferating "secret" societies. Through these they sought to develop instruments for pursuing their struggle against the threatening new order. Yet these very organization instruments became new arenas of contest, for the artisans soon had to struggle to retain their dominance in these organizations and to prevent them from being captured by other "alien" strata. The new organizations, then, inevitably came to express their founders' interests in securing control over these organizations by excluding other strata from power in them. As the working-class movement matured organizationally, there developed a larger sphere of competition for leadership, for control over organization policy, for offices, delegates, editorships, expenses and other perquisites.

By the time Marx encountered the League of the Just, it and other organizations had already experienced open tensions between humanistic intellectuals and "workers" and the latter had already exhibited a clear-cut exclusionary (or "ouvrierist") policy. Hal Draper notes that, for example, in 1847, even after Weitling had been drummed out of the League, Marx and Engels, as "two bourgeois-educated newcomers of higher intellectual attainment . . . were vulnerable to Straubinger prejudices [i.e., artisan prejudices within the Communist League itself] . . . one of the members, Friedrich Lessner . . . recalled that 'the opponents of Marx raised the cry of "down with the 'intellectuals,' " ' not only at the first congress but . . . even at the second congress of November-December where Marx and Engels were assigned to write the Manifesto."[61] The *Communist Manifesto* itself was thus born in an organizational environment in which its authors were defined by some artisans as class aliens who ought to be excluded from their ranks. Some three years later in 1850, Marx complained of anti-intellectual revolutionaries in the movement who "look with deepest disdain on a more theoretical clarification of the workers as to their interests. Hence their irritation—which is not proletarian but plebeian—at the *habits noirs* [frock coats] of the more or less educated people."[62]

Again in 1866, at the first congress of the International Workingmen's Association (I.W.A.), later known as the First International in Geneva, the French communist and engraver Henri Louis Tolain demanded that only manual workers be permitted to be congress delegates. Recognizing that such exclusionary sentiments were widely held in the International Workingmen's Association, Marx kept a low profile, confined himself to influencing its general council, and thought it better not to serve as a delegate to its first congress. The artisans' impulse to exclude intellectuals was strong and was found even in organizations in which Marx had played a role as a principal (I.W.A.) or as founder (the Communist League). The tradition of controlling entry to their ranks was particularly strong among skilled artisans with guild traditions and was easily transferable by them to their new organizations.

Clearly, then, social closure and group protection through exclusionary provision is a tactic not only of an elite or upper class but is used also by subordinated groups. As Frank Parkin writes, "By social closure [Max] Weber means the process by which social collectivities seek to maximize rewards by restricting access to resources and opportunities to a limited circle of eligibles . . . [by] singling out certain social or physical attributes as the justificatory basis of exclusion."[63]

While Weber often stressed the restriction of economic opportunities, there can, as here, also be *political* perquisites, such as the right to have power, hold office, or even to vote, whether as an official of an organization or editor of its press. Intellectuals were stigmatized partly by associating them with capital, partly with their more privileged education, and even as we have noted, in consequence of their dress; a cultural line was drawn (as in the League of the Just) between intellectuals and "true" workers. A cultural "inside" was thus created to which true workers were admitted—and here the criterion seems often to have been *manual* work—and an "outside," to which artisans sought to relegate intellectuals doing merely "mental" work. While any dichotomy between manual and mental work is very difficult to defend in any radical way, for everyone moves his hands and uses his brain while working, the distinction was nonetheless useful ideologically in the course of the struggle to exclude intellectuals from movement organizations.

Our point, however, is not to deny the differences in economic function and culture between intellectuals and other workers, but, rather, to hold that a radical emphasis on such differences was more of a political tactic of convenience, than simply a theoretical achievement. It was useful as a way of *justifying* intellectuals' exclusion from the movement and its organizations.

If workers were culturally marginal to bourgeois society they, in turn, had begun defensively to create a social and organizational space from which the bourgeoisie—whether of money or the diploma, as Tolain called intellectuals—were to be excluded. As Parkin notes, "it is in any case hardly possible to consider the effectiveness of exclusion practices without due reference to the countervailing actions of socially defined ineligibles."[64] One question this suggests for us is what were the countervailing tactics of those who were defined as ineligibles—intellectuals in general and Marx in particular. I shall argue that part of the history of Marxism can be understood not simply as the product of intellectuals-in-general but as the historically specific response of radicalized intellectuals in a special sociological bind: caught in the middle between their interest in workers' movements, and their "alien" social characteristics which made them vulnerable to workers' exclusionary tactics—i.e., to "ouvrierism." The theoretical character of Marxism was, it will be held, in part influenced by the social character of those formulating it, by the fact that they were intellectuals, but, much more specifically, by the *defensive position* into which intellectuals are always thrust when defined as "outsiders" by the very working-class movement to which they are committed. (In some way, this dissonance—the prominent presence of middle-class intellectuals in a working-class movement—must be muted or camouflaged. I shall later argue that this is one of the functions of the Leninist "vanguard" party.)

There are, however, several ways in which this thesis needs to be qualified carefully:

First, an exclusionary or ouvrierist policy is not always successfully imposed; it may not, once-for-all, stigmatize intellectuals as "outsiders." There may instead be a continual, see-sawing contest, visible I believe in the history of Marxism, during which artisans seek to exclude intellectuals while the latter resist vigorously, using all manner of tactics. The most fundamentally exclusionary workers' organizations are trade unions, for these exclude those of different occupations and employment, thus keeping intellectuals on the outside. Intellectuals, therefore, may be expected not only to reject their exclusion in general but, most particularly, to oppose any exclusion based on social characteristics such as type or place of employment or even style of life.

Intellectuals will prefer exclusionary policies that are based either on a lack of ideological qualifications—i.e., a deficiency of beliefs deemed

appropriate—or on a paucity of organizational zeal or loyalty, as exhibited
by the way persons perform organizational tasks or accept organizational
discipline. Ideological propriety and organizational commitment rather
than occupational activity, then, will be the lines around which intellectuals shape exclusionary policies.

Such policies make admission to the organization dependent on things
intellectuals *can do,* rather than on their family or class antecedents, social origins, education, income, occupation, or employment. The exclusionary (or membership) criteria intellectuals prefer are therefore not
those that, in principle, exclude persons by reason of their past privileges
or even because of their ongoing middle-class style of life. The group or
"material" interests of intellectuals, then, shape their selection of (and
reaction to) exclusionary principles.

What organizations *are,* the *kinds* of organization they are, is in part
definable in terms of the kinds of exclusionary principles they employ.[65]
Characteristically, trade unions, like guilds before them, seek to control
admission to occupations and work places and hence limit membership
to those already in these occupations or work places. Political parties, concerned with power in the state, will normally admit those whose ideological conformity or organizational loyalty further their struggle for state
power, excluding only those lacking in these. The interests of intellectuals, then, dispose them to assign greater importance to more purely
political organizations than trade unions. Intellectuals, then, are structurally motivated to induce workers to oppose working-class "economism"
and to encourage "politics." Indeed, this was one basis of Lenin's opposition to trade union "economism," and of his proposal for a political party
of professional revolutionaries, membership in which was determined entirely by ideological qualifications and organizational commitment. For
these are things that intellectuals could learn rather more easily than
could uneducated workers constrained to routine jobs.

Marxism, then, will in part be understood here as a product of intellectuals vulnerable to exclusionary discrimination by workers. In that respect, it is important to insist that the exclusionary tactics of the League
of the Just were not the policies of proletarians "born and bred" but of
artisans. Weitling and other leaders of the League of the Just, whether
of the Swiss or the London faction, were primarily artisans. The tens of
thousands of Germans living in Paris in the mid-1840s from whom the
League might have recruited, were "divided into two sections having
virtually no contact with one another. One consisted of writers and the
other of artisans. Some trades were almost exclusively in the hands of
Germans. In fact, in Paris 'German' and 'cobbler' had almost become
synonymous,"[66] for many German cobblers had migrated because of the

high unemployment in their homeland. The anti-intellectual exclusionism of the League of the Just grew out of that cleavage among the German expatriates and the competition between intellectuals and artisans, as this came into focus in their emerging organizations. As mentioned, Weitling himself was a tailor. Among the League's leadership in London, Joseph Moll was a watchmaker, Heinrich Bauer, a bootmaker, while Wilhelm Schapper had been a former student of forestry and a compositor.[67]

If any social stratum could then compete effectively with intellectuals' growing effort to influence the European working class, it was neither the new bourgeoisie itself, nor newly urbanized workers in factories shorn of skills by the new machinery, disorganized by family separation and urban isolation, and pacified by relatively good wages. The natural and indeed most effective competitors of the intellectuals for influence with the working class were artisans; the anti-intellectual exclusionary policies in working-class organizations were thus largely theirs.

Marx's outrage at this is suggested by his use of the terms *Straubinger* and *Knoten* (which originally meant artisans) to mean louts, boors, or ignorant bumpkins—to heap contempt on his artisan competitors. In a letter of April 16, 1865, to Engels, for example, Marx wrote that "the German *Knote* Scherzer (old boy) came forward and in truly awful Straubinger style, denounced the German 'men of learning,' the 'intellectual workers' who had left them (the *Knoten*) in the lurch. . . ."[68]

Again, in a revealing letter of May 18, 1859, which plainly highlights Marx's dilemma as a middle-class intellectual in a workers' movement, Marx himself described his tension with the artisans as a result of their contest to control the nomination of Party representatives: "Messrs. the *Knoten* have . . . had a very nice lesson. That old-Weitling ass Scherzer thought *he* could nominate Party representatives. When *I* met a deputation of the *Knoten* . . . I told them straight out: We had received our appointment as representatives of the proletarian party from nobody *but ourselves*. It was, however, endorsed by the exclusive and universal hatred consecrated to us by all the parties and fractions of the old world. You can imagine how staggered the blockheads were. . . ."[69]

The point of noting that one group of Marx's and Engels's key competitors was artisans is, of course, not to justify Marx's subsequent attack on Weitling and, more generally, on the *"Knoten."* Our object is to understand the sociological meaning of that attack and of the feelings Marx and Engels developed toward them and, more generally, toward "petty bourgeoisie." The exceptional bitterness of these feelings will be surprising only if one considers the petty bourgeoisie's *powerlessness in society at large*. Marx's critique of Weitling, of artisans, and of the petty bourgeoisie generally, however, was influenced not by the last named's power in society but in the very organizations where they were competitors contending for influence. For competition is keenest not among those most different, or whose social character, skills, or functions differ most, but, rather, among those who are most *similar*. As suggested earlier, intellectuals were then much more nearly like "petty-bourgeois" artisans than they were like factory proletarians.

Perhaps the final ironic twist in Marx's relationship to artisans relates to Freddy Demuth, Marx's illegitimate son with his housekeeper Helen Demuth, whom he had barred from his home as an infant. Freddy, son of the great *Knoten* despiser himself, became an artisan: "The son of Karl Marx was a skilled workman who served the standard six-year apprenticeship and was sufficiently proficient at his job to be admitted into the highest section of the union. . . . 'He was a damn good turner, working on a lathe.' "[70]

In understanding Marxism as in part intellectuals' response to artisan sponsored "ouvrierism," it remains to be added that Marx and Engels were not competing only with artisans but also with other *intellectuals*. Marxism partly developed, then, as a "fight on two fronts" against the exclusionary tactics of artisans, *and* against other intellectuals toward whom Marx, in turn, behaved in exclusionary ways. When oriented toward the exclusionary efforts of artisans, Marx and Engels denounced the "philistinism" of the *Knoten;* when oriented toward the competition of other intellectuals, they would express contempt for them as "servile pedants" who were intellectually incompetent to boot.

Marx's and Engels's own exclusionary tactics against competing intellectuals were advanced in the name of the "self-emancipation of the proletariat." The First International's (I.W.A.) component groups were thus to consist of working men's societies; "sections exclusively or principally composed of members not belonging to the working class" were not to be admitted."[71]

In a letter to Engels of December 10, 1864, Marx discusses how, in order to exclude Louis Blanc from the I.W.A., he had eliminated the category of "honorary member" of the First International: ". . . surmising that an attempt of this sort would be made, I had already put through the by-law . . . that no persons should be an honorary member." (Lenin was in 1903 to take a similar stand in his debate with Martov, to limit the membership of intellectuals in the new Russian Social Democratic Federation to roles in which they would be subject to organization discipline.)

Intellectuals who later sought to ally themselves with the workers' movement, and whose numbers increased in Germany after the anti-

socialist laws were repealed there in 1890, often had impressive credentials as academicians and might be formidable competitors. It is often
forgotten, for example, that Eugen Dühring, the target of Engels's *Anti-
Dühring*, was not anti-socialist but pro-social democratic. Dühring was a
well-known "academic [who] aspired to become the leading theoretician
both of socialism and anti-Semitism."[72] The significant point here, of
course, is that Dühring was launched upon a competition with Marx
and Engels for socialist leadership in the latter's German stronghold, a
challenge to which they had to respond. In like manner and for similar
reasons, Marx took up the cudgels in 1880 against the German economist
Adolph Wagner, using the occasion to denounce "professors who still
stand with one foot in the old crap. . . . From being serfs of the landowners they have changed over to being serfs of the state. . . ."[73]

Marx and Engels's "war on two fronts," then, was not simply a cerebral effort to find an ethereal golden mean. It was an earthy political response stimulated by the competitive challenge to their leadership represented by both groups. It was in substantial part a struggle for power
and influence, and thus for control over party offices and editorships. In
a letter to Becker of September 15, 1879, Engels complained that the
party reformers who were then complaining about the party's "ouvrierism"
actually "lay claim to the leadership of the movement for 'educated' bourgeois of their own stamp." The party reform group to which Engels
had been responding was the Hochberg Movement, which clearly exhibited the leadership challenge that came from other intellectuals—a
competition to which Engels, not being a Herr Doktor, was especially
vulnerable. The essential point, however, is that the influx of new intellectuals into the socialist movement was resisted doubtless in part for
ideological reasons, as Marx often insisted (because they brought with
them reformist views, which doubtless they often did), but additionally,
because they were political competitors for organizational resources.

In this vein, Engels wrote Marx's son-in-law Paul Lafargue on August
27, 1890, expressly complaining that ". . . for the past two or three
years a crowd of students, litterateurs and other young declassed bourgeois has rushed into the party, arriving just in time to occupy most of
the editorial positions on the new journals . . . they regard the bourgeois university as a socialist Saint-Cyr which gives them the right to
enter the party's ranks with an officer's commission if not a general's."[74]
A contest was being fought over who was to lead, and the polemic's cut-
ting edge was then directed against competing intellectuals. In that same
year, Engels wrote an open letter to the rebellious *Jungen*, dissociating
himself from them. "Let them understand that their 'academic education,'" wrote Engels, "gives them no officer's commission with a claim

to a corresponding post in the party . . . that posts of responsibility in
the party will be won not simply by literary talent and theoretical knowledge, even if both of these are present beyond a doubt, but that in
addition what is required is thorough familiarity with the conditions of
party struggle and seasoning in its forms, tested personal reliability and
sound character, and finally, willing enlistment in the ranks of the
fighters. . . ."[75]

Episode No. 2: The Revolution of 1848 and the Communist League

The fortunes of the new Communist League were subsequently shaped
by the accelerating development of the revolution of 1848, especially in
Germany. To anticipate: the revolution often intensified the cleavages
between militant artisans or workers, on the one side, and intellectuals,
on the other, while also sometimes intensifying rivalries among radicalized intellectuals themselves. It would be oversimplifying to suggest that
there were only two policies, and these always at odds with one another.
In the cockpit of revolution, alignments swerved swiftly and alliances
were as important as rivalries. Nonetheless, there were at least two tendencies: Marx (and other radical intellectuals) were exposed to two great
forces, the increasingly radical middle classes and the increasingly radicalized artisans and workers.

As the 1848 revolution surfaced, Marx and Engels sought to weld
these different forces into a single coalition. The major problem this policy faced, however, was the danger that the artisans/workers' increasing
radicalization might frighten the middle classes, as indeed might the
Communist League itself. Marx, then, was caught between the urgent
need to mobilize the middle classes and thus to placate their fear of
lower-class radicalism, while at the same time to give expression to the
growing militancy of the working classes. It was a precarious situation:
too much concern about the fears of the middle classes would cost Marx,
and other radical intellectuals, influence among workers and artisans; too
much concern about the working classes' special needs, however, could
lead the respectable middle classes to bolt the new coalition.

Marx's strategy was to seek a multiclass coalition that was at first essentially under the hegemony of the middle classes. This included the
workers as part of the coalition's left wing, and compensated the latter
for restraining their demands by defining this as only the first stage in a
revolution that would be followed by another in which workers' own
special interests would then be primary. The revolution, then, came to
be defined as a "revolution in permanence," moving from one stage, the

middle-class revolution, to a second, the working-class revolution. Marx's argument was that socialism required the industrial foundation that would be created by the bourgeoisie. Yet if the middle class caught wind that their revolution was to be only a prelude to an increasingly radical revolt, they might pull away from the coalition. Correspondingly, workers might not be inclined to sacrifice themselves to achieve a revolution whose first beneficiary was the middle class. The theory of permanent revolution, then, was a blurred doctrine whose ambiguities were glossed.

Marx defined the emerging revolution as requiring the mass involvement of publics, the open shaping of public opinion, participation in parliamentary politics, and the creation and operation of new media that could mobilize masses. Very soon, he no longer saw it as requiring secret societies such as the Communist League. During the 1848 revolution, especially the "mad year" in Cologne, much of Marx's time, energy, talent, money, and hope were invested in starting and editing a public mass medium, the *Neue Rheinische Zeitung*.

Launching a newspaper is something that workers and artisans are less likely than intellectuals to define as a vital political act. Artisans and workers were also less likely to be committed to Marx's long-term vision, his scenario of a revolution whose first great victory would not be theirs, but the middle class's. The virtues of deferred gratification seemed more rational to middle-class intellectuals than to working-class militants who knew acute deprivation. They would resent radical intellectuals who told them it was necessary to defer their own victory and to temper displays of militancy, sometimes seeing this not as prudence but as a callousness toward their suffering to which those who did not share their lives were prone. In short, many of the same tensions between Marx and his competitors, already exemplified by the Weitling incident, surfaced again in the 1848 revolution.

Two differences, however, are notable. First, that one of Marx's main competitors for working-class leadership is another intellectual, specifically a member of the technical intelligentsia, the physician Andreas Gottschalk. Second, the 1848 revolution makes it increasingly clear that the new organizational forms—first the Communist League and later the First International—introduced a new level of complexity in which even the organization's founders could no longer control events.

Marx in Cologne

The two leaders of the Communist League in Cologne in 1847, Andreas Gottschalk and August von Willich, had strikingly different backgrounds.[76] Willich was the son of an old Prussian military family, a one-

time captain of artillery, drummed out of the army because of his support
for another radical officer. After being discharged, Willich became a
working carpenter. Each morning he would slowly cross the Cologne
parade grounds, wearing his carpenter's apron and carrying his tools,
each proud step provocatively displaying his new status in life to the
soldiery.

Gottschalk's origins were profoundly different from his comrade's.
The son of a Jewish butcher in Düsseldorf, Gottschalk became a physician after studying at Bonn while Marx was there. "From the first he
worked almost exclusively in the working-class quarters of the city as
healer, helper, and friend of the poorest workers. The Cologne workers
idolised their warm-hearted doctor and friend. He was their undisputed
leader."[77]

As the revolution emerged in Cologne, indeed just several days before
Marx's arrival there, Gottschalk moved to expand the League's organizational base, calling for a "Democratic Socialist Union" which subsequently came to be called a Workers' Union or Association. "The success of the new organisation was astonishing," state Nicolaievsky and
Maenchen-Helfen; only two months later its membership was nearly
eight thousand. In short, Gottschalk was the local leader whose political
and personal authority was undisputed among the workers until Marx's
arrival. Half trade union and half political party, the Workers' Union
soon won the enmity of the propertied class. It was not long, however,
before Marx too was at odds with the Workers' Union. ". . . [I]n a very
short time differences of opinion concerning the policy of the Union
arose between Gottschalk and him," note Nicolaievsky and Maenchen-
Helfen because, they claimed, "Gottschalk's programme could not result
in anything but parting the proletariat from the Democratic movement. . . ."[78] Which is to say, Gottschalk resisted the limited place in
the political coalition to which Marx had then consigned the proletariat.

Marx had also wanted the Workers' Union to participate in the elections for the new Frankfurt Assembly, the pan-German Parliament and
one of the first gains of the emerging German revolution. Supported by
the workers, Gottschalk, however, wanted these elections boycotted. In
one rather slanted version, this was said to be because "He utterly rejected all and every compromise and would not hear of even the most
temporary coalition with non-proletarian Democratic groups."[79] Engels
later wrote that in contrast, their own banner then "could only be the
banner of democracy . . . a democracy which emphasized its specifically
proletarian character in details only,"[80] for they wanted a broad party of
action rather than a small, doctrinally pure sect.

Finding the workers' movement in Cologne critical of him, and seeking in any event a broader-based movement, Marx and his friends organized a multiclass Democratic Union that took part in the elections. If Gottschalk had been the workers' undisputed leader, "Marx had won a few supporters in Cologne, mainly among middle-class intellectuals. . . ."[81] Having no control over the Workers' Union, which could legitimately claim to be the Communist League's local heir, and having invested his energies in the new democratic coalition, Marx began to feel there was no longer any role for the Communist League and resolved to get rid of it. "In Marx's opinion the appearance of the *Neue Rheinische Zeitung* did away with the excuse even for the appearance of the Communist League's existence. A secret organisation had become superfluous, and all that Marx had to say . . . could be made public through the press."[82]

Though Marx's desire to shelve the League was opposed by Schapper and others in the artisan-based London group, he nonetheless dissolved it. Still retaining his own Workers' Union, Gottschalk concurred in this decision, although differing from Marx on other issues. Thus, for example, Gottschalk's union collected money to aid the German political refugees that Willich had gathered at Besançon, denouncing Marx and his Democratic Union for failing to help this work. Gottschalk also denounced Marx's *Neue Rheinische Zeitung*—in a manner reminiscent of Weitling's earlier complaint about Marx's control over the left's media—i.e., as bestowed on Marx by the moneyed and rich.

Marx made the *Neue Rheinische Zeitung* the center of his coalition-building policy. In Engels's words, the newspaper was run as a "simple dictatorship by Marx,"[83] which the other editors accepted as a matter of course. Repeatedly, Marx's *friends* (not simply his enemies) describe him as a "dictator"—as had Paul Annenkov in his account of the Weitling incident—often intending this as a compliment. The ambivalence of the *Neue Rheinische Zeitung* coalition policy is suggested by the fact that, on the one side, it spoke of "we Democrats," yet, on the other, state Nicolaievsky and Maenchen-Helfen, Marx ". . . sided just as resolutely with the insurrectionary Paris workers in those days of June."[84]

One way the *Neue Rheinische Zeitung* had sought to cement the shaky democratic coalition was to call for war against Russia. Indeed, it did this from its very first issue, hoping the war would consolidate the alliance and commit the middle class to more resolute action against the mainstay of European reaction, while at the same time winning concessions for the middle class and democracy as the war required their effort. Since the war against Russia was also seen as the essential means of liberating Poland, the *Neue Rheinische Zeitung* "received very generous support from the Polish Democrats . . . [who] sent two thousand thalers in their name."[85]

Gottschalk was soon arrested and imprisoned for six months, allegedly for inciting to violence, and the leadership of the Workers' Union was then vacant. Both Schapper and Moll (then working with Marx) became leaders of the union, Moll being elected temporary president. Marx's influence over the workers in Cologne was thus extended. As the revolution developed in September, Schapper too was arrested and Moll fled, only barely missing arrest. As barricades were being thrown up and workers' tempers flared, Marx attempted to defuse the situation and "declared in the name of the [Rhineland Democratic] Congress that in no circumstances, least of all at the present moment, did they want a rising."[86] Exasperated at the loss of their leaders, the workers listened "with gloomy looks." ". . . Marx declined to consent to a local riot."[87] With Schapper jailed and Moll a fugitive, the Workers' Union was once again leaderless, and this time offered the temporary presidency to Marx who "only after a good deal of hesitation . . . agreed to accept the position."[88]

As the German revolution began to be rolled back, Marx came to believe that the bourgeoisie had failed in its duty to history and had withdrawn from the pursuit of its own class interests. He concluded that the choice then facing Left democrats was either to accept absolutism's successful counter-revolution, or to make a social-republican revolution of their own. "Social republican was the term he used, not 'socialist' or 'proletarian.' . . . Social republicanism involved neither the abolition of private ownership of the means of production nor the abolition of class-conflicts. It meant capitalism still. . . ."[89] While not pursuing a policy against the German bourgeoisie, the *Neue Rheinische Zeitung* nonetheless focused increasingly on tensions between them and the workers. Toward the end of 1848, Marx also increasingly fastened his hopes on a new revolution in France that would revive the flagging revolution in Germany.

Having finally been acquitted by the courts, Gottschalk returned from prison and resumed the presidency (of the Workers' Union) that Marx had temporarily held, and again exerted pressure on Marx's policies. In an open letter, he particularly criticized an article by Marx in the *Neue Rheinische Zeitung* of January 21, 1849. Marx had there diagnosed the political situation as a choice between either the old absolutism or a representative political system under bourgeois hegemony. "The struggle against the bourgeois system of private property could not yet be."[90] In

Marx's own words, "We say to the workers and the petty-bourgeoisie: rather suffer in modern bourgeois society, which by the development of industry creates the material means for the foundation of a new society which will free you all, than step backwards into an obsolete form of society. . . ."[91]

To which Gottschalk replied, "What is the purpose of such a revolution? Why should we, men of the proletariat, spill our blood for this?"[92] His objection was much the same as Weitling's had earlier been when, in his letter to Moses Hess of March 31, 1846, he had complained that Marx had insisted that, "As for the realisation of Communism, there can be no talk of it to begin with; the bourgeoisie must first come to the helm."[93] Nicolaievsky and Maenchen-Helfen astutely observe that Gottschalk's bitter query was identical to "the question that Willich and his supporters were to put a year later, it was the question that Bakunin's followers were to put in the seventies."[94] The pattern was a recurrent one.

Gottschalk's open letter also followed the pattern in denouncing Marx's position as one congenial to intellectuals who "are not in earnest about the salvation of the oppressed. The distress of the workers, the hunger of the poor have only a scientific, doctrinaire interest for them."[95] Seeking proletarian revolution then and there, and demanding that there be no cease-fire until the workers' victory, Gottschalk rejected Marx's policies for a democratic coalition whose first aim was a non-socialist, social-republicanism. (In another time and under different conditions, the intransigent but beloved Gottschalk might have played Che Guevara, another radicalized physician, to Marx's Fidel Castro.) Soon the conflict between Gottschalk and Marx split the Workers' Union which finally collapsed and disappeared. Gottschalk returned to his old life as friend and medical helper to the workers, dying in the struggle against the cholera plague which had spread among them in the autumn of 1849. He had been the first doctor, and for long the only one, fighting the plague in the workers' slums. He died a noble death, succumbing to the disease on September 8, 1849. "Many hundreds of workers followed their dead friend to his grave."[96]

As the revolution was thwarted, efforts were made to resuscitate the discarded Communist League. At first Marx and Engels resisted these, despite repeated entreaties, holding that a conspiratorial group such as the League was superfluous since freedom of speech and the press had emerged. This position, however, opened the possibility of their becoming isolated from the working-class movement and becoming submerged in bourgeois democracy. As, however, the Neue Rheinische Zeitung itself became insolvent and terminal, Marx rejoined the League, though exactly when is uncertain. And when the *Neue Rheinische Zeitung* finally folded, "the last issue . . . warned the workers against any sort of rising,"[97] yet also called for working-class emancipation.

As the revolution wound down and fighting became limited to sporadic rearguard actions, German refugees and exiles once again streamed across Europe. The League's central office was reconstituted in London headed by Schapper, Bauer, and others. Willich was also elected to its central office, after Engels had served with him in the military campaign in the Baden Palatinate, where Moll had died in action. Willich, of course, had been close to Gottschalk and his election to the League's central office is often interpreted, not unreasonably, as an effort to placate the League's left, binding the wounds between the left artisan militants who wanted insurrection *now*, and democratic coalitionists and intellectuals like Marx, who held the process would have to be slower and pass through a bourgeois phase which, however, would lay the necessary industrial groundwork for a proletarian socialism.

Permanent Revolution as Compromise

The central office's first circular letter of March 1850 had therefore to satisfy both groups and paper over the tensions dividing them. Perhaps neither side would have signed it if they disagreed with what the letter actually said, but the letter could not have said all that either faction would have wished, exactly as each wished it. It was a compromise that was susceptible to many differing interpretations, as the long-standing controversy about it among "Marxologists" amply indicates.

The March 1850 circular letter, known as the Address of the Central Committee of the Communist League, begins by reaffirming that the proletariat is "the only completely revolutionary class," applauds the members of the League for their revolutionary leadership in 1848-49, and then gets down to its real business. This is a criticism of those who "believed that the time for secret societies had gone by and the public activities alone were sufficient." (Although he goes unnamed here, among those pursuing just such a policy, clearly the foremost was Marx.) It is complained that they allowed party organization and discipline to grow loose and dormant. In fact, Marx had felt it superfluous, had discarded the League, and indeed resisted initial efforts to resuscitate it, rejoining the League only after the *Neue Rheinische Zeitung* had become insolvent. The letter complained that this policy had left the proletariat "under the domination . . . of the petty bourgeois-democrats."

A new revolution being imminent, writes the document, ". . . the workers' party, therefore, must act in the most organized, most unani-

mous, and most independent fashion possible . . . ," all the more as it
remembers the "treacherous role which the German liberal bourgeois
played in 1848 against the people. . . ." What then shall the relation of
the communists ("the worker's party") now be to the petty bourgeoisie?
It marches with them against the old regime, but "opposes them in everything whereby they seek to consolidate their position in their own
interests."

The address to the central committee then goes on to formulate what
is regarded as the classic statement of the doctrine of "permanent revolution." The demands of the petty bourgeoisie, it says,

> can in no wise suffice for the party of the proletariat. While the demo-
> cratic petty bourgeois wish to bring the revolution to a conclusion as
> quickly as possible . . . it is our interest and our task to make the revo-
> lution permanent, until all more or less possessing classes have been
> forced out of their position of dominance, until the proletariat has con-
> quered state power, and the association of proletarians, not only in one
> country but in all the dominant countries of the world, has advanced
> so far that competition among the proletarians of these countries has
> ceased and that at least the decisive productive forces are concentrated
> in the hands of the proletarians. For us the issue cannot be the altera-
> tion of private property but only its annihilation, not the smoothing over
> of class antagonisms but the abolition of classes, not the improvement of
> existing society but the foundation of a new one.[98]

That, however, was the maximum goal, the long-range prospect. In
the meanwhile, says the circular letter, "during the further development
of the revolution, the petty-bourgeois democracy will for a moment ob-
tain predominating influence in Germany." This "is not open to doubt,"
although the letter does not say how long this "moment" of petty bourgeois democracy may last.

Note that the theory of permanent revolution formulated here addresses itself only to the specific conditions in Germany at that time. It
was not put forward as a general theory of permanent revolution that
might apply to revolutions elsewhere, and certainly not to all countries.
Knowing the economy and society to which the doctrine applied, the
document is thus not required to make a general statement about the social conditions under which the tactics of the permanent revolution may
be applicable. It simply states they are applicable to Germany, then and
there, and nothing more. It therefore is not called upon to make a *general* point about the necessity for the prior development of a mature industrial society before a socialist revolution can be successful. It thus
omits any reference to that capping aspect of "scientific socialism." Noth-

ing about the *economic* requisites of socialist revolution is mentioned anywhere in the circular letter.

The emphasis is upon restoring "an independent, secret and public organization of the workers' party. . . ." Leading the armed proletariat, the workers' party "seeks to dictate to the petty bourgeoisie conditions" (for an alliance with the proletariat) such that "the rule of the bourgeois democrats will from the outset bear within it the seeds of their downfall. . . ." In the course of this developing revolution the workers must "compel the democrats to act upon their present terrorist phrases . . . [and] prevent the direct revolutionary excitement from being suppressed. . . . Far from opposing so-called excesses—instances of popular revenge against hated individual or public buildings that are associated with hateful recollections—such instances must not only be tolerated but the leadership of them taken in hand." As part of this, the workers must themselves be armed and organized as a proletarian guard under the discipline of the central revolutionary councils. These, in turn, are to be centralized "under a leadership established in the chief seat of the movement."

Indeed, workers must oppose petty-bourgeois efforts to decentralize the nation or to form a federated republic. They must, rather, strive for "a single and indivisible German republic, but also within the republic, for the most determined centralization of power in the hands of the state authority. . . ." Again, "the confiscated feudal property [must] remain state property and be converted into workers colonies. . . ." Above all, it must not "be tolerated that a form of property, namely communal property . . . should be perpetuated by a so-called free communal constitution . . . in Germany it is the task of the really revolutionary party to carry through the strictest centralization." The revolution there will thus require a lengthy development whose first act will coincide with the workers' victory in France. "Their battle cry must be: The Revolution of Permanence."

Hal Draper stresses that this circular letter must be regarded as expressing Marx's own authentic views, rather than having been foisted upon him by the exigencies of revolutionary politics and by the Willich-Schapper faction. This is more ambiguous than Draper imagines, for even views that one had normally repressed are also authentically "one's own." Nicolaievsky and Maenchen-Helfen understandably suggest that the March letter's policies diverged from Marx's long-range position. Indeed, they call them an "error" into which Marx presumably fell partly because of the revolution's collapse, partly because of the urgent need to reunite the left in the face of its defeat, and in the expectation that another revolutionary surge was imminent. Nicolaievsky and Maenchen-

Helfen believe that the letter's stress on the revolutionary importance of "resolute, well-organised men" was more nearly Blanquist than Marxist in inspiration. A later, retrospective view might also call it Bakuninist, or even Gottschalkean. Noyes thus writes that Revolution in Permanence had been a slogan "urged upon Marx in the course of 1848-1849 by Gottschalk and others in Cologne and since then by some followers of Blanqui in Paris."[99] Draper, however, denies fervently that the letter entailed even a "Blanquist aberration" on Marx's part, asserting that it is to be understood simply as the maturation of his policy of permanent revolution which, like his earlier policies, allowed for a temporary alliance with bourgeois democrats. The only reason, suggests Draper, that this letter is mistaken as Blanquist is because of its "uncompromising revolutionary spirit."[100]

Yet it is just that which is consistent with Nicolaievsky and Maenchen-Helfen's interpretation of the March letter, for this letter differs from Marx's cautious coalition policies in Cologne when, as Draper admits, Marx might have at *first* preferred to go slow on questions of class antagonism. It is precisely the March letter's "uncompromising revolutionary spirit," then, that signals a shift from the Cologne days. The March letter did represent Marx's views in March, but his views had by then changed, as his acceptance of the letter's critique of the League's earlier dissolution clearly implies. Following distribution of the March letter, the Universal Society of Revolutionary Communists was established which combined Blanquist elements (which Draper admits[101]) with those of the League and left Chartists. This new group was a central committee composed only of organization leaders, rather than of their members. It militantly called on workers to "make an end of the privileged classes, to submit these classes to the dictatorship of the proletariat by maintaining a permanent revolution until the realisation of Communism, which shall be the last form of constitution of the human family."[102] This goal was to be achieved by an internationalism, "between all sections of the revolutionary communist party by breaking down the barriers of nationality. . . ." As the central office letter in March had held, "it is our interest and our task to make the revolution permanent . . . not only in one country but in all the dominant countries of the world. . . ." The revolutionary spirit of working-class autonomy and the idea of "permanent revolution" are evident in both the March letter and in the Universal Society's program.

The doctrine of permanent revolution, then, was a brilliant device for bridging the left artisan militants and the more cautious socialist intellectuals who, envisaging a long and protracted struggle, wanted to avoid what they regarded as dangerous adventures. For on the one side, it reassured the former that socialism and communism had not been forgotten and it reaffirmed a commitment to these in rousing rhetoric; while, on the other, it satisfied Marxists because it still inserted the idea of a series of stages through which the revolution must first go before arriving at the "last form of constitution . . . ," including a prior stage during which the bourgeois-democrats would be dominant. Each could thus read it as a concession to his own central concerns, and, for a while, each did.

In other words, the doctrine of permanent revolution in the March letter does not (as Draper suggests) clearly evidence the *continuity* of the uniquely Marxist views. Rather, it points precisely to the specific strategic mechanism that enabled Marx's evolutionary emphasis (on the need for prior fulfillment of certain preliminary stages as the requisite of socialism) to be accommodated with the most militant proponents of revolution-now. Yet the bourgeois stage of revolution insisted on was portrayed only as a way-station on the road to the final conflict that was to culminate in the dictatorship of the proletariat. The theory of permanent revolution, then, was a shrewd piece of left-wing statesmanship, bridging the militant and revolutionary wings, the artisans-workers and the intellectuals, by providing a formulation in which each could find reassurance.

In my own view, the March letter did indeed express Marx's ideas, but more incipiently and less overtly, and did not express them in their typical manner. As early as *The German Ideology,* Marx and Engels had insisted that alienation "can, of course, only be abolished given two practical premises . . . it must necessarily have rendered the great mass of humanity 'propertyless' and produced, at the same time, the contradiction of an existing world of wealth and culture, both of which conditions presuppose a great increase in productive power, a high degree of its development." They then go on to add that "this development of productive forces . . . is absolutely necessary as a practical premise: first, for the reason that without it, only want is made general and with want the struggle for necessities and all the old filthy business would necessarily be reproduced."[103] What is unmistakably clear, here, is that as Marx and Engels begin increasingly to operate within the framework of classical political economy, they also take over its premises, namely, that the key fact of life is *scarcity*. If this is so, then there is no point in attempting to build an emancipatory socialist society without having first conquered scarcity, but this, in turn, was largely the historical mission of the bourgeoisie who constantly revolutionized productivity.

As the *Communist Manifesto* remarks, "the bourgeoisie cannot exist without constantly revolutionizing the instruments of production. . . . Constant revolutionizing of production . . . distinguishes the bourgeois epoch from all earlier ones."[104] The bourgeois mode of production then, when brought to its maturity, greatly fostered productivity and laid the groundwork for vanquishing scarcity; but the egoistic relations of production within which it operates produce for profit, not for use or for the satisfaction of need. Hence the revolution requires the maturation of productivity brought by the bourgeoisie and thus, for a while, requires the bourgeoisie. This is precisely the point of the remark in the *Communist Manifesto*, that "The distinguishing feature of Communism is not the abolition of property generally, but the abolition of bourgeois property."[105] In short, no bourgeoisie, no revolutionizing of productivity; hence, no bourgeoisie, no socialist revolution. Thus the *Manifesto* characterizes as "utopian," socialists who wrote before the development of the "material conditions for the emancipation of socialism." In Marx and Engels's paradigm, then, it is a central idea that there were economic conditions, especially those making scarcity unnecessary or alleviating it substantially, for socialist revolution. It is a keystone of Marx's scientific socialism that revolution, like all natural phenomena, has certain necessary conditions, which it is the task of science to learn and master.

Yet in the March circular of the Communist League, no mention whatsoever is made of this, in part because the letter is referring to the German revolution in particular, not to revolutions in general. The letter's formulation muted the question of what the general conditions of socialist revolution were, and, indeed, focused directly not on the economic but on the *political* conditions requisite for the revolution— i.e., the maintenance of an independent organization and policy for the workers' party. This political condition indeed comes down to a voluntaristic emphasis on "will"—for which Marx would later chastise Bakunin, claiming he ignored the economic conditions and acted as if only "will" was necessary for socialist revolution. For this *political* condition—the independence of the workers' party—was presumably within their control, and depended only on their insight and determination. The political requisites of the revolution then, need not be awaited, but were already available. Bringing them into existence was indeed a matter of "will."

But while the March letter thus allows the revolution to *start,* the letter also insists that the workers must first support the bourgeoisie. Without a doubt, it says, the hegemony of the bourgeoisie must come first. This would be the start of a permanent revolution, during which the workers' party would build contradictions into the bourgeois democracy thus preventing its consolidation, and would in time come into power in their own right.

The idea of permanent revolution, then, constituted an adaptive response to the cross-pressures situation in which Marx found himself. It allowed him to stress, on the one side, the importance of the prior hegemony of the bourgeoisie as necessary for the socialist revolution, yet without asserting this in a generalized manner as the universal requisite of revolution—Marx's usual formulation. Permanent revolution, on the other side, allowed Marx to define the bourgeois revolution as something which had to be supported, yet defined this support as only expedient, tactical, and temporary—hence more tolerable—and, better than that, as a phase allowing apt occasions when the pressure of the workers' party could build into bourgeois democracy the contradictions that would undo it. Note, however, that the contradictions referred to here are not the economic contradictions mentioned in *Capital,* or even in the *Communist Manifesto,* but refer rather to *politically* inserted contradictions. These depend not on the blind laws of the economy but on the valid strategic insight of the party. Permanent revolution, then, was a doctrine which could placate militant artisans bent on immediate revolution, thus maintaining Marx's identity as a revolutionary, while at the same time, embodying—but only implicitly, and hence non-provocatively—the unique conception of Marx's scientific socialism, namely, that socialism required an overcoming of scarcity that necessitated a prior period of bourgeois development and indeed of hegemony.

It is perhaps also evident from this how the theory of permanent revolution could deteriorate into the straightforward, unembarrassed evolutionism and revisionism, and more broadly, into the Second International's characteristic lip service to the revolution as it was practically combined with accommodation to parliamentary reform.

On September 15, 1850, Marx found himself arrayed against Willich and Schapper, opposing their position as a departure from the March letter. The abiding "error" of Marx's views, to which Weitling, Gottschalk, Schapper, and Willich had all objected, remained implicit in the March letter, being embedded precisely in the stage-like development required by the theory of permanent revolution. They did not object to its prospect of international revolution, namely, that "the development of the revolution in any one country was closely bound up with its development in all countries"; their objection, rather, was to the evolutionary part, namely, "that the revolution had quite definite phases to go through and that the various classes must necessarily come into power in a definite order conditioned by economic facts."[106]

As Engels was to write (in 1852) about the German revolution:

[Our] party never imagined itself capable of producing, at any time and at its pleasure, that revolution which was to carry its ideas into practice. . . . The practical revolutionary experience of 1848-49 confirmed the reasonings of theory, which led to the conclusion that *the democracy of the petty traders must first have its turn, before the Communist working class* could hope to permanently establish itself in power and destroy the system of wage-slavery which keeps it under the yoke of the bourgeoisie.[107]

Weitling, Schapper, Willich, Gottschalk, and, later, Bakunin, all interpreted this position as essentially calling on the working class to sacrifice itself on behalf of bourgeois interest and as defusing worker militancy. One can only imagine what they would have said had they known that Marx's rich uncle, the Dutch banker Lion Philips, communicated just such a cautious policy to Marx, writing him shortly after the founding of the First International, ". . . I believe that *lasting* improvements can now be achieved in a regular way, without violent convulsions . . . *slowly,* but I believe surely, the good aim will be achieved." History, Philips reminded Marx, "always marches without haste. . . ."[108]

In April of 1850, a month after the March circular letter, an article by Marx reverted to his classic position on the economic requisites of socialist revolution and condemned those revolutionary conspirators who sought revolution "without the conditions for revolution. For them [the conspirators] the only condition required for revolution is a sufficient organization of their own conspiracy. They are the alchemists of the revolutions."[109] Whereas Marx, of course, wanted to be its scientist. Three months later, in a letter of July 1850, to P. G. Roser, Marx insisted that "Communism could not be attained at all except by the way of education and gradual development."[110] Marx remembered Weitling's guerrilla army of criminals, and he may have fused this memory with a fear that Captain Willich harbored Bonapartist fantasies of exporting the revolution at the point of arms.

In the September 1850 meeting of the League's central office in London, the group was split four to three, Marx's adherents being the "majority," while Schapper supported Willich in the "minority." Marx complained of the minority:

Instead of the actual conditions, pure will becomes the drive-wheel of the revolution for them. Whereas we tell the workers "You have fifteen, twenty, fifty years of civil wars and peoples' struggles to go through, not only to change the conditions but in order to change yourselves and to make yourselves fit for political rule." You say on the contrary: "We must come to power right away, or else we might go to sleep."[111]

At the September meeting of the League's central office, Schapper rejected Marx's prospect of a period of bourgeois hegemony, stating that he did "not hold the opinion that the bourgeois will come to power in Germany. . . ." "The question at issue," he held, "was whether at the outset we chop off heads or get our own heads chopped off. In France the workers will have their time and thereupon so will *we* in Germany." After the French revolution, says Schapper, "comes our turn, then we take such measures as ensure power for the proletariat . . . I am fanatical about this view."[112] Schapper is thus relying upon the internationalist part of the theory of Permanent Revolution, which sees one country's revolution as environed by those of others, hence as susceptible to aid or to counter-revolutionary pressure. It is this international side of the theory of permanent revolution that Schapper then accented to justify a more militant policy, while Marx accented the internal development of "the actual conditions," particularly of productivity through the rise of the bourgeoisie, to justify a more prudent policy. Each, then, felt his policies continuous with the March letter, and each could do so precisely because of the ambiguous theory of permanent revolution it contained.

To reiterate: the theory of permanent revolution had both a domestic, internal dimension and an international, external dimension. Here, however, I wish to stress the international dimension of permanent revolution. In a *Neue Rheinische Zeitung* article early in 1849, Marx formulated this in a manner clearly foreshadowing Immanuel Wallerstein's thesis about the world system: "The relations of industry and commerce inside every country are ruled by their intercourse with other countries, and are conditioned by their relation on the world market."[113] Again, in his *Class Struggles in France,* Marx argued that French workers mistakenly "thought they would be able to consummate a proletarian revolution within the national walls of France. . . . But the French relations of production are conditioned by the foreign trade of France, her position on the world market and the laws thereof; how was France to break them without a European revolutionary war, which would strike back at the despot of the world market, England?"[114] And in the same study, Marx also asserts that the proletarian revolution "is not accomplished anywhere within the national walls; the class war within French society turns into a world war, in which the nations confront one another."[115]

Other conceptions of permanent revolution current at that time also stressed its international dimension, no less than its domestic and national. Thus Moses Hess's *Red Catechism for the German People,* written in 1849 and published anonymously in 1859, "gives strong emphasis to the international aspect of permanent revolution . . . if the workers win in one country they must immediately go to the aid of their comrades in other countries, since they cannot rule in a single country in the long run: so says the Catechism."[116]

Permanent revolution then faced in two directions, internationally no less than domestically. It was thus profoundly dissonant with the idea of "socialism in one country" that Stalin would later borrow from Bukharin, and explains why Trotsky, proponent of permanent revolution, became Stalin's arch enemy. Domestically, permanent revolution meant that workers must pursue an independent political policy, at first in alliance with the bourgeoisie, but then carry forward their own revolution until communism was fully achieved. Internationally, it meant that a victory of workers in one nation was to be used as a grounding for workers' victories in other countries, whom they were obliged to help against their domestic class enemies. In one dimension, permanent revolution in Marx's view meant the dependence of revolution on industrial maturation through development of the bourgeoisie within a country; it meant that politics was grounded in economics. In a second dimension, however, permanent revolution also implied that, in some countries, revolution might be dependent on the politico-military balance of forces among countries. It did *not*, in short, necessarily depend on the maturation of industrialism *within* a country but on the balance of international politics.

These two dimensions of permanent revolution inserted substantial ambiguities allowing different resolutions: Should the prime criterion of revolutionary readiness be the domestic or the international condition? Or both? If industrial underdevelopment in a country impeded revolution there, could this be counterbalanced (and hence ignored) if this country's workers received help from successful revolutions in other countries? Which was decisive, internal economics or the structure of the international polity? Could a propitious international politics compensate for a backward domestic economy in a country's development toward socialism?

Indeed, even the implications of the *international* dimension of permanent revolution, taken alone, were not without ambiguities: Did the need to protect a workers' state justify its exporting revolution to another country whose domestic economy had not yet matured industrially? Did the revolutionary duty of international solidarity justify endangering a revolution already successful in one country to help a prospective revolution elsewhere? The international dimension of permanent revolution might, on one side, stress the power and duty of successful revolutionaries to help unsuccessful ones elsewhere; or it might, on the other side, be interpreted as implying that even if a revolution occurred in one country, that "socialism in one country" was not feasible. For it was vulnerable to pressures from others that would deform it, and all the more

so if the country in which the revolution had first occurred was not industrially advanced. Hal Draper characterizes Schapper's view as one
that "demands an immediate proletarian revolution with no first stage,"
a view convergent with Mao's when he insisted that "To rebel is always
right." Yet Schapper's view here is also very similar to the one that Marx
would later come (or revert) to concerning the Russian revolution, when
during the 1870s, he allowed that Russia need not inevitably pass
through capitalism (the first stage) to reach a later collectivist society.
But in September of 1850 that was not Marx's view. He then held that
the first stage, passing through capitalism, was necessary, for "if the proletariat came to power [then] it could not take directly proletarian measures but petty-bourgeois ones. Our party can become the government
only when conditions allow it to put *its own* outlook into effect."[117]

I have indicated above that Marx liked to refer to Willich's group as
the "minority," yet Willich controlled the majority in the London branch
of the League as well as in the London Workers Educational Union:

> . . . Willich was closer to [the workers] as a man. While Marx, "scholar"
> and "theorist," lived his own life and only came to the Union to lecture.
> Willich, who had no family, shared in the joys and sorrows of the exiled
> [German] proletarians. He had created [a] cooperative society and lived
> with the workers, ate with them and addressed them all in the familiar
> second person singular; Marx was respected but Willich was popular.[118]

It was in part because of Willich's political strength that Marx then
sought to transfer the Communist League's headquarters to Germany,
and to give the Cologne branch the central office's authority. (Years
later, Marx would do much the same, sending the First International off
to exile in New York City, partly to insulate it from Bakunin.) Having
a "majority" in the League's central office in London, Marx overrode
Willich's objection to the transfer. The split within the League then
broke into the open. Marx gradually stopped attending meetings of the
League in London, isolating himself from exile politics, to intensify and
pursue his own theoretical studies. After the Communist trials at Cologne
in 1851, the League was finally and formally ended at Marx's proposal,
and he then withdrew into the cavernous work of *Capital*. In a way he
now followed Schapper's advice during the September debate, when the
latter had said, "Let us then have two Leagues, one for those who fight
with the pen, another for those who act in another fashion."

In some part, Marx's withdrawal from active exile politics was occasioned by the implications of his own (theoretical and empirical) studies; correspondingly, his return to his studies and their conclusions was
influenced by the failure of his politics. Nicolaievsky and Maenchen-

Helfen as well as Draper concur, in Draper's words, that "around July 1850 his economic studies—as well as the course of events—persuaded him that the return of industrial prosperity meant an end to the ongoing continental crisis, and that the movement now had to reorient."[119]

In his own words, Marx concluded that "with this general prosperity . . . there can be no talk of a real revolution. *A new revolution is possible only in consequence of a new crisis. It is, however, just as certain as this crisis.*"[120] The central point, then, of *Capital* would be to show that the internal contradictions of capitalism would produce the crisis *inevitably*, thereby bolstering the flagging hopes of revolutionaries who had just been defeated,[121] while at the same time justifying Marx's own withdrawal from active revolutionary politics at that painful time. The rhetorical function of the structural *determinism* of *Capital*, then, is to *guarantee* a redeeming crisis.

In effect, however, this meant that only one side of the theory of permanent revolution, that concerned with the *domestic* economy, would now be given systematic development in Marx's mature work, while the *international* conditions also held requisite for proletarian revolution, and no less entailed by the theory of permanent revolution, would now drift to the periphery of Marxist attention. In effect, Marx's program for the analysis of the structural requisites of permanent revolution was never to be more than half completed.

Preliminary Summary

Following the defeat of the 1848 revolution, emerging Marxism was once again subjected to, and shaped by, great internal stresses within the workers' movement which exposed the old fault lines, setting artisans against intellectuals, and intellectuals against one another. The artisan-workers wanted to sustain practical revolutionary activity, but Marx maintained that the time had come to withdraw from it and to deepen theory. Against the activist artisans, Marx repeatedly reiterated the theoretical position he had elaborated earlier, in his 1843 *Critique of Hegel's Philosophy of Right*, his 1844 *Economic and Philosophical Manuscripts*, and the 1845 *Holy Family*. His materialism and "economism," however, came to fullest flower in *The German Ideology* with Engels, which they had started in 1845 but did not finish until summer 1846 after the run-in with Weitling.

Marx's developing theory, sharpened in polemic against the militant artisans' demand for revolution-now, insisted that it was not "will" but objective conditions, and especially economic conditions, on which Communism's future depended. This in turn meant, he indicated, that what was required was a *scientific knowledge* of socioeconomic development—*his* "scientific" Marxism rather than *their* fraudulent "alchemy"—which could reliably gauge when the time was right.

For militant artisans convinced that the time was ripe for revolution-now, what was needed was neither further knowledge or theory, nor the alien intellectuals or theorists who formulated them: What was needed instead was determined, tightly organized action. Those around Marx, however, stressed that successful revolution was contingent on appropriate socioeconomic conditions; revolutionary action depended on a "crisis" that would come "inevitably." They also emphasized that this inevitability would be demonstrated in theory and by theorists. Revolution, in short, now required the sifting and reading of history's intestines, which was the special office of radicalized intellectuals and theorists.

A structuralist account in which socialism was said to depend on, and not only depend on but be guaranteed by, objective socioeconomic conditions, is thus tightly interwoven with a "scientific" conception of socialism. It implied that intellectuals and theorists should hold a special place in the workers' movement, one that was privileged both epistemologically and organizationally. Indeed, it was their epistemologically privileged place that legitimated their organizational authority. If, as Marx had hurled against Weitling, "Ignorance never helped anyone," knowledge did not help everyone *equally;* it gave a special edge to those who claimed to possess it.

In its beginnings, then, Marxism was refracted toward a "scientific" Marxism by the rivalry between artisans and intellectuals. Scientific Marxism was an ideology that intellectuals could and did use against their artisan competitors; it served to justify intellectuals' presence in a workers' movement in which they were all too obviously aliens. Marxism as a structuralist anti-voluntarism, focusing on the "natural" emergence of objective socioeconomic conditions and especially the mode of production, was grounded in this very special set of social relationships, for which it had a kind of elective affinity. Its specific ontology, in which politics is dependent on economics, is thus interdependent with a special epistemology. In the latter, paradoxically, "outsiders" or middle-class intellectuals, are said to know more about the conditions requisite for the workers' movement than "insiders," i.e., ordinary workers themselves.

Precisely because they are outsiders, intellectuals are disposed to deny that workers have a privileged understanding even of their own lives and conditions. For, first (it is said), the latter may see and react only to what is most immediately visible in their everyday lives and, second, they may interpret this in terms of unassimilated ideologies, which may overemphasize economic and trade union issues like the wage question, but ignore the larger political circumference. In this epistemology, it is not simply a fact of nature or society that ordinary workers may be subject to a "false consciousness," and thus are under the hegemony of other social classes. The Marxist critique of workers' false consciousness is also a fact of *politics*, reflecting the competition between artisans and intellectuals in the "workers'" movement, and legitimating the latter's claim to special authority in it.

Intellectuals' claim to a privileged epistemological position was implicit in Marx's admission that "I have always been opposed to the ephemeral opinions of the proletariat." That this epistemology serves to legitimate the authority of outsiders within the workers' movement is suggested in Marx's next sentence, which claimed that "our party can achieve power only when circumstances allow it to put into effect its own ideas," as distinct, one supposes, from ordinary workers' "ephemeral opinions."

The point here, then, deals entirely with the *social function, not the intellectual validity,* of the epistemological doctrine claiming that insiders (or outsiders) are intellectually privileged. The essential point is that the insider-privileged doctrine is part of an exclusionary effort by which socially subordinated groups (whether artisans, blacks, or women), arguing that "it takes one to know one," claim cognitive advantages for themselves, while denying them to other outsider groups. To insist that this doctrine has social functions that serve intellectuals is not, however, to imply that Marx and other intellectuals involved in the workers' movement fostered that doctrine for selfish reasons alone. Doubtless, they did so partly because they simply thought it intellectually correct (just as those opposing it did so partly because they, to the contrary, believed it wrong). The question at issue between them was not simply who can *know* the social world, but also who gets access to its privileges. The doctrine of insider-privileged knowledge was used by artisans against the intellectuals such as Marx precisely as one way of defining them as outsiders and, therefore, as ineligible for the perquisites the group could confer—editorships, leadership offices, incomes, and other "ideal" perquisites such as solidarity.

In one part, Marx agreed that workers were indeed epistemologically privileged, in respect to knowledge of the social world. Or at least he held that, at *some* point in capitalism's breakdown, workers would become better able than others to understand the true nature of capitalism as a whole.

Marx's position in the workers' movement, particularly after the revolutionary years in Cologne ended, was basically that of a *consultant* to various working-class parties and groups. He was never to become the official, full-time leader of a workers' party or a trade union. To be a "consultant" implies that he could persuade and argue for a position, but lacked organizationally endowed imperative authority that could order it. In short, Marx's position in the workers' movements after Cologne rested on his role as a man of knowledge, a thinker and theorist, self-imputedly in possession of something like a social "science."

Marx is drawn to this public self-definition as scientist, even if he did not surrender to it:[122] partly because he really had no other way to ground his authority in the workers' movement, for a "consultant's" claim rests on what he knows; partly because he had earlier concluded that philosophy and philosophers needed to be transcended ("abolished"), yet he knew he was more than a journalist; and partly also because he loved scholarship passionately, and often experienced political action as an enervating diversion from intellectual work. For him, theory was in part a refuge from politics and political failure. He was much happier to get out of exile politics and back into the library than many other eminent exiles after the failure of the 1848 revolution. Later, as we will see, and even though he was a very effective organizer, he also found that maintaining the First International was a grind that kept him from his studies. His scholarly works were his abiding, perhaps truest love. In the end, he sacrificed himself, his wife and children, everything, for his work on *Capital*. It was this he felt to be his calling and historical mission.

We began with a Marx who saw himself as a kind of vessel furthering—in a way altruistically—the interests of a class other than his own. We then argued that this was in part the "appearance" of things, and that the "reality" underneath this was another Marx, egotistically involved in struggles for power against his competitors—artisans and other intellectuals—in the workers' movement. Yet there is no reason to believe that this is the ultimate "essence" and final truth of this matter, if indeed there is any such.

In the next section, we shall see that Marx's "Moriarity," his arch-foe, Bakunin, denounced Marxism as the ideology of a "New Class" of intellectuals, which is really much the same point to which our own analysis seems to have led. Yet we had best not anticipate. For one thing, if Marx sought to enhance *his* political power—and only the worst ideologue would deny it—we still need to ask *why* he did this, what his *intention* was, while also distinguishing that from the *consequences* which flowed from his political victories. After all, to say that Marx was the ideologist of a rising new class of intellectuals does not say enough unless we know what "intellectuals" want or stand for. And Bakunin, as we shall see, unfortunately thought the answer to that plain enough never to have raised the question at all. In short, there are still ironies to be sifted.

6

Marx's Final Battle:
Bakunin and the First International

Marx's encounter with militant artisans and competing intellectuals—his cycle of feuds with Weitling, Gottschalk, and Willich—was the prelude to the culminating conflict of Marx's political life, his prolonged and bitter duel with Mikhail Bakunin. This climactic conflict was largely fought within the organizational framework of the International Workingmen's Association (I.W.A.), later known as the First International. In short, part of what was at stake was organizational power. The struggle was played out during the organization's lifespan which had begun in London in 1864 and ended, for all practical purposes, at the I.W.A.'s 1872 congress in Den Haag. At this legendary convention Marx succeeded in having his carefully mobilized delegates expel Bakunin and then, to doublelock the organization against the latter's growing influence, packed it off into exile in the United States.

This last protracted combat with Bakunin helps us better to understand the earlier ones and to recognize—as Nicolaievsky and Maenchen-Helfen did so brilliantly long ago—that these were all part of a single series, a kind of recurrent bad dream in which Marx found himself inextricably enmeshed. This sequence of conflicts seen in its entirety specifies the micro-matrix from which Marxism emerged and clarifies how Marx's theory acquired certain of its defining accents and rigidities and developed its character. This final battle provides a vivid magnification of many of the features of the previous encounters whose characteristics were at first difficult to see because they were sometimes fleeting and miniaturized. This recurrent (yet evolving) conflict not only casts light on originary Marxism but on later developments in Marxism. Some subsequent episodes may be seen to have been anticipated in embryo by the earlier conflicts. If these early political battles ended in 1872 with Bakunin's expulsion from the I.W.A., the war of which they were a part continued and, indeed, continues still. Lenin's later formulation of the theory of the "vanguard" is continuous with that early history—i.e., it is an extension of Marx's earlier ambivalence toward intellectuals; and it is not without value to regard Mao's antecedents as reaching back through Bakunin to Weitling.

I shall begin with the briefest sketch of the I.W.A. as the organizational setting for the conflict between Marx and Bakunin, following which I examine Bakunin's doctrines and how they related to Marx's, and what they indicate about the social matrix that helped shape Marxism.

From about 1850 to 1864, that is, from the demise of the Communist League, Marx had effectively withdrawn from mundane political responsibilities and especially from organizational involvements. For fourteen years he had largely shut himself into his labors in political economy and his work on *Capital*.[1] His recall to active political service was unexpected, coming about when he was visited by Victor LeLubez, a young French exile, who invited him to participate in a forthcoming meeting of a group that would become the International Workingmen's Association. The preliminary organizing work had been completed well before Marx had been approached and Marx was invited as a representative of the German workers. Marx promptly agreed but then cautiously noted that perhaps a real German worker ought to be added, and asked that his friend, the tailor Johann Eccarius, also be included.

In short order, Marx became the chief theorist, and grey eminence of the new I.W.A. who, while writing its decisive documents and sitting continuously on its General Council, declined to accept the offer of the chairmanship in 1866, and, in fact, rarely attended its congresses. "He spoke at practically no public meetings, he wrote no signed articles, and sufficed himself with the immediate tasks before him, that of 'influencing the workers movement behind the scenes.' "[2]

The new involvement was such a marked shift from Marx's recent practice of insistent unaffiliation that he felt called upon to explain it to Engels. In a letter of November 4, 1864, he wrote that "the reason why I decided to depart from the otherwise inflexible rule to decline such invitations" essentially boiled down to the fact that the new organization had a foothold in the trade union movement and that real "forces" had been mobilized in the new organization. In short, it was the promise of power that tempted Marx from his library studies. By September 11, 1867, Marx wrote Engels that "in the next revolution, which is perhaps nearer than it appears, *we* (that is, you and I) will have this power engine *in our* hands. . . . We can be very well content."[3] Marx had at last made his rendezvous with the "working class," or what he was pleased enough to consider such.

In fact, however, as Saul Padover indicates, the English majority on the General Council represented the skilled trades—"bakers, printers and shoemakers."[4] Subsequently affiliated unions also included masons, pattern drawers, organ builders, cabinetmakers, coach trimmers, bookbinders, plasterers, cigar makers, and trunk makers. In short, while the I.W.A. spoke to and on behalf of the working class and proletariat, it was, once again, another organization largely created by artisans. Among the active members of the I.W.A.'s General Council were Hermann Jung, a Swiss-German watchmaker, George Odger, a shoemaker, Johann Eccarius and Friedrich Lessner, both tailors, Karl Pfaender, an artist, Eugene Dupont, a maker of musical instruments, and a tavernkeeper, Heinrich Balleter. "The French labour leaders who were to be important figures in the International," writes Paul Thomas, ". . . Tolain, Limousin, Fribourg, Varlin and Dupont were, respectively, a carver, a laceworks machinist, an engraver, a bookbinder, and a maker of musical instruments. . . ."[5] Thomas endorses a conception of the matter which holds that the I.W.A.'s trade union following came from "backward" industries, essentially defining "backward" as a dissociation from the modern factory technology, in short, defining it "economistically." A more relevant and accurate perception of the matter is that these artisans were at that historical period from the most *politically advanced* sector of the working class. They along with the peasantry, as Barrington Moore recently reminded us, were in fact the "chief basis of radicalism"[6] in modernizing countries.

And Marx once again encountered the artisans' resistance to himself and other intellectuals. Thus in 1866, at the first congress of the I.W.A. in Geneva, the engraver and French communist Henri Tolain demanded that only manual workers be seated as delegates, arguing that ". . . we have to consider as opponents all members of the privileged classes, privileged whether by virtue of capital or a diploma . . . it is therefore necessary that its delegates belong neither to the liberal professions nor to the caste of capitalists."[7] It was precisely because Marx had expected such exclusionary sentiments that he had kept a low profile, had asked that a "real" worker, Eccarius, be invited to the I.W.A.'s first public meeting, and indeed had refused to serve as delegate to this first congress, although letting it be known that he opposed Tolain's motion. Despite

Marx's opposition, Tolain's motion was defeated by a margin of only five votes—25 to 20—thus a shift of three votes to Tolain would have carried his exclusionary resolution. Radical artisans' exclusionary impulse against intellectuals, then, did not wither away with the death of the Communist League but manifested itself again in the I.W.A.

The International Workingmen's Association was also the setting in which Marx and Engels made plain that they were indeed fighting a struggle "on two fronts"; once more, this time in the I.W.A., they became enmeshed in a contest with competing intellectuals, against whom they developed their own exclusionary tactics, in the name of the "self-emancipation of the proletariat." The I.W.A.'s component sections were thus to consist primarily of workers, while "sections exclusively or principally composed of members not belonging to the working class" were to be denied admittance. Hence sections consisting primarily of students were excluded from membership in the I.W.A., even though there was a rule declaring that "everybody who acknowledges and defends the principles of the I.W.A. is eligible to become a member. . . ."[8] Marx's struggle to exclude competing intellectuals was also evidenced, as mentioned earlier, in his letter to Engels of December 10, 1864, where Marx explains how, in order to exclude Louis Blanc from the International Workingmen's Association, he had eliminated the category of "honorary member" of the I.W.A.[9]

The Conflict between Marx and Bakunin

Although much is usually made of Bakunin's pro-peasant ideology, not to speak of his customary Russian peasant blouse, in point of fact, Bakunin himself was a revolutionary *intellectual*. What makes him different from Marx's other foes, such as Weitling, Gottschalk, or Willich, is precisely that Bakunin wrote extensively and elaborated his own theoretical critique of the social world and of revolution at great length. As John Clark correctly notes, "Bakunin is indeed a serious political thinker whose works deserve careful consideration today."[10] What makes Marx so implacably opposed to him, however, is not simply that Bakunin was his intellectual competitor for revolutionary leadership in the I.W.A., but that the doctrine Bakunin was developing provided a theoretical grounding for the very *anti*-intellectual exclusionary policies so prevalent among the militant artisans—among *"Messrs, the Knoten."* In short, Marx's fury against Bakunin derived in part from the fact that *both* the political competitors Marx opposed in his battle on "two fronts" were personified in Bakunin.

The International Workingmen's Association had begun as a loose coalition of "working-class" groups each vying with the other for hegemony, and each in the beginning often defended by Marx, however much he contemptuously dismissed them privately in letters to Engels. But later, as Marx was spooked by Bakunin, as each became the other's veritable obsession, Marx reverted to the doctrinaire and authoritarian rigidities he had exhibited in his earlier war against Weitling. ". . . Marx in the course of his dispute with the Bakuninists came perilously close to making the International homogenous and doctrinally monolithic, doing much in this way to ensure that future Internationals would be monolithic where the first were not."[11]

In a confrontation between two such great polemicists, it is too easy to overemphasize their differences and to gloss their similarities and convergences. Paul Thomas is thus quite right in insisting that we note the things on which Marx and Bakunin agreed, even if oversimplifying his account of these: "Both believed in the primacy of the economic 'base' over the political 'superstructure'; both wished to overthrow capitalism and were engaged upon working as active revolutionists to this end; both were socialists and collectivists, opposed to bourgeois individualism; both were bitterly at odds with religion; and both had a veneration for natural science."[12] One could add, both began as Hegelians.

One's evenhandedness thus equably displayed, there is still the task of accounting for the conflict. In what follows, I shall focus on their doctrinal differences and, therefore, run the risk of being misunderstood. For I do not at all mean that this (or any) conflict is solely attributable to prior differences of theory and ideology. My own view is considerably more complex: that the conflict was furthered partly by their doctrinal differences but, in their turn, these are also partly due to their conflict. As emphasized in the previous discussion, each party is certainly struggling for power for himself and his group. Yet this struggle is not generated only by the comforts, privileges or powers to be achieved by victory but is, in part, pursued also because each wants to be in a position to implement his *ideas*. Power is sought, in part, so that the "right ideas" —commonly of course assumed to be one's own—may acquire the influence they are thought rightly to deserve. The passionate protagonist believes he and his enemy are profoundly different. He sees *himself* as seeking to defend intelligent and decent principles, while regarding his *adversary* either as misguided by erroneous principles or as unscrupulously using principles as a disguise for selfish interests. From my own standpoint, however, it seems more prudent (and more parsimonious) to assume that both protagonists are alike, each pursuing both material and spiritual interests. What they take to be their principles, ideologies, or theories are, in some part, anterior convictions that genuinely generate the contention; but in some part they are also *post bellum* rationalizations of an involvement fueled by other forces.

Apart from resting on a mistaken rationalist view of the relation between human conduct and theory, any account of the conflict between Marx and Bakunin that wishes to reduce it to their doctrinal differences must also miss the distinctive character of their dispute and how it differs from those earlier ones in which Marx was involved. Marx's previous adversaries had been German or French. Clearly the fact that Bakunin was a Russian (and Marx, a German) made a difference. Each was steeped in his own different culture and ethnocentrism, and this remained an abiding source of mutual irritation and suspicion. Marx *thought* of Bakunin as a Russian, and Bakunin *thought* of Marx as a German, and neither thought the other better for it. Bakunin saw Marx and his socialism as a typically Germanic embodiment of *Obrigkeit*, slavish respect for officialdom and authority; ". . . in his eyes, Germany had been the hub and pattern of despotism for centuries. . . . Bakunin liked quoting the saying of Ludwig Börne that 'other people are often slaves, but we Germans always lackeys.' "[13] "If the Prussians win," wrote Marx to Engels at the beginning of the Franco-Prussian war, "the centralisation of the state power will be useful for the centralisation of the working class"[14]—again confirming Bakunin's worst suspicions about Marx's policies concerning both the state and Germany. Marx, in turn, contemptuously denounced Bakunin's followers as *Kosaken* and declared the Russians a backward nation and the keystone of European reaction. The theoretical differences between Marx and Bakunin, then, are in some part grounded in their national differences, Bakunin being convinced of the *power* and revolutionary potential of the peasantry, while Marx tended to view them as a petty bourgeoisie doomed for the historical dustbin and as having no revolutionary promise.

For those capable of reading the signs, it was plain that social revolution would not spell the end of national rivalries. That the conflict between Marx and Bakunin was embedded in virulent national antipathies indicates, in one part, that their duel was not merely grounded in *doctrinal* differences and, in another, how it differed—despite the continuities—from Marx's earlier conflicts with Weitling, Willich, and Gottschalk (or even with Proudhon). There were, of course, other important differences between these earlier conflicts and the later ones. Bakunin, for example, differed importantly from Marx's earlier artisan foes in that he was the leader of a viable and growing movement of international scope. More than that, while Marx's previous artisan adversaries had all been persons of substance, Bakunin overshadowed them as revolutionary, theorist, and person. He was an outsized charismatic figure, the veritable embodiment of the Romantic revolutionary hero, a giant of a man whose passionate, multilingual oratory could raise audiences to their feet in a paroxysm of thunderous enthusiasm.

In short, Marx began to feel that it was not an ordinary foe but a veritable nemesis that was stalking him. To make matters worse, Bakunin's credentials, as theorist and as practical revolutionary, were substantial. When seen from an academic standpoint, however, Bakunin's written work would not look like "real" theory to Marx who—in an egregiously mistaken judgment—denounced him, as he had Weitling, as a theoretical ignoramus. Thus Marx wrote Paul Lafargue on April 19, 1870, referring to Bakunin as an "ass" who could not understand that every class movement is always a political movement. Again, on November 23, 1871, Marx wrote Bolte from London that as "For Mr. Bakunin the theory (the assembled rubbish he has scraped together from Proudhon, St. Simon, etc.) is a secondary affair—merely a means to his self-assertion. If he is a nonentity as a theorist he is in his element as an intriguer."[15]

For his part, however, Bakunin was considerably more meticulous and decent in giving Marx his full due, as well as admitting that he had learned much from him. Indeed, Bakunin wrote Marx, "You see therefore, my dear friend, that I am your disciple, and I am proud of it."[16] In a letter of October 1869 to Herzen, Bakunin lauded Marx's "enormous services to the cause of socialism, which he has served ably, energetically and faithfully throughout the twenty-five years I have known him, and in which he has undoubtedly out stripped us all."[17] Bakunin also modestly acknowledged that "as far as learning is concerned, Marx was, and still is, incomparably more advanced than I. . . . I greatly respected him for his learning and for his passionate devotion to the cause of the proletariat."[18] Bakunin had a sense of justice and a generosity of spirit toward his adversaries; in this, if in nothing else, he easily vanquished his adversary.

Perhaps one other difference between Marx's conflict with Bakunin and his other struggles worth emphasing here is that it was a protracted struggle and in a way an inconclusive one; for almost a decade it reverberated throughout Europe, publicly fought-out in the open, although often within the precincts of the International Workingmens' Association, rather than being the quick thrust and muffled gasp within a controlled committee room that the Weitling affair had been.

The Bakuninist Synthesis

As Paul Thomas relates, both Marx and Bakunin believed in the primacy of the economic "base" (Thomas uses quotes, apparently queasy about imputing such a crude distinction to Marx). We will see, however, that Marx certainly did not think Bakunin did but, rather, accused Bakunin of being a political alchemist who fantasized he could produce the gold of revolution out of any base social condition at all; not realizing that a specific economic development was requisite for socialism. Far from agreeing that Bakunin accepted the primacy of the economic, Marx held that his adversary substituted "will" for a knowledge of economics and a reliance upon natural economic development. Correspondingly, when Bakunin affirmed the power of the "economic" he did not in fact mean quite the same thing that Marx did. Looked at closely, it is often difficult, here as elsewhere, to be sure whether their theoretical differences produced their contention, or their contention shaped and sharpened their differences in theory.

Both wished to overthrow capitalism, says Thomas. Perhaps, though it would be more precise to say Marx wanted to eliminate the bourgeoisie and *proprietary* capitalism. As for Bakunin, he clearly did not limit his target to what Marx called the bourgeoisie but aimed his revolution at the *state,* no less than the proprietary class. Bakunin was quite emphatic in indicating that moneyed proprietors could be eliminated but that remaining differences in education and knowledge would soon produce differences in power and reproduce class privileges. If both were, as Thomas says, socialists and collectivists, they had very different conceptions of how and when the new society could be brought about and how it would be organized once enacted. Marx's position, as Bakunin elaborated at length, entailed an imposed centralization culminating in the state's ownership of the means of production, while his own was insistently a voluntarily federated set of groups. As Eric Hobsbawm correctly states, "Anarchism is a critique of authoritarianism and bureaucracy in states, parties, and movement . . . [and] also suggests a solution in terms of direct democracy and small-governing groups. . . ."[19]

Finally, if both had a "veneration for natural science," Marx saw science as crucial in alleviating scarcity, thereby making socialism possible. Bakunin, however, saw natural science as providing the cultural base for a "new class" of intelligentsia who would corrupt socialism, make themselves a new elite, and impose their rule on the majority. Indeed, Bakunin's conception of the nature and importance of natural science was greatly influenced by that of Auguste Comte, which Marx thought was largely rubbish. Any view of the relation between Bakunin and Marx which sees them simply as converging or diverging theorists misses the fact that Bakunin was a *post*-Marxist; that he himself had admittedly learned a great deal from Marx and had indeed built upon Marxism; or, at any rate, on his critical appropriation of Marxism. In point of fact, Bakuninism was an Hegelian synthesis of Marxism, Positivism, and Anarchism, each of these doctrines becoming substantially altered as it enters into a new conjunction with the others.

Although usually termed an "anarchist," Bakunin often preferred to call himself an anti-authoritarian communist; and, unlike Proudhon who was anti-revolutionary and individualistic, Bakunin was a collectivist and passionately revolutionary. He is thus linked more closely to Weitling (who had taken Bakunin to his first workers' meeting), Gottschalk, and Willich. In a Comtean vein, Bakunin had once remarked of Proudhon that "his great misfortune was that he had never studied the natural sciences or appropriated their method."[20] Bakunin, then, is not to be understood simply by labeling him an "anarchist" and reducing his doctrine to that single system. Bakunin interpreted Comtean positivism as having in part an emancipatory role because it opposed conventional religion and ancient metaphysics. Bakunin thus spoke of positivism as "the heir and at the same time the absolute negation of religion and metaphysics, this philosophy, which had been anticipated and prepared a long time ago by the noblest minds, was first conceived by the great French thinker, August Comte, who boldly and skillfully traced its original outline."[21] In a similar Comtean vein, Bakunin also lauded positivism which, "having dethroned in the minds of men the religious fable and the day-dreams of metaphysics, enables us to catch a glimpse of scientific education in the future. It will have as its basis the study of Nature and sociology as its completion."[22] Bakunin viewed Comte as a materialist precisely because he was opposed to metaphysics, regarding metaphysicians as those who spiritualized matter and derived it from Spirit, adding that "August Comte, on the contrary, materialized the spirit, grounding it solely in matter."[23] Bakunin was also one of the first to understand the convergences between Comte's change-oriented evolutionism and Hegel's philosophy in which the accent is so much on process and change that *Geist* itself is seen as undergoing the most profound transformations over time.

There are at least three other important convergences between Bakunin and Comte. One is that Bakunin, like the Comteans, had a great passion for "organization," and was continually proliferating revolutionary groups. In this he shared the nineteenth-century passion of the Saint-Simonians who dreamed of canals and postal systems which would link people together. "Organization," of the new economy and of the new

Europe, was a central dedication of the Comteans and of the Saint-Simonians, of whom they were essentially a variant. "Organizing" or pulling things together was regarded by Saint-Simon, the father of Positivism, as a central device of social reformation.

Like Comte, Bakunin stressed the importance of voluntary as against imposed social organization. Indeed, Comte's emphasis on science and knowledge was grounded partly in the expectation that science—producing "positive" (in the sense of *certain*) knowledge—would freely win the consent of persons who then, voluntarily sharing the same science-sanctioned beliefs, develop a common culture which would spontaneously yield consensus and social solidarity. Bakunin's libertarian insistence on voluntary rather than imposed organization and change is part of the basis for his violent antipathy to the state and his preference for a decentralized society held together by a federalism based on mutual choice. (The convergence between this Bakunian federalism and the Comtean preference may be seen in the former's convergence with Emile Durkheim's version of corporative syndicalism, which also had a clear Comtean heritage.) Finally, Comte's positivism provided Bakunin with the clear view of the emerging importance of knowledge and science as the new basis for modern social organization and production, as well as of a voluntary social consensus.

Bakunin, however, rejected the Comtean reliance upon men of science, seeing this as a new priestly elitism, and thus he appropriated a positivist appreciation of science only selectively and critically. He then extended this into a critique of Marxism as the ideology, not of the working class, but of the new class of scientific intelligentsia. Marx's focus on the revolution as an expropriation of the bourgeoisie is thus seen as necessary but insufficient, for there remain those forms of domination grounded in educational privilege. Clearly, then, Bakunin's view of Proudhonian anarchism and Marxist socialism was shaped by his critical appropriation of Comtean positivism, while his acceptance of Marxist socialism and revolution gave him critical distance on both Comte and Proudhon. Bakunin had wrought a distinctively new synthesis whose originality still seems not to have won the appreciation it deserves. Indeed, it would be my own net conclusion that, on three of the main questions on which Marx and Bakunin differed—the oppressive role of the state even under socialism, the elitist role of the new class, and whether it was Germany or Russia that would be the most reactionary force later in nineteenth-century Europe—it was Bakunin's analysis that was more nearly correct.[24]

To elaborate on some of the differences between Bakunin and Marx: Essentially, Bakunin may be understood as holding that Marx was a political utopian, not because he did not see the need to mobilize "political" power, but because he did not see the *dangers* of doing so. Bakunin accused Marx of ignoring the capacity of political power to become a distinct and separate basis of class privilege. Bakunin's conception of emancipation, then, was not simply the removal of the proprietary classes or of inequities based on their ownership of the economy, but, *additionally,* Bakunin opposed all forms of domination, including those grounded in the political system and on educational differences.[25] ". . . [H]aving accepted Marx's critique of bourgeois ideology as the ideology legitimating and veiling the exploitative power relations of capitalist society, [Bakunin] is extending this critique to Marxism itself, as the emerging ideology of a developing social class, a new class whose power is rooted in the growth of centralized planning and specialized technique. . . . This technobureaucratic class absorbs and expands the functions of previous bureaucracies, and utilizes statist ideology, which presents political domination as necessary for social order, to legitimate its existence. . . . Bakunin's originality consisted in his recognition, at a very early stage, of both the political bureaucratic aspects and the scientific-technical side of such a structure, and its legitimating underpinnings."[26]

More precisely, Bakunin derived this judgment from Comteanism (as a variant of Saint-Simonianism). What he added was not this *diagnosis* of modernity, but, rather, a *critical and negative evaluation* of the new elitism of science, which Comteans had uncritically celebrated.

Bakunin's views were developed in terms that resonate the Hegelian dialectic and especially the master-bondsman struggle, the Marxist theory of a struggle between the proprietary class and the dispossessed, the Darwinian struggle for existence, and a Nietzschean conception of human nature centered on the will to power:

> All men possess a natural instinct for power [declares Bakunin. This] . . . has its origin in the basic law of life enjoining every individual to wage a ceaseless struggle in order to insure his existence or assert his rights. . . . If there is a devil in history, it is this power principle . . . this cursed element is to be found, as a natural instinct, in every man, the best of them not excepted. Everyone carries within himself the germs of this lust for power. . . .[27]

In Bakunin's view, power contaminates everyone, even (he says with nice reflexivity) "sincere socialists and revolutionaries"; no one can be trusted with it.

The point, then, is that power itself is one of the things people seek; that power is desired in and of itself, although it has the most intimate connection with wealth, providing a basis for its accumulation. Power and wealth thus have a mutual connection, each providing a means and a motive for seeking the other:

> Political power and wealth are inseparable. Those who have power have the means to gain wealth and must center all their efforts upon acquiring it, for without it they will not be able to retain their power. Those who are wealthy must become strong, for, lacking power, they run the risk of being deprived of their wealth.[28]

Bakunin vs. Marx on the State

The fundamental pivot of the Marx-Bakunin conflict, however, was whether the state could be relied upon as the heir of the bourgeoisie to take over the means of production and to administer them in the interest of the majority of the society, as Marx and Engels supposed in speaking of the new socialist state and the "dictatorship of the proletariat," or whether the state would administer its new property primarily to enhance its own interests and that of its bureaucracy, as Bakunin feared. The difficulty with the latter's conception was that, in its fear of politics and the corrupting influence of power, which had led it to policies of decentralized voluntary federation, the revolution might never mobilize power enough to succeed or, if it did, to hold on to what it had won. The difficulty with Marx's conception was, indeed, precisely as Bakunin had foreseen, that with a socialism where the centralized state owned the means of production, a new privileged class of bureaucrats and educated would arise, the state would grow more powerful than ever, and the mass of society would simply have exchanged one master for another. Thus Bakunin could only think that Engels's formulation— "Do away with capital . . . and the state will fall of itself"—was a fairy tale of which German intellectuals were mindlessly fond.

For Engels, "the abolition of capital *is* precisely the social revolution . . . ," whereas for Bakunin it was only one necessary condition which could not even begin so long as the state, on which capital had been based, was not first destroyed. While Marx and Engels also came to seek a destruction of the old state, as necessary for the "dictatorship of the proletariat," they objected to Bakunin's hostility (as Engels put it) "to any state." They wanted a new workers' state with which, first, to terrorize the bourgeoisie and smash the counter-revolution and, second, to administer the capital expropriated from the bourgeoisie. Above all, then, they wanted to invest, even if only temporarily, all power, military *and* economic, in the state, a prospect which horrified Bakunin, who thought that on no account would such a state in fact be the workers' or the people's. "What does it mean," asked Bakunin incredulously in

1873, "for the proletariat to be 'organized as the ruling class,' "[29] in the *Communist Manifesto*'s conception of successful proletarian revolution. "Can it really be," asked Bakunin, "that the entire proletariat will stand at the head of the [new socialist] administration?"[30]

In his marginal notes (1874-75) on Bakunin's *Statehood and Anarchy,* the volume in which the above questions were asked, Marx replied, "Can it really be that in a trade union, for example, the entire union forms its executive committee? Can it be that there will disappear from the factory all division of labor and differences of function stemming from it?"[31]

The Marxist state Bakunin saw waiting in the wings of history was disturbing but correct:

> . . . the so-called people's state will be nothing other than the quite despotic administration of the masses of the people by a new and very non-numerous aristocracy of real and supposed learned ones. The people is not learned, so it will be entirely freed from the cares of governing, wholly incorporated into the governed herd. A fine liberation. The Marxists sense this contradiction and, realizing that the regime of the learned is the hardest, most offensive and most contemptuous in the world, will in fact be a dictatorship in spite of all the democratic forms, console themselves with the thought that the dictatorship will be temporary and short-lived. . . . They [the Marxists] maintain that only a dictatorship, their own naturally, can create the people's will; we answer: no dictatorship can have any other aim than to perpetuate itself and it can only give rise to and instill slavery in the people that tolerate it.[32]

Once again, history seems to have been on Bakunin's, not Marx's, side, the quotation above accurately portraying the states of Eastern Europe today which arose under the provenance of Marxism.

Bakunin, the New Knowledge Class, and the Egalitarianism of Gracchus Babeuf

Bakunin saw the transition from capitalism to Marxist socialism as a circulation of elites in which the old bourgeoisie would be supplanted not by a new democracy but by a new elite of the educated, those with cultural capital, a New Class. The revolutionary dictatorship envisaged by the Marxists, said Bakunin, means ". . . the ruling of the majority by the minority in the name of the alleged superior intelligence of the second."[33] The new society will be "nothing else but despotic rule over the toiling masses by a new, numerically small aristocracy of sham or genuine scientists,"[34] said Bakunin, not that even genuine scientists were acknowledged as having any right to impose their rule. The Marxists will then divide the society into "two armies—industrial and agricultural armies under the direct command of the state engineers who will constitute the new privileged scientific-political class."[35] The kind of state envisaged by Marx, which controls and plans the entire economy, requires vast knowledge.

> It will be the reign of the scientific mind, the most aristocratic, despotic, arrogant and contemptuous of all regimes. There will be a new class, a new hierarchy of real and bogus learning, and the world will be divided into a dominant, science-based minority and a vast ignorant majority. And then let the masses beware.[36]

Since almost any socially reproduced inequality could constitute the basis of a class system in which one class exploits and dominates the other, then for Bakunin knowledge was essentially a form of human capital acquired largely through education. Those who possessed it would constitute a New Class that was to be the elite of the kind of society that Marxist socialism was seen as preparing.

> Is it not evident [asks Bakunin] . . . that out of two persons endowed with a nearly equal natural intelligence, the one who knows more, whose mind has been broadened to a greater extent by science and who, having a better understanding of the interlinking system of natural and social facts . . . will grasp more readily and in a broader light the character of the environment in which he finds himself . . . that in practice he will prove the cleverer and the stronger of the two? It stands to reason that the one who knows more will dominate the one who knows less. If there were to begin with, only this difference in upbringing and education between the two classes, it would in itself produce in a comparatively short time all the other differences and human society . . . would be split up again into a mass of slaves and a small number of masters. . . . So long as there exists two or several degrees of education for various layers of society, there inevitably will be classes in existence. . . .[37]

Bakunin thus saw class privilege deriving as much from cultural capital acquired through education, as from moneyed capital. Indeed, he expressly invokes the metaphor that education is a form of capital: "What is education, if not mental capital, the sum of the mental labor of all past generations?"[38] It was as Henri Tolain had also said expressly, those having the capital of the "diploma," who ought to be excluded as delegates to the congresses of the I.W.A., no less than the moneyed capitalists.

If class constitution is now seen as generated by knowledge differences reproduced by institutionalized education, then clearly it was not to be expected that the mere expropriation of capital would suffice to usher in a classless society. The revolution, then, could not primarily be a revolution against capital, as Engels described the Marxist position, nor could it only be a revolution chiefly against the state, as Engels had described Bakunin's position. A truly equitable classless society required a "cultural revolution," to use a term employed only much later by Mao, yet intimately connected with the logic of Bakunin's position. This meant that the revolution would have to be directed not only against the bourgeoisie or the state, but also and immediately against educational institutions and indeed science itself. It had to be, in the term Bakunin preferred, a "liquidation" of bourgeois culture and civilization itself, not simply a destruction of the state apparatus or the expropriation of the bourgeoisie. A new integral education was necessary for a new moral and rational man. And new controls over the educated and the scientist were also urgently necessary if class privileges were not soon to creep back in. What was needed, in short, was a cultural revolution. (While Bakunin's suspicion of science and scientists was unrelenting, he seems at one point to have assured Wagner that he had no animus against music, or, at least, would not burn *his* music.) While Bakunin rejected the destruction of science[39] as a "high crime against humanity," he insisted that the scientific intelligentsia would, like the priesthood, "form a separate caste" and that "it would be better for those masses to dispense with science altogether than to allow themselves to be governed with men of science."[40]

So while Bakunin denied that he sought to destroy science, he did not boggle at a kind of moratorium or stasis of science, as necessary for his cultural revolution. "It is possible and even probable," he admitted, "that in the more or less prolonged transitional period, which will naturally follow in the wake of the great social crisis, sciences of the highest standing will sink to a level much below that held by each at present. . . ." Nor was this "eclipse of the higher sciences . . . a great misfortune [for] what science loses in sublime loftiness, will it not regain by broadening its base . . . there will be no demi-gods, but neither will there be slaves."[41]

It becomes clear at this juncture that the intellectual roots of Bakunin's cultural revolution in the name of equality have their ultimate grounding in Rousseau and their more immediate roots in the doctrines of his avid student Gracchus Babeuf. Babeuf's associate, Sylvan Marechal, in his *Manifeste des Egaux* declared equality "the first principle of nature," demanded "equality or death," promised that the French revolution was "only the forerunner of another, even greater . . . ," and swore that "For the true and living equality we shall give up everything. Let the arts perish, if need be!"[42]

In his defense against the charge of conspiracy, Babeuf himself argued that the gulf between rich and poor proceeded in part from the difference in value and price assigned to skilled and unskilled labor, maintaining that "the plea of superior ability and industry is an empty rationalization to mask the rationalizations of those who conspire against human equality and happiness. It is ridiculous and unfair to lay claim to a higher wage for the man whose work requires more concentrated thought and more mental effort. . . . The worth of intelligence is only a matter of opinion. . . . Clever people have set a high value upon the creations of their minds; if the toilers had also had a hand in the ordering of things, they would doubtless have insisted that brawn is entitled to equal consideration with brain. . . ."[43] This egalitarian critique of wage differences is all the more notable considering the backgrounds of Babeuf and his comrades. Babeuf himself had, until the revolution, lived in comfortable circumstances, working as a *commissaire à terrier*—a kind of legal clerk, and keeper of the manorial tax rolls—and was only later to become a peasant leader, journalist, and perhaps the first professional revolutionary. Of his fellow defendants at their Vêndome trial in 1797, many were artisans and "the majority . . . gave their professions as laceworker, embroiderer, clockmaker, printer, turner, goldsmith, weaver, shoemaker. . . ."[44]

Babeuf was also quite clear not only in seeing a parallel between private property and culture as forms of theft, as privilege-bestowing advantages that corrupted equality and therefore needed to be abolished, but, interestingly, Babeuf had also clearly verged on the notion of culture as a kind of *capital:* "the creations of the human hand and mind become the property of society, part of the nation's capital. . . . Invention is the fruit of prior investigation and effort. The most recent workers in the field reap their reward as a result of the social labors of their predecessors in a society, that nurtures invention and that aids the scientific worker in his task. It is clear that if knowledge is a social product it must be shared by all alike."[45] It is noteworthy that this formulation is not only grounded in the premise that private property is in general a form of theft that needs to be restrained or abolished, but is insistently extended to culture and knowledge and to those possessing them. In this, Babeuf was (as he fully acknowledged) a devoted student of Rousseau[46] and not a poor student, at that, if one remembers Rousseau's prize-winning essay in the Dijon competition in which he rejected the idea that the arts and sciences necessarily meant a prospering of human manners and welfare. Like Bakunin, Babeuf before him also held that education needed to be revised:

> . . . if knowledge were made available to all alike, it would serve to make men roughly equal in ability and even in talent. Education is a monstrosity when it is unequally shared, since then it becomes the exclusive patrimony of a section of society . . . an ideological armory with the help of which the privileged make war upon the defenseless masses.[47]

Bakunin's theory of the New Class, as a new elite privileged by culture and knowledge who could not be controlled merely by the abolition of private property in money and things, but required a kind of "cultural revolution" against unequal knowledge and the educational institutions producing it, thus has its intellectual roots here in the *Manifesto of the Equals*, in Babeuf, and ultimately in Rousseau.

The requirements of Bakunin's cultural revolution no less than Babeuf's put science itself at risk.

> Under the historic, juridical, religious, and social organization of most civilized countries, the economic emancipation of the workers is a sheer impossibility—and consequently, in order to attain and fully carry out that emancipation, it is necessary to destroy all modern institutions: the State, Church, Courts, University, Army, and Police, all of which are ramparts erected by the privileged classes against the proletariat.[48]

Bakunin's revolution thus involved the most radical rupture with bourgeois culture and was not to be limited to a war against its state and bourgeois domination of the economy. In this respect, there is absolutely no counterpart in Marx and Engels. For however much they detested other intellectuals as "lackeys" and ideologues of the bourgeoisie—especially if they were competitors seeking influence among the working class—Marx and Engels commonly thought of socialism as carrying forward and embodying the best of bourgeois culture. As Nicolaievsky and Maenchen-Helfen hold:

> In Marx's eyes the revolution was the midwife of the new society which had formed in the womb of the old, and a new and higher culture would be the heir of the old culture, preserving and developing all the past attainments of humanity. For Bakunin the revolution meant a radical annihilation of existing society. . . . Bakunin dreamed of a "gigantic bonfire of London, Paris and Berlin." His was . . . not just the [hatred of] . . . prison and tax office but everything without exception, including schools and libraries and museums.[49]

The point, however, was that Bakunin saw culture and education as a grounding of privilege and domination and the nucleus of an exploitative New Class, so that domination could not be extirpated from society except by the literal leveling of culture itself—at least for a long period of transition.

In contrast, Marx himself took delight in the highest achievements of European culture. He read two or three novels at a time, absorbing his Aeschylus in the original Greek, was devoted to Shakespeare, enjoyed Balzac and Cervantes, took refuge in algebra, and wrote an infinitesimal calculus. As he wrote his daughter Laura in 1868, I am, he said, "a machine condemned to devour books." A product of the German University system, a member of the "Doctors' Club," and himself a doctor, when Marx thundered against the intelligentsia he commonly complained about their intellectual *incompetence*. Rather than seeking a leveling of any kind, he demanded superior levels of intellectual performance from them. He complained, as Babeuf had, about the unequal or high value placed on intellectuals' work but, in fact, held forth the prospect of a society in which rewards would be distributed (at least for a while) on a meritocratic principle that would favor the learned: From each according to his work, to each according to his ability.

Like Marx, Bakunin believed that human emancipation required the socialization of the means of production. Unlike him, however, Bakunin insisted that this alone could not suffice. Domination in its various forms, especially those grounded in the will to power, in the state, and in differences in knowledge rooted in differences in education, also needed to be exorcised in that wide-ranging cultural revolution that Bakunin called "social liquidation." For Bakunin, while economic exploitation and privilege are of crucial importance, they are only one case of domination. One notes (again in passing) how the Frankfurt School converges here with Bakunin, both focusing on a more general "domination," not just on economic exploitation. Jürgen Habermas's quest for the "ideal speech situation," seen as an effort to uproot not just differences in *formal* education or *high* theoretical culture but, more radically, in the practical reason of the everyday life, is a lineal descendant less of Marx than of Bakunin's struggle against the New Class's educational privileges.

Bakunin's Voluntarism vs. Marx's Determinism

The evil against which Bakunin had aimed his revolutionary project, going beyond economic exploitation to all forms of domination seen as embedded ultimately in the will to power, was a more formidable and intransigent foe than the one Marx had conjured up. It was more historically pervasive than the economic kind of exploitation on which Marx focused his studies of capitalism, being entrenched in human nature itself. Inevitably then, Bakunin's optimism must be more restrained than Marx's, if not containing a hidden vein of pessimism. Bakunin's diagnosis of the human condition could lead him to a position adjoining the tragic itself, for it addresses an enemy that is universal if not eternal. It is clearly an enemy he could have hoped to vanquish only with the most extraordinary exertions, being an adversary with countless hiding places in every human spirit. Indeed, such an enemy might well drive its adversary to the most desperate measures.

In contrast, Marxism had gathered strength precisely from its focus on the historically limited, hence more readily vanquishable, forms of exploitation of capitalism, while turning its back on mankind's more ancient enemies. Marxism had thus won its optimism at the cost of a measure of realism. Bakunin's realism, however, also had a price: it was won at the cost of rejecting the reassuring if glib conviction that "history is on our side" and, indeed, by putting human hope itself at risk. Such victories as revolutionaries might achieve, Bakunin held, would result from the suffering inflicted by a society which outraged the human demand of justice, for the passion for justice was as deeply rooted in human beings as their impulse to "live and prosper at the expense of others."[50] In the last analysis, the revolutionary struggle was not *only* a struggle against society and an exploiting class but was also a struggle *within* the human spirit in which mankind's opposing impulses—justice versus power—were pitted against one another. The outcome depended greatly, therefore, on human exertion, organization, and capacity for sacrifice; victory would thus never be secure simply by a change in social structures but also required a change within persons. The new society demanded a new man with a new consciousness, no less than new institutions. There was, therefore, a systematic and explicit voluntarism in Bakunin, unlike the embarrassed and subterranean voluntarism in Marx, whose theoretical presence was occluded by, because dissonant with, Scientific Marxism's determinism.

The trouble with Marxism, declared Bakunin, is that it sees "all human history . . . [as] the inevitable result of economic phenomena . . . the economic material phenomena constitute the essential basis, the main foundation, while all the others—the intellectual and moral, political and social phenomena—follow as a derivative from the former."[51] In calling himself a materialist, Bakunin, then, did not invidiously counterpose "social being" to consciousness or production to ideology. Bakunin conceived of materialism precisely as Georg Lukács had understood Marx's historical materialism, i.e., as a philosophy of the "totality" rather than as an economic determinism:

By these words *matter* and *material* we understand the totality, the hierarchy of real entities, beginning with the most organic bodies and ending with the structure and functioning of the brain of the greatest genius: the most sublime feelings, the greatest thoughts, the most heroic acts, acts of self-sacrifice, duties as well as rights, the voluntary renunciation of one's own welfare, of one's egoism . . . all that constitutes in our view so many different but at the same time interlinked evolutions of that totality of the real world which we call matter.[52]

This totality that is the concern of the materialist "does not by any means exclude, but on the contrary, necessarily embraces the ideal world as well."[53]

Bakunin, then, is no idealist but a voluntarist. He does not, that is, believe that mind, spirit, or ideals primarily determine or control human conduct but, rather, that they constitute a real part of the human situation and that their *interaction* with other parts constitutes the "totality" which shapes outcomes. Persons could thus not achieve whatever they wished, whenever they wished it. Will and consciousness are important and make an important difference in outcomes but are not "free." ". . . [W]e absolutely deny the existence of free will."[54] "Socialism, being founded upon positive science, absolutely rejects the doctrine of 'free will.' "[55] Will itself, held Bakunin, is grounded in need. Yet the human species are unique in having the power of speech and, especially, of abstraction.[56] Thus the human species is grounded in needs as transformed by ideals. While people cannot liberate themselves from their needs, except by suicide, they can modify these in the light of their notions of justice and beauty. Being grounded in man's unique species endowment, the human will can attain "ever greater progress and perfection."[57] Up to a point, a man "can become his own educator, his own instructor, as well as creator. But . . . what he acquires is only a relative independence."[58] Yet precisely because the will is not free, and is subjected to enormous social pressures, it is likewise exposed to and shaped by society's injustices and the suffering it inflicts. Thus "society itself, by its positive and negative action, generates free thought in man and, in turn, it is society which often crushes it."[59] In consequence, free will and thought are not in great supply, and here Bakunin's voluntarism has an interface with its own brand of elitism: "Among a thousand people one can hardly find a single person of whom it can be said . . . that he wills and thinks independently."[60] Yet there are some if not many persons who can withstand the social pressure toward conformity and who, when brought together and organized effectively, can constitute a revolutionary cadre of decisive importance in moments of revolutionary crisis. ". . . [R]evolutions are not improvised. They are not made arbitrarily by individuals nor even by the most powerful association. They come independently of will and all conspiracies and they are always brought on by the natural forces of circumstance."[61] In these moments of great crisis ". . . ten, twenty, or thirty well organized persons, acting in concert and knowing where they are going and what they want can easily carry along a hundred, two hundred, or three hundred people, or even more. . . ."[62] Thus as a voluntarist, Bakunin understands the course and development, but not the emergence, of revolution, to be influenced by a conscious vanguard who guide the new energies then unleashed in the light of their special, positive knowledge.

Bakunin's "good society," then, does not center, as Marx's did, on heightening production and productivity because the central evil in Bakunin's theory was not—as it was in Marx's—scarcity; and the central temptation was not that provoked by scarcity but, rather, the temptations of domination and of power. The central task, then, is not to cultivate the forces of production nor is the central strategic emphasis, as it was for Marx, a waiting for the forces of production to be revolutionized by the bourgeoisie, before committing the cadres to the revolution. The goal was a new man with a new morality able to control his impulse toward domination and the will to power. Bakunin's conception of revolution sees emancipation as in part motivated and guided by the pursuit of certain values, and as in part concerned to reconstruct the social environment so that men will become and behave more morally. Since persons are shaped by nature and society, however, "to make men moral it is necessary to make their environment moral." Bakunin's basic premise is that of the Enlightenment, namely that the ground must first be cleared of the old regime, and that this is the decisive step in social transformation. Unlike the eighteenth-century *philosophes,* however, Bakunin does not believe that persons are inherently good, so that if the ancient superstitions and the institutions supporting them are erased, the automatic drift will then be progressive and benign. For even then the blight of domination will still hang over men and they will remain tempted by the apple of power. The environment must thus be reconstructed so as to assure the triumph of justice, that is, "the complete liberty of everyone in the most perfect equality for all."[63] Bakunin's decisive values were liberty and equality, each being given generalized emphatic and articulate commitment in contrast to Marx's contrasting treatment, which tends to emphasize the derivative superstructural character of morality, the historically limited and emergent character of rights, their link to the bourgeoisie, and their role as a mask for class privilege and oppression. Even in a socialist society, Marx calls only for a distributive principle requiring "from each according to his ability, to each according to his work," later to be superseded in the more mature communism by allocation on the basis of need. In neither case, however, would distribution be equal and indeed Marx stresses that, since persons differ so much in mental and physical constitution, treating them equally is only a form of inequality.[64]

While Marx insisted on the development of certain social requisites before socialism could be achieved, most especially the heightening of productivity through modern industrial technology, Bakunin did not believe that the revolution needed to wait for this maturation of industrial power.[65] Marx was a modernizer who relied on technology and science to overcome scarcity so that history could take its next step forward to socialism. Bakunin, however, did not so much seek a more productive, materially richer and comfortable society but a more equitable one in which people at least shared equally in whatever there was, however little this was. If Marx rejected that societies were more or less backward in terms of the industrial development and modernization of their economies, Bakunin never saw large-scale industry as emancipatory. To the contrary—and in the anarchist tradition congenial to artisans—he wanted small-scale groups for work and residential purposes, federated with one another on the basis of voluntary mutual collaboration, rather than being hierarchically organized in large-scale units that were centrally planned and administered. Marx relied on bourgeois societies (unwittingly) to lay the foundations of socialism, where Bakunin saw traditionalist societies as having a greater potential for revolution and socialism than did Marx. Correspondingly, Marx accented the revolutionary role of the urban proletariat and tended to deprecate the peasantry, while Bakunin, although *accepting* the vanguard role of the proletariat in the revolution, felt that the peasantry, too, approached correctly, also had great potential for revolution.

The Class Basis of the Revolution

A popular stereotype of Bakunin—more distorted by its decisive omissions than in what it says—mistakenly emphasizes that Bakunin, like Weitling, relied greatly upon brigands and the "lumpenproletariat" for his revolutionary cadres, upon the peasantry (because of their violent *Pougatovtchina*), and upon student intellectuals. In this familiar vein, Paul Thomas writes that Bakunin was attracted to the peasantry as a revolutionary force because of its propensity "to unorganized, indiscriminate violence." Thomas also cites Bakunin's florid encomiums to brigandage where, in a path-breaking work that Eric Hobsbawn would later elaborate as a theory of "primitive rebellion," Bakunin held that brigands

"represented the desperate protest of the people against the horrible social order of the time. . . . The brigand in Russia, is the true and only
revolutionary. . . ." "Bakunin believed that the socially outcast, the
marginal, the outlaw and the criminal," says Thomas, "shared with the
oppressed an exemplary victimization and an exemplary desire for vengeance and propensity for violence," also adding that Bakunin "assigned
a major role to disaffected students and marginal intellectuals. . . ."[66]

The truth is substantially different, not because Bakunin was unat-
tracted to brigands, students, or the peasantry, but because Thomas fails
to see that Bakunin was more of a Marxist than he, Thomas, intimates.
Not restricting the revolution to those societies in which an advanced
industrialism had produced a massive urban proletariat, Bakunin observed sensibly that the class composition of the revolution was bound to
differ in industrially advanced Western Europe and in Eastern Europe
where the economy was still largely agricultural. In Eastern and Western Europe, the revolution's class composition will differ: "The initiative
in the new movement will belong to the people . . . in Western Europe, to the city and factory workers—in Russia, Poland, and most of the
slavic countries, to the peasants."[67] Yet even in Eastern Europe, insisted
Bakunin, "It is absolutely necessary that the initiative in this revolutionary movement be taken by the city workers, for it is the latter who
combine in themselves the instincts, ideas, and conscious will of the Social Revolution."[68] Even in Eastern Europe, then, both peasantry and
proletariat were necessary for the social revolution: "An uprising by the
proletariat alone would not be enough" and this would send the peasantry
either into open opposition or passive resistance, and they would then
"strangle the revolution in the cities. . . ."[69] This was a foreshadowing
of what, indeed, the peasantry attempted after the October Revolution
and to which Stalinism was a brutal and bloody response. "Only a wide-
sweeping revolution embracing both the city workers and peasants would
be sufficiently strong to overthrow and break the organised power of the
state, backed as it is by all the resources of the possessing classes."[70]

This is a far cry, then, from the conventional stereotype among some
Marxists of Bakunin-the-anarchist who relied exclusively on the backward
peasantry and ignored the proletariat. Bakunin, however, took realistic
note of the mutual suspicions between urban proletariat and rural peasantry, believing that, in Eastern Europe at any rate, successful revolution
required that these be faced and dealt with appropriately. ". . . [T]he
peasants will join the cause of the city workers," Bakunin held, "as soon
as they become convinced that the latter do not intend to impose upon
them their will or some political and social order invented by the
cities. . . ." He adds that they will join the revolution "as soon as they

are assured that the industrial workers will not take their lands away. It is altogether necessary at the present moment that the city workers really renounce this claim. . . ."[71] In a thrust at the Marxists, Bakunin declared that "To the Communists, or Social Democrats of Germany, the peasantry, any peasantry stands for reaction. . . . And in this hatred for the peasant rebellion, the Marxists join in touching unanimity all the layers and parties of the bourgeois society of Germany."[72]

Throughout their lives, Marx and Engels had indeed steadfastly adhered to just such views. Condemning peasantry as a reactionary "sack of potatoes," they planned to nationalize all land and to turn it over to the state which would then mobilize large agricultural armies in the countryside.

> The proletariat will use its political supremacy [declared the *Communist Manifesto*] to wrest, by degrees, all capital from the bourgeoisie, to centralize all instruments of production in the hands of the State . . . in the beginning, this cannot be effected except by despotic inroads on the rights of property . . . in the most advanced countries the following will be pretty generally applicable: 1. Abolition of property in land . . . Establishment of industrial armies, especially for agriculture.[73]

Since Marx and Engels never repudiated their policy of nationalizing the peasants' land but reiterated it, their policy for a worker-peasant alliance, under the former's leadership, could never effectively be achieved. (Essentially the contradiction between these two policies was never resolved but only concealed in the Third World by revolutionaries who could unite the nation under their leadership on the basis of nationalist, anti-imperialist, anti-colonialist, and ethnic solidarities.)

For Bakunin, it seemed self-evident that the revolution, even in Eastern Europe, required the unity of peasantry and city workers because of the latter's more advanced consciousness. At the same time, however, this very superiority may have induced city workers to impose themselves arrogantly on the countryside: "It is the pretended or real superiority of intelligence or education . . . of workers' civilization over that of the rural population"[74] that disposes workers to impose their will. The socialism of city workers, then, is an ambiguous thing entailing a certain emancipation yet also fostering a sense of superiority by townspeople, even workers, toward what Marx had once called "rural idiocy." The socialism of the city worker not only has an elitist potential but is, suggests Bakunin (in anti-urban formulations later to be echoed in Castroism), an effete and decadent impulse especially in comparison with villagers' natural, even savage impulse toward rebellion:

. . . the more enlightened, more civilized Socialism of the city workers, a socialism which because of this very circumstance takes on a somewhat bourgeois character, slights and scorns the primitive natural and much more savage Socialism of the villages, and since it distrusts the latter, it always tries to restrain it, to oppress it in the name of equality and freedom, which naturally makes for dense ignorance about city Socialism on the part of the peasants, who confound this socialism with the bourgeois spirit of the cities. The peasant regards the industrial workers as a bourgeois lackey or as a soldier of the bourgeoisie . . . so much that he himself becomes the servant and blind tool of reaction.[75]

Bakunin thus regarded Marx's socialism as a bourgeois socialism—not because Marxism sought to secure the future of the bourgeois economy or its bourgeois proprietors but, rather, because Bakunin felt Marxism was imbued with bourgeois *sentiments* and *culture* and expressed the elite ambitions of a New Class of intellectuals that had grown out of the old moneyed capitalists. To grasp what Bakunin regarded as Marx's bourgeois sentiments one need only recall the florid encomiums to progressive capitalism expressed in the *Communist Manifesto* and compare them with Bakunin's own more somber judgment on the bourgeoisie. Despite its final condemnation of the bourgeoisie, when it reached (and for *having* reached) its moribund state, the *Manifesto*'s praise of the bourgeoisie's emancipatory historical role is barely less than a celebration:

The bourgeoisie . . . has been the first to show what man's activity can bring about. It has accomplished wonders far surpassing Egyptian pyramids, Roman aquaducts, and Gothic cathedrals; it has conducted expeditions that put in the shade all former Exoduses of nations and crusades. . . . The bourgeoisie, during its rule of scarce one hundred years, has created more massive and more colossal productive forces than have all preceding generations together. Subjection of nature's forces to man, machinery, railways, electric telegraphs, clearing of whole continents for cultivation, canalization of rivers, whole populations conjured out of the ground—what earlier century had even a presentiment that such productive forces slumbered in the lap of social labor?[76]

In contrast to Marx's memorialization of the bourgeoisie for having revolutionized productivity, Bakunin's more tempered appreciation of the bourgeoisie praised them for having engendered *revolutions* against the crown, the aristocracy, and the church, and for having once been the embodiment of the hope for fraternity and union—at least prior to 1793. In those days of its vigor, the bourgeoisie is praised for having supported "the great principles of liberty, equality, fraternity, reason, and human justice. . . ."[77] Such technical progress as the bourgeoisie brought, mentions Bakunin, briefly benefited "only the privileged classes and the power of the states . . . they have never benefited the masses of the people."[78]

While Bakunin had no Marxist contempt either for brigands as a "lumpenproletariat"—the passively rotting "social scum"—or a suspicion of peasants as a doomed and reactionary class—Bakunin's position is convergent with Marx's. He views the revolution as grounded in an alliance between the peasantry and the proletariat. The latter are the more "conscious" element and the former, having retained their folk integrity, are the more natural, instinctive, and necessarily "savage" in their rebellion. Far from ignoring the proletariat, then, or subordinating them to the peasantry in the revolution, Bakunin insisted that ". . . in order that the peasants rise in rebellion, it is absolutely necessary that the city workers take upon themselves the initiative in this revolutionary movement . . . ,"[79] although rejecting any doctrinaire assumption that the revolutionary alliance and leadership would be identical everywhere in the world. Bakunin, then, was a post-Marxist Marxist, who readily took what he thought valid from Marx's *oeuvre* but felt no impulse to canonize it. Unlike Marx, who knew only Western Europe, Bakunin knew and knew at first-hand both Western and Eastern Europe, and he understood at once that Marx's theory had been limited by the special conditions of its origin and development.

Bakunin vs. Marx: Revolution as Negation, Revolution as "Aufhebung"

How Bakunin had conceived revolution, and what its requisites might be, were naturally enough connected issues. Having conceived the revolution as a radical break with the past and as the extirpation of previous inequities, Bakunin envisaged it as a kind of destructive "liquidation," akin to the *philosophes'* conception of *écraser l'infâme*—annihilate (liquidate?) the mess. Bakunin believed that before there could be substantial forward movement, the iniquitous past had first to be liquidated and that this itself was the decisive prerequisite of subsequent progress. So revolution was not viewed as something which had a requisite, but as clearing the ground for the subsequent liberation.

This, of course, is quite different from Marx, whose decisive characteristic as a scientific socialist is—as he admonishes Bakunin—the idea that economic conditions, the maturation of the industrial economy, and not "will," are the foundation of the social revolution. In his notes about Bakunin's *Statehood and Anarchy,* Marx fulminates:

Schoolboy drive! A radical social revolution is connected with certain historical conditions of economic development; the latter are its presuppositions. Therefore it is possible only where the industrial proletariat, together with capitalist production, occupies at least a substantial place in the mass of the people. . . . Herr Bakunin . . . understands absolutely nothing about social revolution; all he knows are its political phrases. For him its economic requisites do not exist. Since all hitherto existing economic formations, developed or undeveloped, have included the enslavement of the working person (whether in the form of the wage worker, the peasant, etc.), he thinks that a *radical revolution* is possible under all these formations. Not only that! He wants a European social revolution, resting on the economic foundation of capitalist production, to take place on the level of the Russian or Slavic agricultural or pastoral peoples and not to overstep that level. . . . *Will power* and not economic conditions is the basis of his social revolution.[80]

For Marx, then, social revolution was not a destructive but a *constructive* action, a kind of deliverance from a moribund social system. The communist served as a midwife to the new system which had been gestating, and had finally matured, in the womb of the old regime. Marx basically believed that this revolution consisted of destroying the old state apparatus, then taking over the technologically advanced industrial basis developed under capitalism and placing it under the direction of the new state, the dictatorship of the proletariat. This, for him, was the decisive act from which all else would follow. The old division of labor and the old culture with its distinction between mental and manual labor—while ultimately to be scrapped—would survive in this reckoning, for a long while. There was to be no cultural revolution concomitant with the political; the industrial plant and equipment developed by the bourgeoisie were in effect to be placed under a new management, with the smashing of the old state and the bourgeoisie's expropriation. For "Herr Bakunin," however, the object was not a limited excision of bourgeois proprietorship, but the veritable "annihilation of bourgeois civilization" where revolution-in-permanence would pursue unending civil strife through permanent "cultural revolution."

Bakunin expected that the revolution would usher in at once a "full and complete social liquidation," and he opposed any revolution that allowed the political to precede the social and economic transformation: ". . . both have to be made at the same time . . . ," he insisted.[81] For Marx, the essential requisite of the revolution would be the maturation of industry that had developed naturally and without plan in the midst of bourgeois society. For Bakunin, the revolution itself was the first requisite of social transformation. After the liberating social liquidation it brings, there is a protracted struggle during which this beginning is consolidated. "It is necessary to overthrow that which is," said Bakunin, "in order to be able to establish that which should be."[82] Bakunin observed—as against Marx's stress on the importance of the revolution's economic requisites—that "even poverty and despondency are not sufficient to provoke a social revolution. . . . That can take place only when the people have a general idea of their rights and a deep, passionate, one might even say religious, faith in their rights."[83] Which is precisely why, for Bakunin, the revolution must "have economic equality as its immediate and direct aim"[84] and not the mobilization of power, conquest of the old state, or expropriation of the bourgeoisie. This is the authentic anticipation of later Western "Critical Marxism," of Georg Lukács's self-styled "revolutionary messianism," of Gramsci's and the Council Communists' Marxism, which also insisted that economic conditions did not suffice for social revolution and that a change of *consciousness* was necessary. This begins to suggest that Bakunin was the first articulate Critical Marxist; that Critical Marxism is grounded in what Scientific Marxists simplistically condemned as "anarchism" and in the entire tradition going back from Bakunin to Weitling. Put otherwise, Critical Marxism is repressed (not repressed "by" but) *in* Marxism because it is identified with, and historically embedded in this continuous sequence of political adversaries that Marx faced and fought.

The revolution for Bakunin was thus first of all to be an act of thoroughgoing destruction; going well beyond a political or even economic change, it would level the ground for a new beginning: "In order to humanize society as a whole, it is necessary ruthlessly to destroy *all* the causes, and *all* the economic, political, and social conditions which produce within individuals that tradition of evil."[85] If Marxism is a paean to productivity, Bakuninism was thus a hymn to destruction. "On the Pan-German banner [Bakunin's code-name for Marxism] is written: Retention and Strengthening of the State at any cost. On our banner, on the contrary, are inscribed in fiery and bloody letters: the destruction of all states, the annihilation of bourgeois civilization, free and spontaneous organization from below upward, by means of free associations, the organization of the unbridled rabble of toilers. . . ."[86] With the revolution there will come, says Bakunin, "first the terrible day of justice, and later, much later, the era of fraternity."[87] It is only in passing through this bloody "animal struggle for life" that the revolution can arrive at a human society. Bakunin conceives revolution as a kind of human volcano and his mind glows in anticipation of its unbridled animal savagery: "A rebellion on the part of the people, which is by nature spontaneous, chaotic and ruthless, always presupposes a vast destruction of property . . . when the exigencies of defense or victory demand it, they will not stop at the destruction of their own villages and cities. . . ."[88] (One is reminded of the destruction of Phnom Penh and other cities by Pol Pot's Communist regime in Cambodia.) Again: ". . . inasmuch as property in most cases does not belong to the people, they very often evince a positive passion for destruction . . . without that passion the revolutionary cause is impossible of realization, for there can be no revolution without a sweeping and passionate destruction, a salutary and fruitful destruction, since by means of such destruction new worlds are born and come into existence."[89] This revolutionary liquidation was to prepare the liberated future by an abreactive and cathartic expressive explosion. Bakunin was not about to have his revolution without this "salutary and fruitful destruction," in which the people would give vent to a pent-up savagery born of their centuries-long suffering. "There is only one science for the revolutionary," declared Bakunin, "the science of destruction. Day and night he must have but one thing before his eyes—destruction."[90] For Bakunin, a revolution without sustained violence was not only unlikely, but would be devoid of the purifying fire of holy retribution. The concentrated justice of the revolution was in its terror. "I drink to the destruction of public order and the unleashing of evil passions," toasted Bakunin.[91]

A revolutionary with such a conception of revolution could only view with revulsion Marx's cautious edging forward to his own revolution of which each step was strategically measured and paced off; coalitions and organizations diligently knitted and used for as long as they produced increments of power, and then discarded when better targets and opportunities appeared; the sordid bargaining and negotiating for political handholds; the concern with how things looked so that allies in other classes would not bolt—all this had to strike Bakunin as a very respectable "bourgeois" socialism indeed. And it was. Marx was proceeding toward his revolution with the same instrumental rationality and impersonal energy with which the bourgeoisie planned and built, bought and sold, all that it needed. At first the bourgeoisie attempted to conflate Marxists and Bakuninists, portraying both as wild-eyed fanatics. When the need arose, however, the bourgeoisie could do business with the Marxists; and indeed has in numerous domestic coalitions with social democratic parties and in international *détentes*.

Marxists and Bakuninists have had very different constituencies. The Bakuninists have recruited among artisans, peasants, unemployed, uprooted students, and intellectuals, while Marxists have often recruited children of the middle classes and those in full-time factory jobs to their leadership cadres. The Marxists saw Bakunin's following as an undisciplined rabble and lumpenproletariat. Bakuninists might see Marx's following as those who had surrendered their autonomy to become mercenaries and servants of the bourgeoisie. Bakuninist conceptions of small autonomous communities coming together voluntarily in federated systems would appeal to the peasantry, for both are drawn to a "political programme [that] was republican and anti-authoritarian . . . [and] envisaged a world in which the self-governing *pueblo* was the sovereign unit, and from which outside forces such as kings and aristocracies, policemen and tax-collectors and other agents of the supra-local State, being essentially agents of the exploitation of man by man, were eliminated."[92] Marxists and bourgeoisie alike have been drawn to the promise of abundance and are sworn to the overcoming of scarcity and both, therefore, were devotees of productivity. The peasant and artisan poor, however (and Eric Hobsbawm speaks of them here, as I do not, as the "pre-industrial" poor), ". . . always conceive of the good society as a just sharing of austerity rather than a dream of riches for all."[93] In contrast, Marxists and bourgeoisie both believed in progress and both believed that this largely depended on the sheer expansion of the forces of production, on producing "more." Neither saw that people would never be contented simply by having more than they had had, unless it also conformed to what they believed they might rightfully expect: justice. Both Marxists and bourgeoisie alike believed that this Promethean expansion of the forces of production would continue forever, and could not be slowed or stopped; and rather than viewing this as the symptom of a pathological insatiability, both saw it as a normal and healthful vigor. The Bakuninists were right about the affinity between the Marxists and the bourgeoisie. Forced to a choice, the bourgeoisie would recognize the common interests, while the Marxists, feeling themselves mortally compromised by this misalliance, could only deny it vigorously or define it as only a temporary expedience required by the revolution in permanence.

7

Marx vs. Bakunin:
Paradoxes of Socialist Politics

Marx and Bakunin differed also in their very understanding of the everyday process of social transformation even in its pre-revolutionary, more routine moments; they differed in their conception of how to relate to and make politics and indeed on what "politics" was. Much of the struggle between Marx and Bakunin, especially within the International Workingmen's Association, often took the explicit form of a discussion of "politics," of Marx's insistence that the International involve itself in parliamentary elections and of Bakunin's resistance to this (which, however, was never as intransigent as Marx liked to portray). This publicly visible conflict was at bottom about "opportunism," i.e., communists' and workers' everyday participation in capitalist institutions and parliaments and the extent to which this would produce a trade union economics and a parliamentary reformism that would tame the proletariat rather than arouse it to revolution, would sell its revolutionary future for modest and precarious gains within the limits of the *status quo*. Marx confirmed the Bakuninist's suspicions when, at the last congress of the First International at Den Haag in 1872—the very same congress in which Marx maneuvered successfully to expel the Bakuninists—Marx capped the meeting by declaring that there were indeed some countries which, because of their democratic heritage, might allow socialism to come about through parliamentary reform. Having eliminated the Bakuninists, Marx had also eliminated the repressive effect that their policy of direct action had had on his gradualism. Bakunin gone, Marx no longer had to be "more revolutionary than thou."

The differences between Marx and Bakunin are important from my standpoint here, because they help us understand Marx and his theory. Bakunin was a key boundary whose contours helped shape Marxism's own identity. We cannot know either adversary without knowing something of both. For Marx, the difficulty with Bakunin was his theoretical ignorance which led him to ignore the industrial and economic requisites of revolution and thus, presumably, to overemphasize the importance of sheer "will." In short, for Marx, Bakunin was a proponent of free will—a radical voluntarist—which, we have seen, Bakunin himself firmly denied. Bakunin, of course, defined his struggle with Marx differently, largely seeing it—in one part—as a struggle against Marx's Germanic impulse to centralize the International Workingmen's Association and to endow its general council with too much control over local sections, thereby intruding on their rightful autonomy. In another part, however, Bakunin also saw these differences centering on the Marxists' refusal to proceed directly from the "political" to the "social" revolution, and their greater reliance upon the "political"—whatever that was.

Much of the struggle between them in the I.W.A. was focused on the question of participation in politics and this commonly came down to whether or not to participate in various elections. In short, the differences between Marx and Bakunin were quite convergent with those exhibited in Marx's conflict with Gottschalk in Cologne in 1848. Like the latter, ". . . at the end of 1869, the Bakuninists started proclaiming the principle of not taking part in elections for any kind of parliament, and with this their struggle with the Marxists in Switzerland began."[1] Yet it was not so much that Bakuninists opposed all political action but rather that they only supported those kinds of political action that aimed at an immediate or coincident emancipation at the social, cultural, and economic levels. For Bakuninists, political struggle must lead on directly to social and cultural revolution without long pauses or delays. They could, in fact, even countenance electoral participation if they believed that it might spill over immediately into the social revolution. The differences, then, were not that the Marxists allowed "politics" while the Bakuninists did not; but rather that they disagreed about the amount of autonomy that each was prepared to allow to political activity and hence how each conceived politics itself.

If Bakunin demanded a politics of direct action that had direct and immediate social effects, Marx saw the whole process as a longer and more protracted one, with many historical layovers and side trips. Marx saw the process as dependent on complicated, slow-working mediations. He saw it also as requiring difficult and delicate preparations, as requiring the disciplined deferring of any quest for emotional gratifications by the workers, as the preparation and planning for a kind of social war that could not tolerate a surrender to impulses, including those for "passionate destruction." For Marx, it was not only necessary to change the society by excising the proprietary class, but also to change the workers themselves, to make them competent for emancipation. The revolution, for Marx, then, proceeds within the framework of a system of instrumental or utilitarian action aimed at the mobilization and control of increasing increments of power. It is power that was being garnered and anything that impaired, slowed, or threatened the cumulation of this power was held to be a manifestation of the class enemy. Anything, therefore, that impaired the forces of production or their efficiency, once in the hands of the revolution—and, indeed, even before then—was held to be dangerous to the revolution, undermining its ability to make war against the counter-revolution or to satisfy its material needs. Thus a "cultural revolution" that involved proceeding *immediately* from the political to the social revolution, that weakened experts' support for the revolution, or which undermined industry's infrastructure in science and the university, was held to be hazardous and was likely to be tabled.

For Marx, the culmination of power was the "dictatorship of the proletariat." Paul Thomas remarks that "the anarchists' fears that Marxist revolutionary politics pointed towards and would lead to proletarian dictatorship were well-founded. Marx's advocacy of the dictatorship of the proletariat was . . . central to his doctrine. . . ."[2] While literally true, Thomas is somewhat disingenuous here, for the anarchists did not actually accuse Marxism of preparing a dictatorship of the proletariat but, rather, *over* the proletariat.

Something of the difference between Marx's and Bakunin's idea of politics may be stated, in first approximation, by suggesting that Marx concentrated his politics on the *means* he took to be necessary for achieving the social revolution, while Bakunin sought to protect the *ends* for which that struggle was undertaken, the social revolution itself. Marx thought that once power was achieved and the dictatorship of the proletariat installed, there would be nothing to prevent the gradual achievement of the social revolution, especially the development of the forces of production. Bakunin thought that if this produced a concentration of power in a newly centralized state, that in itself would resist the development of the egalitarian, free society he believed to be the real essence of the social revolution. Marx was, we might say, a realist—a *Realpolitiker*—about the importance of mobilizing power—i.e., pursuing a "politics"—within the framework of the *status quo*; he was quite utopian, however, in expecting the voluntary self-dissolution of the new socialist society's power center and its new class elite. Bakunin, while far more realistic about the role of power in Marx's *future* socialism, was utopian in his inclination to avoid politics and the mobilization of power in *present* bourgeois society, and to treat it as quickly dispensable by moving on immediately to the social revolution. He is utopian too in his belief that the costs of cultural revolution could be paid without risking the revolution itself. Marx's basic attitude was that everything is achievable in time if only we come to power in a maturely industrialized society; the main task of politics, then, was to come to power, and to choose the right moment for doing so. Bakunin's basic attitude was that in politics all depends on using instruments compatible with your ends and that, if coming to power means the concentration of power in a new state and elite, they would surely never surrender it and allow a classless society to come into existence. Marxist politics, then, was instrumental; Bakunin's was a pre-figurative politics which situates him in the camp of those Marx stigmatized as "utopians."

Politics then has a special and delimited meaning for Marx. It is a long and protracted struggle which aims at the capture of power at the national and state centers, rather than a practice limited to the factory plant level and concerned with local wages or working conditions. Centered as it is on mobilizing and capturing power, Marx's conception of politics is, presumably, not an end in itself but only a means to other ends, especially aiming at a broader emancipation which is the "social" revolution. Thus the first statute of the International Workingmen's Association formulated by Marx in 1864 expressly stated that "the economic emancipation of the workers is the great aim to which all political action must be subordinated as a means." Each was focusing then on a different danger. Marx sought to avoid a dependence on the good will and voluntary consent of the class that was to lose out in the revolution, by creating specialized standing centers of coercion that could be used against them; he sought to protect the revolution's capacity to act against the certain and intransigent resistance of a powerful class that felt itself threatened with the loss of its essential privileges and position. Bakunin, however, expected that this old class could be totally smashed by an era of mass terror, and that, therefore, the problem was not to create specialized centers of coercion that fought the old class from above, but to prevent the emergence of a new class by ruthlessly and promptly extinguishing every social difference, privilege, or institution that might become the locus of a new hierarchy. Marx expected that the struggle for power would continue even after the old state was smashed and the dictatorship of the proletariat installed and he believed that the way to proceed was to create and institutionalize power instruments available to the revolution. Bakunin premised that the revolution could be defended by letting mass terror paralyze the old class's opposition, by eliminating all institutions that permitted it cultural and ideological hegemony, by activating the masses and maintaining them in a state of high mobilization. Whatever his own anti-statist predilections, then, Marx was impelled inescapably toward state-building both by his realistic conception of the need for centralized power available against the old class and its remnant influence, as well as by the need for an apparatus to administer and plan the newly expropriated means of production. Bakunin, however, believed, no less realistically, that it was precisely this that made Marxism continuous with bourgeois society and which would lead it to give birth to a new system of privilege.

In their differences about the role and nature of "politics," Marx and Bakunin were operating within an emerging set of linguistic distinctions in Western European culture. Thus among the activists pursuing radical change prior to the revolutions of 1848, the issues would often be formulated as to whether the "revolution of 1848 would assume a *social* character, or be confined within *political* channels. . . ."[3] In the then current usage, the "political" and the "social," especially the political and social *revolutions*, were terms contrasted and counterposed to one another, implying first, that the choice of one—the political—*might* be achieved without the other, the social revolution, and implying, second, that the social revolution was a kind of extension of or extreme outcome of a political revolution, while the latter might simply be the means or the opening act of a social revolution. Tocqueville thus distinguishes politics and class struggle: "This was . . . not a political struggle . . . but class-war, a kind of slave-war."[4] Again, F. Palecky in drawing up a memorandum of the Czech members of the Austrian parliament about their policy during the revolutionary period, "distinguishes between the social, political, and national elements in the revolution, making 'political' cover the problems of self-government and the freedoms. . . ."[5] The "political," then, bore upon those issues of a public character which arose out of the elimination of dynastic governments in Europe and the emergence of the nation state as a "public" affair whose governance was to be in the hands of all qualified citizens. This public business had its unifying and salient occasion in the conduct of parliamentary elections. The political revolution was, then, widely understood to be something less than the social revolution; it was something concerning and expressing the interests of the propertied middle classes and as ensuring that those of property could exercise an influence on the affairs of the state commensurate with their wealth, and from which the poor might be excluded. It is precisely because he premises these rather widespread if tacit understandings of the "political" that Bakunin dismissed parliamentarianism as a fraud. The workers, he said, cannot make use of political democracy because "they lack two 'small' things: leisure and material means . . . it is certain that the bourgeoisie knows better than the proletariat what it wants . . . first, because it is more learned than the latter, and because it has more leisure and many more means of all sorts to know the persons whom it elected. . . ."[6] A merely political revolution, then, does not serve the interests of workers but, allowing them empty freedoms, binds them the more closely into the old system of domination. Consequently, ". . . those who call upon them to win political liberties without touching upon the burning question of Socialism, without even uttering the phrase 'social liquidation' which sets the bourgeois trembling, tell them in effect . . . 'Win first this freedom for us in order that we may use it against you later.' " While Bakunin regards the impulse to power as central to human nature, he does not regard the political institutions of bourgeois society as possessing a measure of autonomy enabling them to be used to protect and extend workers' conditions. These political institutions, like those of the socialist society conceived by Marx, were seen as useless or dangerous for the working class.

Marxist Politics

From Marx's standpoint, and however much he held that political institutions were essentially a superstructure grounded in the economic foundation, class interests, and antagonisms, Marx was never disinterested in "politics." He believed that liberal and democratic institutions could and should be used to advance working-class emancipation. Certainly, and as Paul Thomas notes correctly, in Marx's view these institutions "are not to be despised or ignored but recognized and . . . put to good use . . . in revolutionary emancipation. . . ."[7]

As early as 1847, in his critique of Proudhon in the concluding paragraphs of *The Poverty of Philosophy,* Marx attempted to integrate his insistence on the priority of the economic with a concern for the claims of the political. The tension between these two impulses in Marx's work is evident here, yet there is no question but that he leaves room for the political. On the one hand, the political is defined as grounded in class conflicts: "there will be no more political power properly so-called, since political power is precisely the unofficial expression of antagonism in civil society . . ." once the working class excludes classes and their antagonism. "It is only in an order of things in which there are no more classes and class antagonisms that social revolutions will cease to be *political revolutions.*" On the other hand, "Do not say that social movement excludes political movement. There is never a political movement which is not at the same time social." Despite his emphasis on the priority of the economic, then, Marx nonetheless retained a distinct place for the political and, while insisting on its connections with the social movement, also recognized its relative independence.

While Marx insisted on the importance of political action, never despising politics as Bakunin sometimes did, still Marx's commitment to it was not as unambivalent as his polemics against Bakunin seem to suggest. The basic structure in which Marx thinks about politics is, first, his distinction between the governing economic infrastructure and the governed ideo-political superstructure. This parallels then current European political discourse, with its deep structure distinction between the society and state, its auxiliary distinction between the society and state, and its further distinction between social and political revolution. In the established distinction between state and society that Marx inherited, the emphasis had been on politics and the state as superordinate elements. Marx maintained this fundamental social topography but critically revalued it, assigning priority to *society,* especially to the relations and forces of production within it, thus making politics a kind of epiphenomenon dependent on economic development. Here economic development is the back country from which politics emerges.

At some level, then, Marx's differences with Bakunin, his strenuous insistence on using political opportunities to the fullest, is sharply dissonant with Marx's economic determinism. Because of this the role of the political is never articulately theorized in Marx. And for all of the importance attributed by the March 1850 circular letter to the political requisites of revolution and to the revolution in permanence, the textual foundation of these views is at best half a dozen pages. The explicit discussion of permanent revolution is hardly more than a page. And if Marx encourages workers to wring all the political concessions they can from the state, he also tells them that what they can get is limited by the kind of state and society it is, and that no ultimate emancipation and social revolution is possible within capitalism and its state. Use all the electoral and parliamentary machinery you can, Marx tells workers, and use it to the hilt, but remember that this can never emancipate you from wage slavery.

Underneath Marx's articulate theory of history—i.e., his "historical materialism"—underneath the articulate political economy expounded at great length in many places and especially in *Capital*—there is a less articulate level, the background assumptions by which Marx guided himself in his *organizational activity and political life*. These are the tacit rules of his political *modus operandi*. By reason of his organizational involvement, Marx was thrust willy-nilly into politics. Yet he never theorizes this politics, at most alluding to it as a "means" of economic and human emancipation against his organizational competitors, the "anarchists." Marx's conception of politics can only be extracted from the various usages in which it is found, rather than in developed texts. Yet there also were rules of a sort that Marx seems to have followed—or which we can *view* him as having followed—in making politics, no less than in understanding it. The following is a preliminary and provisional effort to codify these *subtextual* rules of Marxist politics:

Rule One: Open struggle is preferable to secret, conspiratorial struggle, for it can more readily involve and change masses.

Rule Two: Prepare for and expect a long and protracted struggle.

Rule Three: It is therefore necessary to guard against expending all the movement's resources and energies on some specific issue, or in pursuit of some limited public policy. The movement must also develop and husband organizations that can serve as the general staff of the revolution, which can economize its resources and maintain policy continuity over a long period of time, after as well as before elections.

Rule Four: Since the struggle is open, the organization guiding it—or parts of it—and some of its leaders, also need to be public.

Rule Five: Victory will require a long, protracted struggle and will not come as the result of a swift coup aimed at capturing public functions and buildings (e.g., Blanqui) in which the seat of government would be seized by a small band of determined men, but by building organizations and movements.

Rule Six: Victory in the end requires the prior maturation of industrial productivity to overcome scarcity, and the spontaneous unfolding of the natural laws on which this development depends.

Rule Seven: In the meanwhile, victory also requires influence over the minds of men, a mobilization of mass public persuasion.

Rule Eight: Victory also requires instruments of propaganda and agitation and the creation of movement newspapers and other media, to counter the cultural hegemony of the bourgeoisie. Thus in order to stabilize and channel workers' alienation, what is required is both organization-building and media-development.

Rule Nine: The focus around which the public struggle develops at first is the struggle to pass laws favorable to the working class—e.g., the eight-hour day—and which allow them to organize openly.

Rule Ten: In order to pass such laws, it is necessary to make publicly visible and to elect candidates favorable to them.

Rule Eleven: Such parliamentary efforts require alliances, temporary or permanent, with other social classes and various groups.

Rule Twelve: Temporary concessions have to be made to these allies without, however, losing sight of or commitment to the long-range goals, the "social" revolution of the armed workers. It must be accepted that the early stages of the struggle will involve concessions to and the hegemony of bourgeois and petty-bourgeois classes and parties.

Rule Thirteen: Maturation of a parliamentary politics and the consolidation of the working class is facilitated by developing a national society without divisive localisms; and also implies a territory freed from domination by foreigners and possessing resources adequate to support self-determination, and one should therefore support movements for national self-determination.

Rule Fourteen: Since the struggle will be long and protracted (Rule Five), requiring alliances with various classes (Rule Twelve) having aims different from those of the working class, one should develop a timetable, dividing time up into different phases, so that one knows which rules apply at any given time, so that one can apply rules at the later time that differ from those of the earlier, and so that the earlier alliances and compromises are not allowed to continue indefinitely.

Rule Fifteen: The struggle is not to be carried forward in pacifist ways, but may at one (earlier) time require legal parliamentary struggle and at another (later) time, armed force. Military skills should therefore be acquired and studied, while persons competent in them should be cultivated.

Rule Sixteen: (a) All struggle—parliamentary, military, or para-military—aims at winning and optimizing power; it must culminate in destruction of the old state and in construction of a new state: the "dictatorship of the proletariat." (b) All struggle must seek the mobilization of power for the revolution here and now; its ultimate point is participation in the state or the formation of a new state. (c) All political activities are to be judged in instrumental ways, i.e., from the standpoint of whether and how much of a power increment they produce. The party movement, then, is to be appraised in terms of its efficiency as a tool to mobilize, seize, and wield power.

The object of political struggle, then, is primarily the acquisition of power with which to destroy the state supporting the old capitalist mode of production, and to introduce a new one compatible with a socialist mode of production. Yet it is not that alone. Marx also maintains that the function of the struggle is to transform those involved in it so that their own human nature will now be more compatible with the new society. At their present stage of cultural development, workers and others bear the dross of centuries which can be shed only with time and struggle.

The Cultural Context of Politics and Power

What, then, did the struggle about the "political" mean? Which is another way of asking, what did the contest between Bakunin and Marx mean? Part of the answer can be discerned if we return and compare the ambitions of disaffected artisans and intellectuals during the 1848 revolution. Artisans sought (a) a more expressive discharge of their hostilities—a kind of Luddite direct action—against the emerging factory system and owners, ruining them economically and declassing them socially. Artisans also (b) wanted something of a restoration to the guild system, but for many journeymen this was to be a modified return that would not restore the hereditary privileges the guild masters had acquired.

What, however, did disaffected intellectuals want? Part of what they sought was improved market opportunities, whether in the private sector or the state bureaucracy. The new technical intelligentsia would, however, be the prime beneficiaries of an expanding private sector. Those with "traditional" forms of training could be aided primarily by state programs that would require bureaucratic expansion. This, in turn, meant that they wanted institutions that could pursue such state-expanding policies, essentially the political process and parties. What traditional intellectuals were directed toward, then, was an expansion of the entire framework of *politics through which,* first, state-expanding policies could be furthered and, second, *within which* a whole host of new "political" careers could be directly pursued by them.

This is an appropriate place to connect our earlier discussion (see pp. 113-120) of how the exclusionary policies of worker-artisans and intellectuals differ. Recall that I had argued that each prefers different policies, worker-artisans seeking to exclude intellectuals by limiting membership to those employed in certain manual occupations, while intellectuals reject such an occupational test and prefer ideological and organizational commitments as membership tests. Intellectuals then reject purely "economistic" or trade union principles of exclusion and foster organizations to which they have access because these are not linked to manual labor in the work place but are "political" in character.

The struggle between Marx and Bakunin about politics, then, did not just represent a disinterested or purely theoretical difference concerning the most effective ways of making the revolution or transforming the world. For in some ways, the strategy of deferred action, of parliamentary and other instrumental politics versus direct expressive action, each had a different elective affinity for different groups, the latter being more attractive to artisan groups, the former to intellectuals. Support of the "political," then, was a demand especially congenial to intellectuals whose own social origins, educational background, and communication skills allowed them to profit from the institutional changes implicit in the new politics. They could now have expanded career opportunities as deputies and ministers in the new parliamentary politics, and as experts or lawyers, in the newly expanding bureaucracies of the state apparatus. Artisans could at most hope for an improvement in their conditions through changes in the laws. Intellectuals, however, could hope to participate in the very management of the new politics rather than simply be its clients.

Hal Draper and other Marxologists have commonly seen this in a one-sided way, noting that *anti*-political Bakuninism was supported by a specific social stratum, the artisans. While often overstated, there was a strong tendency in this direction. Yet this is one-sided because it assumes that Marx's *pro*-political line in opposition to Bakuninism's policy of direct action was simply a cerebral decision which had no corresponding grounding in the interests of a social stratum or distinct class. Our point here, then, is that *both* sides in the struggle—Marx's pro-political position and Bakunin's anti-politics—had a class grounding.

For Marx and Marxism, however, this represented something of a problem. For the pro-political interests of the intelligentsia as a social stratum were fundamentally dissonant with Marxism's deprecation of politics and its impulse toward certain forms of economic determinism. In other words, the class interests of the intellectuals supporting Marxism were not fully expressed in Marxism as *articulate* theory and were indeed inhibited by it. In some part, these interests could be pursued more openly and are given fuller expression in Bernstein's revisionism with its genteel voluntarism. Revisionism represents in part the growing influence of intellectuals in the German social democratic movement, especially after the repeal of Germany's anti-socialist laws. The limited public apparatus of Leninism, however, dwarfed by Czarist repression, allowed intellectuals many fewer opportunities for career fulfillment as politicians or state bureaucrats. Leninism, then, represents the ideology of intellectuals whose political ambitions in the public life are more sharply thwarted; who are thus more severely alienated from the *status quo;* and who had relinquished hope for normal political influence in society. That, on the one hand. On the other, Leninism also represents the repression of just such political ambitions for public careers within the *status quo,* offering intellectuals instead compensatory "careers" *against* it, as "professional revolutionaries," and fostering the vanguard party itself as the decisive site for the revolutionary's political career, a kind of substitute sphere for the pursuit of political ambitions.

Intellectuals and the Consolidation
of the Revolution

For Marx, then, workers are prepared for their new socialist future both
by the natural evolution of the mode of production and by conscious political struggle. Despite this preparation, however, many of them are also
expected to remain under the hegemony of bourgeois culture and to retain a measure of false consciousness. There is, then, a genuine continuity—continuity, not identity—between originary Marxism and Leninism as
it called for a political vanguard which was to be more theoretically and
culturally advanced and which would lead the workers and diffuse a
correct, socialist consciousness among them.

Marx's assumption, however, is that most decisive of all is the mobilization of power by communists. It is assumed that, with the seizure or
peaceful assumption of power, this new state, together with the mature
industrial mode of production that made this revolution possible, will
suffice to produce the remaining necessary changes in workers' consciousness and culture. Controlling the economy and the new state,
workers and their representatives will now be in a position simply to sift
through the old culture and to remove administratively whatever is in-
appropriate to the new society. Hence no "cultural revolution" will be
needed to prosecute an active struggle against the old culture and its
bearers. The educationally privileged will be needed in the new socialist
society although terror is foreseen as possibly necessary to command the
obedience of the old, technical intelligentsia.

As Engels remarked in a letter to Bebel on October 24, 1891, the allegiance of the technical intelligentsia to the movement is necessary for
a smooth transition to power. If, however, we come to power too early,
he adds, ". . . the technical people will be our main enemies, and they
will betray us wherever they can; we will have to use terror against
them, and still get done in anyway. . . ."[8] Here there is a clear foreshadowing of the exigencies that would lead the new Soviet state to Stalinism's purges and show trials which, if culminating in mass terror
against the entire populace, began in the Shakty trials against the
engineers.

For Marx, many elements in the old culture were useful and necessary to further the forces of production. So long as those embodying the
old culture did this faithfully, there was no question of whether they
possessed, by reason of that very culture, an ideology inimical to the
ideals of the revolution. The technical utility of the old culture and
the faithful compliance of its bearers were paramount issues shaping the
attitudes of the new political authority. The "workers'" possession of po-

litical and economic power was assumed sufficient to decontaminate ideologically dissonant remnants of the old culture, for this was seen as primarily an infrastructure dependent on the forces of production. As
Carmen Claudin-Urondo puts it in discussing Leninism, ". . . Western
civilization is to be accepted as it is, for, once separated from the political
interests that have led it astray, it can serve even better the interests of
socialist society."[9] There is, therefore, never anything in Marxism calling
for a distinct and special effort against the ideological embedding of the
old regime in the old culture that is transmitted to the new society. This
ideological residue is, rather, regarded as if it were an archaic vestige
which, with the development of the new material foundations, is destined
to die out in time of its own accord. It is not defined as borne and reproduced by a social stratum—the intelligentsia—with special interests of
its own; a stratum which passes the old culture from the old regime to
the new society and which, because of its utility, is supported by the new
society insofar as it is dependent on old culture skills. For all of Marx's emphasis on the importance of ideology critique, he never regards science
and technology as a sphere of ideology with its own impulse to social
domination. Instead he sees them as a largely neutral culture capable of
being transplanted into the new socialism without side effects. Here
their new context will assign them a new role. Nothing could be farther
from Bakunin's notion of "social liquidation," with its call for a moratorium on elite science and its denunciation of the educated as a new
class of exploiters. According to Marx, however, what makes science and
culture ideologically distorted is nothing intrinsic. There is therefore
nothing that needs uprooting by a special cultural revolution. Culture is
distorted only by the bourgeois *interests* it serves under capitalism, and
these limits are more or less automatically removed with the latter's overthrow. Implicit, then, is a notion of the "automatic crash" or entropy of
bourgeois culture with the demise of the bourgeois mode of production;
that culture, therefore, needs no special critical sifting.

Since culture and technology are not intrinsically ideologically distorted, even the old intellectuals and intelligentsia who are its bearers
may be relied on to serve the purposes of the new socialist society, once
they realize there is no way back to the old society. It is important to use
the old experts and intellectuals, especially during the period of transition to the new society, because they have the skills necessary to help
fight the counter-revolution and to keep the machinery of production
going so that the needs of the new society may be met. Intellectuals and
intelligentsia, then, are largely seen as the "functionaries" of the ideological superstructure—to use Gramsci's terms—and, like the superstructure, they too simply reflect the interests and direction of the dominant

class and its mode of production. They thus have a technical neutrality, making them as useful in the new as in the old society. Without learning from technical specialists and intellectuals and using their services, the new socialism will be unable to defend and feed itself. With the rise of socialism to state power, it is not power but skill that becomes the salient problematic for communists. Increasingly their tasks will be less those of politics than of administration whose effectiveness depends on educated, technically competent personnel. This, then, is the logic of Marx's position, particularly when formulated as an economistic determinism.

The society that is premised, as well as the political measures through which Marx proposes to bring it about, both entail building the state apparatus, its centralization, increasing the scope and variety of its functions, the extension of its powers, and, along with this, an increasing role for intellectuals and other technical specialists whose skills are a kind of cultural capital acquired through specialized education. Even before the socialist movement wins power, however, it provides opportunities for intellectuals to secure editorships in movement journalism, to attain parliamentary offices, and to win jobs in the movement's own technical bureaucracy. State- and nation-building are a proclivity of intellectuals, as is political contest; for in this "open struggle," "argument" counts. In open political struggle, the everyday life of the movement cadre can be more or less normal and its sacrifices limited. Far from going underground, it publicizes itself as candidates for parliamentary selection. Open political struggle is thus more compatible with the life style of middle-class professionals and intellectuals. Revolutionary politics becomes another "profession." Indeed, Lenin will later promise that the communist revolutionary "vanguard" will be led by "professional" revolutionaries—a rhetoric serving to normalize revolutionary life for middle-class intellectuals. Both the political life of revolutionaries during the struggle for power—which requires planning, persuasion, and negotiation—as well as the state they construct after seizing power become preserves in which intellectuals have a privileged place. Indeed, the state becomes the pre-empted career ground of intellectuals, where positions are allocated on meritocratic and educational bases, and where merit is commonly measured by educational certification. The open struggle of "politics," then, is more compatible with the life styles and educational privileges of intellectuals.

Marx's inclination to vest importance in the political sphere, and in liberal or democratic institutions, culminated in his remarks at the last congress of the International Workingmen's Association in 1872 where, after decisively defeating the Bakuninists and expeling them from the I.W.A., Marx had the last word, endorsing the importance of these institutions, and denying that socialism must everywhere require a "social liquidation" as Bakunin had insisted. ". . . [W]e do not deny that there are countries like America, England (and, if I knew your institutions better, I would add Holland)," said Marx in Den Haag, "where the workers can achieve their aims with peaceful means."[10] In a letter of December 8, 1880, Marx wrote Henry Hyndman to much the same effect as his remarks of 1872, namely, that our "party considers an English revolution not necessary, but . . . *possible*."

The Bakuninists were essentially correct in insisting on the gradualist potentialities of Marx's emphasis on the political, although mistaken in implying that Marxism can be reduced to such a gradualist tendency. While these gradualist tendencies grow stronger in mature Marxism and are continuous with later full-grown revisionism, the latter is only a one-sided culmination of Marxism; for Marx never doubted that in certain countries socialism could be achieved *only* with force or that it might, in any country, need to defend itself against counter-revolution with force. Yet when contrasted with Bakunin, Marx was certainly much more the gradualist. His politics was a mediated process requiring deferred gratification. It increasingly excluded the remnant apocalyptic elements from the political process and lodged these in the inherent economic contradictions of capitalism. He placed much less emphasis on direct action and violence than Bakunin and stressed the need for a protracted struggle using the political institutions of the old society, while expecting to carry forward into the new system the best culture of the old. If Marx was an Hegelian in his philosophy of struggle, his was an Hegelianism of the "reconciling" dialectic whose final movement entailed a synthesizing and healing sublation, an *aufhebung*, in which the past is both transcended and partially included in the future. Bakunin's Hegelianism, however, was a negative dialectic that did not point toward a culminating "reconciliation."

Critical Marxism as a Recovery of Bakuninism

For Bakunin and Marx alike, the problem was how to unite the political and the social revolutions. For Bakunin, this meant passing from the political to the social revolution—via "social liquidation"—as quickly as possible. Marx, too, faced the problem of integrating the social with the political revolution and formulated the "permanent revolution" as his central conception of this. Marxists believed that there must, indeed, first be a political revolution before the social revolution can be effected, that the "dictatorship of the proletariat" must be achieved first. Marx also held that this could be built only on ground that had first been cleared by the bourgeoisie, through the development of national public institutions of liberal democracy which could protect their hegemony. He and Engels both repeatedly warned that there were great dangers for a workers' revolution that had erupted in a society in which this bourgeois economic evolution and political revolution had not occurred.

The essential difficulty with Marx's position, however, was that the social revolution, socialism, required the prior maturation of an industrial economy that was to be wrought by the bourgeoisie. The development of the economic requisites of socialism, therefore, also meant that the bourgeoisie was becoming ever stronger economically and, if it secured the political institutions appropriate to its hegemony, it would become stronger politically as well. The revolution, as Marx saw it, required a prior economic evolution of the forces of production being fostered by the bourgeoisie. The bourgeoisie were thus becoming stronger, both economically and politically, at the very moment when the conditions imputedly requisite for socialism were at high tide. Having not defined such an economic development as the requisite of socialism, but seeing revolution itself as that prime requisite, Bakunin's socialism could feel free to seek power *before* a capitalist economy secured bourgeois hegemony. Bakuninism was, paradoxically, a strategy that facilitated the political revolution as a transfer of power, but which once victorious would be badly impeded in its effort to move on to the social revolution. Even though the entire point of its strategy deprecated the political and extolled the social revolution, Bakuninism might more readily achieve a successful political revolution but be unable to pass over to the successful social revolution it sought.

One implication of this internal Marxist flaw is that Marxism could never make a successful revolution by adhering to its original scientific socialist vision of industrial maturity as the vital requisite of revolution. A second implication derives from our observation that the flaws of Bakuninism and Marxism had a certain complementarity. This suggests that Marxism as a scientific socialism could begin to overcome its flaws by accommodating to Bakuninism and taking over certain of its features, although one could never expect this to be done openly. The subsequent history of Marxism seems to bear out these expectations.

Marxism developed increasingly from a Scientific to a Critical Marxism that was much more voluntaristic and stressed consciousness and conscious organization—rather than emphasizing a spontaneous economic evolution that first develops the forces of production. This long-term shift in Marxism is visible in Leninism: Leninism formulates a conception of a "vanguard" revolutionary organization more nearly akin to Bakuninism than to Marxism and adapts the old conspiratorial secret society to a Marxist rhetoric of theory and science by speaking of the vanguard cadres as "professional" revolutionaries. It also devoted increasing attention to the peasantry as an ally of the proletariat with a revolutionary potential. If, as Marx had noted during the 1848 revolution, a secret organization had no point where there was expanding freedom of speech and press, it was precisely this that proved effective in the repressive atmosphere of Czarism. Both Castroism and Maoism are more uninhibited movements in the direction of a voluntaristic socialism. They also go much farther than Leninism in their correspondingly greater reliance upon the peasantry. This is especially the case with Maoism and its repeated "cultural revolutions" which sharply accelerate Marxism's convergence with Bakuninism. This increasing world drift of Marxism toward a less economistic and more voluntaristic theory has more usually been called a "Critical" Marxism, when found in Western Europe. Critical Marxism has, therefore, seemed to some, such as Merleau-Ponty or Perry Anderson, a distinctively "Western Marxism." This, however, misses the point of the greater political success of Critical Marxism in the Third World. In these less industrially advanced countries, Critical Marxism's reliance upon the peasantry has been even greater and its convergence with Bakuninism even more obvious. In Asia—including Czarist Russia—and other less-developed regions, Scientific Marxism's insistence upon a prior industrialization made it seem irrelevant and generated apathy and passivity among revolutionaries who did not want to spend their lives making a bourgeois revolution. To use the resources they did—i.e., to rely on the peasantry and countryside rather than the city—to pursue a program of revolutionary militance at once, revolutionaries in the Third World moved toward a Critical and away from a Scientific Marxism. This shift suggests that there was a potential mutual transformability of Marxism into Bakuninism. Each might, under certain conditions, become the other.

This was, of course, most visible in the earlier or "youthful" Marxist work that was more saturated with apocalyptic sentiments. Perhaps the watershed year for the violent repression of these Bakuninist components in Marxism was 1850. The floodtide of "Bakuninism" in Marxism is the publication of the March letter of the Communist League's Central Committee on revolution in permanence (very soon, however, to be followed by Marx's sharp renunciation of exile politics and his fourteen-year immersion in theory and writing).

My point, then, is that Bakuninism and Marxism cannot be understood as two adversaries, each external to the other. Rather, they were doctrines which had certain communalities and overlapped at important points. Each had a living part of his enemy *in* himself. I have already indicated that, in one part, Bakunin was a Marxist, and ready to acknowledge this debt generously. Indeed, the authoritarianism of some of Bakunin's organizational schemes sometimes "went far beyond the most extreme ambitions of the dogmatic and dictatorial Marx."[11]

If Bakunin condemned the Marxists and Lassalleans for planning a despotic government over the masses by a "new and numerically very small aristocracy of real or alleged learned men," Bakunin himself, according to Max Nomad, secretly planned just such a dictatorship. His "societies were to be limited to a small number of persons, but would include, as far as possible, all men of talent, knowledge, intelligence and influence, who, while obeying a central authority would in turn exert a sort of invisible sway over the masses."[12]

The war between Marx and Bakunin was so bitter because it was something of a civil war within the soul of each. The enemy was all the more dangerous and had to be squashed without qualm because he was already within the fortress of the self. Marxism and Bakuninism then, each had an interface with the other. Each—to its own horror—could become the other under certain conditions. Each was an adaptation of elements of a deep structure that both shared; they were two different but adjacent niches in the revolutionary terrain. Critical Marxism was an evolution of Marxism toward Bakuninism that developed where a peasantry was weak. Maoism was an evolutionary adaptation of Marxism toward Bakuninism in a different historical terrain, one with a larger, more powerful peasantry.

Nowhere, however, did Marxism come to power through revolution without a measure of "regression"—i.e., a reversion to the elements of Bakuninism contained in the March circular letter. In noting affinities between Bakuninism and Critical Marxism—where the latter is either a Western Marxism or a Maoism—it is well to recall that Bakuninism itself was the outgrowth of a long, insistent development. Bakuninism was the *last* (in Marx's lifetime) of a series of emergents that had begun with Weitling and continued through Gottschalk and Willich, all of which had been opposed and repressed in Marxism. Critical Marxism, then, through insisting on its own legitimacy as a Marxism, was an extension of this developmental tendency that matured after the period of Bakuninism. Its claim to Marxist credentials was legitimate enough, considering the acute ambivalence embedded in originary Marxism and its opening to Bakuninist elements which were the successor to Left Hegelianism, utopian socialism, and anarchism.

To characterize the development of Marxism as an "evolution" is to imply that its earlier and originary forms—no less than later, more recent forms—were partly an adaptation to the changing circumstances in which it found itself, including the competitive situation of its leadership.

Marxism was thus never simply the outgrowth of earlier theories. The forms it took were never simply the result of an intellectual borrowing from the past but were also and always a response to a larger practice in the present. The problem of the forces that shaped Marxism's character thus never reduces itself to the theories it borrows or adapts, or to their truth. Anything that enabled Marxism to survive repeated failures and changed conditions, and thereby to move on, edged its way into Marxism's doctrine and political rules. To characterize Critical Marxism in particular as the product of an evolution in which it is a successor to Bakuninism is surely not to define it as identical to Bakuninism; for that, of course, would not be an evolution but mere reproduction. Finally on this point, to characterize the development of Marxism as an evolution is not at all to define it merely as responding to the "force of circumstances." It was also a process entailing a selective response mediated by human consciousness and theoretical commitment. Yet the presence of consciousness did not preclude a good measure of blindness and false consciousness in the evolutionary process through which Marxism developed. Indeed, it is the very nature of consciousness which, in part, allows and requires that very unconsciousness.

III

Against Fragmentation

8

Marx into Marxist:
The Confrontation of
Theoretical Resources

Clearly, no Marxist would ever attempt to account for the origins of Marxism primarily in terms of prior technical traditions and earlier theoretical achievements. For this would only diminish the originality of Marxism, inevitably present it as dependent on "bourgeois" science, and define its emergence as a natural if not a routine event. At the same time, however, accounting for Marxism in terms of its cultural, organizational, social, or class origins generates difficulties of its own.

One such is the embarrassment of accounting for Marxism in the work of non-proletarians and, worse still, among those who were clearly part of or close to the ruling class itself. This not only creates a rhetorical dissonance but a technical problem for Marxism. For since it stresses that "consciousness is determined by social being," how could those without a proletarian social being have produced a "working-class" theory? Moreover, any accounting of Marxism that dwelt on its social origins could make it seem that it was just another partisan ideology, rationalizing the class interest of its founders, and thus lacking intrinsic intellectual merit. It is because of *this* dilemma, because Marxism seems to be diminished by *any* accounting of its origins, that Marxists have persistently failed to produce a Marxism of Marxism.

Louis Althusser's work is in part an effort to find a way out of this impasse. His first strategy, as we shall see below, was to stress the *technical* origins of Marxism as science, rejecting any suggestion that *mature* Marxism was a class ideology, but also minimizing Marxism's dependence on bourgeois science by invoking the idea that it developed through a "leap," a *coupure épistemologique,* i.e., a discovery that went far beyond the normal bourgeois theory of the time. This is perplexing because, as Marxism is no longer held to originate in the technical traditions and languages, i.e., in the *structures,* we are thus paradoxically shunted into an *anti*-structural accounting in which the emergence of Marxism is (tacitly) *recentered* in the *person* of Marx. The account is thus essentially *humanistic,* in blatant contradiction to Althusser's militant anti-humanism.

Until recently, at any rate, Althusserians usually rejected analyses of the *social* origins of Marxism as a "sociology of knowledge." When these origins are invoked, as they are in Göran Therborn's work, they are of course riddled with the very contradictions discussed above. Thus when Therborn makes the rediscovery that Marxism was invented by *intellectuals,* he is also embarrassed about their *bourgeois* character, about the fact that Marx and Engels were indeed *bourgeois* intellectuals, and the focus is diverted from their dissonant *class* origins by identifying them as "non-bohemian," rather than as bourgeois intellectuals. But this will not cut the Gordian knot. For if those who founded Marxism were not bourgeois but merely "non-bohemian" "intellectuals," then intellectuals need not have a bourgeois class character, *and* hence need not have limiting special class interests of their own, but are "free floating intelligentsia" (in Karl Mannheim's term); free, that is, of all special "material" interests, whether derived from their own or from the class situation of others.

An effort to escape these difficulties leads Marxists to a mirror epistemology—i.e., these intellectuals—Marx and Engels—are said to have discovered the working class and its historical role because, unlike the "utopian" socialists who wrote before there was a developed working class, Marx and Engels worked after its maturation. In short, Marx and Engels presumably discovered the proletariat's role because the proletariat was there to be discovered. (Obviously, however, not everybody saw the proletariat as the agent of history and of the socialist future, even though it was there to be seen. Most embarrassingly, the working class itself did not see its *own* historical mission.)

The sociological premise here was that the social position of these intellectual discoverers need not have misshaped or interfered with their perception of history. The premise, in short, was that Marxism's founding fathers lacked class or other interests that could distort their perception. Yet this is fundamentally at variance with the strongly sociological perspective of Marx and Engels themselves. They themselves never doubted that a group's consciousness—whether true or false—was shaped by its social position and by special interests that corresponded to this.

We will find, then, that Therborn's account of Marxism's social origins among intellectuals does not refer (as Marxist logic would require) to any of the special interests and patterned experiences of intellectuals themselves. Instead, intellectuals are tacitly presented as having achieved this task simply because they were untainted, or because their own intellectual work enables them to surmount their class bias, which is to say, because they are "objective scientists." In the end, then, I conclude that Therborn's is not an analysis of Marxism's *social* origins but an Althusserian fantasy about Marxism's immaculate conception.

To grasp Althusser's understanding of the origins of Marxism one must begin with his early stress on the autonomy of science-in-general and of Marxism-as-science in particular. His emphasis on the autonomy of science was essentially an argument about the slippage of science from society.

There were two parts to their argument: (1) socialist "science" was not brought into existence simply by the needs of society or even by the needs of any class, a view consistent with the Leninist judgment that it would be necessary to bring Marxist science to the working class from the outside. (2) Not being produced by societal or class needs, science could then be produced only by events internal to the knowledge system, by science and theory. It could be produced only by a distinct, specifically theoretical practice (Althusser had by then reduced science to theorizing, and had elevated theorizing to a "practice").

Such a standpoint, however, is exactly what Marx had denounced as idealism, i.e., philosophical idealism, the accounting of ideas in terms of other ideas. The idealism of Althusser's view of science is thus more than incipient. In addition, it also contains a strong if subterranean infusion of *voluntarism*. For Althusser maintained that Marxism, like any other science, comes into existence by a *coupure épistemologique,* the latter concept being derived from his teacher, Gaston Bachelard. The ideological bondage Althusser imputed to the young Marx and the scientific attainments of the older Marx were then bridged by the *"coupure."* But this, however, only attended to the gap between the young and old Marx: it could *explain* nothing. What needed explaining was how Marx moved across that gap.

How, then, does Althusser account for the transition from the young to the old Marx? Essentially, his account entails a tacit Nietzschean-like "leap" and thus depends on some quality of the leaper. This, however, is a romanticism of science in which science is allowed to escape its own normal evolution. For someone who exalted a scientific Marxism, Althusser thus had (from the beginning) a surprising opening to voluntarism. Indeed, it is Althusser's suppressed voluntarism that is one of the grounds for his flirtation with Maoism and his apologetics for Stalinism. While declaiming in the best structural dramaturgy that "history is a process without a subject" and that it is not persons but structures that really make history, Althusser also insists on the great difference between his theory and others and repeatedly admonishes his readers: "You have a choice, you have a choice,"[1] notwithstanding that such a choice is supposedly a delusory opiate, i.e., "humanistic" humbug.

We must start at Althusser's own starting point: This centers on (1) his effort to establish that Marxism is a science; (2) his contrary effort to set off this Marxist science from non-science, i.e., from "ideology," including the ideology of the young, "anthropological" Marx who still focused on alienation; and (3) his effort to connect the young and older Marxes by an alleged *coupure épistemologique*.

Initially, this rupture in Marx's writing was held to have occurred in 1845, but it soon became altogether clear that Marx's early concerns with alienation continued into his *Grundrisse* studies for *Capital* which were started in 1857 (the same year in fact that Marx returned to the study of Hegel's *Logic*), as well as continuing into *Capital* itself. Criticism finally drove Althusser to the desperate position of contending that Hegelian influences on Marx had finally disappeared only in 1875, in his *Critique of the Gotha Program,* and in 1882, in Marx's notes on Wagner's "Lehrbuch." Since Marx died a year later, it has of course been observed that Marx managed to remain "young" for most of his life.

Althusser now admits he was mistaken in having held that, after 1845, alienation disappeared from Marx's work. But Althusser's is no abject surrender. He notes, for example, that two of the works in which alienation did appear after that, *The German Ideology* and the *Grundrisse,* had never actually been published by Marx and Engels but were published only posthumously. While this is true, it has also been observed that even though Marx himself did not publish Volumes II and III of *Capital,* Althusser never doubts that *they* constitute authentic Marxism. In any event, Althusser now acknowledges that alienation appears in Volume I of *Capital.* While he now holds that the differences between the younger and older Marx are not as radical as he had earlier maintained, Althusser nonetheless continues to insist—and I believe correctly—that there was a substantial shift in Marx's focus after the 1844 manuscripts which centered on "the human essence," or alienation, and alienated labor and that, with the different focus of *The German Ideology,* "something new and unprecedented appears in Marx's work."[2] Specifically, concepts such as forces and relations of production, social classes, class ideologies, and class struggles now become central. Even this more attenuated claim has been contested, however, and it has been

pointed out (for example, by John Lewis) that even in the 1844 manuscripts the concepts of political economy had already appeared. Althusser replies that, at that time, Marx had not yet made these concepts his
own and only gave them substantially different interpretations than they
had received in classical political economy. Nonetheless, the claim for
the differentiation of the concepts of Marx's own political economy from
classical political economy is never given convincing development.

Marx's concept of production forces, or powers, *Produktivkrafte*, is
simply his translation into German of a term used by the English political economists, to whom it was at least important enough to have found
its way into the subtitle of Adam Smith's *Wealth of Nations: "Of the
Causes of the Improvement of the Productive Powers of Labour. . . ."*
The continuity between Marx's *vocabulary* of political economy and that
of classical political economy is substantial. And previously, Henri Saint-
Simon and the Saint-Simonians, Bazard and Enfantin, had already
formulated the concepts of social class and class conflict, as well as fully
articulated the idea of a correlation between ideological systems and
social classes. This is not to deprecate the creative originality of Marx's
own formulating; but it is difficult to accept Althusser's exaggeration of
its *dis*continuity. Although Marx's is a work of major originality, it is
simply an ahistorical mystification to speak of it as "a theoretical and
political event unprecedented in human history."[3]

Continuity and Creativity in Marx

Marx's contribution was possible only because—as Lenin himself noted—
of the prior work of the Saint-Simonians and other French utopian socialists, the English political economists, and German philosophical
idealism. Althusser's view of Marx's originality actually diminishes it by
reducing Marx to a species of political economist. Above all, Althusser
really has no grasp of the *sources* of Marx's intellectual creativity; indeed,
it is because he has no theory of intellectual creativity that he is forced
into a reliance on the mystifying and romantic notion of a *coupure*.

In this respect Lenin's view of Marx's grounding is much more nearly
accurate. Lenin did see the *multiplicity* of Marx's sources in English
political economy, French utopian socialism, and German philosophy. It
is precisely this conjunction of multiple traditions and their mutual confrontation and confluence *within Marx*, that grounds his originality.
Marx begins with the tradition of German idealism and moves increasingly into the tradition of English political economy; in this respect,
Althusser is correct. Political economy concentrates Marx's and Engel's
attention (together and independently) on the importance of productive

forces. But Marx does not make this concept "his own" simply by relating it to other technical concepts already developed within English political economy. Indeed, had that been his direction, he would have been assimilated indistinguishably into political economy. Rather, and as Göran Therborn notes, Marx develops the concept of the forces of production uniquely because he moves *outside* of political economy and links it with his critique of German philosophical idealism: "It [forces of production] plays a part in a polemic against idealist theories that see society as constituted by a certain 'spirit' or culture."[4] The forces (and relations) of production become the materialist alternative to the *Geist,* as the driving force of evolution. They serve as an accounting for consciousness, or *Geist* itself, which is now seen to rest (as Marx and Engels remark in *The German Ideology*) "on the productive potency of men conditioned by a definite development of their productive forces and of the intercourse corresponding to these. . . ."

Put another way, Marx's opposition to German idealism centered on the *autonomy* it had imputed to the self-developing Idea. At the purely philosophical level, Marx often proceeds by inverting idealism, holding that it is not consciousness that determines social being, but social being that determines consciousness. But on this purely philosophical level, "social being" is an empty, formal abstraction; it is given substance only when "interpreted" in the framework of political economy, where it becomes the *forces and relations of production*—the "infrastructure." In thus linking philosophy and political economy, Marx is enabled to use each to *contextualize* the other, and it is precisely this new contextualization that uniquely transforms each of them. The forces and the relations of production then become the basis of an interpretation and critique of the dualistic sociology—centered on the civil society/state relationship—in Hegel's philosophy. The philosophical context situates the forces of production so that it is not only significant for the "wealth of nations" but is now also critical for their system of *ideas,* consciousness, or culture.

The "forces of production" are thus not only newly interpreted by their new conjuncture with consciousness or ideas; they are also recontextualized by a new conjuncture with the relations of production, most especially with *property* institutions, of central concern to the Saint-Simonians. (The Saint-Simonian influence on Marx had begun as early as his acquaintance in Trier with the Baron von Westphalen, later to become his father-in-law; with the Trier teacher Ludwig Gall, a Saint-Simonian publicist; and with Eduard Gans, Hegel's successor at the University of Berlin whose lectures Marx attended.)

In the eighth session of the exposition of the doctrines of Saint-Simon, dealing with theories of property, the Saint-Simonians note that the elimination of the privileges of birth had been all but completed, with the exception of property: "This heritage of our fathers is surrounded by an aura of respect. It is the forbidden ground upon which even the hothead cannot tread." Reactionary and enlightened factions alike, complained the Saint-Simonians, have "a truly religious susceptibility" for the rights of property. The moderates had focused on the importance of science, technology, and the advance of industry, while the radicals had centered on the quest for equality. But the Saint-Simonians, while giving special attention to the importance of modern technology and science for industry, linked this with *property* rather than equality and, indeed, rejected "dreams of equality." Saint-Simonianism much like Marxism centered its policies on the reconstitution of property, not on the institution of equality. In this vein, the *Communist Manifesto* plainly asserted that "the theory of the Communists may be summed up in a single sentence: abolition of private property."

It needs to be noted, however, that a decisive step toward Marxism had already been taken by the Saint-Simonians when they linked the new industrial technology (the forces of production) with the new *property* system, i.e., the *relations* of production. In grounding himself in Saint-Simonianism, Marx could thus make problematic what the political economists had taken as given, namely, the *property* question; in grounding himself in political economy, Marx secured a tradition in which to analyze the production process in dense technical detail.

The Saint-Simonians, however, had already gone beyond the mutually contextualizing linkage of technology and property (i.e., forces and relations of production). They had, in addition, plainly asserted (in contrast to the common sense of the contemporary bourgeois) that this relationship between the forces and relations of production was not only mutually supportive but that property relations sometimes *blocked* the new technology. Indeed, the fundamental Saint-Simonian concern was with the private *inheritance* of property precisely because they believed that this permitted incompetents to inherit and mismanage a societal resource, the forces of production.

The Saint-Simonians, then, saw the link between the new technology and bourgeois property as a *problem* because the property system might block technological development. Marx was later to develop this, in his Introduction to *A Contribution to the Critique of Political Economy*, as the "contradiction" between the forces and relations of production, which as he and Engels had earlier noted in *The German Ideology*, was the very motor of historical development. Marx's conception of the contradiction between the forces and relations of production was thus prepared by the Saint-Simonian critique of property as existing "by right of birth and not by right of ability." Marx learns from the Saint-Simonians that private property in the forces of production may be socially irrational. Marxism thus took it as a *given* that, with socialism, private inheritance of the forces of production will end, although it is not merely efficiency that Marx aims to protect in eliminating private inheritance. That property was the foundation of the social order was indeed the common assumption of respectable bourgeois political economy; that private property was an *irrational limit* on the new forces of production, which it itself had unleashed, is Marx's decisive inheritance from the Saint-Simonians.

The Saint-Simonians made sociologically tangible, at the level of concrete class and historical analysis, the Hegelian philosophy of contradiction. In part, therefore, Marx's Saint-Simonianism and Hegelianism were consistent with one another, even if at different levels of generality. Hegel could provide conflict-sensitive change-oriented elements as philosophical foundations for Saint-Simonianism, as Saint-Simon provided a conflict sociology consistent with an Hegelian philosophy of contradiction. Actually, however, even this *conjunction* between Hegel and Saint-Simon did not have to be developed by Marx from the beginning; *this, too, was part of his inheritance,* being transmitted through his teacher, Eduard Gans, who had already begun that synthesis.

Correspondingly, Hegel's philosophy had already been linked to political economy by Hegel himself. The two could be intergrated because Hegel was, of all German philosophers of his period, the most fully alert to political economy, as Georg Lukács's study *The Young Hegel* demonstrates. Unlike Schelling, who focused on the aesthetic, and Kant, who accented the importance of play, Hegel stressed *labor*. While Hegel's views were consistent with classical political economy's own judgment on labor as the source of economic value, he ultimately advanced to a larger conception of labor's role in transforming both nature and man himself.

Marx's own understanding of the critical importance of labor was largely developed under Hegel's influence. Indeed, Nicholas Lobkowicz is essentially correct in holding that "almost every thing which Marx says about labour can be traced back to Hegel."[5] Marx never repudiated Hegel's doctrine of labor, that is, never denied the *positive* functions Hegel attributed to labor, although he did criticize him for focusing primarily on labor's positive side and neglecting its negative side.

It was through labor, said Marx echoing Hegel, that man appropriated nature. For Hegel, too, labor was the means through which men asserted themselves as proper subjects over the world of objects, fulfilling their inherent destiny as Subjects. For Hegel, also, labor mediated between men's needs and the materials that could satisfy these needs; labor enabled men to transcend the merely biological kingdom, taught men discipline and self-control, and induced them into a civilizing co-operation with one another. For Hegel as for Marx, then, labor is not simply a way of satisfying men's biological needs but of removing a limit on their personhood and achieving their true human character; through labor man does not only satisfy his needs but also *transforms* them and with this himself. Hegel holds that labor teaches men to control their passions and to defer the gratification of appetites, thus building character and morality. In large part, Hegel's was a secularized "gospel of labor."

It is not from political economy but from Hegel that Marx first comes to focus upon the instruments of labor, tools and machines, "which the labourer interposes between himself and the subject of his labour," and on the role of labor in "the appropriation of nature by the individual within and through a definite form of society. . . . In production, men act not only on nature but also on one another. They produce only by co-operating in a certain way and mutually exchanging their activities."[6]

It is on the basis of this complex interaction between English political economy and Hegel's secularized gospel of (the humanizing function of) labor, in which Hegel had moved to historicize elements of English political economy as part of a cryptic theory of human evolution, that Marx radicalizes classical political economy. It is precisely because political economy is already cryptically embodied *in* Hegel that the young Hegelian, Marx, resonates to the political economy that he later encounters and can quickly accept its importance. Hegel had in effect prepared Marx for political economy. It is because political economy has already been invisibly transmitted to him via his Hegel studies, and because of the central focus on labor in Hegel, that Marx can commit himself to and redefine the political economy he encounters.

Classical political economy had been centered on the *market* and on the exchange of commodities; Marx, however, redirected it into a theory of *production* centered on labor, on the relation between workers and capital, in particular, and on the extraction of surplus value from workers by capitalists. Maurice Dobb formulates this transition with admirable succinctness:

> The progress and maturing of Marx's thought, indeed, lay in the direction of deepening it in a sense quite opposite to the development of "bourgeois economics" with its increasing formalisation of purely quantitative market relations and linkages. Marx started, indeed, from concepts such as supply and demand, competition and the market. . . . In the

course of criticising and explaining these concepts—of revealing the *essence* behind the phenomenal *appearance* of market relations, as he frequently put it—he was led progressively into the examination of production and of production relations (division of labour in general terms initially, and then to the specific forms assumed by the division of labour under capitalism) and of the social and class roots of a society dominated by exploitation and the pursuit of surplus value.[7]

This transition, from market relations to production relations, is in part the result of Marx's fusion of the Hegelian philosophy of *labor* with classical political economy. Hegel's philosophy also contextualized political economy by indicating the historically limited character of societies (and thus of the laws of capitalism formulated by political economy), allowing for the transcendence of capitalism as a transient stage in human development. It did this, however, without simply accepting the relativism of an individuating historicism focused only on the unique character of each different society.

The discussion above of the origins of Marx's work focuses on its roots in three different intellectual traditions, two of them "technical"—political economy and German philosophy—and the latter even fully grounded in an established academic culture. Even the critical reworking of Hegelianism by Marx's youthful associates, namely, the Young or Left Hegelians, had its origins in university teaching and literature and in student reaction to it, organized, for example, in Berlin's "Doctors' Club." This certainly speaks to the question of the continuities in Marxism.

Several points may now be summarized, which focus on the problem of continuity and creativity in Marx:

(1) Marx's creativity is indeed grounded in his mastery of several established, highly developed, intellectual traditions; one cannot imagine Marxism without them. (2) This mastery, however, did not simply entail a knowledge of their technical details but a *critical* assimilation of them; this, in its turn, is based partly on Marx's capacity to see each of the three from the standpoint of the other two. Each tradition provided a perspective that enabled him to be "outside" of the other two, to see their *limits* or *boundaries,* and to see certain potential values in them not readily visible to ordinary participants normally submerged in each specialized tradition. (3) By reason of his *simultaneous* command of these multiple traditions, Marx is not captured and not limited by the paradigm of scholarship "normal" to each tradition; he can therefore adopt a critical position with respect to the basic paradigms of each of the traditions. (4) Central to Marx's creativity, then, is his unconven-

tional *relationship* to three established intellectual traditions, his sheer possession of *multiple* intellectual traditions and their simultaneous *conjunction* within his own outlook. Marx, then, does not "become Marx," simply by virtue—as Althusser seems to think—of his movement *from* philosophy *to* political economy, but only because, in moving to the latter, he does not surrender but *takes his philosophical perspective with him.* (5) The simultaneous presence of multiple intellectual traditions now constituted a new symbolic context, a *re-*contextualization, of each of the constituent traditions, endowing each with a changed interpretation and novel meaning. The mystery of Marx's genius, thus, is dissolved by an analysis of (a) the well-developed intellectual traditions which he assimilated critically and commanded in technical detail, (b) by noting their multiple simultaneity and the (c) resultant mutually recontextualizing effect on each component part, and (d) the partial syntheses that had preceded Marx. Note that all this is possible only because these traditions are not "decentered" but are centered within and by Marx. (6) It is especially noteworthy that the process of establishing a new conjuncture of intellectual elements, a new symbolic system, does not begin with Marx confronting *atomized* elements. Rather, he already has available to him *partial* syntheses—prefabricated links—so that his own system is a larger synthesis of smaller syntheses: for example, of the Saint-Simonians' synthesis of property with the new technology or forces of production; or the partial synthesis of Saint-Simonian concerns with the Hegelian philosophy formulated by Eduard Gans, a favorite of the young men of Marx's *Doktorsklub.*

Marxism, then, scarcely comes into being simply with one *coupure,* or with the singular leap of a great genius. It comprised a synthesis of smaller prefabricated syntheses, rather than of uninterpreted raw materials or intellectual traditions. There was, in short, an ongoing *vector* of *syntheses* in which Marx's work was totally immersed, with which it was fully continuous, without which it would have been impossible, of which it was a culmination.

I am now in a better position to formulate my own theoretical position concerning some of the *sources* of Marx's creativity and, in particular to explain how it (or similar intellectual *coupures,* leaps, or novelties) comes about. We are now able to de-mystify the notion of the *coupure épistemologique,* to specify certain of the conditions under which it can occur, which be it noted, is not the same as denying all discontinuity. It is not our intent to denigrate Marx's own great creativity, but to *account* for it; the object here is not to deny "genius," but to contribute to a sociology of genius.

A Boundary-Transgression Theory of Creativity

Intellectual creativity predicates *paradigm-distancing:* i.e., the ability to adopt a position apart from, outside of, or in critique of the established paradigms of normal science or scholarship. Persons may indeed be "competent" within such a paradigm; "normal" scientists are committed to *technical* interests and to the solution of technical "puzzles" which, in Thomas Kuhn's important (if tacit) critique of science, are definable as cases of patient, puzzle-solving work within the established paradigm(s) of a science. The normal scientist's competence and originality are *within* a paradigm and involve the *application* of the principles, explicit or tacit, already exhibited by the paradigm.

"Creativity," as distinct from routine competence, implies valuable novelties, however, that do not limit themselves to exploring the space within a paradigm, or extending it to new fields. Creativity entails paradigm-distancing—a capacity to discern and a willingness to transcend paradigm boundaries. The smaller forms of creativity taking place *within* paradigm boundaries are forms of "competence"; the major forms of creativity taking place *beyond* these boundaries, sometimes characterized as works of "genius," involve boundary *transgressions.*

The fundamental source of major intellectual creativity, with its seeming *"coupure,"* entails an ability to *cross the boundaries* of an intellectual tradition and thus to escape control by a single perspective. This is facilitated by involvement in multiple traditions. The structure of creativity entails (1) a multilinguality in which (2) each of the different languages used is *conventionally* assigned a distinct function in a linguistic specialization or intellectual division of labor, and where (3) this division of labor has been "violated," i.e., where there has been an *unconventional* switching from one language to another and, (4) finally, where the multiplicity of languages is given a firm *hierarchical* ordering.

The creative theorist is thus more likely to be bilingual or multilingual—or bi- or multi-theoretical—which implies an ability to switch languages or theories. It implies a skill at "translating" back and forth between them, and thus an ability to see things, hitherto visible only within one of the languages, from the perspective of another *which had not conventionally been used for that purpose.* It is such an unconventional perspective—in Kenneth Burke's terms, a "perspective by incongruity"—that is systematically generative of intellectual novelty and creativity.

Major forms of creativity thus entail a kind of intellectual *deviance.* It is a break from some tradition made possible by a multilinguality that facilitates an incongruous perspective and distances the theorist from the paradigms dominant within an intellectual specialization. Major creativity, then, involves bi- (or multi-) linguality. The more creative speaker-theorist knows several distinct languages or theoretical traditions, is able to bring them into *interaction* with one another, to switch and to *translate* from one to another, in dealing with his problematic topic, thereby violating the conventional intellectual division of labor which has usually kept them separate. For example, "labor" may be seen as the source of value within the framework of political economy, but also as the source of human development, as in the master-bondsman dialectic of Hegel's philosophy. The normal, paradigm-limited political economist was not likely to see labor as the ironic resolution of a contest in which the loser, forced to labor by the victor, so deepens and develops himself that, in time, his human development exceeds his master's. Yet for those knowing both languages, "labor" becomes *one* bridge (among others) by which the theorist can escape the limits of one tradition and move across to the other, thereby developing a perspective on elements within it that are unexpected to those remaining encased within its traditional boundaries. Creativity, then, entails *linguistic boundary transgression*.

It is in these terms that the familiar *phenomenology* of "genius" may be understood. The phenomenology of genius centers on the "black box effect" which amounts to this: a problem, and materials bearing on it, are presented to several problem-solvers. In short, a number of theorists seems to be working on a similar problem with seemingly similar resources, but one (or a few) of them produces a novel solution, i.e., a *coupure* or *rupture*. How can this be explained? Why is it that, although the *input* to a variety of thinkers was the "same," their *output* varied so considerably? Since something special has happened *inside* the thinker, and since what this is is not visible to the outside observer, it is chalked up to the theorist's special gift, his unique talents, his "genius"—that is, his exceptional personal qualities. The imputation of "genius" is an effort to account for a seeming disparity between a successful theorist's input and his output, to throw light on the "black box." But this simply explains the novel solution in terms of the thinker's imputedly special ability to construct special solutions, without specifying *how* that special ability is itself *produced*.

From my own standpoint, what is crucial to the production of a *coupure*—now definable as, "ordinary input, extraordinary output"—is that it does not, properly speaking, depend upon events internal to a creative person but rather on his critical assimilation of and unusual relation to established intellectual traditions, upon his access to *multiple* traditions, as well as his capacity to *switch* or translate from one to another. The reason that the extraordinary output or novel solution was possible was that the thinker was not limited to the language or theory conventionally used in dealing with his problem; indeed, he may have used a tradition that was forbidden. In short, creativity is often a function of cognitive deviance—because it uses resources that one is *not supposed to use* in the traditional division of intellectual labor. Creativity, in short, entails cultural rebellion. Thus the novelty of a solution often depends upon the novelty of the *resources* brought to bear on the problem. It only *seems* as if all were using the *same* resources, when in fact some had mobilized extraordinary resources.

Moreover, since some of the resources used may be *improper,* the forbidden tradition actually employed may be hidden, repressed, or glossed over, particularly when the new solution is communicated to members of an intellectual community who would regard its use as improper. For example: a philosopher who wants to communicate his novel analysis of, say, surplus value to a group of normal, "scientific" political economists will not talk about "alienation"; his use of philosophy might make his work suspect. It is this motivated concealment of the boundary transgression that makes it difficult for outsiders to notice the role of a novel resource in producing a novel, "creative" solution, thus producing the characteristic "black box" dramaturgy of "genius."

The presence of an unconventional tradition may also be invisible because the conventional specialist simply does not *expect* it to be present. Not expecting it to be there, he will "normalize" his perception of the situation; he will see but not notice the alien element. In both cases, however, there is an invisibility of some intellectual resources actually used. The observer is thus led to a mistaken accounting for the novel solution, attributing it only to a special personal quality within the person. The solution offered here, to the problem of the *coupure,* then, has the advantage of, on the one side, offering an account of the production of sharply novel solutions and, on the other, of accounting for the common, everyday *accounting* of valuable novelties.

At the beginning of these remarks, I urged that it was not only multilinguality that was conducive to creativity but a specific ordering of that multilinguality, namely, that the arrangement of the several languages must be firmly *hierarchical* or "anchored." Not all of the traditions can be equally important; there must be one around which the theorist's work pivots. Given an ambiguous hierarchy or an equality of traditions, within one speaker, the results may be a wavering eclecticism: i.e., seeing diverse sides of a problem but not reintegrating them into a coherent structure. Eclecticism is a situation of multilinguality in which there is no resolution concerning which of the languages will be central. Unless multiple languages, traditions, or theories are focused simultaneously on one region there will not be "incongruity of perspective," generative of sharp creativity; unless these multiple traditions are anchored or structured *hierarchically,* the resultant creativity is limited by the disintegrative tendency of eclecticism. One of the common ways in which such hierarchical ordering occurs is when the several languages spoken are not on the same level of *generality,* so that there is a more general and abstract language in which it is possible to speak about the less general and abstract ones; in other words, where one of the several languages is a *meta*-language.

A specific condition under which this occurs is where one of the languages is a *philosophy.* It is possible to speak about the internal structure of political economy in the language of philosophy; but what can be said about the internal character of a philosophy from the standpoint of a technical political economy is very limited indeed. The original period of great intellectual ferment and creativity in the social sciences, when their paradigms were being established, was characterized precisely by that specific type of multilinguality, that is, where one of the several (technical) languages spoken is a philosophy.

This is why the "classical" works within a social science (a social theory) tradition are often written by those who are also grounded in philosophy. To be a "technician" or a "professional" is to be *one no longer in command of a philosophical language.* "Professionals" are those whose more limited forms of creativity are "competencies" in applying already established principles to areas in which they have not yet been applied, and whose self-defensive occupational ideology is: continuity, cumulation, "adding another brick to the wall of science."

From this standpoint, then, Marx's grounding in German philosophy was of decisive importance for his own creativity and, far from having been a language that Marx spoke but gave up, that is, far from being important only as an archaic survival, his philosophy was the intellectual foundation of all that followed, enabling him to surmount the weaknesses of eclecticism.

Rather than being an unheralded revolution in theory, then, Marxism was a significant variation of a cognitive structure commonly employed for the historical analysis of society in the eighteenth and nineteenth centuries. Here I want to turn directly to the nature of the more fundamental modal on which Marx's contributions were variations, specifying its character, while exhibiting Marx's relationship to it. In effect, the discussion here will focus on what may properly be called the "deep structure" of Marxism, i.e., the basic language of which it itself is only a dialect.

This deep structure, i.e., the *communalities* of this cognitive structure, has been well formulated by Ronald L. Meek.[8] To collate his remarks at several points:

> The essential idea of the theory is that societies undergo *development* through successive *stages* based on different *modes of subsistence*. The important point is that the stages should be based on different *modes of subsistence,* rather than on (for example) different modes of political organisation.[9] [Suggesting that the Scotch scholar John Millar was the first to have "ever used a materialist conception of history,"[10] Meek quotes from Millar's lectures:] "The first object of mankind is to produce subsistence . . . their next aim is to defend their persons and their acquisitions against the attacks of one another . . . the more inconsiderable the possessions of any people, their political regulations will be the more simple. And the more opulent a nation becomes, its government ought to be the more complicated. Property is at the same time the principal source of authority, so that the opulence of a people not only makes them stand in need of much regulation, but enables them to establish it. By tracing the progress of wealth we may expect to discover the progress of Government. I shall take notice of 4 great stages in the acquisition of property. 1. Hunters and Fishers, or mere Savages . . . 2. Shepards . . . 3. Husbandmen . . . 4. Commercial people[11] . . . the dispositions and behavior of man are liable to be influenced by the circumstances in which he is placed."[12] [Meek holds that] By 1780, indeed, Millar's master principle was beginning to appear as something very like orthodoxy.[13]

If the mode of subsistence is decisive for the evolution of society, Meek also notes that it was not long in becoming evident that "commerce," although obviously of the first importance, was not a mode of subsistence in the same sense as agriculture or pasturage. It is in part as a response to this problem that Marx moves away from formulating the "master principle" as a mode of *subsistence* and (under Hegelian influence) moves toward conceptualizing it as the "mode of production" which includes and distinguishes between the *forces* of production and the *relations* of production. That these concepts are so basic to Marxism, but are given little systematic and explicit specification, is in part (but in part only) due to their involvement in what was then a long familiar deep structure. It is obvious, too, that the work of Saint-Simon and the Saint-Simonians, including Auguste Comte, was also grounded in the same deep structure, which "took the form of a theory of development, embodying the idea of some kind of 'natural' or 'normal' movement through a succession of different modes of subsistence."[14]

While Meek is exceptional in the incisiveness with which he specifies the *general analytical* characteristics of the materialist deep structure on which Marxism was grounded, others had earlier made a similar point concerning the continuity of Marx's historical materialism with that of previous thinkers. Not least of these was Roberto Michels in his essay "The Origins of Economic Determinism and Social Class Theories,"[15] which seeks to demonstrate that "historical materialism . . . has never been the monopoly of Marxism."[16] Michels develops his thesis with ready examples:

> that Ferguson declared in 1776 "that any kind of economic occupation produces in a man a special mentality and that each single trade 'requires different talents and inspires different sentiments'." . . . James Harrington (1611-1677) affirmed the existence of a causal connection between the economic conditions of a country and its political constitution, in the sense of a dependence of one on the other. . . . Early in the nineteenth century, Guiseppe Pecchio . . . advanced the theory of the absolute supremacy of the economy over other manifestations of life in the political field and in literature . . . the Neapolitan . . . Gaetano Filangieri . . . said in 1780: "Observe the state of all nations, read the great book of societies; you will find them divided into two irreconcilable parties: the owners and the non-owners or hirelings." . . . [I]n the period between 1830 and 1840, some writers devoted themselves to writing histories of the proletariat, among them a member of the French Parliament, Robert du Var and the German, Bensen . . . Adolphe de Cassagnac wrote in 1837 his *Histoire des classes ouvrières et des classes bourgeoises* . . . an attempt to trace the history of the proletarian class [and] George Wilhelm Raumer recognized in 1854 the "necessity to understand that political events are the consequence of changes in the methods of production."

Meek's and Michel's observations of the general model of social materialism, which Marxism embodies and which it develops consisted of the following elements:

The Deep Structure of Marxism

1. That societies were developing, in some ways cumulatively and progressively;
2. That this development passes through different stages which succeed one another;
3. That this development depends upon the mode of subsistence;
4. That each different stage has a distinct mode of subsistence;
5. That movement into a new stage does not derive from or depend on the policies of political leaders but is a "natural" evolution;
6. That, on the contrary, politics, government, and the state vary with the mode of subsistence and the level of wealth in the society;

7. That the sentiments, ideas, behavior (indeed, some of the diseases) of men are structured and constrained by the economic circumstances in which they find themselves.

The deep structure outlined above expressed itself in terms of a dichotomous distinction between "civil society" and the "state," widely used in the eighteenth century. This was a linguistic expression of the deep structure; i.e., it was the most important manner in which the deep structure was recovered and spoken in ordinary language. The particular formulation of this distinction between Civil Society and the State which most directly influenced Marx was Hegel's, especially as expressed in the latter's *Philosophy of Right*. For Hegel, civil society was the sphere of the concrete person, whose relations with other concrete persons take the contradictory form of competing private egoisms and of a simultaneous mutual interdependence; pursuing their own particular interests through work, men simultaneously contribute to the satisfaction of others' needs.[17] This mutual gratification is not the end being pursued but is, rather, an *unintended* consequence of the private struggle each carries on against all, and is in tension with the universal interests of the state. ". . . [T]he creation of civil society is the achievement of the modern world. . . . In civil society each member is his own end, everything else is nothing to him . . . others are means to the end of the particular member. . . ."[18]

In Hegel's version, the sphere of civil society (the *burgerliche Gesell-schaft*) is the sphere of the private, the egoistic, and the particularistic; the state is the sphere of the public, the altruistic, and the universalistic. If civil society was riven, the state was the sphere of the communal; if civil society centered on interests, the state was an ethical ideal. In this dichotomous structure, civil society as the sphere of private interests is also the sphere of the *economic,* while the state is the region of the *political*. It remains only to be added that, for Hegel, the state was the ideal, higher realm, civil society being the lower.

Implicit within this dichotomy there is then an hierarchical arrangement of the spheres: civil society is the infrastructure, the "base," i.e., the *lower* on which the state is a superstructure, a superior plane that stands over civil society. What Marx does is to *transvalue* this. *At one level,* Marx maintains the hierarchical arrangement, but assigns different power and value to the different spheres, making the base into the foundation, the *grounding,* which becomes that on which the superstructure *depends;* and transforming the superstructure into a recipient of influences so that rather than being the source of influence, it is now only the topmost *appearance.* Marx accepted the hierarchical topography; but he had redefined the economic bottom rail so that it was no longer the *lowest* but the *first* step: As Engels put it, "the state—the political order is the subordinate, and civil society—the realm of economic relations—the decisive element."[19]

"My inquiry [wrote Marx] led me to the conclusion that neither legal relations nor political forms could be comprehended whether by themselves or on the basis of the so-called development of the human mind, but that on the contrary, they originate in the material conditions of life, the totality of which Hegel, following the example of English and French thinkers of the eighteenth century, embraces within the term 'civil society'; that the anatomy of this civil society, however, has to be sought in political economy."[20]

Plainly then, and on Marx's own testimony, his fundamental topography of infra- and super-structures—i.e., economy vs. state/ideology—is a development of the familiar dichotomy, civil society–state, as this was formulated by Hegel, who in turn had derived it from the eighteenth-century English and French theorists who established the deep structure of historical analysis from which Marxism emerged and differentiated itself.

That deep structure was fully visible in Marx and Engels's *Communist Manifesto,* whose "fundamental proposition" Engels himself expressly characterizes in this way: ". . . in every historical epoch, the prevailing mode of economic production and exchange, and the social organization necessarily following from it, form the basis upon which is built up, and from which alone can be explained, the political and intellectual history of that epoch."[21]

There is, then, both *continuity and discontinuity* in Marxism's relation to the dichotomy civil society–state, which it inherits from Hegel. Marxism retains the developmental and hierarchical aspects of Hegel, but rejects its *Geistliche, idealistic* character as Marx stands Hegel "on his feet" again. Thus the elements remain separated as they had been, i.e., they remain in the old spaces, together with the other things with which they had formerly been associated, and apart from others with which they were contrasted. What had been changed was the meaning of the spaces or locations. The bottom (economics), formerly the lowly and base, was now transvalued and made the "basic" grounding; the upper (politics, state, ideologies), formerly the high and superior, was now the superficial and dependent.

In effect, Marx had used the Hegelian version of the dichotomy civil society–state to tunnel his way back to the deep structure of materialist analysis as it had developed in the West. Marx had moved the Hegelian formulation back in the direction of the Western deep structure, *naturalizing* and de-spiritualizing it, but retaining its developmental and hierarchical character. Marx had thus naturalized the Hegelian structure of analysis by endorsing the more Western and materialist versions of the deep structure as the normal model.

The shift that Marx makes here is a radical one only relative to Hegel's idealism; but it is considerably less radical *relative to the Western materialist deep structure of social analysis.*

In examining how Marx made that shift, my focus here on the boundary transgression theory of creativity has rested largely on the special conjuncture of "internal" intellectual and technical traditions centering in Marx. This focus, however, is not incompatible with the influence of certain "external" social influences,[22] as we have seen.

APPENDIX: ON CREATIVITY
KAREN G. LUCAS

The analysis of creativity and of the roots of intellectual *coupures* in Chapter 8 developed out of a study of Marx's innovative synthesis of several traditions. Our search for the sources of the extraordinary creativity of Marx's contributions lead us to a general sociology of genuis. This is a rather different outcome from what might have been expected had we asked the abstract question: What are the origins of creativity? Having now developed a theory of creativity based in the specific Marxist context, we might do well to examine some other views of creativity, both traditional and current—some from psychology, others from philosophy, none firmly established as authoritative—which touch in various ways on our theory of creativity.

The first problem addressed by theorists of creativity is usually: What is the nature of the creative work?, What characteristics must an art work or scientific achievement have in order to be creative?. George Kneller, in his *The Art and Science of Creativity*,[23] argues that any definition of creativity "must include the essential element of novelty" (p. 3), adding that "creative novelty springs largely from the rearrangement of existing knowledge—a rearrangement that is itself an addition to knowledge." But as he stresses, "Novelty alone, however, does not make an act or an idea creative; *relevance* is also a factor. Since the creative act is a response to a particular situation, it must solve, or in some way clarify, the situation that has caused it to arise" (p. 6). In other words, the fact that an act results in something strange or unusual is not enough to qualify the act as creative, but rather it must have some *effect,* teach us something, show us something, tell us something, must be capable of changing the ways we think or behave.

Thus some theorists hold that creativity is a particular kind of problem-solving—one in which the problem is especially difficult and the solution is unexpected. While this should not be taken to exhaust the field of creativity, it certainly is in accord with our description of Marx's creative work. Of course not all theorists agree that creativity is a form of problem-solving. Among psychologists, psychoanalysts in particular argue against the conception of creativity as problem-solving on the grounds that while actual problem-solving is a fully conscious process, creative thinking is shaped strongly by unconscious or preconscious processes. If there is error here, one is inclined to fault psychoanalysts not so much for claiming unconscious influence on creative efforts, as for overlooking unconscious influence on dull and routine problem-solving as well. If this is the case, the presence or absence of unconscious activity can obviously not be used to discriminate creative from routine efforts.

Actually only a thin line separates the definition of a creative work from that of a creative person. It is commonly held that the creative person must have several different mental abilities. "These include the ability to change one's approach to a problem, to produce ideas that are both relevant and unusual, to see beyond the immediate situation, and to redefine the problem or some aspect of it" (p. 13). The boundary transgression theory of creativity stresses particularly the ability to see a problem regarded as the "property" of one discipline in the light of one or more other disciplines.

Since ancient times it has been repeatedly suggested that the creator has no special abilities of his own, but rather is divinely inspired, that when a person does something creative it is not really his or her action, but that of a "higher being." Thus a writer may feel that the creative output was actually designed by some muse, some spirit which merely used him as a tool for the physical production of the creative idea. Plato holds this view in the *Ion*, saying it is actually God who expresses himself when a mortal seems to have done some creative work. Another ancient and recurring theory of the creator's nature is that the creative person is insane, that the creative achievement is something that a normal, adjusted, non-mad person could not or would not have executed. Perhaps the more modern philosophical theory of creativity as a nonrational intuitive process can be traced back to this creativity-is-madness conception. In addition to the divine inspiration view he advanced in the *Ion*, Plato also subscribed to the madness view, saying in the *Timaeus* that "No man, when in his wits, attains prophetic truth and inspiration; but when he receives the inspired word, either his intelligence is enthralled in sleep, or he is demented by some distemper or possession."

All these views that appeal to inspiration, madness, or nondiscursive intuition for creativity's source see evidence for such appeal in the frequent statements by artists and scientists attributing the original basis for their creative achievement to some sudden "flash," "mental vision," or insight, coming seemingly from nowhere and for no reason, which, they say, provided the plan for the creative project to come. But in stressing that part of the process, which may or may not be a *necessary* part, one may tend to forget that the next part, the hard work of carrying out the plan, coping with unexpected difficulties, having the painting or symphony or biological theory fulfill the original mental image, is also crucial in achieving a creative work. Not to mention the many inspirations which turn out not to be workable at all.

Psychological descriptions of creativity are dominated by the debate between behaviorists, existentialists, and gestalt theorists that continues in psychology generally. In the nineteenth century the dominant school of psychology in England and the United States was *associationism,* which grew out of the work of John Locke. It continues to have influence today, especially on behaviorists. The basic idea here is that, faced with a problem, the thinker summons one combination of ideas after another until eventually he finds an arrangement that solves the problem. Thus, according to associationism, the more associations a person has acquired through experience, the more ideas he or she will have on hand, which will in turn result in a higher level of creative output. One of the more obvious difficulties with this theory is that while it would seem to predict increasing creativity with age, actual examination of creative works reveals that for the most part they are the prerogative of youth (though there are some important exceptions). Despite their ever growing stores of associations, most people tend to become more rigid and conventional, less experimental and open to new ideas, more socialized along narrow paths, as they age. Such discrepancies as this suggest a major fault in associationism: it is not how many experiences we have had but rather what we are able to do with them that matters most here. Nonetheless this theory does provide some insight into the creative act, which *does,* as we have said, consist of forming new combinations (associations) of ideas. In fact, the boundary transgression theory accounts for people tending to be less creative as they age. If creativity requires distancing oneself from the problem, refusing to deal with it in the prescribed terms, then as a person becomes more immersed in a given tradition, has strengthened his habits of approaching a topic in a particular way, he will find it more and more difficult to escape the limits of that tradition, to break the habits he has developed in working on problems in the past.

Unlike the atomistic theory of associationism, gestalt theory explains the creative phenomenon in terms of the larger whole, treating creative thinking as primarily a reconstruction of gestalts or patterns that are structurally deficient. Thus the creative thinker, confronted with a problematic situation, deals with that problem as a whole, and characterizes its solution as one which will restore harmony to the whole picture. As in making the gestalt switch from seeing the face of a young woman to seeing the old woman in the familiar double-aspect picture, creating a problem solution involves noticing elements that were there all along, but had been overshadowed by the prejudice of one's expectations. Gestalt theories of creativity aim more at explaining the creativity of artistic works than that of intellectual theories, but their analysis of creativity parallels ideas in the boundary transgression theory we have developed. Thus, in gestalt theory's terms, on the question of theoretical creativity, one might speak not so much of switching attention from certain lines of the puzzle to others as of switching routinely prescribed intellectual lines of thought to other approaches not previously thought related to that situation. Here the creative theorist suddenly "sees" a hitherto hidden dimension by reaching out for insight to disciplines treated as irrelevant or even forbidden by other theorists. Thus the creator not only gives us an unexpected *solution,* he recasts the original *problem* as well, finds in it aspects the rest of us missed entirely.

The Freudian psychoanalysts who see creative thinking as highly sensitive to unconscious (preconscious) processes actually hold creativity to be the result of unconscious conflict within the creator. Thus, given certain desires that conflict with consciously held values, the id produces a "solution" to that conflict, which, if acceptable to the ego, will manifest itself in creative behavior. On this analysis, a person with a highly protective ego will fail to be creative since few "solutions" offered by the id will meet the rigid specifications of the ego's scrutiny. This theory roughly anticipates ours, with, of course, the stipulation that our theory pays particular attention to the difficulties of achieving *theoretical* creativity. In psychoanalytic terms, we might say that the theorist's consciously held values are determined by his or her training in a particular tradition, which teaches that certain problems are to be dealt with in certain ways. Hence when that theorist is tempted to turn to other traditions or use methods other than those he has been indoctrinated to use, his ego will tend to suppress that temptation, to ward off the impulse to engage in the forbidden. The creative theorist is one who is able to bypass those conscious restraints. Strict Freudian theory has of course a limited vision of what kind of impulses the id might have, namely sexual-aggressive ones, whereas we are recognizing a wider range of tendencies that one is socialized to repress. For Freud, creativity is an **adult form** of childhood play, serving the same "acting-out" function of otherwise perhaps unacceptable urges of the id. This function is one of reducing tension, ending conflict. Many writers have attacked this psychoanalytic view of creativity on the grounds that such a "sublimation" theory fails to capture the significance of worthwhile accomplishment, that by reducing highly sophisticated achievement to mere by-products of primitive hostile or sexual drives, it limits rather than aids our understanding of those achievements as skillfully produced creative works. Psychologists such as Carl Rogers have attempted to meet this objection, agreeing with psychoanalysis that creativity may serve a drive-reduction function, but seeing that as only one aspect of creativity. Thus Rogers suggests that the creative act is not used as a means only but also as an end in itself. His theory takes a wider range of human drives into account, postulating not merely sexual-aggressive tendencies, but a drive to produce, to affect the world positively, to create, as well.

In our own boundary transgression theory we have not been as interested in understanding people's motives in trying to create, either as individuals or as members of a species, as we have been in determining what factors in their nature, history, and approach are responsible for their creativity. We have identified one crucial factor as the ability to step back from the problem, to see it from a variety of vantage points. One who has the skills and knowledge of several traditions, schools, or disciplines and who can apply them all, both to one another and to a given topic, is more likely to develop a creative view of a topic than is someone who keeps those perspectives compartmentalized and isolated from one another, and who uses one exclusively when addressing a given area. By bringing a tradition or field usually considered irrelevant to bear on a problem, one may highlight hitherto neglected aspects.

Arthur Koestler's theory of creativity converges with our own in interesting ways. He points out some interrelated aspects of the psychology of the creative act: "the displacement of attention to something not previously noted, which was irrelevant in the old and is relevant in the new context" and "the discovery of hidden analogies" which is a result of that change in attention.[24] Note that he views the creative person as one who gives a problem a "new context" and who thus finds elements of the problem which were previously hidden. A "Gestalt-switch" is being made here—the picture has not changed, but the viewer is seeing it in a new light.

Our boundary transgression theory refused to place creativity's burden on the creator's personal attributes. One model envisages several thinkers, all posed a certain problem and provided a common set of materials for its solution; such a model postulates that a mysterious process occurs in only a few of those thinkers, resulting in a creative solution to the problem. Our model, however, argues that the creative thinker did not use the *same* set of materials in solving the problem. Rather he was able to call upon multiple resources, to bring a number of traditions to bear on the problem. Koestler, with his notion of "bisociation," agrees with our view: creativity consists not only in special internal processes but also in the diversity of materials employed. He says the creative act is "a new synthesis of previously unconnected matrices of thought,"[25] that "The essence of discovery is that unlikely marriage of cabbages and kings—of previously unrelated frames of reference or universes of discourse—whose union will solve the previously unsolvable problems."[26] "The creative act is not an act of creation in the sense of the Old Testament. It does not create something out of nothing; it uncovers, selects, re-shuffles, combines, synthesizes already existing facts, ideas, faculties, skills."[27] Koestler too sees the importance to creative problem-solving of bringing in the conceptions of "foreign" disciplines. These allow one to go beyond the stale answers proffered by whatever discipline is routinely held to be sovereign over the problem at hand. "The Prejudices and impurities which have become incorporated into the verbal concepts of a given 'universe of discourse' cannot be undone by any amount of discourse within the frame of reference of that universe. The rules of the game, however absurd, cannot be altered by playing that game."[28] Thus, for Koestler, real progress in a field is dependent upon knowledge being brought to the field from without. "All decisive advances in the history of scientific thought can be described in terms of mental cross-fertilization between different disciplines. Some of these historic bisociations appear, even in retrospect, as surprisingly far-fetched as the combination of cabbages and kings. . . ."[29]

Just as we stress the modification of each discipline by the others in the thinker who has assimilated several, so too Koestler recognizes that "the integration of matrices is not a simple operation of adding together. It is a process of mutual interference and cross-fertilization, in the source of which both matrices are transformed in various ways and degrees. Hidden axioms, implied in the old codes, suddenly stand revealed and are subsequently dropped; the rules of the game are revised before they enter as sub-rules into the composite game. . . ."[30]

We have seen that once Marx redirects political economy from centering on market relations to production relations, by bringing philosophy to bear on "technical" problems, those issues could never again be viewed in the terms of classical political economy. Koestler recognizes such a change in possibility as one of the natural products of creativity. "When two frames of reference have become integrated into one it becomes difficult to imagine that previously they existed separately."[31]

It seems that most theorists who have seriously considered the nature of creativity see the importance of escaping conventional approaches to the problem, of conceptualizing it in nonstandard ways, of a "placing of things in new perspectives."[32] Yet many have only recognized the *internal* aspect of this, the fact that the creator is doing something different with his materials. We have shown, however, that the variety and conjunction of those materials selected from the *exterior* world is an even more crucial feature. Our theory also implies that the thinker must exercise critical ability in order to utilize such a range of intellectual traditions in working out a theoretical problem. Thus, such critical ability as the capacity to liberate oneself from any one given technical paradigm is an essential element in theoretical creativity.

One might well be tempted at this point to respond that critical ability, so important to producing creative responses to intellectual problems, is paradoxically a double-edged sword. For we all know how a "critical" mind can mercilessly destroy fledgling innovations, focusing on those unresolved difficulties which plague any theory's infancy. This suggests a contradiction: critical ability is required for creative contributions but it is also the harsh repressor of potentially creative deviation. This contradiction is only apparent, however, arising from an ambiguity in the meaning of "critical ability." In fact, it refers to two quite different attitudes or activities. The adherent of a particular school or field who uses "critical ability" to attack all creative formulations of a problem or solution which result from the temptation to take a different perspective, to use a forbidden tradition, is in fact judging those formulations *in terms of his old theory*. Here, exercising critical ability means using the norms, beliefs, and, in general, the language, of standard practice in one's intellectual community to determine the truth and usefulness of a proposed problem solution. Naturally then, to the extent that creativity is dependent upon escaping the boundaries of single traditions, *such* critical activity has negative consequences for creativity.

But this is a very narrow, almost mechanical kind of critical functioning, whereas the critical ability we have identified as central to achieving creative works is a much rarer, deeper talent. This second kind of critical ability does not generate a mere evaluation of the consistency of any new proposal with the principles of the accepted view. Rather, it turns the critical mind to the very norms and standards with which the "critical" defender of the standard view in question judges deviance. This second kind of critical activity involves the assessment of normal theory *in terms other than its own,* employing an assortment of "imported," "outside" tools, including discoveries and insights from alternative traditions (traditions that the creative theorist will also have examined critically and modified in light of his own interpretation of the world). Thus while a theorist exercising the first kind of critical ability will automatically reject any claim which is inconsistent with the normal theory he has been trained to use, the creative theorist employing the second kind of critical ability effectively challenges theoretical normality with fresh combinations of ideas from surprising directions.

9

Enslavement:
The Metaphoricality of Marxism

While Marxism derived its special creativity from its boundary-transgressing impulses, it is no less true that its eclectic theoretical origins and its specific cultural and organizational ecology have made it intellectually troublesome in many respects. I will expand on this in the final chapters. In spite of these intellectual failures, however, Marxism has in no realistic sense been a failure as a *politics*. For if "politics" is the struggle for power in the state, then Marxist politics has had an historically unparalleled success. Indeed, it is impossible to understand most twentieth-century revolutions without seeing the role that Marxism and Marxists have played in them. In about half a century, something like one-third of the world has come under the governance of those defining themselves as Marxists. No other system of thought in human history has ever had so extensive a success in so brief a period.

The Context-Freeness of Marxism

Still, there is a problem here which has to do with how Marxism was able to play such an important role in these revolutionary movements. This is problematic because Marxism was a theoretical system focused on capitalism and advanced industrial societies, quite unlike the underdeveloped economies in which recent collectivizing revolutions actually occurred. The problem, then, is how Marxism could be so politically successful in societies so greatly different from those in which it had developed, which it knew most about, and on which its critique of "capitalism" centered. How is it possible for Marxists to pursue revolution in societies that may scarcely have a proletariat and be only marginally capitalist?

Faced with the failure of socialism in the industrially advanced societies, and its coming to power in the backward ones, some Marxists have been constrained to redefine the very essence of Marxism, detaching it from the specific Marxist concept of a "proletariat" to the more diffuse notion of a "working class," thus allowing Chinese and other peasant societies to be subsumed by Marxism. And to hold that Marxism is not specifically focused on the proletariat is also to imply that Marxism is not necessarily about capitalism *per se*. The proletariat thus increasingly becomes a metaphor for any social system exploiting its "working class."

Much of this tendency to distinguish the working class from the proletariat, and to treat the proletariat as a special case of a working class, is visible in Paul Sweezy's discussion with Charles Bettelheim, where Sweezy sees the importance of trying "to be more specific about what is meant by the 'proletariat' in the kind of underdeveloped countries in which most of the anti-capitalist revolutions of the twentieth century have taken place. In classical Marxian theory . . . the concept of the proletariat was, of course, quite clear and specific: it referred to wage workers employed in large-scale capitalist industry who, in the advanced capitalist countries, constituted a majority of the working class and a very substantial proportion of the total population. . . ."[1] It seems certain, however, that this cannot describe the majority of workers in those countries in which the revolutions of the twentieth century succeeded, including the Russian revolution whose urban proletariat was then only a minuscule minority of that society's total working class. In Serge Mallet's words:

> Socialist political regimes in Eastern Europe all came about under sociohistorical conditions different from those foreseen by Marx. . . . In Russia and China, the political revolution occurred in the framework of an agrarian revolution for land and peace. In Yugoslavia, it was the expression of a movement for unification and national liberation. In the other Eastern European countries, it was exported into the country as a consequence of the Red Army's victories and the refusal of traditional forces to collaborate with it. Whatever the case, the political revolutions were never principally the product of a revolutionary class, which in those countries was still too small to constitute a decisive political force.[2]

This discussion is about *how* an historically sensitive theory, focused on the distinctive character of capitalist society and its industrial proletariat, could be refocused to encompass societies that were not capitalist and hardly had any proletariat at all. Basically, my answer will be that

Marxism exists as an archaeologically stratified symbolic system, in which its historicist political economy is only the more recent layer, a "technical" or extraordinary language, an EL, that does not exhaust Marxism. Underneath this there is an older, more elemental layer of language, an ordinary language or OL, nucleated with "paleosymbolic" elements on which there is continuing if unnoticed reliance but to which recourse is had especially when difficulties are encountered in using the EL. The discussion here develops an archaeological conception of Marxism as multi-tiered.

I shall, in addition, argue that an important clue to this transferability of Marxism to the less developed countries lies in what I shall call the "metaphoricality" of Marxism, and in its capacity for metaphorical "switching."[3] In the course of this discussion, I will suggest that, for Marx, the "proletariat" and "socialism" were in part metaphors, and I shall try to clarify the nature of these underlying metaphors. It is only when we attend to the metaphoricality of Marxism that it becomes possible to understand how Marxist-socialists can speak of "socialism" in such different ways: as the dictatorship of the proletariat; as the democratic dictatorship of the "people"; as what exists in Russia, Cuba, China, Algeria, South Yemen, Yugoslavia; as existing in industrially advanced and in economically backward countries, etc. It is the metaphoricality of socialism, and the use of metaphorical switching, that permits that interchangeability. A similar interchangeability of proletariat, peasantry, and people also suggests that the proletariat too must be understood as a metaphor. It is the metaphorical openness of Marxism that also explains how it is possible for some Marxists to drop, or to contemplate—as some recent Marxists have—dropping the proletariat as "historical agent," and to search for a different one.

The metaphoricality of Marxism is one of its greatest sources of political viability and adaptability. It enables Marxists to see revolutionary agents in almost any oppressed strata, in almost any kind of society, at almost any level of industrialization or economic development. It is through its metaphoricality that Marxism may place revolution on the order of the day, almost anywhere and anytime.

The Paleosymbolic in Marxism

Rather than being a superficial stylistic embellishment, it is Marxism's metaphoricality that provides clues to its deeper structures and better enables us to see Marxism as a duplex system of surface and deep structures. Marxism consists on its manifest (technical and ideological) level of categories and rational discourse with a concern for evidence. It also exists, however, on a deeper level, embedded with highly condensed and affectively charged symbols. On this "paleosymbolic" level, as I will call it here,[4] Marxism has more liquid, less firmly boundaried meanings which, in certain ways, give it a measure of maneuverability. On the paleosymbolic level, the limits of Marxism are different and broader than its surface technical structures. This paleosymbolism constitutes part of the symbolic grounding, i.e., part of the OL, within which elements on the technical level will be interpreted, especially when they are ambiguous or contradictory. The deeper structure symbolism specifies what are allowable interpretations of upper level symbols, usually permitting a greater looseness, interchangeability, and a larger set of equivalences, than might be allowed on the technical surface alone.

The deep structure is a submerged level, a kind of silence that cannot be reflected upon. This paleosymbolic layer constitutes the last *immanent* code for interpreting the technical communication. It contains the system of final rules, the code of last referral, the authoritative ambiguity-resolving interpretations of the manifest message on the upper technical layer. It is a symbolic structuring mechanism, sorting, sifting, and rearranging the symbolic contents on the manifest level, establishing the governing hierarchy of value-interests within which the technical code operates. This deep structure, then, is the analytic of last resort.

It is precisely Marxism's grounding in this deeper paleosymbolic layer that allows its manifest, technical, upper level to survive contradiction; to accommodate to false predictions, without being disoriented or demoralized by defeats. For this paleosymbolic level has switching rules that allow an interchangeability of metaphors without generating a sense of Marxism's non-rationality, incongruity, insincerity, or inauthenticity. It is Marxism's grounding in a deeper paleosymbolic structure that is one central explanation of how it has been possible for it to survive countless reversals of party line, falsified predictions, and political betrayals. For these are often within the boundaries of acceptable ultimate meaning in the framework of the deep structure.

A *final caveat:* To speak of Marxism as existing on these two levels does not imply that it is different from any other social theory, including "normal" academic sociology. As I showed in *The Coming Crisis of Western Sociology,* normal academic social theory also exists on and derives strength from such different levels.

Three Kinds of Metaphors

There are, of course, different ways of constituting metaphors, different bases on which things may be counted as equivalent within the com-

munity of Marxism-speakers, as in others. Among these different bases
of metaphoricality are the *iconic*, the *conceptual*, and the *functional*.[5]
In a *conceptual* form of metaphor, equivalences are established by defining a set of particulars as cases of some analytic connotation or definition, or by assigning them to some one conceptualized category. In an
iconic form of metaphor, equivalence is established perceptually; one
sees—or learns to see—certain particular cases as similar to some visually
concrete form and thus as similar to one another. Finally, in the *functional* basis of metaphoricality, one imputes a similar function to diverse
objects. They are defined as functionally equivalent in what they do for
some object, or as functionally equivalent insofar as our use of them is
concerned.

To illustrate the latter, functional bases of equivalence, in Marxism:
vis-à-vis the uses to which a vanguard intelligentsia put them, a proletariat, peasantry, or even lumpenproletariat, may all commonly become
objects of political mobilization. It is because of their equivalence on this
functional level that they may, also, come to have a conceptualized
equivalence as "historical agents." Again, countries may be judged as
socialist or revolutionary nations because they are the "enemies of my
enemies." Concretely, opposition to the United States is, in different
parts of the world, a basis for claiming acceptance as a revolutionary person or country.[6] Arab countries' claims to being "socialist" have sometimes rested on little more than that.

In what follows, I shall suggest that the most profound and perdurable
basis of metaphoricality in Marxism has been *iconic*, and that this is con-
cretized in the paleosymbol of "enslavement." Enslavement is a paleosymbol with an elemental visual imagery of body confinement: an im-
prisonment of the body and a repression of the flesh and instinct that
inflict gross indignities on the person. The imagery of enslavement in
Marxism is also fused with a *conceptual* metaphor of debasement: to
enslave is to treat persons as "objects" rather than "subjects," thus making them passive, deadened things. Enslavement is a condensed, elemental symbol evoking an imagery of crushed bodies, humiliated spirits, su-
pine and beaten persons, and confinement in chains. The *Communist
Manifesto*, it will be recalled, ends with a call to the proletariat who
"had nothing to lose but its chains." Subsequently, the Communist song
"The Internationale" promised that "no more traditions' chains shall
bind you." The symbol of enslavement evokes notions of an archaic
cruelty abiding into a later, seemingly enlightened time and thus intimates that a grotesque, brutal primitiveness underlies the civilized "ve-
neer" of more modern class systems. (The *structural isomorphism* with
the *id* of Freudianism is noteworthy.)

In his critique of Proudhon, Marx had contended that "modern peoples have only succeeded in disguising slavery in their own countries, while openly imposing it on the New World."[7] In Engels's early draft of the *Communist Manifesto* in June of 1847, the question was asked: "In what way does the proletarian differ from the slave?" The answer given was: "the slave is the property of a master and precisely because of this has his existence assured, be that existence ever so wretched. The proletarian is as it were the slave of the whole bourgeois *class*, not of one single master, and thus has no assured existence. . . . The slave may therefore be able to secure better conditions of life than the proletarian, but the proletarian belongs to a higher stage of development."[8] Ironically, this view paralleled the position taken by outright apologists for slavery in the United States and England who argued that free wage-labor in the North was only a disguised form of slavery, sometimes worse than the open slavery in the South.[9] Given a tacit rule that all historically specific class systems are, can be, become, or may regress to, an enslavement—and that this is their true reality and proper interpretation—then the differences between Fascism/Nazism and liberal democracy diminish or disappear and all may now be viewed as more or less equivalent forms of "enslavement," and may be treated in much the same way.

The revolutionary must then struggle to make manifest the brutal essence of enslavement underlying the liberal disguise, thereby polarizing the choice between his enlightened socialism and their brutal barbarism.

Although Marx and Engels later gave unequivocal support to the North's cause in the American Civil War, their earlier, more general view was equivocal indeed, emphasizing that there had been a period when slavery was necessary and, indeed, historically *progressive* in character. Thus, in 1846, Marx in *Misère de la philosophie* had held that "without slavery, North America, the most progressive of countries, would be transformed into a patriarchical (i.e., tribal) country. . . . If slavery disappears, America is removed from the map of nations." Engels, for his part, had averred that "without the slavery of antiquity, no modern socialism."[10] For Marx and Engels, slavery was once necessary, but now archaic; a past that was still present, living on formidably, coexisting with and underlying the more modern forms which were its "disguise." The enslavement metaphor in Marxism thus had a certain dissonance with Marx and Engels's articulate theory with its materialist "appreciation" of slavery's historical "necessity."

The enslavement metaphor, then, is part of the seen but unnoticed paleosymbolism lodged in Marxism's selective adaptation to ordinary language. As such, it is an element that is spoken by Marxists but is not easily spoken *about* by them. Although of restricted reflexivity, this paleosymbolism is a major source of Marxism's capacity to ignite and mobilize rebel political motivation; it is a near-invisible mover secreted in the vicinity of Marxism's technical theory.

Metaphoricality of Early Marxism

The early history of Marxism allows considerable visibility of the metaphors and of the rules of metaphoric switching in which some of the deepest structures of Marxism are to be found. The fundamental syntax of Marxism is displayed in its metaphoric switching between God, universal rationality, man, and proletariat. Much of Marxism begins with an effort to clarify the relation of these elemental symbols: ". . . the critique of religion is the prerequisite of every critique," wrote Marx in his *Critique of Hegel's "Philosophy of Right."*[11] Marxism inherited the general achievement of the Young Hegelians that "the foundation of irreligious criticism is this: man makes religion; religion does not make man." Here the metaphoricality of religion and man is unequivocal. The only qualification made is that it is presumably only a one-way switch: "Man → Religion" is correct; "Religion → Man" is *in*correct.

Along with Feuerbach and the Young Hegelians, Marx expressly affirmed a metaphoricality of religion, religious theology, metaphysics, and even rational philosophy. That metaphoricality is, in fact, the basis of the critique of Hegelian philosophy as embodying a suppressed religiosity. "The secret of theology is anthropology," said Feuerbach, "but the secret of speculative philosophy is theology."[12]

That this critique was thoroughly merited is clear from the metaphoricality of Hegel's contention that reason *is* the "divine in man." Again, in his *Philosophy of History,* Hegel celebrates Christ as the Man who is God—God who is man."[13]

The metaphorical switching between man/God—philosophy/religion is evident also in the following commentary by Marx: "Religion is only the illusory sun about which man revolves so long as he does not revolve about himself." It is the task of philosophy, says Marx, to move from the critique of religion to the critique of the world in which it grew, so that the conditions that foster and reproduce illusions will themselves be overcome. Philosophy, says Marx, is now "in the service of history."[14] Thus, philosophy/history—theology/God.

As Marx and the other Young Hegelians moved from a critique of theology to a critique of philosophy, from a critique of topic to a critique of resource, even the rational theoretical self is seen as having a "false consciousness"; as not having transcended theology, as having failed in its tacit, self-imposed requirement to obey the rules it imposes upon others. Philosophy itself must therefore be transcended and actualized on earth, by changing the social being of which it is the flawed consciousness. But now, having come down to earth, philosophy required a material basis that could actualize it there, the proletariat.

"The critique of religion ends in the doctrine that man is the supreme being for man . . . with the categorical imperative to overthrow all conditions in which man is a debased, *enslaved,* neglected, contemptible being. . . ."[15] Two points are worth mentioning here. First, note that in making man the "supreme being" there is a clear metaphoricality switching between God and Man. This "transformative critique" entails the usual "inversion" which is not as profound a change as may at first seem, because the claims made for religion and God are reassigned to Man, as the assets of a bankrupt business are assigned to the court-appointed receiver.

A second point: note that the imperative is, at this point, to overthrow "all" enslaving conditions. "Capitalism" is thus a metaphor of "enslavement": It is precisely because Marxism starts with a quest for a universal human emancipation that it may later move from a *particular* theory of revolution against capitalism to a more *general* theory of revolution, in almost any society.

This theoretical shift is subsequently most visible in Georg Lukács's "methodological" reading of Marxism which emerges following the failure of the Hungarian and German revolutions. But this is in the nature of a reversion, for early Marxism *began* with a theory of "universal emancipation" and was a general philosophy of revolution; Marxism only subsequently historicized "enslavement" and moved to a narrower theory of proletarian revolution in capitalist society. Lukács's thrust toward a general theory of revolution was thus a rediscovery of what had been suppressed in Marxism, as it developed from a more universal to a more specialized theory of proletarian anti-capitalist revolution. In their encounter with the world, then, what Marxists had discovered was—*themselves.*[16]

The Enslavement Metaphor
and Hegel's Master-Bondsman Conflict

The later Marxist political economy of the increasing "misery" of the proletariat, and the early Marxist philosophy of a *universal* emancipation, both center on a metaphor of enslavement. Marx's formulation of this metaphor is in part derived from and continuous with Hegel's analysis of the dialectics of the "master-bondsman" relationship. In this, the slave's autonomy continues to develop, by reason of his need to work and cope with necessity, in time making the master dependent upon and inferior to him. Encysted within the subsequently historicized Marxist focus on class struggle and, in particular, its sociologically specific struggle of proletariat and bourgeoisie, lies a paradoxically timeless paradigm of human conflict, Hegel's protean mythos of the master-bondsman struggle.

Although most fully elaborated in his *Phenomenologie des Geistes,* Hegel's concern with the master-bondsman paradigm is to be found in a large variety of his work including the so-called "theological essays." George Armstrong Kelly is surely correct in speaking of "the symbolic power of the master-slave image throughout most of the corpus of philosophical writings."[17] In Josiah Royce's anglicized version: "The master essentially recognizes that he needs somebody else in order that this other may prove him, the master, to be the self. . . . I can only know myself as this individual if I find somebody else in the world by contrast with whom I recognize who I am . . . the slave, to be sure, has no rights, but he has his uses, and he teaches me, the master, that I am the self . . . the master hereby becomes dependent upon the slave's work. . . . The master's life is essentially lazy and empty. Of the two, the faithful slave after all comes much nearer to genuine selfhood. . . . The slave, so Hegel says, works over, reconstructs the things of experience. Therefore, by his work, he, after all, is conquering the world of experience, is making it the world of self, is becoming the self . . . who in the end must become justly proud of the true mastery that his work gives him."[18]

The metaphor of enslavement embedded in Hegel's master-bondsman dialectic like other, less systematic uses of that metaphor, provides the central switching house in which rebellion against *any* kind of master is sanctioned. It allows Marxism's specific theory of proletarian revolution against capitalism to cope with that rebellion's failure in advanced capitalist societies and, by regressing to the paleosymbolic layer, to re-emerge in Lukács as a generalized theory of revolution.

Subject and Object as Master and Slave

The historically sensitive Marx knew well enough that the working class of capitalist society was not *identical* with the slaves of antiquity, or for that matter, with those of the New World. To the extent, however, that he thought of both as commonly "exploited"—as creating the "surplus value" that others appropriated—he is fully aware of the two classes as sharing some essential properties, and of holding that they do. The slavery metaphor in Marxism is thus not altogether blind or unwitting. There is, however, an even deeper level in which there is an *unlabeled* metaphor of slavery that pervades Marxism's most fundamental intellectual resources. This unlabeled metaphor is tacitly implicated in German idealism's central distinction between "Subject" and "Object," actor and acted-upon, knower and known, which Marxism continues to employ even if critically. From the standpoint of idealism, the Subject is in the nature of a Self, the true self, which is the locus of all the most basic dimensions of meaningfulness: goodness, potency, and mobility. The Subject is thus the potential repository of potency and goodness, or at least of the norms to which potency will conform. The Subject, in short, is the generalized. The Subject-Object differentiation in German idealism is the grammatical infrastructure of the master-bondsman mythos.

The crux of the relation between Subject and Object (physical world, nature, Other) is that the Object is constituted by the Subject (self) as, indeed, is the Object's very *foreignness* to the self. Composed of contradictory and opposing forces, the self is at first unconscious of its own masterful nature and of the powers which it successively unfolds and develops. The Subject is thus the realm of both a consciousness and an *un*consciousness. Above all, it is precisely as knower that the Subject lacks awareness of itself, for it first takes the world in a common-sense way, as an Object existing apart from it, rather than as a produced thing of its own making. The Subject is thus at first "objectivistic." The self's maturation entails its growing recognition of its own power, its overcoming of the foreign-ness and Object-ness of the world, and its mounting awareness of the way it itself is world-making. The Subject-self's ultimate achievement is the recognition of its own world-constituting master-nature.

The confrontation of the self with these "external" alien objects leads it to the discovery that it is *both* Subject and Object, knower and known, self and other. Indeed, this is the mark of the subject's maturation. It is in achieving this unity or harmony, this new wholeness, that there is an overcoming of all contradictions and a new, culminating oneness, the Absolute. The Absolute is the philosophical sublimation of deity, the completion of perfect being, the surmounting of limitation, the end of change and time, and the transcendence of all contradictions. German idealism, in short, entails the sublation of God in Reason.

Seen from one perspective, this is a Protestant *mythos* of the overcoming of fragmentation *recited in the idiom of logic;* it is logic anthropomorphized and historicized. This reunification, in Hegel's version, is an historical progression, going through various stages of development each of which has both its falsity and its limited truth or necessity; and in which each subsequent stage incorporates the earlier and transcends it. Each stage has a certain unavoidable necessity; at any given moment and place, depending on what has been before, only a certain limited kind of movement toward the ultimate unity and wholeness can be achieved.

The unity finally attained, however, is not in the nature of an even-handed "reconciliation" or compromise in which the opposing Subject and Object come to tolerate and co-operate with one another as equals, maintaining their separate and sovereign identities. Rather, their culminating unity will be one in which one side, the Subject, ultimately masters the other, the Object, and in so doing thereby eliminates its own subjectivity. The ultimate unity thus takes place under the domination of the Subject, and by reason of *its* initiative. At last, the Subject has so deepened its awareness that it recognizes that the Object is part of its own being; thus what seemed like an autonomous foreign being, an Other, now appears in its true light as only a different guise of the Subject-self.

For the Marxist, the comparable culminating moment comes when the proletariat has been transformed from a weak, exploited class—*from an enslaved Object of the system*—from a class *as such,* into the master class with a new awareness and with a new self-consciousness. In becoming a class for itself, the proletariat becomes a true Subject, a master rather than a mere slave Object. In overturning the society, the proletariat ultimately transforms itself; it ceases to be an enslaved "proletariat" and is now neither Subject nor Object. This ends man's pre-history and is the culmination of all of history hitherto. It takes the form, especially in the Hegelian version of Marxism, of the overcoming of man as a *passive,* enslaved Object and humanity's transformation into an active Subject mastering the world: humanistic imperialism.

The basic aim of revolution and the deepest meaning of human liberation and of socialism itself were, then, first conceived by Marx in terms of (and remained deeply rooted in) this structure of the Hegelian Subject and Object which are unlabeled metaphors of master and slave. Marxist socialism is the political economy generated by a discourse whose fundamental grammar premised (and sought to overcome) the subject-object differentiation.

Two of Marxism's fundamental critiques of the pathology of capitalism—those of alienation and of reification—are, like "socialism," intelligible at the deepest levels only in terms of the language and tacit assumptions of the Subject-Object differentiation. The Marxist critique of "alienation" is an indictment of a society in which men make their own history without knowing that it is they who are making it, and without having control over the history they make.

If workers are "alienated from the means of production," then, they have no control over these but, on the contrary, are used by them. If men have been alienated from other men and from themselves, this means that the Other has an alien Otherness, an unrecognizability and difference from the discerning Subject-self, with the result that there is less understanding of self and Other, and, also, less self-control and control over the Other. To be alienated means to rupture connections of understanding and of control over things. To be alienated is to confront a situation in which men's access to "things" is impaired.

In the later Marx and Marxism, enslavement and the tacit obligation to resist enslavement were increasingly historicized. Marxism was rationalized historically and politically, and grounded tacitly in terms of a Kantian norm of the moral that holds: ought implies can. Which is to say, one is *obligated* to fight enslavement *when* that enslavement is not historically *necessary* at a given stage of historical development, and *when* there exists an "historical agent" who can provide the "material" basis for that struggle.[19] Correspondingly, enslavement is no longer necessary when there is a political force—and a technological force—whose needs coincide with what rational diagnosis indicates. Yet however much Marxism turns toward an historicized political economy, it never totally disengages itself from its first impulse toward a *universal* human emancipation and its paleosymbolism of enslavement, an impulse to which it reverts increasingly as history falsifies its expectation of a proletarian revolt in advanced capitalist society.

On page 55 of the *Communist Manifesto,* utopian socialism is roundly condemned on historicist grounds, as premature, as seeking to launch socialism before its material conditions were prepared, and it is further denounced as voluntaristic: "historical action is to yield to their personal inventive action."[20] Only five pages later, however, indeed, on its culminating last page, the *Manifesto* declares with its recurrent ambivalence that "communists everywhere support every revolutionary movement against the existing social and political order of things . . . *no matter what its degree of development* at the time . . . [and] they openly declare that their ends can be attained *only* by the *forcible* overthrow of *all* existing social conditions."[21] In short, if a central motif of the *Manifesto* was its historicist emphasis on political emancipation's dependence on material prerequisites, and if its focus is on emancipation under capitalism, nonetheless, its culminating declaration is a call for a universal human emancipation, for the overthrow of all existing conditions, and it pledges its support to every revolutionary movement, regardless of how economically and industrially backward its society.

Capitalism and Subject-Object Inversion

Fundamental to the Marxist notion of "critique"—one of its central rules—is the ideal of a "transformative criticism," which is also grounded in the subject-object distinction with its tacit rejection of enslavement. Transformative criticism inverts the mystifying relations claimed between Subject and Object, showing that what had been claimed to be the Object was actually the Subject, and *vice versa*. In J. O'Malley's formulation:

> Feuerbach made explicit his technique of the subject-predicate conversion utilized earlier in *The Essence of Christianity* and presented it as a general method of criticizing speculative philosophy. . . . "All we need to do is always make the predicate into the subject . . . in order to have the undisguised, pure and clear truth. . . . We need only . . . invert the religious relations—regard that as an end which religion supposes to be a means—exalt that into the primary which in religion is subordinate, [and] at once we have destroyed the illusion, and the enclouded light of truth streams in upon us."[22]

Leaving aside the glowing conclusion, it is clear that here the paradigm of "mystification" is conceiving of religion as having made man. The essence of *de*-mystifying "critique," then, is to invert that Subject and Object, now making man the Subject and religion the Object he has made, thus releasing humanity from *bondage* to its own creation.

In the course of the decades-long discussions about the relationships between Marx and Hegel, and the old and young Marxes, it has become clear that even the mature Marx's political economy is grounded in a concept of critique as an inverting de-mystification. Bertell Ollman's study *Alienation: Marx's Conception of Man in Capitalist Society* (1971) documents this in convincing detail. Similarly, Dick Howard's work also stresses that

> The critique of the mystification of the Hegelian state has its analogue in Marx's political economy. In *Capital* . . . Marx devotes an important part of the analysis of commodities to the "fetishism" which makes them independent subjects. . . . Marx speaks of the "inversion of subject and object" and notes later that: "In the labor process looked at for itself, the worker utilizes the means of production. In the labor process which is equally a capitalistic production process, the means of production utilizes the workers. . . . The domination of the capitalist over the

worker is thus the domination of the thing over the man, of dead labor over the living, of the product over the producers. . . . This is exactly *the same* relationship in the material production, in the actual social life process . . . which presents itself in the ideological domain in *religion:* the inversion of subject and object, and vice versa."[23]

In his famous aphorism about turning Hegel right side up, and standing him on his feet, Marx puts his own relation to Hegel essentially in terms of such a notion of transformative criticism. In these terms, inversion is presumably at the heart of mystification, and therefore, reversal of the received Subject-Object relationship—that is, affirming the contrary— is the heart of *de*-mystifying critique. In effect, then, (the *early*) Marx saw social relationships as *on the order of speech processes;* as entailing a language and grammar. The effort to analyze social processes was seen as akin to formulating sentences about subjects and objects; a de-mystifying critique of such an analysis, then, was the proper re-ordering of the inverted Subject-Object relationship.

Two implications of Marxism's grounding in the grammar of Subject-Object discourse are of considerable importance. One is that, given the commitment to critique as transformative inversion, the falsification of reality tends to be seen as only a grammatical or logical error. The decisive cognitive tool of critique thus becomes formal and linguistic repressing the *empirical* dimension as unproblematic. The problem is to find the right transformation, to move from one to another equation. Thus the question of the empirical and factual, whether the facts at hand are sufficient or whether they need "testing" and development, is defocalized. The empirical, in short, becomes secondary.

Second, given the Subject-Object distinction as a conceptual framework, a very specific social ontology is generated in which, for example, things are *either* Subjects or Objects but not both. Despite Engels's determined efforts at *eluding* this *implication,* the fundamental Marxist distinction between the economic infrastructure and the socio-ideological superstructure is grounded in and invisibly reproduced by that Subject-Object grammar. Given the Subject-Object grammar, some are masterful Subjects, who produce others, while others are the made, receptive, acted-upon Objects. That is, some must be masters, others slaves. One is thus impelled to categorize things as *either* makers or made, and to see this as entailing a one-directional relationship. A subject-object grammar always comes back to the question: Who is master here? It generates a social ontology of hierarchy and hidden hierarchy. Thus the full possibilities of a wholistic theory, in which all are *both* Subjects and Objects, can only be explored with difficulty.

To recapitulate: Underneath the Marxist critique of capitalism with its diagnosis of capitalism's pathologies and conception of its remedies, there is a generalized notion of "enslavement," a labeled metaphor as well as Hegel's master-bondsman mythos; and under *that* is the powerful but unlabeled metaphor of Subject and Object. It is largely in terms of this nested system of metaphors that it becomes possible to understand how Marxism, which in its mature political economy was an historical critique of capitalism, could transcend this to become a *generalized* theory of revolution, justifying revolution at almost any time and any place in the modern world.

Enslavement and the Fusion of Private and Public Spheres

Marxism's use of the paleosymbolism of enslavement permits it to fuse diverse modalities of human degradation—man as a tool used in a modern factory, or a thing-like commodity bought and sold on the labor market, or an animal brutalized by the misery of urban slums, or any repressed being subjected to irrational constraint. These diverse symbols are now brought together, condensed, and made equivalent in the notion of enslavement which, in all the instances above, carries the sense of an unjust subjugation of persons.

The great mobilizing power of the enslavement metaphor derives from its ability to fuse sentiments against otherwise separated sectors of *authority*. In particular, "enslavement" fuses the rejection of an irrational public authority grounded in the private life of the family system. The diffuse paleosymbolism of enslavement, then, powerfully compresses feelings directed toward public and private life, and especially political and family structures, for both may be defined as regions of enslavement. The worker brutalized by capitalist exploitation and the child brutalized by patriarchal authoritarianism find a common denominator in the symbolism of enslavement.

The metaphor of enslavement facilitates the development of "deviant" political values especially when economic or social disruption undermines the father's ability to fulfill his family obligations and provide nourishment, protection, attention, understanding, connections, or love and where, in consequence, there is little or no compensation for the costs inflicted by the father's patriarchal discipline. Above all, the middle-class father's ability to reproduce his political values declines when his status cannot be inherited, when the father has no property to transmit and when, at the same time, emerging systems of public education become agencies of status conferral no longer controlled by the father. Family rebellion against the father and his political values grows as his public authority wanes, and as his capacity to confer privilege and status on his children is assumed by other institutions and authorities. The disruption of public authority and the failure of family authority are then interwoven. The enslavement metaphor plays a part in these linked developments, facilitating the transfer of sentiments felt toward disappointing family authorities and permitting them to be attached to public or political authorities. The enslavement metaphor can capture and redirect family-centered affect and energy, placing it in the service of revolutionary politics. It structures the fusion of public resentment and private rage; it organizes and gathers up energies long accumulated and blocked during the life cycle, allowing them a concentrated discharge within the public sphere. The paleosymbolism of enslavement in Marxism invisibly taps the vast energies of the private life, making them available for political goals, and specifically for a politics *opposed* to established authorities.[24]

APPENDIX: PALEOSYMBOLISM
AND THE THEORY OF DISCOURSE

The essence of the paleosymbolic is that it is more readily accessible primarily in private or intimate circumstances, rather than in the public and anonymous settings that are the grounding of rationality. It entails symbols saturated with affect, and thus lives at the mutually meshing interface of cognition and sentiment. They are, also, symbols acquired at a relatively earlier period in the education and socialization of persons, well before university education, well before the age of intellectual consent. They are, therefore, locked-in symbols, not easily accessible to critical examination by those using them, partly because of their surrounding affectivity. They are also difficult to isolate as cognitive objects, to make visible and problematic, in part because they are so closely interwoven with the concrete social positions and relationships in which they are encountered.

They are conveyed to us by "significant others" on whom we are dependent, whom we love, whom we fear and hate, and from whom at first we dare not be separated. Paleosymbols are thus integrated with individual character structure, on the one side, and, on the other, they are implicated in family structure and family-referencing sentiments. In consequence of this family implication, paleosymbols are linked also to the class and other systems of domination.

Among the paleosymbols to be found among many Europeans of the nineteenth century were the following: greed, venality, money, material interest, egoism, selfishness, lust, sexuality, the "flesh," sexually, "liberated" women, power, domination, force, violence, fraud, Jews or Jewishness, sensual enjoyment, industriousness, labor, hard work, *Geist*, Christ and Christianity, mother and father.

For example: among Saint-Simonians such as Enfantin and Bazard, or for Schlegel's *Lucinde*, the flesh was beginning to be resurrected; the former launched a "dizzying" discussion of "free love" and lurched off to the Middle East in search of a Jewish "femme libre" as priestess of their new cult. The flesh was being opened to public communication by spiritualizing it, often by imputing to women a greater sensitivity and capacity for feeling. Think, for example, of Comte and Clotilde de Vaux. For the Comteans, the Saint-Simonians, and the group around the Schlegels, the flesh was being talked about, rediscovered, probed. Surely, however, this was not the case for the Pietists, members of churchly orders, and good bourgeois families. And what bourgeois family talked publicly about its own money, how much it earned or owned—did the children or even wives know?—how it was allocated, and who controlled expenditures? This was a great bone of contention between parents and sons. Think of Marx or Max Weber. Some groups might talk freely of God, but how much of their own feelings about this did people know; and what could be spoken by churchgoers about the inward death of God; and how far could proud atheists venture an inward exploration or public expressions of their own religiosity? For some among the learned classes, God had literally become "unspeakable." And surely modernizing Jews who wanted to break free of the cultural web of the ghetto and dreamed of university jobs spoke quite differently than the orthodox about Jews and Jewishness. And, of course, the same paleosymbols' bodily gesture is lacking. The connection to a particular context is so strong that the symbol is not independent of covarying actions. Although the paleosymbols represent a pre-linguistic basis for the intersubjectivity of mutual existence and joint action, they do not allow public communication in the strict sense of the word. For the identity of meaning is not yet granted and the private meaning associations are still prevailing. The privatism of pre-linguistic symbol organization originates in the fact that the usual distance between sender and addressee as well as the differentiation between symbol signs, semantic content, and items of reference have not yet been developed. The reality levels of being and appearance, of the public and the private sphere, cannot yet be clearly differentiated with the help of the paleosymbols."[25] Habermas's discussion helps clarify our own formulations. First, and most importantly, he sees the tension between the paleosymbolic and the grammatic. Certainly this is correct for the usual notions of grammar which premise a set of rules "mastered" by the speaker, whereas the point of the paleosymbolic is to make reference to the opaqueness of the paleosymbolic even to the speaker. This is an opaqueness partly derived from the fact that the symbols do not confrom to rules the speaker *knows* and can acknowledge as correct. For it is mastery of grammatic rules that enables speakers to distinguish between correct and incorrect speeches.

In my own view of the paleosymbolic, however, I have tried to emphasize the distinction between public and hence a grammatical speech, on the one hand—the kind of speech an ideology facilitates—and, on the other, more privatized or intimate speech which, if it has a grammar, has one that differs in important structural characteristics from that of ordinary and "artificial" languages or ideologies. This suggests that *how* speakers understand one another in the two cases differs importantly. It is not so much the common mastery of grammatical rules that enables them to establish communication in more private intimate communication. In other words, certain kinds of communications, indeed symbolic and linguistic communications, are possible without common mastery of a grammar, enabling the paleosymbolic to transcend the purely privatized and to attain social intersubjectivity, at least among intimates even if not among strangers in an anonymous public.

Obviously, speakers continually understand one another despite their mistakes, lacunae, and grammatical failures. Some speakers, of course, do this better than others: those sharing common experiences, histories, and life-situations, and thus common understandings based on the indexicality of speech. They may share a common experience and assign a common meaning to speech because they share common icons and paradigms of memory, not necessarily because they have a common grammar. Grammars (like contracts) become more important when tacit understandings dwindle and are no longer grounded in shared images, when histories cease to be common, when situations and "fates" are less likely to be shared: We who fought together, went to war together, were wounded, suffered and bled together; we who were hungry and unemployed together; we who sat in the back of the bus together; we who had the same nourishing and dominating mothers and fathers together—we can begin our conversations by saying: remember the time when. . . .

The speech of intimates may be ungrammatical but intelligible to intimates, being less like discursive dialogue and more nearly like a monological "inner speech"—in Lev Semenovich Vygotsky's sense. That is, speech omitting reference to the subject; for as Vygotsky says, "we know what we are talking about." And so do our intimates. Vygotsky adds the decisive sociological point that "psychological contact between partners in a conversation may establish a mutual perception leading to the understanding of abbreviated speech . . . a practically wordless communication of even the most complicated thoughts." This, he tells us, contains a greater preponderance of the sense of a word over its "meaning"; a richness of association rooted in its historicality, contextuality, indexicality, thus being more fluid and shifting and less context-free than the "meanings" of words. Much the same is true for the more privatized conversation of intimates who, knowing the ramifying sense of what is being said, need not launch discourse. They also know the things *not* said, the alternatives omitted, the unspoken *sub*-textual implications of what has been spoken.

The relationship between ideology (or theory), on the one side, and the paleosymbolic, on the other, is thus profoundly ambiguous. Ideology—and, indeed, any rational social theory—attempts to overcome the barriers to communication among strangers by giving them a new and common language having a common grammar. Yet even this step toward a new sharing premises an old sharing. It premises an ordinary language with a set of older common paleosymbols, some of which remain shared. And it also generates new paleosymbolic intimacies among the new, once mutually unknown, adherents of the ideology. In that sense, then, every ideology or theory is grounded in an old, and generates a partially new, paleosymbolism, changing old tacit undertandings and generating new ones. To that extent, every ideology has a tacit doctrine, a sub-textual meaning, that cannot be decoded except by excavation of its paleosymbols.

I do not limit the paleosymbolic to the *pre*-linguistic. I allow for a conceptual and linguistic paleosymbolism which is partly social or intersubjective, not totally privatized; which is cultural and not uniquely personal; which can be transmitted and taught and not patterned only unwittingly or non-normatively.

It is therefore also capable of being correctly or incorrectly used, and is thus also susceptible to being grammatically generated, in principle. It seems to me that there is sometimes an ambiguity concerning the meaning of linguistic "competence." Does mastery imply "awareness" by the *speaker* of the rules to which his speech conforms? Can mastery and awareness differ? Much of the thrust of Basil Bernstein's distinction between "restricted" and "elaborated" language codes, and particularly the context-freeness of the latter, calls attention to awareness (of the code) as related to but not identical with mastery.

Thus the paleosymbolic, even as the pre-linguistic, could also have a generative grammar of its own (Freudianism), if we did not insist that the speakers must be *aware* of its rules. Again, conceptual categorization is not the only basis of classification, for iconic and functional equivalence is possible. A grammar of the pre-linguistic, then, can use iconic and functional classification. The pre-linguistic paleosymbolic, no less than the linguistic, can thus in principle be grammatically generated. But since its grammar differs from the grammar of ordinary language, we had perhaps best say the two constitute different languages with consequent problems of mutual access and translation.

But to repeat, my use of "paleosymbolic" is on the linguistic, the cultural, and the social levels, although otherwise resembling Freud's (and Habermas's) pre-linguistic paleosymbolic. For example: affective saturation, situation fixity, or indexicality, rather than freeness, fusions of symbol and gesture, or action, a lower degree of differentiation of sign, meaning, and referent. Being linguistic, the paleosymbolic, as I use it, is therefore closer to a restricted language code or ordinary language with its situation-and-position-embeddedness. In this view, then, "restricted" and "elaborated" codes are differentiated *levels within* a language system; the former OL being the deeper and genetically prior, the latter EL being grounded in the former and genetically later. Most basically, however, the paleosymbolic construed as a restricted linguistic code is relatively lower in reflexivity, is subject to rules that are difficult for speakers to speak, although they can *use* them to the satisfaction of other speakers. In general, it depends much less on rules and grammar, and requires relatively specific and concrete avoidances and performances; its standards of correctness are relatively more paradigmatic, iconic, or functional than conceptual and analytical. Alternatives are, therefore, fewer and more difficult to generate, and action is *relatively* more stereotyped.

An important consideration for us is the relationship of the paleosymbolic to discourse, particularly to the world-referencing discourse of either "ideology" or "social theory." The concern here is in the *relation* between the paleosymbolic, on the one side, and ideology and theory, on the other. Still more particularly, our concern is with the manner in which the paleosymbolic is involved in the production of ideology or theory. In *The Dialectic of Ideology and Technology,* I sketch a model of the production of discourse (that is, of an ideology or theory) that encompasses the role of the paleosymbolic, although also going beyond it to a more general formulation.

10

Recovery:
The Rationality of Marxism, I

Marxism's fundamental epistemology is often said to be a correspondence or reflection epistemology which holds that truth is that which mirrors "what is." This view of Marxism is correct as far as it goes, but it omits several things, one being that the reality supposedly mirrored is further preconceived by Marxism in a specific manner. It is viewed as a "whole" and, in particular, as a whole whose parts are not harmoniously arranged but internally contradictory. To exhibit truth, therefore, a Marxist must show how social reality constitutes a whole, and second, display the contradictions by which that whole is riven but which, at the same time, define it. In this respect, Marxist epistemology critically appropriated the Hegelian view that "the truth is the whole," including the idea that the whole is internally contradictory. I shall try to reconstruct the tacit logic of this Marxist epistemology, and in particular, to make explicit certain of its aspects that are often left undeveloped by reason of the conventional over-emphasis on its correspondence principle.

I begin by relating Marxist epistemology to the idea of a "false consciousness." This is neither a deliberate lie nor an accidental mistake, but, rather, a wrong view produced systematically by the speaker's social position within the whole. The idea of a false consciousness is grounded in the premise that reality is a *whole,* for it is not possible to locate the speaker except by reference to that whole; it is also grounded in the further premise that the whole is internally contradictory, which ultimately accounts for the *falsity* of his consciousness. The idea of a false consciousness means that not all persons or groups are—whatever their good will—able to see the whole and its contradictions and speak the truth about them. False consciousness, then, is neither deliberate dissembling nor a sequence of random technical mistakes. It follows that neither moral probity, technical training, logical precision, nor meticulous research suffices to enable persons to see the whole, for this depends (also) upon their position in a riven society. Marx's epistemology, then, does not really deny the value of the knowers' moral character or his scholarly competence, but, rather, merely takes these as givens. His focus is elsewhere; what is problematic to him is neither research method nor moral character, but, rather, a kind of *sociology* of knowledge. It remains only to be added that the idea of "false consciousness" is also central to the Marxist idea of "ideology," that latter being any view professing the false consciousness that it simply grows out of other ideas, not understanding its embeddedness in class interests.

Marx's epistemology involves an ideology "critique" that attempts to show that what persons know of the whole is either aided or distorted by their social position and by the everyday life experiences and interests that this systematically generates. Marxist critique culminates in showing how persons' consciousness or knowledge is not autonomous but always depends on their social location. "Critique" in general, then, embodies a critique of philosophical idealism, centering on the denial of the independence of ideas, persistently linking them to the enshadowed social position of the persons holding them, and exhibiting how their ideas are systematically limited by their position. It is in this very linking of beliefs to believer, or knowledge to knower, and in linking knowers to their social positions, that Marxism's epistemology parallels its anti-fragmenting politics and sociology.

This holistic epistemology implies that the avenue to truth is most essentially blocked by the deficiencies of single propositions about "what is." In this view, truth is not reducible to the question of the reliability of any single proposition, for these are always generated within the shaping perspective of speakers' social positions. Any one statement might be correct, factually reliable, but nonetheless fail to convey the whole and thus lack truth. Neither the "correctness" nor "reliability" of statements necessarily entails a truth-bearing portrait of the whole. What persons can see and say depends on where they are and to whose side they are committed, especially in a riven world. Their location fosters an ideology whose perspective impedes or facilitates truth. Each will be more fully open to truths that facilitate his interests, or are consonant with his typical everyday experiences and with the ideologies emerging from these. A "vulgar political economy" pretending that the categories of capitalism are eternal, says Marx, is distorted by the interests of the bourgeoisie whose perspective it takes; contrariwise, when thinkers adopt the standpoint of the proletariat they are liberated from these distortions of the bourgeois perspective.

Marx tacitly and dubiously assumes that a working-class perspective imposes no limits of its own on truth since it is a universal class that cannot emancipate itself without overthrowing *all* exploitative class systems; he assumes that its revolution will overthrow class differences without imposing a new exploitative class, and will thus emancipate society from all class-limited truth-distorting perspectives. Since it is class exploitation that distorts, truth requires the elimination of exploitation. Thus the point is not to add another new interpretation of the world but to change it and, through this, provide a new grounding of truth, and, in that very process, to learn about ourselves and the world. It is not by accepting the world that one acquires truth—for that would be accepting what is in any event only a transient appearance—but only by a struggle to overcome and reveal its deceptive, ephemeral appearance, and by showing not "what is" but what is becoming.

The Struggle for Recovery

The Marxist epistemology of truth-as-whole is not the same as the liberal conception of truth which says: there are "two sides to everything" and that we attain truth by seeing them both. For one thing, Marxism does not maintain that there are always two sides to everything, a functional or rational side as well as a pathological or irrational side, at any given time. Marxism holds that certain groups can be historically progressive and necessary during certain limited historical periods, but can cease being so at a later period.

Moreover, to see all sides of a question often results in crediting a social definition of reality that is already widely believed because it is supported by dominant groups and contributes to their hegemony. This simply lends them further support and leaves the world as we found it. That kind of liberal holism is a form of intellectual bookkeeping that always reinforces the *status quo*. Far from being the truth, Marxism believes *that* whole is a *lie*. For it ends by crediting the already familiar, self-serving definitions of social reality useful to the hegemony of the dominant and must, therefore, maintain silence about things embarrassing to them. Marxist "critique," however, does not aim to repeat what is already well known; it does not speak even-handedly about the widely known and the unknown, the already familiar and the unfamiliar, the repressed and the advertised. Marxist critique, rather, focuses on what has been silenced and repressed systematically; hence it must also speak

about and against those social forces powerful enough to censor definitions of social reality at variance with its own interests.

Marxist epistemology is grounded therefore in a rejection of passive
contemplation and in an emphasis on struggle. Knowing is not regarded
simply as a frictionless retrieval or direct discovery of truth but, rather,
as the combating of error. To this extent, Marxist epistemology is directly continuous with the epistemology of classical antiquity. For Greeks
of Hellenic antiquity, *aletheia* (truth) is that which has now been rendered no longer concealed or forgotten; it is that which has been cleansed
of deceit. The knower, therefore, must engage in a contest to remove the
disguises and distortions that hide things; the intellectual sublimation
and expression of that truth-questing contest during antiquity was the
dialectic, the friction of minds. Truth, then, is not what is immediately
visible through mere acquaintance; it is attained not by a surrender or
passive opening of the self to the world, but by active struggle against
the world's resistance.

Marxism's epistemology fundamentally accepts and builds on this
classical notion of truth but sociologizes and politicizes the struggle
by which it is to be attained. In part, this may be seen in its critique
of dominant definitions of social reality that exhibit their inversion of
reality. Marxist critique, in one form at any rate, entails the idea of
"transformative criticism," in the course of which one shows that that
which had been conventionally treated as the subject was really the
predicate, and vice versa. The former view is not only held to be wrong,
but upside down. This is a very aggressive posture. Here truth is being
sought through intellectual combat: by taking issue with tradition, defy-
ing the common sense, challenging definitions of social reality fostered
by dominant social classes. But Marxism's fundamental aim is not simply that of *aletheia,* to reveal what has been hidden, but rather to reveal
and *transform* what has been hidden.

Critique also entails a "de-mystification" which proceeds by showing
that even the most technical, esoteric, or learned idea is grounded in the
mundane practice of the everyday. Critique rejects the conceit of the
learned that they are in any way autonomous, as a self-serving ignorance.
To de-mystify is to exhibit the repressed connection between the highest
ideas and the basest interests, between spirituality and earthiness, between the speech and the speaker in his social role.

Critique premises that definitions of social reality—the picture of what
society is like—always have implications for maintaining or changing
society and are, therefore, always grounded in something outside of
themselves. They will be supported by the powerful when they further
their hegemony, but opposed by them when impairing their hegemony.

To search for truth, then, means to confront powerful forces prepared to impose their views and, indeed, to maintain distortions, when this suits their interests. To search for truth means that one either prepares for combat against real social forces—and not just against an abstract "nature"—or else knuckles under. Truth is produced in struggle; it is not simply a product of intelligence but also of courage.

Fetishism: Recovering the Secret

There is little question that Marx conceived his intellectual work as uncovering that which had been *hidden;* and he conceived the hiddenness of certain features of capitalism as of decisive importance in maintaining its class character. Marx, himself, repeatedly presented his work as revealing what had hitherto been a secret and mystery. Thus Marx spoke of ownership as the deepest mystery and the concealed basis of the whole social system: "it is always the direct relationship of the owners of the conditions of production to the direct producers . . . which reveals that innermost secret (*innerste Geheimnis*), the hidden basis of the entire social structure, and with it the political form . . . in short, the corresponding specific form of the State."[1] It is thus not just said that the direct relation of workers to owner is the foundation of the society and state, but more specifically, that it is their *hidden basis and innermost secret.*

The idea that social reality is hidden and that its disguise contributes to the maintenance of capitalism's class character is intrinsic to Marx's notion of "fetishism." This refers to "a definite social relation between men . . . [which] assumes in their eyes, the fantastic form of a relation between things . . . their own social action takes the form of the action of objects, which rule the producer instead of being ruled by them."[2] This fetishism is a form of mystification which disguises human relations as *object* relationships; it inverts reality, transforming men who should be the subjects of history into its objects. De-mystification, then, clearly requires a transformative criticism that inverts appearances, allowing object relations to be seen as human relations, and restoring men to their legitimate subjecthood.

From this point, then, the most generalized form of mystification is the transformation (disguise) of social and human actions into natural, non-human things. The remedy, de-mystification, thus requires that the "natural" be revealed, as the doing or making of human beings in a specific kind of society. Men must be called back to the knowledge that they are implicated in history, that the world became what it did (at least partly) through their own actions (and can, therefore, be changed by them). In critique's de-mystification, then, what occurs is the over-coming of men's forgetfulness. Critique, then, is *the recovery of a knowledge that they had already had,* at least at the tacit level. De-mystification, therefore, is not just remedying ignorance, for ignorance is a knowing that had never existed—a kind of emptiness. Forgetfulness, however, is a knowing that had existed but was lost; it is once having known. But men cannot be supposed to have had no glimpse at all of what they themselves were doing in the world, of their own implication in events. Rather, they had been subjected to certain social forces that made their role opaque, even to themselves.

Marx's epistemology, then, implies an untheorized, tacit "doctrine of recovery," calling men back to a knowledge of themselves and their ac-tion, knowledge that they at least had developed tacitly, but which they subsequently repressed or forgot. This forgetting, repression, silence, or inarticulateness about their own lives and actions, however, is not simply some inner cognitive condition, but is produced by determinate social forces; it thus cannot be recovered simply by reminding them of it. The social forces conducive to the forgetting need to be removed before the recovery can take place in public life.[3]

Marxism's tacit doctrine of recovery, then, is clearly continuous with the Hegelian unfolding of the *Geist,* an unfolding in which the Spirit at last recognizes that the world is not just full of alien objects but discovers its own presence in them, finally recognizing itself in them. Yet this continuity with Hegel is only a partial one; for the recovery that Marx premises cannot take place simply through an inner or self-unfolding of consciousness but only through human action in and upon the world, removing the forces disguising reality. That this doctrine of recovery is also manifestly convergent with Freudian psychoanalysis, in which there is also a recovery of the unconscious, is due not to a tacit Freudianism here but rather to the historical fact that both Marx and Freud oper-ated—however critically—within the framework of the Hegelian grammar of the unfolding spirit seeking to overcome its own fragmentation.

Marxism: Economism or Recovery

We are now in a better position to state more precisely what Marxism is *about*. It is not *only* about proprietary classes, or only about class strug-gle and exploitation, but about a capitalist society in which these are all *disguised*. Marxism is about *hidden* classes, *hidden* class struggle, and *hidden* exploitation. Marxism is about a class, the proletariat, that exists at first only as an object of history, in itself, but without consciousness of itself, without knowing itself, and unable therefore to be "for itself," and which does not yet know its great historical mission and destiny. Marxism is not only about the importance of the mode of production as the grounding of civil society and the state but, also, about the way this grounding has been secreted from public view. Marxism is not only about the importance of the economic infrastructure but about the importance of an infrastructure that had been disguised. Marxism, in short, is about how disguise is an integral part of the way social things produce their effects. It is about the role of knowledge, and the *lack* of knowledge, in maintaining and in changing capitalism's social world.

Marx makes it perfectly plain that capitalism is not unique in being exploitative; it is only the latest in a long line of class exploitative societies, but it is unique, he tells us, partly by reason of the *hidden* character of its exploitation. The world of capitalism seems to be one in which the commodity and its relation to other commodities is its central defining essence, and in which "capital" seems to be another "factor" in production. But this conceals the way in which capital is actually a social relationship, in which the owners of the means of production produce by buying the labor power of workers who, lacking property, are constrained to sell their labor power and work under the constraint of others.

The relations among commodities, expressed in their different prices, conceal the relationships among men and classes. So what is characteristic of capitalism, then, is not simply general commodity production but the *fetishism* of commodities, a specifically *cognitive* condition, among other things. Under slavery, products were produced by slaves under the direct command of their owners and it was quite clear to everyone that masters were appropriating what slaves produced. Marx makes a similar point about the openly exploitative character of feudalism. Capitalism, then, is held to be unique partly in the *hidden* character of its exploitation.

Yet at this point there is a certain tension within Marxism. As a "materialism," Marxism stresses that capitalism's character is an objective one, that it does not depend simply on what men think—or know; it assumes here that cognitive processes are a reflection of the forces and relations of production. Here, knowledge about class relations is separate from and secondary to the infrastructure of production. In the specific conception of capitalism as a fetishizing economy, however, this knowledge—the sheer knowing and forgetting of men's relations—is intrinsic to capitalism's character and is embedded within its relations of production. From the standpoint of Marx's theory of fetishism, the *disguised* character of worker-owner relationships is thus at the very core of capitalism—not a peripheral epiphenomenon—preserving and protecting uniquely the hegemony of owners.

Recovery and Tacit Knowing

One version of the doctrine of recovery—as already suggested—was formulated in the Hegelian philosophy of the unfolding *Geist* whose quest culminates in its recognition that it itself is implicated in what it had first thought to be a world of alien objects. That doctrine is probably a lineal descendant of classical antiquity's theory of remembrance which, in its Pythagorean form, premised a notion of reincarnation: i.e., being reborn, man forgot what his past life had taught him, but, under certain conditions, comes to remember it.

The core of the doctrine of recovery is that the truth is not totally unknown or new to those receiving it; that it is something anticipated by the knower or learner; that various forces have somehow led him to lose sight of it; and that to offer truth is to offer *back* what was once known but had been forgotten. It is knowledge from which the person has become alienated and that he could not hold-in-view but had only glimpsed fleetingly. It implies that truth is preceded and prepared for by a knowing—as Michael Polanyi terms it—that is *tacit*.

The doctrine of recovery, then, implies that truth does not simply face "forward" into the social world but also reaches "backward" into the knower's life. In the doctrine of recovery, truth is not just another bit of impersonal information but a knowing about how our lives are implicated in the world and touched by knowledge of it. Truth is a knowledge for which our lives have readied us. Truth is not simply externalizing. It addresses something already experienced, implying that these experienced things elude recovery through the *ordinary* language and thus remain elusive or opaque in the *everyday* life.

The doctrine of recovery implies that truth is trapped in the limits of ordinary language, and hence that it is at first known only in a gauzy, tacit, and hence unstable way. "Recovery" enables these limits of the everyday life, the common sense and the ordinary language to be overcome; enables the tacitness to become an explicitness; permits the fleeting glimpse to be held firmly in view; helps the merely private to become public.

The doctrine of recovery sees truth as a condition which persons recognize because they have previously encountered it, but could not grasp and speak it. Recovery is the overcoming of a charged silence; one that wanted to speak but could not. The doctrine of recovery thus premises the view that truth resonates a memory and produces the sense of *déjà vu*.

"A genuine learning is . . . an extremely peculiar taking," remarks Heidegger, "a taking where he who takes, takes only what he already has. . . . True learning only occurs where the taking of what one already has is a self-giving and is experienced as such. . . . The most difficult learning is to *come to know all the way what we already know*."[4]

Such a learning, however, cannot simply be accomplished by a research, for this does not set aside the truth-distorting and inhibiting social forces. The learning and achieving of truth is not like filling a receptive vacuum, but the overcoming of a resistance. The Marxist version of the doctrine of recovery premises that the truth requires a critique of the social forces distorting knowledge as well as of the distortion in the knowledge itself. Critique culminates in a transformation of the social world that revolutionizes institutions inimical to truth.

While Marxism embodied a specific version of the doctrine of recovery, however, it never spoke or theorized it more generally. The doctrine was there, it was operative, but it remained silent. The effort here has been to recover that doctrine of recovery in Marxism. In doing so, however, and in any more general appraisal of the doctrine of recovery, it is important to see that it does not necessarily entail the assumption that all forgetting is motivated, as Marx's emphasis implies. Certainly, motivated forgetting, forgetting induced by sociological or psychic pressures, is *one* important type of forgetting. There are, however, at least two others: there is forgetting induced by the structural and lexical features of a specific language which may not enable persons to fix a particular thought or object in view, thus causing it to be forgotten readily. There is also forgetting induced by "problem-distraction." To focus on one thing is to occlude others. Here forgetting occurs simply because immersal in an immediate problem distracts attention from other things, letting them become remote and lost to view. Here concentration in one direction necessarily means an inability to attend elsewhere. Indeed, it is one of the main functions of holistic analysis to overcome the limits of *ad hoc,* problem-centered thinking, with its tendency to forget that there is more than one type of problem and its difficulty in carrying forward into the analysis of a new problem what had been learned from an old one.

Marxism: Recovering What for Whom?

Marxism's attraction and success in the world is due in part to the fact that Marxism *is* a recovery of what was formerly only tacit knowledge, is due also to the *specific* things it recovers, and is due, further, to the particular *publics* to whom it *offers* these recoveries and *for whom* they constitute a recovery. Something can be a recovery for *some* person, but rarely for all. Something is a recovery only for those to whom it had hitherto been known tacitly. What is a recovery for some may have little interest and value to others with different experiences.

How did Marxism function concretely as a doctrine of recovery? In a preliminary way, it has to do with the dialectic between technology, as the then most recently visible force of production, in its interaction with a property system driven by private venality. Engels's field work in Manchester, as well as his experience as a businessman, clearly focused his attention on the importance of the developing industrial and technological revolution. Modern technology was changing dramatically and it was clear that concern with subsistence-getting did not altogether encompass that new development. What Marx and Engels did was to link the two, making both focal, and proceeded to show how the significance of modern technology depended importantly on its rooting in commerce. In short, while the industrial revolution was fully visible, what was less so was the manner in which it had been called forth by bourgeois commerce.

Marx and Engels revealed the grounding of the new technology in commerce rather than treating it as Saint-Simon had, as the direct outgrowth of advances in science. But more than that, they also held that the private property form did not simply foster but also *limited* the new forces of production, generating a contradiction between the forces and relations of production. It is this contradiction and, in particular, *the inhibitory effects of the property system on technology*, that are systematically occluded in the everyday understanding of the system.

Marxism could thus indicate the ambiguity of commerce, acknowledging its revolutionizing effects upon technology, while also deploring that it uses technology only insofar as it produces profit. Marxism promises that there will come a time when the forces of production will be blocked by the property form and will then need to be overthrown. Thus commercial venality is seen as generating short-run benefits and long-run costs. While technology, itself, is also viewed as ambiguous, its short-run benefits are primarily to owners while its immediate costs are paid by the masses of workers; but in the long run, technology lays the groundwork for the overcoming of scarcity required for socialism.

In this dialectic between the forces and relations of production, it is clear that the former, forces of production, are not reducible to technology, yet this is its concrete paradigm of most importance to Marx and Engels. The forces of production and technology are mutual metaphors. It is the new technology that promises to release mankind from bondage to ancient scarcity, permitting the movement to socialism to go forward. It is the property system that exploits this technology for private gain and which ultimately blocks its continuing development, even though at first accelerating it. Thus the *Communist Manifesto* asserts that ". . . the theory of the Communists may be summed up in a single sentence: Abolition of private property." And more: "The distinguishing feature of Communism is not the abolition of property generally, but the abolition of bourgeois property."

Now in this respect, Marx's socialism clearly and firmly transcended the common sense of the Enlightenment which had held private property sacrosanct. Marx could do this, however, because he could build *upon* the critique of private property formulated by the Saint-Simonians, to whom inheritance had been a fundamental problematic. The Saint-Simonians believed private property in the means of production implied its possible inheritance by incompetents and could thus be wasted as a social resource. They saw this largely as a problem of the rationality of production at the level of the individual manager's relation to his firm and not, as Marx came to see it, as a problem of collectivizing and integrating the separate firms. In many other respects, however, one is dumbfounded by the convergences between the Marxist and Saint-Simonian views about property.

The crucial account is that of the eighth exposition of the Saint-Simonian doctrine, the night of March 25, 1829, which deals with modern theories of property. This begins by noting that the historical progression from the abolition of slavery to the French revolution has meant "the destruction of almost all privileges of birth. . . ."[5] "Almost," for there remains the inconsistency of an abiding privilege—inheritance of property. "This heritage of our fathers is surrounded by an aura of respect. It is the forbidden ground upon which even the hothead cannot tread. This truly religious susceptibility," said the Saint-Simonians, is found not only among reactionary people but also and miraculously "among the enemies of superstition and fanaticism, among the apostles of the emancipation of thought, free enquiry and doubt, but above all among the partisans of human perfectibility."[6] A critique of property, insist the Saint-Simonians, will not be found among the political economists, the majority of whom "and above all Say (in whom nearly all the others are summed up) consider property as an existing fact, the origin, progress, and utility of which they do not examine."[7]

What had captured the attention of the Enlightenment and its *philosophes* was the explosion of *knowledge,* the deification of reason, and the advance of *science;* and, in the German case, the culmination of all philosophy in Hegel—as he himself was not too modest to mention. In contrast to the *philosophes,* who had extolled liberty, equality, fraternity, the Saint-Simonian and Positivist—the two then still being intimately linked—argued that what the revolution had really instituted was industry and science, and above all, science *applied* to industry and thus newly capable of eliminating scarcity.

If, on the one side, every respectable element of society focused on science, technology, and the advance of science, on the other (noted the Saint-Simonians), radicals such as Babeuf and Buonorotti had centered their grievances upon the need for an absolute *equality*. But these "dreams of equality" were not the Saint-Simonians': "Saint-Simon's doctrine cannot give rise to such an absurdity. . . ."[8] This converges with the Marxist position in which, too, equality is not the central project, but rather, the reconstitution of property which the Saint-Simonians had earlier made central.

The Saint-Simonians' enemy is "property by right of birth and not by right of ability, it is inheritance."[9] They thus condemned all the economists because "they all speak of the necessity of maintaining property. But slavery and serfdom were also rights of property."[10] Finally, and Marx never said it more plainly in his discussion of the relation of infra- and super-structures, "the economists of the eighteenth century based their political system on the interest of owners." Inheritance gives birth to a class of men created merely for pleasure, allowing the children of the privileged to devour wealth which, were it better divided, would serve to establish all.[11] The proletariat is now invoked by name; it is expressly characterized as the "disinherited"—those who inherit no property. What is done today, asked the Saint-Simonians, "for the wretched proletarians disinherited. . . . Nothing; misery, isolation, despair and death are their destiny and future." The solution, then, is ". . . to determine through law in a general way that the use of workshops or instruments of industry always passes, after death or retirement of the man who used it, into the hands of the man most able to replace the deceased."[12]

It is because Marxism builds upon this analysis that the *Manifesto* plainly states that the distinguishing feature of communism is the abolition of property, meaning the abolition of inheritance in productive property. Marxism takes the abolition of inheritance as given; this is its own inheritance from the Saint-Simonians. In making property focal, however, it does not patiently wait for the death of owners, and its attention is directed to the question of *who* exactly does replace the private owner, to which the *Communist Manifesto* answers quite plainly, the State. Then Marxism asks, *how* shall it be replaced, and the *Manifesto* again answers clearly and plainly: by "forcible overthrow." It is because Marxism raises and answers these questions as it did, that it conceives itself as having gone beyond its predecessors. It conceives them as "utopians" because they had not understood the task as requiring the mobilization of *power* for the *struggle* against the capitalist class and its state.

But there are problems here: if the idea that property was the "foundation" of the social order was a commonplace of political economy, and indeed of popular, everyday materialism, and if even the Enlightenment had held it sacred, how, then, could Marxism offer this "commonplace"— the importance of property as the grounding of political and social order—as such an eye-opening revelation?

Indeed, a better question is: to *whom* can these "discoveries" seem so striking? Primarily to *intellectuals*. The Saint-Simonians' emphasis on the priority of merit over inheritance, as the basis for allocating property, signals a new historical situation in which property and educational privilege were no longer united. Saint-Simonism was the ideology of the *educationally* privileged, and it is built into the very grounding of Marxism. The defense of privileges in terms of "ability" is the vested interest of the educated and intellectuals. Moreover, that a social reconstruction of the property system would be brought about by a power struggle is, again, a striking idea primarily to intellectuals, whose enlightenment traditions had hitherto drawn them to reform through *education and rational persuasion*. Intellectuals generally regarded ideas, not property, as the prime mover of society, most especially if, like Marx, they had been steeped in the tradition of German philosophical idealism. In short, property as the foundation of the social order appears as an earth-shaking discovery only to intellectuals. It appears so because their common ideology had normally stressed the primacy of ideas, theories, language—consciousness. Thus, radicalized intellectuals recover the experience of their parents; that which had been told them and which they had rejected.

To put the matter more precisely: the idealistic Mandarin culture of intellectuals was dissonant with the experience of their own everyday life in an emerging bourgeois culture whose "vulgarity" gave pride of place not to ideas, but to money and property. (Look at Marx's tirade against money.) A status group such as intellectuals could then maintain a culture nucleated by philosophical idealism only by fostering a radical isolation from the rest of society and/or by a massive repression of bourgeois society's dissonant materialist assumptions. Marxism releases intellectuals from that isolation and from that repression. It enables intellectuals to "recover" the importance of property and money which, while plainly exhibited in their own everyday lives, and in their parents' lives, was simultaneously shrouded by the very different conceptions of their specific occupational culture and education. Marxism not only enables intellectuals to bring property into firm view, but at the same time offers the comforting promise that its days are numbered and calls for its abolition.

Still more: Marxism regards the forces of production as being blocked and thwarted at some point *by the property system*. The thwarted forces of production are plainly associated with a different group—with the practitioners of science and technology. Thus while Marxism's text speaks of the future as an emancipation of the proletariat, its sub-text implies that it is a liberation of the scientific intelligentsia from the ignorant hegemony of owners. Marxism thus offers a future which is comfortable both to humanistic intellectuals who believe that higher values have been vulgarized by property, and liberating to the technological interests and ambitions of the scientific intelligentsia. Marxism thus uniquely provides a grounding for the *unity* of the New Class, which is otherwise divided among older humanistic intellectuals and modern technicians and scientists. Marxism is thus at once a *manifest* critique of moneyed capital and the bourgeoisie, but it is the *latent* ideology of the educationally privileged, of a cultural bourgeoisie with "human capital." Its promise to resolve the contradictions between the forces and the relations of production has "liberative" implications not only for society-in-general, nor just for impersonal "technology" or "science," but for a very specific social group, the New Class of educated intellectuals and intelligentsia. For a function cannot be liberated without liberating the functionary.

Yet if Marxism were a recovery gratifying to the New Class alone, it would isolate New Class members rather than enabling them to attract a large following that could mobilize power in society. We must, therefore, consider how Marxism succeeded in generating favorable attention in a broader public, recovering things of interest to a larger group.

On the Necessity of Evil

In larger measure this has to do with the manner in which Marxism brings the "economic" into focal attention. While in popular, everyday materialism, property is commonly believed to be the "foundation of social order," at the same time, property and the economic are also the object of suspicion and distrust. For example, it is commonly held that "money is the root of all evil," and widely felt—and not only among the educated—that property and the economic are the realm of the selfish, the dirty, the base, the uncharitable, the egoistic. From the standpoint of believing (as distinct from a Sunday) Christianity, economic interests may be defined as selfish and inimical to Christian charity and brotherhood. The economic, then, while widely praised in popular materialism is, nonetheless, an object of ambivalence in a Christian culture.

This ambivalence toward the economic is organized in a special way; there is considerable awareness of and respect for its *power* in the world, but considerably less conviction that the economic is a morally "good" thing, or that its effects upon the world are desirable. Marxism helps resolve these ambivalences about the economic. It does this in part by confirming the potency of the economic, by enabling this potency to be seen as something more than a personal motive or "human nature" but, rather, as an historical force. Marxism both allays and represses unease about the "goodness" of the economic. It acknowledges the suffering it produces for the poor, but maintains that this is only a transient evil, for the bourgeois mode of production is laying the groundwork of emancipation from the realm of scarcity. Marxism also largely de-focalizes the question of the *goodness* of the economic, viewing this as a moralizing sentimentality with which it has nothing in common. Marxism instead stresses that the economic is the realm of necessity, that the evil it does is also *necessary,* until the conditions requisite for the elimination of present suffering have matured.

Yet while de-focalizing the immorality of the economic and subordinating it to necessity, the evolutionary narrative drama of Marxism always intimates an ultimate punishment. In time, the knell of history will ring out, signaling what is clearly a retribution, namely, that "the expropriators will be expropriated." They will reap as they have sown. They will pay. The reconstitution of property so central to Marxism is thus both a political deed and a passion play in which justice is done. Its culminating, most vivid act, however, is not giving property to those who had suffered, but taking it away from the bourgeoisie; it is not an act of restitution but of retribution.

Certainly Marxism does not newly reveal the evil of technology and economic development to the *proletariat*. As Engels saw in his study of the working class in England, the source of their misery was plain. What Marxism does, however, is to make their suffering meaningful and therefore more bearable. Defining it as a necessary but transient stage in their ultimate emancipation, their suffering is transformed into an occasion for a self-redeeming discipline. Marxism guarantees the proletariat both its emancipation and the necessity of its temporary suffering, teaching them to bear it in anticipation of a new world. Workers ought to understand, wrote Marx, that ". . . with all the miseries it imposes upon them, the present system simultaneously engenders the material conditions and the social forms necessary for an economic reconstruction of society."[13] Again, "Fanatically bent upon the expansion of value, he [the capitalist] relentlessly drives human beings to production for production's sake, thus brings about a development of social productivity and the creation of those material conditions of production which can alone form the real basis of a higher type of society. . . ."[14] In this dialectic, there is a unity of opposites, of evil and good, a necessary link between the misery of the present and the emancipation of the future. Marxism thus teaches—peripherally but powerfully—the necessity of evil and the need to harden oneself to it.

The standpoint is Hegelian, in seeking the rational kernel of any economic system, viewing it as having a period during which it is historically progressive and cannot yet be superseded. Each socio-historical system is thus an historical epoch in a larger evolutionary pattern, arising out of what has gone before, yet transcending it and laying the groundwork for the stage that will succeed it, and toward which it moves via its own internal contradictions. Even the capitalist system, then, has a progressive role to play during certain periods of its development, i.e., while it still contributes to the development of productive forces rather than blocking them.

Indeed, a socioeconomic system inflicts costs, pain, and suffering—even during its progressive phase. But these must then be borne, paid as necessary costs on the bill history submits. Insofar as capitalism continues to expand the forces of production, it is a progressive society and the costs it inflicts must be met. Human suffering cannot be surmounted at any time one wishes. Conditions must be ready and developed before the system inflicting the costs can be supplanted by a better one. The Marxist project is thus directed not simply against suffering but, more specifically, against suffering defined as historically *unnecessary*.

To take up arms too soon is the mark of the utopian or of the political adventurer seeking a mere *coup d'état*. Taking up arms too late, however, is accommodation. One must therefore teach the proletariat to bear their suffering, to endure it, as well as to fight those inflicting it when conditions are right. Marxism thus has an undertow of a Christian, tragic element which can sometimes justify brutality and callousness to suffering by the very movement seeking proletarian emancipation. One must learn to "harden" oneself to suffering, to endure it, and indeed to use it as a lever of social change. One must so "harden" oneself to suffering as even to be capable of inflicting it on behalf of historical necessity, expecting that "history will absolve" us.

This is not simply a "lesson" for the working class; it has a special resonance for intellectuals as well. It contains a lesson to them about what leadership entails, one that every battle commander must learn, namely, that he is required to inflict losses not only upon the enemy but also on his own troops. More than that, intellectuals, and romantic intellectuals especially, are told that they too must discipline themselves and control their revulsion against the new society. They must not bolt from society, burrowing into bohemias, but understand that even a society personally repulsive to them is, for a period, under the protection of historical necessity and must be borne. Inhibiting romantic revulsion as a fastidiousness unbecoming the sewermen of history, Marxism reconciles intellectuals to the durability of capitalism. While stressing the inevitability of its demise, Marxism does not claim this is imminent. Thus the need to work out some personal accommodation to capitalism during its reign is sanctioned and, indeed, the enjoyment of bourgeois life styles is not ascetically forbidden. Engels rode to the hounds and sent the Marxes cases of champagne on holidays. As Göran Therborn says, Marxism is the product of non-bohemian intellectuals. What mattered was not a vow of poverty, but the will to struggle, and whether or not conditions were right for struggle. So for romantic intellectuals—and, indeed, especially for romantics—the lesson is about discipline, waiting, preparing, marshaling forces; enjoined to accept blows and suffering while they are the anvil, they are given the compensatory promise that they will someday be history's hammer. This is a politics of deferred gratification which is, of course, more consistent with middle-class ideology than with that of the proletariat. Young middle-class revolutionaries are, in effect, being told that not everything their fathers had to teach them was useless.

To view Marxism as a cryptic doctrine of recovery, then, gives us a rather different perspective on what it is (and is about) than the conventional view that sees it as uniquely concerned with the importance of the economy, economic surplus, of social classes, and of class conflict. Marxism as a doctrine of recovery is, among other things, a theory about the role of knowledge in society and is thus interfaced with the doctrine of the "unity of theory and practice."

From the standpoint of Marxism as recovery, its concern with the economic is no longer a reference to the eternal anatomy of society or a social ontology; in this perspective, Marxism is only manifestly a statement that the economic determines in "the last instance," but is, rather, a metaphor about forgetting and the importance of forgetting. From this perspective, the emphasis on the economic is *contingent,* derived from its having been forgotten by *some relevant group.* The economic is emphasized not only because of its inherent importance but because its importance was forgotten. It says, in effect: in the analysis of society many things are important, but the ones we choose to elaborate on are those in danger of being forgotten or those some key group has forgotten—these have a *special importance*. Marxism is thus not only a theory about the underprivileged, but about underprivileged *reality*.

Why does anyone wish to speak the unspoken? Because the human situation changes in a special way when knowledge about it varies. Knowledge recovered as explicit recognition differs from merely tacit knowledge because it is now possible to reflect upon it more critically and rationally. The commitment of the doctrine of recovery, then, is not to the economic as such but to the economic as hidden (thus unexamined) force and, indeed, to any social force that is hidden. To that extent, Marxism is at least tacitly a theory about the role of rationality in society rather than simply one that accents the power of the economic.

Recovery and the Syntagmatics of Power and Good

The Hegelian/Marxist conception of the necessity of evil is only a concrete instance of a larger aspect of their rationality dealing with certain basic rules of syntagmatics, which is to say, with the kinds of conjunctions of attributes prescribed or allowed. If we hold with Charles Osgood that two of the basic predicates of all objects are, first, their value/goodness and, second, their potency/strength, then one rule of an universal grammar prescribes certain conjunctions of the two: that which is good is also supposed to be weak. To repeat, this is a grammar of morality syntagmatics, prescribing these conjunctions as modes of moral equilibrium.

In effect, the syntagmatic rule stipulates two kinds of social worlds or cultural objects: (1) *prescribed* social worlds or objects, in which (a) goodness and strength or (b) evil and weakness coincide, and (2) *forbidden* social worlds/objects in which evil and power or goodness and weakness coincide. An important part of theology has long been concerned to account for the existence of forbidden worlds, attempting to rationalize how it happens that the good fail to get their just rewards and that an imputedly all-powerful deity permits evil in his world.

To understand the Hegelian/Marxist contribution, a second consideration needs to be added, namely, that there is a powerful tendency for those in whom this grammar of syntagmatics has been internalized to deny, gloss over, rationalize away, repress, or minimize the importance of forbidden worlds/objects. Encountering what seems to be conjunctions of weakness and evil, or of goodness and weakness, there is a powerful impulse for persons to deny what they saw and, instead, to repress or to refract what they in fact saw into something which they did *not* see, but which conforms with the grammar. This common impulse to transform forbidden into prescribed worlds/objects is here called "normalization." To "normalize" a forbidden world is to deny its abnormality, to repress its existence, or to subject it to a perceptual transformation in which one of the two dissonant terms in the conjunction is so changed as to reduce the dissonance; for example, an evil/powerful world/object is perceptually transformed into one that is evil/weak or good/powerful.

We may now better understand the implications of the Hegel/Marx conception of the necessity of evil. Above all, it is an effort to inhibit the common normalization of forbidden worlds/objects, and to resist the common grammar of syntagmatics. To that extent, it is a powerful force toward realism. It says, in effect, that these forbidden worlds can and do happen, that we must be prepared for their occurrence, rather than deny it when it happens. In this, there is an opening to positivism which is lodged in Hegelianism and Marxism alike, both insisting that we must at times accept the world as it is. Hegel, especially in his doctrine of "reconciliation," stresses the rationality of "what is," arguing a cunning of history in which some evils are historically necessary, even if transient. Marx's view of the necessity of waiting for the maturation of objective economic conditions before overthrowing the present, his emphasis that even capitalism with its evils can for a while play a progressive role, is a bit more ambiguous. On one side, this fosters a positivistic accommodation to what is; for in part, it may be read as normalizing a forbidden world—i.e., arguing that an evil capitalism prepared the grounding for good socialism and is, therefore, not "really" evil. In part, Marxism may also be read as condemning any impulse to normalize capitalism as a sentimentalizing claptrap. While neither Hegel nor Marx absolutely rejects the conventional grammar, for in the *final* culminations both envisage goodness and power will again converge, both also produced a significant reinterpretation of that grammar. By firmly demarcating the grammar with its stipulated proprieties from actual performances, they allow systematically for departures from propriety and they inhibit normalizing impulses that would reduce actual performances to the expected proprieties. Marxism thereby enhanced the rationality and realism of social analysis. But to some degree it shared this achievement with positivism.

Positivism, like Marxism, constituted an important epistemological advance. In its opposition to the proliferation of metaphysical invisibles, positivism placed itself in abrasive opposition to conventional and established religion, and much of its rational kernel still resides in that. Even in its mistaken self-understanding as a presuppositionless scholarship, positivism's emphasis on the *empirical* resolution of public contention, makes any society's self-understanding—its common sense and its elites' definitions of social reality—problematic.

There are now no social groups—neither priests, bourgeoisie, nor revolutionaries—whose pronouncement about themselves need be taken as authoritative simply because they had been self-confidently asserted, or because of the authority of those asserting it. Opposing the most ancient traditionalism or the newest dogmatics, positivism's empiricism insisted that a person's social position or political allegiance did not suffice to establish the truth of his declarations. To that extent, positivism also adhered to the culture of critical discourse, although it expected arguments to be resolved finally by reference to some observables. Its sheer empiricism, no less than its culture of critical discourse, however, necessarily created tension for all elite definitions of social reality. These claims had now to be established "empirically," or else be challenged as unproved or meaningless.

Positivism thus affirms that it accepts the reality but not the authority of the world or of groups in it. It assumes that the social conditions it requires to pursue knowledge are secure and will continue to be provided to it. It argues that silence must be open to the reality of the Other; not to the Other's *self*-understanding, but only to inferences that the knower himself makes on the basis of his own observations. The Other thus no longer expresses "truth" but now simply "gives evidence" which must be interpreted. The Other then has been de-authorized as a source of truth and, indeed, has been made suspect as such. He is allowed to retain a compelling claim on our attention, not because of his authority, but because of his sheer existence. In this respect, early positivism too was a *critical* doctrine.

Yet the prestige of science was rising everywhere, at least in the secular world; all manner of honors and material support were being bestowed upon it by the public and by elites, partly in the premature expectation of its utility, partly in the hope that science could win political consensus and resolve social differences, and partly as a symbol of the benign Enlightenment and universalism of these elites. Indeed, the positivists expected the fullest support from *les industriels*. Its enemies were men of the *past*, not those to whom the future belonged and who were already increasingly powerful in the present. The new positivism, then, did not see itself as proceeding against resistance, and as having to extricate knowledge of the *social* world from its concealment and disguises.

Living in a transitional world, between an old regime fighting a rearguard action and a new bourgeois order still only half-born, the positivists' reliance on the "empirical" and rejection of "blame and praise" was possible because neither of these contending social forces then had credit or power enough to impose its views. Indeed, the empirical allowed positivism to hold both at a distance, refusing to concede automatically to either group's definition of social reality. At the same time, the celebration of the empirical filled the vacuum produced by the mutual discrediting of Old Regime and New Bourgeoisie. Positivism saw the new element in society, science (their science and therefore themselves), as lending virtue to the secular powers and yielding a new social equilibrium.

Marxism saw the problem of disequilibrium differently, namely, that the power it required did not yet exist, was still only stirring in the weak proletariat, and had to be brought into being. The positivists, however, at first backed away from the new industrialists when ignored by them and, largely repressing their critical proclivities toward the new order, waited for the powers that be to change tack and give them support—which did, indeed, come to pass.

Marxism's alliance with the weak had consequences as profound as positivism's accommodation to the strong. It meant that Marxists were not dependent on established power elites who, being stronger than they, could impose their definitions of social reality. If Marxism's epistemology developed a tinge of paranoia, at least it escaped positivism's Pollyanna prattle about soaring beyond praise and blame. Marxism could thus block the reduction of performances to proprieties, could see power (capitalism) as evil and the weak (proletariat) as good; it inhibited the distortions of normalizing definitions of social reality sponsored by the powerful. Its crucial epistemological maneuver was that it had not allied itself with forces stronger than it was. Yet however much this strengthened its rationality, it did not fortify its moral sensibility.

The Anomie of Marxism

Marxism's capacity to control its normalizing impulses involved the simultaneous inhibition of its moral capacities and subjected it to an endemic *anomie*. This was closely connected with the way it inhibited normalization, i.e., by diverting the issue away from the goodness of some social world or object and substituting concern with its *necessity*. Necessity was an alternative to and inhibitant of moral judgment, and was indeed presented as superior to morality's sentimentalizing. Marxism's disjuncture between economic infrastructure and ideological superstructure also implied that the moral consciousness was a mere epiphenomenon, derivative of the power of the infrastructure, and not to be taken seriously.

The central strategy of the Marxist project, its concern with seeking a remedy to *unnecessary* suffering, was thus in the end susceptible to a misuse that betrayed its own highest avowals. The root of the trouble was that this conception of its own project redefined pity. Sheer human suffering alone did not qualify, in the Marxist view, to justify concern for others, or efforts on their behalf, or to invite sympathy, or to feel solidarity with the afflicted. The human condition was rejected on behalf of the historical condition. In short, Marxism, like any ideology, shunned the tragic. It shunned that suffering to which the flesh is universal heir—indeed its historicism casts doubt that any such is universal—and attended to the suffering which men at certain times and places may, through struggle, avoid.

The trouble here is not only that this limits the scope of Marxism's capacity for human solidarity and sympathy. The trouble, rather, is that if the Marxist project is the reduction of *needless* suffering, one may not only turn one's back on certain sufferings, holding them to be presently beyond correction, but then, going one step further, one may now claim the highest moral sanction for the infliction of new suffering under the justification of necessity. The historically necessary becomes the sacred. Men acting in the name of this higher necessity are acting on behalf of something which can sanction almost any cruelty. Convincing ourselves that we are acting only as the agent of necessity, we may then become the Grand Inquisitor and Sacred Torturer of History.

11

Holism:
The Rationality of Marxism, II

I want to begin summing up my thoughts about Marxism, asking once again, how it came to be that Marxism had such a tremendous impact upon the world and how it found such widespread acceptance with a speed known by no other system of thought. What won it such acceptance?

In asking this question we need to be mindful of the different ways it can be put. In one respect, to which I am sympathetic, our concern is not simply with all the reasons why Marxism has made its way so effectively in the world, but especially with a certain, limited kind of reason—with, one might call them, the *good* reasons for Marxism's acceptance. Here, the question asked is both moral and factual. The premise is that, at least for a period, there were good reasons for Marxism's being accepted, that the millions believing in it were not totally deluded, misguided, or stupid, and that there were (or are) aspects of Marxism that, given the conditions in which people found themselves, *deserve* to have been accepted. In other words, the question here is: what is the rationality of Marxism?

This is very much the Hegelian framing of the question which, despite its manifest virtues, also has certain costs. Most notably, there is the temptation to assume that, if there are good reasons for accepting Marxism then, whatever acceptance it is given, is always for a "good" reason and due to Marxism's rationality. Indeed, this is also Marxism's own self-understanding. Yet we had better be careful not to totalize; not to assume that simply because there were some good reasons for accepting Marxism that *all* reasons for doing so were good or rational. In short, we must not assume, with Hegel, that whatever is real is rational.

Hegel's inclination—at least, the Hegel of "reconciliation"—is to assume that the reality or power of things blends harmoniously with their goodness (= rationality). The trouble is that this assumption is often accepted simply because it is comforting. Hidden in it is an apologetic impulse to accommodate to what is, a certain "positivism" which appears odd for so dialectical a philosophy because it implies a readiness to normalize the world. It is not only promised that the good and the powerful will live together happily ever after in the Great Absolute but, even more comforting to secular minds, they are also said to have cunning ways in which they already dwell together in bliss. Like the good magician, the normalizing theorist edifies his audience by his dexterity, exhibiting the unexpected rationalities of the world. In anthropology and sociology, this intellectual legerdemain was called structural functionalism or just plain functionalism. It had a certain vulgarian Leibnizianism in which even our own jungle is portrayed as a paradise, "the best of all possible worlds." The tendency to reduce accounts of the survival of social phenomena to their rationality manifests the pathetic fallacy of intellectuals whose everyday ideology affirms the power of right thinking—that very unity of the good and powerful that Hegel projected into a systematic metaphysics of the identity of the real and rational. While such a standpoint is in my view generally wrong, it does particular violence to our subject, to Marxism and its "materialism." Equating the rational and the real is essentially the conceit of philosophical idealism which, since Socrates, has assumed that the nucleus of the good life somehow centered on the cognitive and the rational, and believed that evil was essentially a kind of ignorance.

If we cannot tolerate a standpoint that equates the real and the rational, neither can we pretend that the forces sustaining Marxism are only the need and greed of its users or that it has prevailed (where it prevailed) simply because it was powerful, as if its ability to mobilize power had no connection at all with its own kind of intelligence and rationality. We cannot set ourselves above and apart from Marxism in this way, pretending that we study it as we might a rock or a fish, that it has nothing to teach us, that it is merely an object to be learned about rather than learned from. In short, while we cannot allow a standpoint that equates the real and the rational, neither can we dehumanize our study and forget that we are studying men and women who are not only as real as but every bit as rational as we who study them. We cannot understand their work unless we see it as exhibiting their achievement of rationality as well as certain specific limits on their rationality.

The Emancipatory Horizon

Marxism itself is, after all, not simply post-Hegelian but anti-Hegelian—
as well as anti-idealistic and anti-rationalistic. While Marxism's project
aimed at enhancing rationality, at extirpating false consciousness, at de-
mystifying the world, still its aim was not rationality as such; it included
but went beyond rationality. Any failure to understand this is to make
the egregious error of confusing Marx with Jürgen Habermas and of reducing Marxism to a philosopher's project. Rather than aiming at rationality as such, Marxism had a broader horizon—*emancipation*.

Marxism's object was to transform the everyday life by subjecting it
to a critically appropriated grammar of rationality brought to focus on a
political project. This project aimed at world reconstruction through
political struggle for which rational diagnosis, rational persuasion, and
critique were subsidiary, were necessary but not sufficient, were a part
but not the whole. Marx believed that "social being" which in its sociological version meant (in his words) "sensuous human activity" determined social consciousness and with this, rationality; making rationality
historically possible under some but not all social conditions; strengthening or debilitating it under different social arrangements.

Marx never focuses, therefore, on the general and universal social conditions necessary for rationality; for him rationality was an historical
achievement which could have diverse forms. Moreover, his aim was to
produce revolutionary institutional changes which would somehow foster
a human emancipation that would by itself dissipate all false consciousness and de-mystify society—in short, heighten rationality. The issue here
is not whether Marx was mistaken (as I believe he was) in adopting
such a mechanical view of the prospects of rationality but, rather, to see
that his project subordinates rationality to a larger vision of "emancipation." Marx never doubted that rationality was only part of "emancipation" and only part of the struggle through which he expected to bring
it about. Thus in the oft-cited passage in *The German Ideology,* Marx
and Engels note that "in communist society . . . it is possible for me to
do one thing to-day and another tomorrow, to hunt in the morning, fish
in the afternoon, rear cattle in the evening, criticize after dinner, without ever becoming hunter, fisherman, shepherd, or critic."[1]

Marx's vision of the good man was not, therefore, someone with a
huge bulging brain from which there dangled a matchstick body and
spindly limbs; nor was his a vision of man as the coolly self-possessed
strategist. Marx also admired strength and passion in men (as his daughter Laura tells us) and the will to struggle courageously. In this, Marx
resonated with the classical Greek search for "roundedness" and with the

romantic striving for emancipation of the body. Marx sought a unity of theory and practice, not the dominance of theory over practice. This further implies that insofar as Marxism is committed to rationality, it is committed not only to pure reason—not only to reason for its own sake—but, rather, to practical reason which is not simply consciousness-raising but, more broadly, life-supporting.

Marxism, then, is not a philosopher's bony rationalism; it rejects contemplation dissociated from sensuousness, thought separated from action, the theoretical attitude isolated from practical reason, philosophy separated from life. Marx himself made this plain when he summarized his disagreements with Feuerbach in what have been dubbed his "Theses on Feuerbach." The chief defect of previous forms of materialism, says the first thesis, is that they conceive of reality only in the "form of the object or of contemplation." Feuerbach, he holds, mistakenly "regards the theoretical attitude as the only genuinely human attitude, while practice is conceived and fixed only in its dirty-judaical manifestation. Hence he does not grasp the significance of revolutionary, or of practical-critical, activity." The second thesis argues that men "prove the truth . . . in practice." The third maintains that not only are men changed by circumstances but that they also change themselves, and that the two, world-changing and self-changing, can only be understood and produced by "revolutionary practice." The fourth thesis observes that the religious world grows out of the secular which must "in itself be understood in its contradictions and revolutionized in practice." This evocation of man as sensuous and active, rather than simply as intellective, culminates, of course, in the final and familiar eleventh thesis: "The philosophers have only interpreted the world in various ways; the point is to change it."[2]

Marx's is not a condemnation of interpretation (or of the theoretical attitude) as such, but only of its perverse transformation into an end in itself, into a passive contemplation of the world that leaves everything as it was found. Nor does Marx pursue a critique of interpretation because he aims to substitute for it a joy in sensuousness and a delight in the sheer appearances of things. There is small doubt that Marx shared the familiar "masculine" conception that conceives of interpretation as a piercing of the surface and a getting to the bottom of things. He is not worried that interpretation is an act of aggression on the world, the intellectual's way of reconstructing reality. Rather, Marx is worried that a pursuit of interpretation *alone* feeds the intellectual's specific arrogance: presenting his limited talent as the world's supreme salvation, and exalting mind and rationality as panaceas for all the world's ills.

Marx's critique here is kin to his central objection to idealism; his insistence that "consciousness" cannot be understood in isolation; his conviction that rationality is part of a larger array of human talents no one of which can be understood in isolation from the others, and that reason is partner in, not master over, the human enterprise. Most basically, Marx's views of consciousness, rationality, and interpretation are a critique of any tendency to substitute part for whole; they are an affirmation of the whole, of "social being," of sensuous praxis. Marx's project of emancipation, then, is at bottom a critique of and drive to overcome *fragmentation*. The most fundamental character of his project is to make the world whole, to connect the disconnected, to integrate the isolated, to remember the forgotten and the repressed, and to overcome old contradictions. The deep structure of Marx's project moves toward a vision of a new human unity overcoming the divisiveness of competitive, possessive individualism, of a civil society where the common interest is no one's business. At this level Marx's macroscopic sociology and his epistemology share a common structure, the sociology seeking to reconstruct the class-riven society into a solidary human community, and the epistemology aiming at the reconstruction of discourse, in which meaning is established by the joining of hitherto disconnected fragments, by a *recontextualizing* analysis, by pursuing the understanding of "superstructure" in the light of the underlying infrastructure of the forces and relations of production. It is thus a move toward both a new world and a new rationality.

Marx directs himself, then, toward a critique of man's alienation from the world and from himself; of the cleavages wrought by the division of labor, of the separation of manual from intellectual labor, and of town from country; he directs himself to the need to overcome the separation between philosophy and the everyday life, or the gap between theory and praxis. He seeks to overcome traditional religion as an obsolescent and mystified wholeness, and the modern sciences as a new specious wholeness, when they do not simply augment fragmentation.

Marxism's epistemology, its sociology, and its politics thus all share a common deep structure, reunification of a fragmented world; and it is at this level that Marxism achieves its fullest rationality. Yet, as Marx might well have expected, this reunifying rationality is not without its own new contradictions. In one, Marxism's reunifying drive smashes up on the powerful monopoly of economic and political powers that it uniquely bestows upon the state. As a result, such reunification as it achieves is regressive and external, devoid of the inner adhesiveness of the free community Marx had sought. Marxism's reunifying drive was also directed against post-Enlightenment cultural fragmentation—spurred partly by the decline of religion and the church and by the rise of fragmenting intellectual specializations—but this, too, was distorted by Marxism's transformation into an official state doctrine which did not hesitate to impose unity through bureaucratic censorship.

Reunifying the World:
Positivism + Romanticism

The eighteenth century's rapidly expanding commercial and industrial order and the burgeoning world market to which it was linked were other sources of fragmentation whose effects ramified in every direction, undermining all older social structures: threatening the pre-bourgeois elites and the old political institutions they had fashioned, threatening the old family system by separating its members during the day and for even longer periods as they left to find work in the city. With the spread of enlightenment criticism and of science in the eighteenth and nine-teenth centuries, and with the church's insistence on allying itself with the losing aristocracy, even the once unifying clerical authority waned. The rise of markets in landed property threatened the economic position of the old elites as well as their family integrity; the decline of the guilds threatened the artisans and their families with a loss of security and privilege; indeed, it had been they, far more than the new industrial fac-tory workers, who most militantly supported the revolutions of 1848. And both the artisan and old elites were threatened by the rise of the middle class as well as of the factory system and its workers.

This historical junction saw vast social damage and growing conflict as the cities exploded with new rural migrants, often unattached men unfamiliar and unhappy with city life. As the movement to emancipate the serfs grew, tensions also spread into the countryside, and disorders and jacqueries became more frequent. From all directions a profound sense of widespread change emerged, a sense of the decline of the old order, of the rise of a new one whose character still remained unclear and undeveloped, a sense that the two were in opposition and that the new era was one of transition and social conflict. The sense of the social "order" as a predictable, familiar, and manageable system waned. The mappings of the old social order no longer enabled persons to move around the emerging society effectively and to understand it.

One massive, widespread reaction was a surge of new, comprehensive map-making efforts at different levels and in different quarters of society. On the state level, there was an intensive development of "constitution"-making which was, in effect, an effort at the comprehensive legal specifi-cation of new structures for the new society, an effort to bind it up and organize it in minutely legislated detail. From another direction, which was an important source of Marxism itself, there emerged "utopian socialism"—the socialism of Fourier, the Saint-Simonians, and of Cabet—which presented its own image of a counter social order often in equally minute and even more comprehensive detail. Utopian socialism's comprehensiveness was the emerging left's map-making counterpart to constitutionalism, while the latter was the map-making utopianism of the respectable middle classes. Utopianism was also, we might say, the future-oriented counterpart to the backward-looking historical novel of the romantics. In both cases, social worlds were being designed and mapped in imaginative detail, were offered as new social "wholes" alternative to the fragmentation of the present.

Two of the great social movements that responded to the intensified fragmentation were particularly important for Marxism. One was the growth of French positivism around Saint-Simon and the Saint-Simonians, which thus overlapped with utopian socialism, and the other was the growth of romanticism as a European-wide development. Marxism itself, is, in substantial part, to be understood as an effort at the fusion of these two great social movements, both of which were efforts to revitalize European culture, to reorganize it, to express the new fragmentation, and to help overcome it.

The Saint-Simonians, for their part, had an articulate sense that it was their task to contribute to the *completion* and maturation of the new society around them. Above all, they conceived their task as one of "organizing" the new society, of bringing its dismembered parts together. One way they expressed this, and sought to do something about it, was in their development of new systems of transportation, railroads, postal systems, credit and banking systems, and, in a way oddly, their unique interest in the building of canals. Indeed, when Saint-Simon was with Lafayette during the American revolution, he conceived the project of building what, in effect, later became the Panama Canal; subsequently, it was the vision and preparation of the Saint-Simonians that laid the groundwork for de Lesseps's later development of the Suez Canal.

The Saint-Simonians saw society as almost physically dismembered, and as needing to be reknit. They believed that the new society would be held together by a new theology and religion that would have to be consistent with the new science and so invented a new "religion of humanity." At the same time, seeking to extend the principles of science to the study of man—so that knowledge would then have one rather than multiple systems of principles—they also invented the positive "science of society." Having earlier been one of Saint-Simon's promising young men and secretaries, Auguste Comte fashioned a new "sociology" that was simply one variant of Saint-Simonism.

The point of the new social science was not simply pure knowledge about men but the practical reconstruction of a unified society; indeed, this was also the understanding that Pecquer and Leroux had of the new social science. The central point of Saint-Simon's new "positivism" was that it would provide a science of politics. He believed that the advent of a truly scientific study of man meant that social and political questions could now be resolved authoritatively. Applied to human affairs, social science could produce "positive" (certain) conclusions to which all would consent, thus unifying the fragmented, anarchic society within a new social consensus. The new science and technology, moreover, were also expected to heighten productivity, thus providing greater economic welfare for the working class and thereby winning their loyalty for the new society. Finally, science was to provide the basis for a new system of administration, enabling decisions to be made and enacted without force and violence, merely by winning the voluntary consent of subordinates. In these three ways, then, positivism expected science to overcome social fragmentation.

Sociological positivism was related to the breakdown of traditional mappings in one unique way, in its sense of the irrelevance of all past dominant mappings and in its search for the new *method* of mapping and defining social reality. Hostile to lawyers and metaphysicians, it sought for new elites that could authoritatively re-establish social order on modern bases. For positivism, the new authorities were to be scientists, technologists, and *industriels;* its new method, of course, was to be science.

Much the same mapping problem was then also being confronted by the romantics who, however, did not define the task as a cognitive, scientific, or even rational one but often viewed it as requiring a feat of imagination, spirit, and faith. As I have discussed elsewhere,[3] however, it would be totally mistaken to think of French positivism and of romanticism as two entirely separate responses; indeed, French positivism was at first undoubtedly a blend of science and romanticism.

The German version of romanticism, however, developed along special lines because it was a response not only to problems and developments in its own society but, in addition, was affected by the earlier responses that the French had made to similar problems. The Germans' negative judgment of the latter was due partly to the Napoleonic presence and French cultural hegemony in the Germanies. The romantics expressed their sense of modern fragmentation and disunity in part through their call to an intense "organic" society, and in part, through their notion of the "grotesque" which they saw as the incongruous and ominous conjunction of cultural incompatibles. The strange world of the grotesque was also viewed in a special way; it was looked on as one looked at events in a dream, as a passive onlooker who felt alienated from what he saw. Romantics also expressed their sense of living in a twilight world of transition, between an unsatisfactory past and as yet unworkable future, by developing an aesthetic that saw objects as blending into one another rather than as well demarcated by hard-edged boundaries. They felt that to seek truth by the careful dissections of analytic reason was an alien (French) perversion that could only produce a vivisection that destroyed living reality. The separation of objects was overcome by blurring; ambiguity became transvalued. Faced with a changing social reality in which social structure and the traditional ways of understanding it were both dissolving, the romantics sought to rescue meaning by "romanticizing." That is, by endowing the ordinary, everyday world with the pathos of the extraordinary—by idealizing mundane reality. As Novalis said, to romanticize was to see the infinite in the finite, the universe in a grain of sand. The romantics' characteristic concern with the symbolic was thus another way in which they sought to overcome the split in the world, linking immediate appearances with underlying essence, observation with imagination.

Moreover, many romantics—as for example, the young Goethe—sought to discipline themselves into a wholeness that joined reason with sensuality, will, and feeling. (The young Goethe said, "Feeling is all.") Others, however, rather than seeing feeling and reason as complementary, held they were incompatibles. For many romantics, love—"romantic love"—assumed importance as a way of overcoming human isolation and distance; they stressed mood and feeling because, in mood, one feels whole and overcomes inner conflict, while with intense feeling, internal ambivalences are overcome. Love, said Coleridge, can make the self whole. In a similar vein, the romantics began the redemption of the flesh and the modernization of sexuality, defining the true social unit as bisexual combination of men and women. The "liberation of women" begins here in romanticism.

Thus, in Western Europe, romanticism and positivism overlapped, because they both were responding to the same sense of the early nineteenth century's fragmentation. Marxism shared with them this sense of fragmentation and the effort to overcome it. So, when the young Marx remarks that "philosophy is the head of emancipation, and the proletariat is the heart," he is politicizing the Goethian effort to reunite reason and feeling. Certainly, for Marx, reason alone could achieve no worldly political reconstruction—and that, he said, was the whole point, not just another interpretation of the world. For Marx, political reconstruction was not simply a laboratory experiment but required a commitment of the whole person, of the passions no less than of the intelligence. Marx's abiding aim to transcend "alienation" is a characteristically romantic effort to mend the split between and within men, reuniting rational man with active, sensuous man. It was in the horizontal division of labor in which workers became alienated from their own faculties, and it was the vertical division of labor which reproduced the property system in which men lost control over the products of their own labor. Wanting a society in which all human faculties could find a home, Marx thus rejected the Socratic rule—one man, one task—and looked to a time in which men could play several roles in the course of a single day, uniting manual and intellectual, aesthetic and cognitive activities.

Marxism Against Fragmentation

The point here, to reiterate it emphatically, is *not* that "Marx was a romantic" but, rather, that like the romantics (and the positivists) much (no, not *all*) of the deeper problematic of his work was that of fragmentation. Yet how can this view be reconciled with the manifest importance that Marx attributed to class differences and with his commitment to the class struggle and the proletariat? Marx chose the working class as his "historical agent" precisely because he believed that its position of total deprivation and increasing misery made it a "universal class" whose suffering would lead it ultimately to reject not only its own wage slavery but the entire system of exploited and exploiting classes. It cannot achieve its own emancipation, Marx thought, at the cost of fastening the yoke of repression upon another class and does not seek, as other classes had, simply to produce a new system of exploitation. It represents the interests of the majority in the beginning and, ultimately of all: "All previous historical movements were movements of minorities, or in the interest of minorities," notes the *Communist Manifesto*, but "the proletariat movement is the self-conscious, independent movement of the immense majority, in the interest of the immense majority."[4] After the proletariat is raised to the position of the ruling class, says the *Manifesto*, then "in place of the old bourgeois society, with its classes and class antagonisms, we shall have an association, in which the free development of each is the condition for the free development of all."[5] In short, fragmentation can then give way to community. Rather than rejecting anti-fragmentation, class struggle was Marx's way of healing class antagonisms—an incongruity scarcely intolerable to the romantic tradition's fascination with the grotesque and to the Hegelian committed to the "unity of opposites."

In this, as in so many other ways, there was an important continuity between Marx and Hegel. The notion of a "universal class," as an agency to unify and represent the interests of society as a whole, was largely derived by Marx from Hegel. Hegel's own starting point had been a German classicism in which the modern world was tacitly or explicitly contrasted with the supposed unity of the ancient Greek city-state, where men's personal existence was intimately bound up with the *polis*.

In a similar vein, Marx sees private property as instigating an egoism and individualism inimical to social solidarity: "Marx comes to the conclusion in the *Critique* that private property is essential to the achievement of the socio-political ideal of the *Gemeinwesen*. . . . Genuine human emancipation . . . is achieved only with the elimination of such conflict and duality. . . ."[6]

Concerned with the atomization wrought by private property in civil society, Hegel had earlier sought to reunify society and had believed that this was primarily to be done through the Estates General and state bureaucracy. While rejecting Hegel's solution, Marx accepts the general framework of the problem, in which the task of modern reconstruction is formulated in a very special way—as the overcoming of divisions, disunity, fragmentation. Here, to reconstruct is to make the split world whole again. The task, here, is thus not to find a solution to this or that partial "social problem" in different spheres of life but to overcome the sheer disconnectedness of the several spheres.

So Marx accepts the basic contours of Hegel's problem, that some kind of pulling together of society, some kind of "organizing" of it—in the positivists' words—was necessary. They differ, of course, in the agency of this unification, Marx substituting the proletariat for Hegel's bureaucracy. "Marx took seriously Hegel's notion of a universal class, that is, a class within society whose interests are identical with the interests of society as a whole, and therefore of man himself as a naturally social, species-being."[7] As distinct from its power as an historical agent, nothing makes the proletariat a *legitimate* agent except its supposed universality; it is this which legitimates the proletariat's mission in terms of the classical requirement that authority in the state be nonpartisan and "serve the people." Marx thus selects the proletariat as historical agent as much for its legitimacy as for its efficacy. But the essential point, for all its "false consciousness," is that the proletariat is conceived by Marx as the agent of history and of the general interest; the interests of the whole are conceived as vested in part; this part undertakes a struggle not for itself alone, but for the reunification of the whole; and it seeks human peace through class struggle. Marx's commitment to the proletariat and class struggle thus does not contradict but exhibits the essential anti-fragmenting drive of his theory.

Central, if subliminal, to Marx's work there is also an effort to unite the value perspectives of the classical world, its intense commitment to the importance of "contest" and agonic struggle,[8] with the modern world's accent on the redemptive power of work, the gospel of labor. Here, too, Marx is trying to make the world one. Much the same may be said of Hegel's earlier analysis of the master-bondsman dialectic which is also an effort to integrate new and old, modern and classical, work and struggle. In this, Hegel exhibits the dialectic between heroism and routine disciplined work. Although Hegel extols labor's transformative power, he does so only by treating it as a kind of sublimated struggle which aims to "annihilate" or dominate nature. Labor is tacitly treated as a mode of domination on the model of the heroic struggle. In Hegel's master-bondsman dialectic, there is an echo of the classical Greek notion that it is better to die than live as a slave, yet death is also feared as one of the most terrible disasters. There is an ambivalence between fear of death and hatred of submission. In Hegel's dialectic, however, a Christian and bourgeois note has been added: the bottom rail becomes the top through work. The conquered who was forced into slavery redeems himself through the discipline of his labor and becomes superior to his conqueror and master. Ironic romantic reversal thus parallels Christian parable. Hegel's master-bondsman dialectic attempts to harmonize Greek classicism and its accent on struggle with Christian meekness, bourgeois work, and romantic irony. This ambitious syncretism is at the heart of his master-slave dialectic.

A similar (but not identical) fusion is central to Marx. It is interesting, however, that, when asked to summarize his philosophy in one word, Marx chose "struggle" rather than "work." When he concludes the *Manifesto* with the ringing call to a struggle in which "the proletarians have nothing to lose but their chains," he is echoing the agonic ethic of classicism, not simply in its stress on struggle but, also, in its "heroism," apparently deeming it unworthy of mention that proletarians may, indeed, lose their very lives in this struggle, especially since in the same breath he has already declared that their goals "can be attained only by the forcible overthrow of all existing conditions."[9]

This is the heroic ethic of a classicism that assumed that men would willingly risk death rather than live as slaves. Marx's fusion of struggle and labor offers a political sphere in which heroic struggle compensates for degrading labor in the economy. At the same time, revolutionary struggle in the political sphere is to be infused with the discipline learned in the industrial system, i.e., it is to become methodical and organized, a kind of political work, while (as for Hegel) labor becomes a struggle against nature, a mode of domination.

Holism and Epistemology

Marx's epistemology—his assumptions of how to proceed toward and ensure knowledge—is also grounded in his opposition to fragmentation as
inimical to truth; as Hegel had said, "the truth is the whole."[10] Systematic concern with holistic analysis was thus, in large part, derived
by Marx from Hegel. Hegel had viewed entire societies as integrated by
an enveloping "spirit of the age" or of the people—a spirit which was
seen to pervade all its institutions and infuse all its parts. This spirit of
the age was the historical expression at the national level of the unfolding world *Geist*. For Hegel, then, the whole is constituted as a whole
(that is, integrated) by the common spirit pervading its several parts.

Two other features characterize the Hegelian whole: One is that it is
not, at any given moment, a finished and perfected entity, but is continuously evolving in a *progressive* manner, such that its later state has
assimilated the rational part of the previous state and has reorganized it
into some larger, more comprehensive entity. Second, the movement of
this whole proceeds by the unfolding of its own internal *contradictions*
and of efforts to compose and transcend these contradictions. The Hegelian whole is neither complete nor harmonious, although it is integrated
by diffusion of the *Zeitgeist* or *Volksgeist*.

The whole here is thus integrated at the *cultural* level, by reason of
common ideas and understandings distributed among the parts. The parts
of the Hegelian whole then are united "inwardly" by their participation
in a common spiritual substance and not merely outwardly, by the different functions they perform for one another. For Hegel, to know the
whole, one must know the spirit pervading the parts. The parts are the
work of the spirit; they are its epiphenomena, uniformly shaped, as it
were, by the anterior code or logic of the spirit. The fullest secularization of this formulation is the anthropological concept of *culture* as a
"super-organic" domain of shared understandings which is not imprinted
by men's bio-genetic nature, and which is transmitted by learning from
generation to generation, or from one territory to another.

The Hegelian "spirit of the age" as it pervades and unifies a total society is thus an esoteric cultural determinism. As a determinism, the
Hegelian whole retains an hierarchical metaphysic, the lower parts being
imputedly determined by the higher cultural or spiritual code. The integration existing among the elements, then, is not the solidarity of peers
based on their mutual aid and need, but a "Lutheran" hierarchical integration entailing domination and subordination. The vision of the "father" set over his sons lurks here.

Marxist theory is based on the assumption that the world of conscious-

ness and that of the "social being" of the infrastructure are not two separate realms, but, rather, two different sides of a single totality. This is its
"materialism." If for Hegel the whole is held together by the common
spirit infusing its several parts, Marx's materialist counterpart has a similar integrating role. If Hegel moves against fragmentation by a monistic
integration wrought by the *Geist,* Marx moves toward a monistic materialism to accomplish the same task. Either monism is a unity-produc-
ing machine. If for Hegel the split world is made one by being made of
Geist, Marx (as he himself tells us) merely turned this all upside down,
assimilating ideal and consciousness into the material. As the *Communist
Manifesto* says in direct address to the bourgeoisie: "Your very ideas are
but the outgrowth of your bourgeois production and bourgeois property,
just as your jurisprudence is but the will of your class made into a law
for all, a will whose essential character and direction are determined by
the economic conditions of existence of your class."[11]

The point of such a materialism, however, is not only the identification of a controlling substance fundamentally different from what it controls but, rather, the assertion of the unity of the world in that (material) substance. The point of this materialism, then, is not tangible
matter but intangible unity. It is, paradoxically, a very "spiritual" materialism. Like Hegel, it assumes that there can be unity only when things
have the same or a common substance permeating the whole. Such a
unity premises one substance, whether that substance is a Spirit, or "material"; both contrast with the kind of unity involved in the notion of
"system" which premises a division of labor, the togetherness of essentially diverse but equally real substances. In Marxism, the "whole" is the
tacit, *un*theorized, structural implication of the materialist analytic. It
is tacit and untheorized because Marx's focus is on only *part* of the
larger context, specifically the economic-production-technological-prop-
erty-power elements: i.e., the "infrastructure." But these are, indeed,
unmistakably part of a larger societal totality, an encompassing socioeconomic *system,* a "capitalist system."

Marx moves toward the societal totality by way of its governing "economic" infrastructure, which is always understood as part of a larger societal whole. Marx's conception of production as an infrastructure implies
that it is a part which in turn premises a context-establishing whole.
This, however, is obscured by the focus on the infrastructure as a *determining* part. Marx's move to the totality bogged down while passing
through the territory of the socioeconomic. The ideological superstructure was seen as determined by the socioeconomic "in the last instance,"
so that their joint constitution of an encompassing whole remains largely
tacit. Marx's own holism is thus less emphatic than his specification of

the infrastructural part that governs the whole, "in the final instance." It is the socioeconomic part that is situated in his peripheral, auxiliary awareness. The former was his problematic; the latter was a "given" to him, his Hegelian inheritance.

Marx's analytic strategy for *integrating* the whole is, I have suggested, similar to Hegel's. Like Hegel, he focuses on a *single* sphere or substance which imposes a monistic integration on a societal whole seen as evolving via its internal contradictions. Since the whole retains a hierarchical integration, Marx retains the topography of Hegel's structure even as he "inverts" him, "standing him on his feet." Hegel's *Geist* is now transformed into the "material" forces and relations of production that govern the whole. At the level of his most general domain assumptions—as distinct from his topic-focused, concrete historical studies—Marx thus remains within the deep structure of the Hegelian analysis of the whole; like Hegel's, Mark's whole entails a hierarchical, two-tiered totality: a manifest (super) structure of appearances governed by a deep or latent (infra) structure. The latter becomes the analyst's cognitive problematic, the hidden, silent element to be revealed, "recovered," and spoken in each new concrete case. For Marx, to *analyze* means: reveal and recover the historically special and contradictory character of the *infra*structure in each case, and its distinctive interplay with other forces, which together are conceived to be a totality.

Marxism is thus open to two different strategies of theoretical development: *One:* In polemicizing against idealism's assertion of the autonomy of ideas, it sometimes re-contextualizes these simply by counter-asserting against them the importance of another "factor," the socioeconomic, thus limiting re-contextualization to the assertion of a competing, "hidden" factor. Here Marxism remains within a tacit single-*factor* model, where each model affirms its own different (but still single) factor. *Two:* In another outcome, however, Marxism's re-contextualizing critique of idealism only *negates* the affirmations of idealism, simply saying, no, ideals are not autonomous. It does not counterpose to these the socioeconomic treated as just another single factor; while noting the importance of the socioeconomic, it stresses the re-contextualizing *logic,* and focuses on some larger whole in which outcomes are patterned differently for *all* the totality's constituents, whether ideas or socioeconomic sub-systems.

The first Marxist strategy reproduces a factor model; the second moves toward a cryptic, holistic model of which there can be different types. Counterposing the "economic factor" against "consciousness," arguing that consciousness was determined by social being, the factor model was a Scientific Marxism that degenerated into "vulgar Marxism." The second development of Marxism—toward cryptic holism—which simply holds that consciousness is not autonomous but an aspect of the whole—was Lukács's vision of a Critical Marxism that focused on the "totality."

Each of the two models is thus produced differently: The factorial model of Marxism is produced by focusing on an overcoming of philosophical idealism that re-contextualizes consciousness by affirming its alleged contrary, the economic factor. Lukács's cryptic totality model, however, is produced by re-contextualizing the *economic itself*, and in addition, it (1) rejects factorialization as a species of *mechanical* model, (2) accepts a tacit organicism, and (3) formulates a critique of idealism that does not simply counter-assert the contrary of consciousness but negates the logic of "the last instance" as an epistemological principle.

Factorial model, materialism-as-contrary, vulgar Marxism, is economistic, sociologistic, and structural. It focuses on socioeconomic structures as having their own unswerving impulsion, their own autonomous blind laws; as fundamentally ("in the last instance") impervious to other regions surrounding it. It interposes a *one-way* osmotic membrane between itself and them and is thus not as open to other "factors" as they are to it. It is not as reciprocally exposed to fundamental transformations from the larger eco-system, its links with "nature" being only residually acknowledged. Nor, for that matter, does it link the socioeconomic subsystem to the psychodynamic level, to the psychology and physiology of persons. Operating with a hierarchical metaphysic, a *factor model* of Marxism treats some things as real and others as not, or at any rate, treats some things as more real than elements in the ideological superstructure. Its holism, then, is patriarchal.

The more truly holistic perspective of Critical Marxism is, by contrast, a *general* social science (or theory) in *embryo*. A general social science or theory is not one, such as economics or sociology, but, rather, assumes that any accounting of human behavior always implies a number of different "levels." All of these are always implicated in affecting outcomes, although some levels may not be focal to the work conventionally done by a special social science. A general social science or theory implies a levels analysis which holds that, for any proposition about human behavior to be true at any one level, something must be the case at each and all the other levels. While the concrete "parts" examined in an analysis vary with the specific system/totality being studied, each level must always be touched explicitly (or is otherwise used implicitly and hence uncritically) in any analysis of any concrete system/totality. All levels must in principle always be considered.

Among the different levels that a levels-focused general social discipline might, *for example*, encompass, there could be the ecological, the psychological, the social system, the cultural, the class, status, or role level. A general social discipline implies that no analysis can avoid having implications or making assumptions at each of these levels. To emphasize, as I have above, that Critical Marxism is a general social science in *embryo* means that its spread does not "now" encompass the variety of conceivable levels, but that its commitment to totality analysis moves it *toward* a more inclusive coverage of the levels. Certainly, a general social discipline does not merely premise but articulately insists that a society's functioning cannot be understood apart from its class system or that its class system and economy cannot be understood apart from the other levels. A general social discipline thus generalizes Marx's denial that the "consciousness" level (or culture) is autonomous.

An impulse toward a general social discipline, however, may be said to be "utopian" (in Marx's sense) without the prior maturation of the several special social sciences or theories. In their absence or during their immaturity, the impulse toward a general social discipline can be expressed only through philosophy, which overshoots the required level of generality. Here philosophy usurps the place of social science and theory. Another possible result, however, is that Marxism itself tends to become just another special social science, for example, a radical political economy. Here philosophy is abandoned. In both cases, however, Marxism's capacity for scientific and theoretical generality is damaged.

With the repression of Marxism's impulse toward a general social discipline, and with its movement toward a *special* theory, philosophy itself must be repressed, and Marxism becomes just another "normal" social science specialization, thus competing with and substituting itself for "bourgeois" sciences. This is a maneuver of Scientific Marxism. Correspondingly, Critical Marxism's move toward a *general* theory always entails—in Lukács, Korsch, and Gramsci—the *rehabilitation* of philosophy; while downplaying the relevance of the special social sciences, rather than critically incorporating their new contributions within the framework of philosophical critique. Marxism thus seems to oscillate between ignorance of the special social sciences and capitulation to them.

A critique of the specialized social sciences that simply negates and eschews them as "bourgeois ideologies" leads Marxism toward a singular dependence upon philosophy which is totally inconsistent with Marx's own clarion call to *aufhebe* or sublate, transcend, and indeed abolish, philosophy. The naïve assimilation of the social sciences, which is to say, an assimilation that is only technical without being critically reflective, is a philosophical regression; just as the first tendency—ignorance or denunciation of the technical sciences as bourgeois ideologies—is a technical and scientific regression.

The Metaphysical Pathos of System and Totality

Holistic analysis in Marxism takes two forms, a focus on "system" in one case and on "totality" in the other; each is embedded in a different set of domain assumptions, each generates a different structure of sentiments, and depends on different metaphors. Totality analysis is the holism of Critical Marxism while systems analysis is the holism of Scientific Marxism. System is more fully infused with a mechanical metaphor, while totality is suffused with organicist import. To see the whole as system is to see it as man-made as, for example, a clock; the metaphysical pathos invoked here is unsentimental, secularized, part of the everyday life, part of the ordinary. In contrast, to view the whole as totality links it to an organicist metaphor and with that which is not man-made, with "life" which is a *given* rather than a produced thing; which is the premise of all making, and, indeed, precedes mankind itself, retaining an aura of the transcendent, and possibly the sacred and extraordinary.

The complexity that "system" invokes is forbidding but relatively intelligible because it is man-made through "organization" and work. The complexity of "totality," however, is even heavier and denser, evoking the weight of the past, tradition, history, and can be discouraging, at least to those committed to changing the world. Both system and totality, however, are complexity-intimating and both are in *some* measure dissonant with voluntarism, for each indicates the difficulties of deliberate intervention. Each indicates the multiplicity of considerations needing to be weighed; each induces an awareness of possible unanticipated consequences of intervention which may, indeed, discourage the entire project.

Because of this, each needs simplifying strategies, in effect, enabling it to bypass the intimating sense of complexity yielded by notions of system and totality. One such is to stress the special weight of some *one* factor, to simplify the system/totality by focusing, for example, on determination by the economic "in the final instance." A second dodge is to make the internal *native* disposition of the complex whole parallel the intention sought. Here it is held that the goal sought is guaranteed by the system's own natural evolution, as, for example, in vulgar Marxism's theory of the automatic economic crash.

There is, then, a certain dissonance between political intervention and all holistic analysis. Holistic theory continually intimidates and threatens praxis. The more sensitive an actor is to complexities intimated by system or totality models, the more *anxious* he becomes when faced with the need to decide and act. One result is that he may suspend action altogether, amputate the praxis side of the theory-praxis equation, and *academicize* Marxism, transforming it into another contemplative social science. Both system and totality models heighten anxieties about the very possibility of rational social action, about its outcomes, and, indeed about whether or not it is controllable at all. Yet cognitive uncertainty is not equally conducive to anxiety in all persons. The more rigid, the more hierarchically minded, and the more "authoritarian" will have less capacity to tolerate cognitive ambiguities and will be pressed harder toward solutions for dealing with it. Some may flirt with the mystique of "revolutionary leaps," others rely on a controlling bureaucratic authoritarianism.

The "system" analysis of Scientific Marxism is a methodical effort to take hold of the many elements involved in any action situation, to trace out their interconnections, and to provide a dynamic social geography of the action terrain in which political intervention is to occur. That, on its rational side. On another side, however, its formulation of limited neatly specified "variables," and their careful permutations, has a ritual, anxiety-controlling import affording a *sense* of control that is not altogether technically justified.

This is so because of (1) the inevitably great simplification it entails, i.e., the relatively small number of "variables" with which it deals, and (2) because it can have reference only to situations of a certain average type—those covered by the explicated variables—rather than the unique one concretely at issue. In that sense, systems analysis may be regarded as *in part* a ritual for reducing the very anxieties about complexity that it itself heightens, effected by a process of simplification, selectively focusing attention on a well-boundaried fraction of the situation, cognitively decomposing it into a small number of simplified entities. In effect, the metaphysics of *systems* analysis may persuade persons that the world is manageable partly by the usable technologies it provides, and partly also by its "sober" rhetoric which simplifies and vulgarizes complexity. Its happy motto is: things are really simpler and more controllable than they look.

The metaphysics of Critical Marxism's *totality* analysis, however, is committed to the view that the world is more complex and devious than it seems; it holds that simplicity is only skin deep, and resonates a sense of mystery. To it, life is not a machine that can be taken apart and politics is not just a technology for "making" history. Situations have a certain impenetrability not only because they are complex, but also because they are touched with pathos, are the site within which men work out their destiny and in which the most fateful issues hang in the balance. (This resonates Lukács's "revolutionary messianism.") Here the metaphysics of the *totality* demands intervention even as it heightens anxiety about intervention. In the metaphysics of the totality, the whole contains ambiguities, uncertainties, and important lacunae; it has both fulfilling and calamitous possibilities, a great destiny toward which there is no assured technology.

While systems analysis deals with average entities, thus guiding action in a set of cases, totality analysis conceives the whole as a unique, singular identity, as an "individual" different from all others in its structure and operation, and seeks to grasp that unique individuality as the grounding of its practical intervention at some specific moment. But to take hold of such individuality is no routine matter; it requires a probing dynamic assessment—a "leap"?—rare theoretical skills, and the most extraordinary personal qualities.

Lukács's insistent characterization of Lenin as a "genius" may be taken as an effort to reassure those who confront the complexity of totality. In other words, dealing with the totality is conducive to charisma-mongering. I am inclined to call this the irrational side of totality analysis. Yet is it really altogether irrational to assume that understanding a unique individual case is an art requiring exceptional experience, rigorous training, and rare talent, rather than being a standardizable scientific judgment producible by any number of interchangeable persons? A judgment concerning an individual case at a given moment can only be made by those knowing the current condition of the "individual," and for this no knowledge of scientific generalizations, however necessary, can ever be substituted. While many persons may be competent with respect to the generalizations bearing on a *class* of systems, the number competent to speak of any *one* case in this class, and then of its *current* condition, is always considerably smaller. And the number competent to *intervene* effectively in that unique system is fewer still. The optimistic assumption concerning the essential interchangeability of large numbers of analysts using standardized procedures is not so readily granted for practitioners of the political hermeneutic.

Intellectuals as Functionaries of the Totality

Both system- and totality-analysis represent the unifying efforts of different intellectual communities to reintegrate a knowledge system fragmented by the increasing scientific division of labor. "System" is the reunifying work produced by the culture and cadres of science. Its fundamental effort is to reintegrate by creating a new *special* science of action—for example: operations research, cybernetics, Skinnerian behavior modification, Scientific Marxism—rather than a *general* science, thus essentially bypassing all the other special social sciences. But in bypassing the other social sciences, the new systems analysis cannot constitute an integration of their *knowledge;* it instead provides only a general theory of *instrumental control* over social systems and human behavior. Such systems analysis thus only papers over and reproduces the fragmentation of knowledge. It is primarily an administrative tool; disinterested in knowledge *per se,* it increasingly equates knowledge with control. What it integrates, then, is not knowledge but *action,* and in particular, instrumental administrative action by bureaucratic management.

The sociological infrastructure of systems analysis's reunification effort is the growth of separated communities of technical specialists ecologically adjacent to one another within the framework of the modern bureaucracy. The object of a bureaucracy is to *act* effectively on its environment and its technical experts' knowledge is seen as instrumental to that end. Its problematic, to which systems analysis corresponds, is thus the synthesis of special sciences at the level of social action. Systems analysis is thus the ideology of a *technical intelligentsia* whose various specializations have to be integrated because they are responsible to a common bureaucratic authority for a common project.

Correspondingly, totality analysis is the ideology of non-specialized, boundary-transgressing humanistic "intellectuals" who—with the decline of the once universal church and the rise of fragmenting scientific specialties—seek to reknit intellectual unity, restore a common value system, and, by bridging ordinary languages with technical languages, to infuse the everyday life with enhanced meaning. The quest for totality expressed a longing for a community-building coherent vision that transcends the multiplicity of diverse and shifting perspectives—seeking, indeed, to vanquish perspectivity as such—and to overcome the barriers in the emerging intellectual division of labor.

The search for totality is also a quest for that site where scholarship or science comes together—not should, but no, in *fact,* comes together—with religion's impulse, particularly the impulse of religions of salvation, to make men brothers.[12] The quest for totality, then—even when presented as a problem of secular philosophy—always has subterranean links with religion and, especially, with religions of salvation. The process is the outcome of the secularization of German philosophy's evolution from God to *Geist* and from *Geist* to "totality."

This clearly cannot be read to mean, however, that there is no rational content in the quest for totality, or that it is "mere" religion. It does not mean that the concern with totality is "only" a rationalization of the religious interest without independent secular content and devoid of intellectual validity. The quest for the totality is the hidden place of the sacred in secular social theory, a palimpsestic archaeological site in which the secular tradition builds its new altar overlaying the old pagan worship place, hiding it, yet affected by its presence. At the secular level, this is expressed in a search for a common "public interest" that, facilitated by a new, liberating knowledge, transcends conflicting egoisms and partisan group interests. In Marxism, the "public interest" or "universal" cannot be pursued by the whole itself for the whole is internally contradictory, fragmented; instead the interests of the whole can be pursued only by the struggle for some part—the proletarian "historical agent." The quest for the totality is the modern secularized descendant of antiquity's quest for Logos, the sacred whole which was the fusion of reason and the god, of goodness and power, embodied in the Word.

Then as now the problem was: who speaks for the totality? Then as now, the totality was the province of the specialists who strove to connect appearances and the realm beyond, who united phenomena and noumena, the secular and the sacred, and who bridge the ordinary languages of the everyday life and the extraordinary languages of arcane learning. With the decline of the church and the rise of fragmenting intellectual specializations, the problem of seeing and speaking for the whole grows more acute. To speak for the totality becomes the self-assumed mission of those intellectuals with ties to the older humanistic disciplines, intellectuals who are alienated by the rise of the new sciences and technologies that supplant them in public esteem and support. The quest for the new secularized Logos becomes the mission of alienated intellectuals convinced that the culture they bear is a great tradition, but embittered at the indifference of the new technological society. In effect, these intellectuals serve as brokers bridging technical languages with the ordinary languages of the public life, thus rejoining the fragmented world.

"Totality" becomes the war banner which these intellectuals raise against the partiality of the technical intelligentsia and the increasing irrelevance to the everyday life of the old religious specialists: Intellectuals become the new functionaries of the totality.

Any general theory of intellectuals, then, must see them as "vulnerable" to a certain kind of vision, the vision of uniting the totality; and it must be noted especially that they do this through their control of diverse languages, by bridging ordinary and extraordinary languages. Revolutionary intellectuals in particular serve to bridge the extraordinary languages of the "great" cultural traditions of the cosmopolitan world—science, philosophy, "theory"—with the ordinary languages of local "little traditions," of insulated workers and peasants whom (they aver) they serve.

12

Dialectic of Recovery and Holism

If the doctrine of recovery is often used to restore something to its authentic wholeness, holism is often aimed at overcoming some sensed limit and recovering what has been excluded or forgotten in a given epoch. The two doctrines face complementary difficulties. On the one side, holistic analysis risks treating all elements as if they were of equal importance. It runs the risk of objectivism, of human irrelevance, and of commitment to the banality which says, everything is related to everything else, hence nothing is more important to attend to than anything else. On the other side, the doctrine of recovery risks confining attention to only a small part of the whole—that which had been forgotten, thus overshadowing important forces that were already well known; it creates a new forgetting.

Holism—the objective side—is an attempt to overcome the inevitable partiality of a focus on the forgotten whose circle of illumination, while intense, is narrow in circumference. The doctrine of recovery—the subjective side—can compensate for a holism that, continually extending its boundaries aiming at inclusiveness, loses a clear organizing center. Every "grand theory," including Marxism, is involved in a precarious dialectic between (1) its effort to provide a comprehensive picture of the totality and (2) its wish to accent only a limited part of the totality that it takes to be a precarious, cognitively underprivileged bit of reality—i.e., in danger of being forgotten, neglected, or underestimated. In what follows, I shall give two examples of where this happened in theories other than Marxism, in Max Weber and Talcott Parsons, and then return to show how this is true also of Marxism.

Concerning Parsons

No social theory has been more emphatic than Parsons's in insisting on the general importance of conceiving of society (and other, smaller groups) as "social systems" composed of an interacting "Ego" and "Alter" and of other mutually interdependent parts; and no social theory has been more insistent in attempting to overcome fragmentation and make the world whole. Parsons's theory focuses repeatedly and most generally on such questions of systems analysis as the character of system "interdependence," of system maintenance, of boundary exchange and system equilibrium. Parsons's central assumption is that it is not possible to interpret any single social pattern except by referring it systematically to some larger whole, and he is led forthwith to the *ex cathedra* specification of the system's interdependent parts, its entire social anatomy, on the supposition that—since all social parts are mutually influential—no one of them can be understood unless seen in its linkages with all the others.

Much of Parsons's emphasis on system interdependence is a polemical response to social theories such as Marxism that he interprets as improperly emphasizing the importance of the economic, or some other single factor. Nonetheless, Parsons's work at the same time has sometimes been called a "value Marxism" because it often elides into a one-sided focus on the importance of values, moralities, or normative elements. If Parsons's social systems theory understands society as a whole composed of many interdependent parts, his "social action" theory focuses more narrowly on normative elements which he felt had been neglected by "utilitarian" and "Hobbesian" models—among them, Marxism. For Parsons, then, the social world is not merely a system of which the "moral" element is one among many equally influential peers, but is a uniquely moral world in which normative elements play a role to which he assigns a special force.

When Parsons analyzes a social system, then, he gives special attention to the way behavior conforms to or deviates from the legitimated, value-underwritten expectations of others. As part of the special emphasis Parsons gives to such normative elements, there is, also, the unique significance he repeatedly attributes to religion, in general, and (for Western European cultures) to Christianity, in particular.[1] Parsons's work thus manifests the ambivalence between holistic analysis focused on incorporating the largest, most complicated variety of factors, and a dissonant but unmistakable emphasis on one limited area, the moral and normative.

Concerning Weber

Max Weber's own work manifests a similar vacillation, operating in some cases with an effort to incorporate complexity and variety, while, in others, aiming to bring into focus a limited and precarious factor. Actually, however, Weber had *two* different kinds of factors that he wished to focalize. One of these was a normative element such as the Protestant Ethic, while the other was sheer "domination" without moral support. *Both* are central to his analysis.

Weber thus faces two directions simultaneously. In one, when he focuses on the importance of religious elements, he is essentially developing a critique of Marx's "forgetting" of the moral and religious factor and of his treatment of it as derivative of "material" forces. In particular, Weber is developing an *historicist* critique that stresses the uniqueness of Western society and capitalism and, indeed, of the Protestant Ethic as a spur to rational economic activity, work, and commerce. Weber is in effect arguing that Marx was over-generalizing when he held that social being determined social consciousness in *all* societies. Weber insists that, in *some* societies and at some times, consciousness shapes economic being. *The Protestant Ethic and the Spirit of Capitalism* is essentially an argument to that effect.

Weber, in short, was attempting not only to recover morality and religion from Marx's forgetting but, more than that, to recover the sense of the historical specificity of the West and its dependence upon a special religious ethic. He was trying to recover the sense of historical texture from theoretical schematization. At the same time, it is crucial to remember that Weber is a post-Marxist. He wants to draw a line between his own theoretical standpoint and Marx's without regressing to pre-Marxist idealism and without surrendering to a compulsive anti-Marxism. He wants to incorporate and transcend Marx, not simply oppose him.

Marx's critique had not left idealism unscathed; it had penetrated a German university culture that had once been nucleated by idealism. Marxism had produced a distancing from idealism even among many German academicians themselves. Their own involvements with state power and German nationalism had grown. It is partly on these grounds that Weber also focuses on domination and on the Darwinian struggle for survival among representatives of different cultures, views the state as an amoral power instrument with a monopoly on political violence, and stresses the importance of political prudence (the ethic of "responsibility") which he contrasts with political moralism (the absolutist ethic).

Weber wants to recover Marxism's realism, its recognition of the amoral dimension of much social domination, protecting this from the university's impulse to regress to a pre-Marxist, idealistic view of politics and the state. In focalizing the role of morality, he means to draw the line between Marx and himself in an exacting manner, refusing to allow respectable opposition to Marxism to make him overstate his own position. His recovery of religious elements was therefore cautious and qualified; he refused to claim a universal independence for them to match Marx's assertion of their universal dependence. He thus argues that in the modern era, religion had little of its earlier influence in generating the development of capitalism. He stresses the historical difference: "The Puritans wanted to work in a calling, we are forced to do so."

In short, it was not only the religious and moral factor Weber wanted to recover, but the element of realism and historical specificity, in both politics and scholarship. He sees scholarship and politics as heroic activities and as realms for the clash of heroes. He is not, as he was once called, the "Marx of the bourgeoisie" but, if anything of the sort, the Lenin. He wanted men who could not only choose conscientiously but who could also fight for what they chose, rather than passively submit to the emerging system of impersonal domination. He wanted to recover the importance of the individual in a social world where massive economic forces and great gray organization machines were overwhelming him. In seeking this within the framework of an insistent realism that rejected romantic illusion, he could not have been optimistic. He sensed that the "Iron Cage" was upon us, that the times were wrong for his project. Yet he was not about to throw in his hand.

Weber, then, faced two ways: one, in the holist direction, toward the construction of a broadly comparative canvas with a finely textured portrait of historical complexity, with a "multi-dimensional"[2] stress on the mutual tensions and mutual elective affinity of both "ideal and material interests"—a formulation which heightens the salience of the moral element precisely by placing it within the "interest" framework of Marxism. But Weber also faced in the "recovery" direction, on the one side, forward to the recovery of the religious ethic from Marxist deprecation as a factor in historical development, though without totalizing its significance; and, on the other side, toward the recovery of a realistic focus on domination and struggle from the regressive impulses of German university culture.

Reverting to Marx

The same tensions evident in Talcott Parsons and Max Weber were earlier displayed in Marx and Marxism: the dialectic between (1) an effort to encompass the larger whole, to provide a picture of the social whole in its complexity, on the one side, and (2) to rescue fugitive elements of cognitively underprivileged social reality, on the other. Marx is repeatedly and unavoidably talking about two things at once: the importance of property (of mode of production) in its relation to the ideological and political superstructure. Marxism is at pains to talk about the capitalist "system" with its intimately interconnected, mutually influential parts and, at the same time, to characterize its dominant part. The notion of a "capitalist system" does both, establishing capital as a system of social relationships while clearly focalizing the center of that system in capital.

Much the same may be said about the broader, more general mode of analysis, Marxism's "historical materialism." It operates with partially tacit, partially explicit, distinctions between those sectors that control "in the last instance," the economic infrastructure, and those that react back on the former but are controlled in that last instance, i.e., the political-ideological superstructure. The importance attributed to the former takes the form of exhibiting its ramifying influence on a multiplicity of other, dependent social parts, which could constitute a whole only with and by virtue of the determining sector.

For Marx, however, holism was important but not problematic. It was an intellectual inheritance given and presumably vouchsafed by his Hegelian antecedents. What was problematic to him, therefore, was the recovery of property and the economic factor, of the fugitive part that was cognitively precarious, i.e., underprivileged reality. This part could be focused on precisely because the holistic perspective was already firmly established for Marx. Yet it is typical that, in the very process of recovering the neglected part, the previously consolidated larger whole itself, and its once firmly established other parts, could become precarious.

Discussions of Marxism's distinction between, and linking of, economic infrastructure and ideological/political superstructure, usually, and correctly, recognize that his particular system diminishes the importance attributed to the superstructure. Yet if no importance at all is attributed to the superstructure, why include its elements? By making systematic reference to superstructural elements, by locating them in relation to others, Marx's theory (like any form of holistic thinking) stabilizes future referral to it, makes an abiding place for it. The superstructure need not later be invoked only in an *ad hoc* way, thus in effect preventing its recurrent forgetting.

All holistic thinking, including systems analysis or totality analysis, functions to prevent forgetting, seeks to consolidate in the system elements that had previously been seen and recovered, and to lay down a memory channel from which the rescued element can later be retrieved, without having on each new occasion to reproduce the initial struggle for its recovery. It is, therefore, only the *particular* form of Marx's system that acts to diminish the ideological and political superstructure; its general aspect as a holistic analysis necessarily but subliminally preserved the superstructure from being forgotten. There is, then, a built-in tension between the particular and the general aspects of Marxism's holism. For if, on the one side, Marx's particular version of holism diminished the superstructure's importance, its general character as a holistic analysis refused to allow the superstructure to be forgotten altogether and contains an implicit warning: You forget the superstructure only at your peril! At that level, the theory contains an inner tension if not a contradiction. Pay special attention to property, it says explicitly; do not forget about the superstructure, it says tacitly. It is this tension internal to Marxist theory that contributes to the recurring structural differentiation between Scientific and Critical Marxisms. The latter seeks to revise the devaluation of the superstructure deriving from the explicit doctrine, while retaining the tacit holism, i.e., polemically involving the "totality." It is the function of Critical Marxism to recover the superstructural elements that Scientific Marxism forgets.

Amnesia and Discontinuity

Inherent in the dialectic between the doctrines of recovery and holism, despite holism's best efforts, is an everpresent danger of discontinuity. Old recoveries can once again be forgotten; continual progress, continuity and cumulation are not inevitable. Indeed, every new recovery can generate a new repression or regenerate an old one; can create a language change that defocalizes and unstabilizes what was once known. A new recovery can distract attention from other factors, allowing them to flit around in the half-world of merely auxiliary attention. If a theory expresses, it also represses and distracts; if it sensitizes, it also desensitizes, papering over intellectual lacunae or conflicts and creating a sense of unity that is partly spurious. Narcissistically dwelling in its own limited circle of new illumination, it may let the learning of the past lapse into a darkness penetrable only in an *ad hoc* way.

The outcome of the Marxist theory of the state, for example, suggests that, in the dialectic between the doctrine of recovery and the holistic perspective, it is the latter that is the more precarious. If one of the objects of recovery is to make the self whole again, then this is surely ironic. The doctrine of recovery gains strength from the interests of individualistic intellectuals in establishing their intellectual originality and from their competitive drive to demarcate their own contributions from others', thus inducing them to overemphasize the recovery of the part with which they happen to have been associated. The capacity of theorists to pursue the recovery of some part is distorted by a background rule peculiar to the theorist's community. This condemns the speaking of the commonplace as a trite bathos; even though that commonplace may actually refer to something important; if it is already known, it may be given less emphasis than something less important but newly discovered. To this extent, then, the culture of the theorist's community betrays the needs of the everyday life, and the needs of theory *contradict* those of practice.

Limits on Holism and Recovery

While it may seem to some that the doctrines of holism and of recovery are both unexceptionable—for who does not want to see clearly what he has only glimpsed, and who does not want to be whole and have his world whole again?—nonetheless, each of these doctrines has important limits to its rationality. The call for wholeness is more ambiguous than it seems at first glance. If it is taken to imply that there is only one kind of wholeness, then it is plainly doctrinaire, asking obedience to an unexamined premise. There is the wholeness of the society of ants and that of the pile of sand; neither is the more compelling because of the gross defects of the other.

The call to wholeness is tainted by a romanticism which—donning the mantle of religions of salvation and only faintly secularizing them—interprets wholeness as "brotherhood." It views wholeness as an organic growth overcoming the pervasive loneliness of a society atomized by competition. It looks forward to a society in which each feels an inner communion with all others, which implies that all share the same ideology and morality. Here a solacing solidarity is purchased at the price of what may readily be the crushing of individuality, the blunting of individual differences on behalf of group integration, and a deadening consensus. Such a conception of holism easily becomes the ideology of an overbearing, paranoiac state apparatus, and can be convincing only to those whose religious sensibility allows them to expect the imminent resolution of all conflicts between individuals, on the one side, and the society or state, on the other. One may also guess that this ideal of brotherhood appeals more to older than younger brothers. The joy of brotherhood, tacitly based on the family paradigm, always premises an area *outside of the family;* but the state and society as a brotherhood would have no such free space to which persons might escape. If one does not expect the imminent end of all contradiction, one wants to take care that any planned society allows the open expression of contradictions rather than having them papered over and repressed by an imposed consensus.[3]

The Marxist notion of what limited the achievement of wholeness was itself all too limited. It conceived of the limiting as a "material" force, and therefore, as an "interest"; it thereby linked the limiting force primarily to sensuous satisfactions, venality, producing incomes or avoiding their loss. It took these as limiting because it premised that scarcity was at the bottom of the matter. Eliminate scarcity and you do away with egoism, it assumed, and with this the grounding for selfish class interests. Why, indeed, be selfish if there is enough for everyone? But how much and when is enough, enough? Marxism thought about scarcity in an objectivistic manner, as if it depended only on the object-side, on the *amount* of goods produced in an economy, rather than depending (not instead of, but) *also* on the expectations, ambitions, and moralities of people, i.e., on the subject-side. It altogether missed the fact that material interests were fully and intimately interdependent with ideal interests and that each defined and shaped the other; and it was led to do so systematically, by reason of its materialism which polemically held that it was not consciousness that determined social being, but social being that determined consciousness.

In its systematic theorizing, Marxism focused on scarcity as economic and not political in character, and thus could never systematically incorporate what it plainly saw; the ambitions of the power hungry to be first, to be dominant, to have repute, honors, and glory. The will to power is grounded not only in economic scarcity, and it will not, therefore, be overcome when or if economic scarcity is eased or overcome. Russia and China struggle no less furiously than Russia and the United States. Members of the Politburo struggle to be party leader; cardinals strive to be Pope; members of the company board of directors scheme to become chairman. Indeed, historically, men have repeatedly squandered goods and incomes in order to achieve pre-eminence and power. The pursuit of power is thus not simply an effort to ensure selfish incomes or to prevent their loss. Indeed, the pursuit of power is often at its most ruthless when it is least selfish in anything like the ordinary sense, i.e., when it is pursued in order to secure the highest, most sacred value and ideal interests, and where the goal is not mere personal pre-eminence or vanity but reproduction of one's own kind.

If Marxism's search for wholeness deepens modern rationality by denying the autonomy of speech and linking it to the speaker and his class interests, Marxism was also naïvely utopian, because it did not go far enough in exploring the diversity of factors that might distort understanding. Marxism's critique of "ideology" focused on the manner in which truth was corrupted by interest. This, of course, opened the door to a nihilism which held that, since truth rests on interests, each man's truth is as good as any other's. Marxism, however, sought to close that door, not by denying that truth was grounded in interest, but by denying that all interests were equal, particularly in the limits they imposed upon truth claims. In claiming that the proletariat was a "universal class" whose interests coincided with most others' in society, Marxism claimed that the proletariat could speak a truth closed to the bourgeoisie, and that this would not be limited by the special interests of other narrow elites. But this very affirmation itself, with its myth of the proletariat as ruling class under socialism, concealed the role of the New Class and its growing hegemony; the very conception of the proletariat as the universal class was a mystification behind which a new elite prepared its hegemony.

This false consciousness on behalf of a new elite was scarcely the only way Marxism failed in its effort at a new wholeness. Marxism had assumed that central to the failure of holism was class exploitation and conflictive class interests. It therefore assumed that the main enemy of understanding was ideology—the partisan distortion of wholeness on behalf of a limited class interest. But to hold that ideology is the sole or central distortion of truth is to impose another distorting partiality. It ignores the role of desire, of the passions, and even of "selfless" love, all of which may generate their own forms of domination. These may be a bondage generated by loving, not due to the inability to love. As Willard Waller once observed, those who love most are controlled by those who love less. Nor is it simply "When you are in love," as the old song went, that "smoke gets in your eyes." For this means that we do not wish to see the failures of our beloved—nor wish them to see ours—out of a need to protect *ourselves*. But we also often wish to protect *them* from anything that might hurt them, including *their own* failures.

The vision of the whole is thus limited by our altruistic no less than our selfish interests, by our noblest aspirations and ideal interests no less than our base material interests. We are limited, then, not just by our animal nature but our very humanity—by our very capacity for idealism and morality. It is not selfish interest alone that keeps the whole beyond our reach, but limits embedded in our very effort to overcome partisanship. To attempt to place all the many forms by which the understanding can be distorted under the single rubric of "ideology" is a utopian oversimplification; it desperately attempts to conceal its own limitations under a specious totalization.

The doctrine of recovery, no less than holism, has its own important limits, of which I can here briefly mention only two. First, we may note that, insofar as a theory makes its way by generating recoveries, it wins acceptance for what it offers precisely by reason of its familiarity, i.e., its evocation of the sense of *déjà vu*. It thus not only commands our attention by sensitizing us to what we already believed but elicits our conviction in the truth of the recovery offered precisely because we already believed it. The doctrine of recovery thus invites a specious confirmation. We say, in effect, yes it must be like that! For confirming us in what we have already believed, it relieves any tension we might have felt about it, and we now pronounce the recovery a truth ratified, rather than an hypothesis yet to be confirmed. It is much as if we had passed on a bit of gossip to a friend who passed it on to another who, not knowing its source, then told us of it and we, in turn, hearing it again are now more inclined than ever to believe it.

Second, the doctrine of recovery is, in its modern form, appealing because it is in effect a counterbalance to positivism. If positivism externalizes, directing itself to problems of observation and their reliability, the doctrine of recovery internalizes our attention, and reminds us that it is hard to find things unless we know what we are looking for. To paraphrase Pascal, the Doctrine of Recovery says, we would not be looking for something unless we had already found it. It says that we cannot possess what we do not already have, or understand what we do not already know. It is a version of the hermeneutic circle. This emphasis on the internal is rational only insofar as it counterbalances positivism's externalization; but when it replaces this focus, it becomes another partial view inducing us to lose contact with the world, with the stimulation it can provide, as well as with the serendipity and genuinely emergent novelty of which the world is capable.

Elements in a Rational Social Theory

Rational social theory, then, requires the careful maintenance of a delicate dialectic between holism and recovery; between the effort at consolidating the past through deliberate cumulation and continuity, and the doctrine of recovery that illuminates narrower concerns that had become dim, overgrown with empty formalisms, or repressed, but which now assume special importance. The special, rational task of the doctrine of recovery is to link the theoretical systems of the past to the special problematics and sensitivities of the present; to add what the present needs but is short of; to press the old system toward a new reorganization better enabling it to cope with new tasks, internal and external.

"The Old Theoretical System." This, of course, is an objectivistic way of talking about the cumulated theory of an intellectual community as if

the theory lived apart from that community's experience. But it does not. "The Old Theoretical System" (tradition) may be a veritable paragon of diligent continuity and cumulation, "objectively" balanced, increasingly whole and comprehensive. But we will never know, for "The Old Theoretical System" is the Kantian thing-in-itself, a noumena that no one can speak. The theoretical community's *interpretation* of the Old System is another matter; there are those who can speak. Invariably, their interpretation has shadings and accents that focus on limited elements while enshadowing others. In practice, then, even a holistic Whole is never without its silences. Indeed, the doctrine of recovery is a mechanism for dealing with this.

Moreover, the intellectual community is always part of a larger society in which its members play other social roles, which influence and constantly change their interpretations of the theoretical tradition, creating ever new accentings and new forgettings. The doctrine of recovery also serves this recurrent need. Finally, a theoretical system always has lacunae and contradictions which it hides. Its wholeness always proceeds faster than the grounding for it. As both Engels and Nietzsche suggested, the "system" is always a bit of a noble lie and a false consciousness. Members of the theoretical community, however, sense this lie; for after all, they are the ones perpetrating it. It is a function of the doctrine of recovery to speak these silences too. There is no way forward for a theoretical community without striving toward a systemic wholeness which provides its members with logistical retrieval of its past nor without a doctrine of recovery that enables the community to adapt the system to the present and to deal with its silences.

Several stipulations to be outlined below may clarify the general program compactly indicated here, making it more concrete and specific. The first calls for a focus on "hostile information" as central to a critical theory and as the target of a doctrine of recovery. A second, a special case of the former, focuses critical social theory on detecting and criticizing "normalization." A third has to do with developing critiques of the tendency to "credit" elite definitions of social reality. Fourth and finally, a few comments will be offered concerning the *organizational* requirements for fulfilling a program such as this. In particular, I will focus on the implications of the theorist's group involvements—especially his employment and party affiliations—for his capacity either for wholeness or recovery.

1. *Centering on Hostile Information*
Studies of the social world must (a) protect the autonomy with which technical interests are pursued, inhibiting censorship of them on political

or other grounds, while also (b) insistently clarifying the relation between technical interests and those in the everyday life. No one is protected if technical interests are defined as if they had in *fact* developed autonomously. Marx was altogether correct about this: elements of a distorting false consciousness are embedded in suppositions about the autonomy of the technical; things are mystified when a norm is identified with reality. Indeed, it becomes a total mystery why private or public resources should be and are invested in technical interests, if technical interests were actually independent of societal or class interests. It must, therefore, be shown insistently that reports about "what is" are never only bits of technically relevant information but are, also, always "news" relevant to those playing other, non-scholarly roles in the everyday life. If the community of theorists is to function with reflexivity, it must help its own members and the larger society develop and sustain consciousness of the connection between interests, desires, material groundedness or "social being," on the one side, and information, reports, studies, and all references to social worlds, on the other, clarifying the manner in which the latter always constitute "news"—i.e., has relevance for social roles in the everyday life.

It must be a central principal of any community of rational theorists that the reception of "news" is structured by how it impinges on people's hopes and aspirations in their everyday roles. The reception given their reports about society, then, depends in part on whether it is "good news" that is welcome or "bad news" that is unwelcome, and, therefore, denied, glossed, or readily forgotten. Reports consonant with persons' beliefs about the social world, and about the self holding them, constitute good news that will more readily be credited as true and remembered; news dissonant with the assumptions of the everyday life is more likely to be resisted, doubted, ignored, misplaced, or forgotten by those accepting that everyday life.

Good news tends to be credited more readily—by those to whom it is good news—than is bad news, because good news is dissonance-reducing. Bad news is credited *less* readily—by those to whom it is bad news—because it is dissonance-generating. So the actual process of crediting and discrediting reports about social reality never depends entirely on their evidence. Indeed, what is taken to be "evidence" depends partly on its character as "news," which is to say, on its implications and relevance for the everyday life, and the interests, desires, ambitions, policies, commitments, and plans of people in it—including theorists themselves, who, be it remembered, also live in that everyday life.

Reports about the social world are news when relevant to men's intentions in their everyday world and this relevance influences its reception.

Good news will be "credited"—i.e., more loosely and informally tested, whatever criterion is employed—before being *accepted,* than bad news. Bad news will not be credited and will be more loosely tested before being rejected, than will good news. Whether a report is ultimately accepted and acted upon, or filed and forgotten, depends in important part, then, on whether it is good news or bad. (And, as I will further discuss below, it depends also upon *who* thinks it good news or bad.)

The problem here comes down to the question of avoiding cultural *censorship,* that is, avoiding systematic silences about or repressions of reports dissonant with some group's policies or ambitions. The special task of the theorist's community from this perspective, then, is never simply to "tell the truth, nothing but the truth, and the whole truth" but, rather, to consider the *news-*value of its reports, and to attend especially to communicating and preserving hostile information. The task of the community of critical theorists is to help persons maintain access to news their society is systematically silent about and which members of some group will regard as hostile information. The task is to help persons and groups remain critical even of *good* news, to insist that even this be double-checked, and, correspondingly, to help them accept and remember bad news. From this standpoint, then, wholeness is paradoxically pursued by stressing insistently and one-sidedly the repressed and silenced side of reports. It is an effort to overcome the limitations of groups and persons through the recovery of what their everyday lives have systematically repressed, distorted, forgotten, or lost.

Hostile information, bad news, is not information about the state of the social world *per se.* It is, rather, the relation of reports about the social world to the purposes of some specific groups that makes a report either good news or hostile information. The same information may be both hostile to some groups and friendly to others. Reports certifying the power and stability of some government are hostile information to revolutionaries there but good news to conservatives. There is, therefore, almost no news that is glad tidings for all groups or persons, for all times. What is repressed and silenced, and therefore what needs accenting, varies with each group and its historical position. To tell the "whole" truth is not to say the same thing to everyone in the same way; it is not to repeat the same message at all times. The "whole" truth cannot be spoken, once for all. To speak the truth about the social world, then, means to understand that knowledge is never a bit of information in the head, but always a communication; which further implies that to speak the truth about the social world requires that one not only know that social world, but in addition, know the specific publics to whom it is being communicated, and thus the theorist's own position in the world and his relationship to those publics. A sociological epistemology, then, implies a theory of communication and thus, in part (as Kenneth Burke might have it), a rhetoric as well.

2. The Critique of Normalization

If a special task of a community of critical theorists is to focalize and recover bad news and to question good, the recovery of one particular kind of bad news especially concerns it. It is generally bad news for persons or groups to discover or believe that forces in the world they see as powerful are also inimical toward them—i.e., bad. The same is essentially the case when they discover that social objects or forces they define as good are weak. Both of these, as previously discussed, are "unpermitted worlds" which are a very special sort of bad news and which, like others, tends to be silenced or subject to distortions. The characteristic distortion with which persons respond to unpermitted worlds is to "normalize" them, i.e., redefining the strong but evil object as either "actually" weak, or not "really" good, thus reducing the dissonance.[4] Inhibiting the normalization of unpermitted worlds is thus a special task of the community of critical theorists. This is one of the most powerful and rational inheritances of Marxist/Hegelian syntagmatics. Indeed it was a major step in the development of a rational social discourse when the central objects of Marxist analysis—"capitalism" and "proletariat"—each allowed for a stable dissonance between its power and its goodness, capitalism being powerful but (for the most part) bad, the proletariat being weak but clearly good, in Marx's analysis.

3. The Critique of Establishment-Credited Definitions of Reality

Any definition of social reality accepted by power centers, elites, and establishments is more likely to be "credited"—that is, publicly attended to and offered credence in advance of critical inspection—than definitions of social reality held by the lowly. It is thus a special task of the community of critical theorists to recover not only underprivileged reality that is bad news, but (a) also to rescue from neglect underprivileged sources of definitions of social reality, and (b) to inhibit the crediting of establishment-sponsored definitions of social reality. Which is to say, it must scrutinize closely those definitions of social reality congenial to the expectation of power elites and hegemonic classes.

Establishments and counter-establishments may treat one another's views with a similar suspicion and subject them to especially close scrutiny, but the conclusions that each draws about the other's definitions of social reality do not make their way into the world with equal ease. For their differing views are not credited equally by publics. Most publics

will more readily accept a dominant group's definitions of reality, subjecting them to less rigorous testing than they do beliefs of counter-
establishments.

Moreover, establishments exert more influence on the very conditions
under which their definitions of social reality are appraised. The prob-
ability of discrediting a belief is (other things equal) a function of the
size of the resources devoted to the task. Establishment groups can commonly mobilize more resources to discredit discrepant beliefs than lowly
groups can acquire to inspect establishment views. This is part of the
way in which dominant views are commonly proved right and true,
while views challenging them are usually undermined. Again, the question of how carefully some claim should be investigated is just another
belief that will be resolved as other beliefs are, that is, as a function of
differences in the power, prestige, and resources of disputants. Establishments in politics (and in science as well) influence the very conditions under which their own claims are appraised, arranging the examination to favor their own survival. Establishments appoint the juries whose
findings will determine whether they are to be impeached or retained.
Counter-establishments, however, commonly have to face juries not of
their peers but of their adversaries.

It is common, then, that levels of credibility vary with the social status
of the speakers, the superior status conferring a "halo effect" on its occu-
pants' claims. It follows from this, then, that upper classes and elites have
a better chance than others of having their definitions of social reality
attended to and credited, which is how they become and remain hegemonic classes. Marx was correct: the views of the dominant tend to
become dominant. Since there is already ample yea-saying about dominant views, it therefore also follows that the community of critical theorists has a special responsibility to cast a particularly cold eye on definitions of social reality already dominant and a similarly critical eye on
the processes by which counter-establishment views are thrust aside. It
follows, further, that the ability of a community of critical theorists to
speak truly about social worlds depends on the nature of its social relationship to, and dependence on, hegemonic groups and dominant establishments.

4. The Social Situation of the Community of Theorists
It would seem to follow that there are two fundamental requisites for
the theorist's community to develop a more holistic view of society:
(a) their capacity to achieve some consensus in their internal relations to
one another and (b) their ability to maintain distance and tension not
simply with "society-at-large" but most especially from its hegemonic

elites. It is precisely this twofold need, for internal consensus and external tension, that characterizes vanguard political parties. They must have great internal solidarity to pursue a conflict against the *status quo* and escape the gravitational pull of its definitions of social reality. Internal solidarity of the vanguard is thus not only a requirement of political battle but, also, a cognitive requirement for defining social reality. At the same time, the political battle may be so hazardous and so intensify anxieties that pressures are generated which distort critical discourse. Theorists associated with political vanguards are under pressure to manifest their loyalty by giving consent to merely authoritative definitions of social reality, i.e., to follow "the line" initiated by their own counter-elites.

Universities, too, no less than political vanguards, are also characterized by the twin need for internal solidarity and external friction as a grounding for their cognitive rationality. Universities, however, are dependent upon public or private sources of support; being vulnerable to their pressures and definitions of social reality, they are characteristically less combative and more accommodative. They seek to preserve their cognitive rationality not by combat and friction with establishments but by maintaining distance, by lying low rather than rising up. Here, rationality and the ability to see the whole is subverted not by anxieties born of harsh battle, but by the dependence and temptations generated by establishments. Here cognitive rationality is subverted by complacency, by the drift toward the maintenance of creature comforts, by security derivable from accepting the establishment and friendly discourse with it, and by immersal in narrow puzzle-solving which blocks a view of larger contexts.

It follows that neither involvement suffices to sustain theorists' efforts to develop understanding of the social totality, although ironically both Party theorists and University academicians agree that each of their (different) group environments already suffices for that very purpose. My own conclusion is to the contrary. I therefore believe that one of the central tasks of social theory in our time is to attempt to rethink the position of theory's own group involvements and to re-examine the conditions, social and organizational, requisite for the development of an effective community of theorists committed to the understanding of the social totality.[5]

Notes

Frequently Cited Titles

KMTR	Hal Draper, *Karl Marx's Theory of Revolution* (New York: Monthly Review Press, 1978)
CC	A. W. Gouldner, *The Coming Crisis of Western Sociology* (New York: Basic Books, 1970)
Dialectic	A. W. Gouldner, *The Dialectic of Ideology and Technology* (New York: Seabury, 1976)
Enter Plato	A. W. Gouldner, *Enter Plato* (New York: Basic Books, 1965)
For Sociology	A. W. Gouldner, *For Sociology* (New York: Basic Books, 1973)
Future	A. W. Gouldner, *The Future of Intellectuals and the Rise of the New Class* (New York: Seabury, 1979)
TTM	A. W. Gouldner, *The Two Marxisms* (New York: Seabury, 1980)
Capital	Karl Marx, *Capital*, 3 Vols. (New York: International Publishers, 1967)
CM	Karl Marx and Frederick Engels, *Communist Manifesto*, authorized English edition (Chicago: Charles H. Kerr, 1888)
GI	Karl Marx and Frederick Engels, *The German Ideology* (New York: International Publishers, n.d.)
MEW	Karl Marx, Frederick Engels, *Werke* (Institut für Marxismus-Leninismus beim ZK der SED, Berlin, Dietz, 1956-68)
N and M-H	Boris Nicolaievsky and Otto Maenchen-Helfen, *Karl Marx: Man and Fighter* (Philadelphia: J. B. Lippincott, 1936)

1. The Social Origins of Marxism

1. Indeed, as Perry Anderson observes, "virtually all the major theorists of historical materialism to date, from Marx or Engels themselves to the Bolsheviks, from the leading figures of Austro-Marxism to those of Western Marxism, have been intellectuals drawn from the possessing classes: more often than not, of higher rather than lower bourgeois origins. . . . The conventional appellation 'petty bourgeois intellectual' is not appropriate for most of the figures discussed above. Many of them came from families of wealthy

manufacturers, merchants, and bankers (Engels, Luxemburg, Baner, Lukács, Grossman, Adorno, Benjamin, Marcuse, Sweezy); large landowners (Plekhanov, Mehring, Labriola); senior lawyers or bureaucrats (Marx, Lenin)." Perry Anderson, *Considerations on Western Marxism* (London: New Left Books, 1976), p. 104.

2. Yvonne Kapp, *Eleanor Marx*, 2 Vols., Vol I, *Family Life, 1855-1883* (London: Lawrence and Wishart, 1972), p. 109.

3. *Ibid.*, p. 108.

4. *Ibid.*, p. 30.

5. *Ibid.*, pp. 35, 36.

6. Cited in David Gross, "Introduction to the Luxemburg-Jogiches Correspondence," *Telos* (Fall 1978): 157-58.

7. *Ibid.*, p. 160. Italics by R. L.

8. Rosa Luxemburg, *Reform or Revolution?* (New York: Three Arrows Press, 1937), p. 5.

9. *CM*, p. 26.

10. *GI*, pp. 68-69.

11. *Ibid.*, p. 39.

12. *CM*, p. 26.

13. *Ibid.*, p. 27.

14. *MEW*, p. 454.

15. *Ibid.*, pp. 468-69.

16. V. I. Lenin, *What Is To Be Done?* (New York: International Publishers; trans. 1929, original publication 1923), pp. 27, 32-33, 40.

17. Samuel H. Baron, *Plekhanov; The Father of Russian Marxism* (Stanford: Stanford University Press, 1963), p. 250. The quotation is from Plekhanov himself, cited by Baron.

18. *Ibid.*, p. 220.

19. Cited by Baron, *ibid.*, p. 103.

20. *Ibid.*, p. 183.

21. Norman Geras, "Louis Althusser—An Assessment," *New Left Review* (January/February 1972): 84 *et seq.*

22. Göran Therborn, *Science, Class, and Society: On the Formation of Sociology and Historical Materialism* (London: New Left Books, 1976), p. 317.

23. *Ibid.*

24. Antonio Carlo, "Lenin on the Party," *Telos* (Fall 1973): 257-58.

25. Cited by Carlo, *ibid.*

26. Therborn, *Science, Class, and Society*, p. 325.

27. George A. Kelly, *Idealism, Politics, and History: Sources of Hegelian Thought* (Cambridge: Cambridge University Press, 1969), p. 268.

2. *Marxism as Politics of the New Class*

1. Göran Therborn, "The Working Class and the Birth of Marxism," *New Left Review* (May/June 1973): 7.

2. See my *Dialectic* and *Future*. See also my "Prologue to a Theory of Revolutionary Intellectuals," *Telos* (Winter 1975-76).

3. It is precisely this dilemma that was posed most acutely for Marx and Engels by Max Stirner's *The Ego and Its Own*, and why they wrote—"Saint Max"—a vitriolic reply of 320 pages, two-thirds the full text of *Die deutsche*

Ideologie. For a good introduction to this problem, see John Carroll's *Breakout from the Crystal Palace* (London and Boston: Routledge and Kegan Paul, 1974), and Nicholas Lobkowicz's master work, *Theory and Practice* (Notre Dame, Ind.: University of Notre Dame Press, 1967), especially pp. 390 *et seq.*

4. *CM*, p. 41.
5. V. I. Lenin, *Collected Works*, Vol. 27, 4th ed. (Moscow: International Publishers, 1960-70), p. 310.
6. *Ibid.*, Vol. 29, p. 70.
7. *Ibid.*, Vol. 25, p. 105. Italics by A. W. G.
8. *Ibid.*, Vol. 27, p. 240.
9. *Ibid.*, Vol. 26, p. 110.
10. *Ibid.*, Vol. 41, p. 258.
11. *Ibid.*, Vol. 27, pp. 268 *et seq.*
12. *Ibid.*, Vol. 31, p. 420, and Vol. 27, p. 257.
13. Carmen Claudin-Urondo, *Lenin and the Cultural Revolution* (Atlantic Highlands, N. J.: Humanities Press, 1977).
14. Lenin, *Collected Works*, Vol. 33, p. 194.
15. *Ibid.*, Vol. 28, p. 381. Dec. 25, 1918.
16. *Ibid.*, Vol. 29, p. 448.
17. *Ibid.*, Vol. 27, p. 248.
18. *Ibid.*, Vol. 32, p. 144.
19. Merle Fainsod, *How Russia Is Ruled* (Cambridge: Harvard University Press, 1965), p. 231.
20. *Ibid.*, pp. 225-26.
21. Cf. Leonard Shapiro, *The Communist Party of the Soviet Union* (New York: Random House, 1970), p. 435, and Nicholas DeWitt, *Education and Professional Employment in the USSR* (Washington, D. C.: U.S. Government Printing Office, 1961), p. 537.
22. For the detailed argument, see my *Future.*
23. Thomas Cottle, "Show Me a Scientist Who's Helped Poor Folk, and I'll Kiss Her Hand," *Social Policy* (March/April 1974): 35-37.

3. *Popular Materialism and Historical Origins of Marxism*

1. See his letter to Bolte, Nov. 23, 1871, *Selected Correspondence, 1846-1895*, trans. Dona Torr (New York: International Publishers, 1942), p. 317. In the preface to his *Poverty of Philosophy*, Marx also refers to himself as a "German economist."
2. One reason being that he himself had been subjected to the anti-Semitic vitriol of his onetime friend, Proudhon, who listed him, along with other "Jews," as "evil, irrascible, envious, bitter, etc." Leon Poliakov, *The History of Anti-Semitism*, Vol. III, *From Voltaire to Wagner* (London: Routledge and Kegan Paul, 1975), p. 379. His onetime collaborator, Arnold Ruge, also denounced him as a "skunk and shameless Jew."
3. Yvonne Kapp, *Eleanor Marx*, 2 Vols., Vol II, *The Crowded Years* (London: Lawrence and Wishart, 1976), p. 260.
4. The following account of conditions in Germany leading to the revolution of 1848 was gleaned from various sources but is heavily reliant on Theodore S. Hamerow, *Restoration, Revolution, Reaction: Economics and Politics in Ger-*

many, 1815-1871 (Princeton: Princeton University Press, 1958), for most of the statistical data and qualitative materials cited in this section, although sometimes centering my interpretation somewhat differently. Karl Marx's own *The Class Struggles in France 1848-1850* (in *Selected Works in Three Volumes* (Moscow: Progress Publishers, 1969-70)), as his *Eighteenth Brumaire of Louis Bonaparte* (various editions) may still be consulted with profit. So, too, may L. B. Namier, *1848: The Revolution of the Intellectuals* (London: Oxford University Press, 1944); Priscilla Robertson, *Revolutions of 1848: A Social History* (Princeton: Princeton University Press, 1952); J. H. Calpton, *The Economic Development of France and Germany, 1815-1914* (Cambridge: Cambridge University Press, 1936); Georges Duveau, *1848: The Making of a Revolution* (New York: Random House, 1965); Agatha Ramm, *Germany, 1789-1919* (London: Methuen, 1967); P. H. Noyes, *Organization and Revolution: Working-Class Associations in the German Revolutions of 1848-49* (Princeton: Princeton University Press, 1966); Golo Mann, *The History of Germany Since 1789* (London: Chatto and Windus, 1968); Ernest K. Bromstead, *Aristocracy and the Middle Classes in Germany* (Chicago: University of Chicago Press, 1964); and Frederick B. Artz, *Reaction and Revolution, 1814-1832* (New York: Harper, 1934).

5. Cited from a contemporary account by Hamerow, p. 163.
6. *Ibid.*, p. 176.
7. *Ibid.*, pp. 211-12.
8. *Ibid.*, p. 179. Italics by A. W. G.
9. *Ibid.*, p. 249.
10. *Ibid.*, p. 87.
11. Lorenz von Stein, *The History of the Social Movement in France, 1789-1850* (Totowa, N. J.: Bedminster Press, 1964), p. 11 of introduction by Kaethe Mengelberg.
12. *Ibid.*, p. 12.
13. *Ibid.*, p. 13.
14. *Ibid.*, p. 14.
15. *Ibid.*, p. 27.
16. This is basically a discussion of the deep structure of the grammar of materialist discourse. Its basic rules, unlike those governing the CCD, hold certain things unproblematic and non-discussable. A materialist grammar of discourse has a principle of censorship: interest. See Chapter 2, pp. 30-33, and my *Future,* for the CCD.
17. K. Marx, *Wage-Labour and Capital* (New York: International Publishers, 1933), p. 3.
18. K. Marx, *Value, Price and Profit,* ed. Eleanor Marx Aveling (New York: International Publishers, 1933), p. 61.
19. Loyd D. Easton and Kurt H. Guddat, eds. and trans., *Writings of the Young Marx on Philosophy and Society* (Garden City, N. Y.: Doubleday, 1967).
20. Tom Bottomore, ed., *Karl Marx, Early Writings* (New York: McGraw-Hill, 1963), p. 164.
21. *Ibid.*, p. 63.

4. *The Binary Fission of Popular Materialism*

1. My colleague, Steven S. Schwarzschild, observes that "when Marx comes to give the term 'relation' ('*Verhaeltnis*') his new, Marxist meaning, it is no longer primarily an epistemological Hegelian notion but an ethical one, connected with '*verhalten,*' 'to behave . . . toward others,'" citing Albert Massiczek, *Der menschliche Mensch—Karl Marx' judischer Humanismus* (Vienna: Europa Verlag, 1968), p. 87.

2. Tom Bottomore, ed., *Karl Marx, Early Writings* (New York: McGraw-Hill, 1963), p. 191.

3. Steven S. Schwarzschild has noted that "at the time with which we are concerned, the popular mind in France, for an example, sang an old song, '*L'argent est un dieu sur terre,*'" i.e., "money is a god on earth." See Steven S. Schwarzschild, "Karl Marx's Jewish Theory of Usury," in *Gesher* (New York: Yeshiva University, 1978), p. 30.

4. Bottomore, *Karl Marx*, p. 193.

5. *Ibid.*

6. *Ibid.*, p. 34.

7. *Ibid.*, p. 40.

8. *Ibid.*, p. 34.

9. *Ibid.*, p. 35.

10. *Ibid.*, p. 38.

11. *Ibid.*, p. 39.

12. Saul Padover, "The Baptism of Karl Marx's Family," *Midstream* (June/July 1978): 43.

13. Leon Poliakov, *The History of Anti-Semitism*, Vol. III, *From Voltaire to Wagner* (London: Routledge and Kegan Paul, 1975), p. 393.

14. *Ibid.*, p. 396.

15. See Julius Carlebach, *Karl Marx and the Radical Critique of Judaism* (London: Routledge and Kegan Paul, 1978), p. 36, certainly one of the most learned studies of this complex issue.

16. Poliakov, *Anti-Semitism*, p. 380.

17. Marx, *Capital*, Vol. I, p. 131.

18. *Ibid.*, p. 336.

19. *Ibid.*, p. 132.

20. *Ibid.*

21. *Ibid.*

22. *Ibid.*, p. 137.

23. *Ibid.*, pp. 138-39.

24. *Ibid.*, p. 140.

25. *Ibid.*, p. 141.

26. Max Weber, *General Economic History* (New York: Greenberg, 1927), pp. 175-76.

27. Marx, *Capital*, Vol. III, Bk. I, p. 207.

28. There are also other rules: for instance, that any alteration in a product belongs to the buyer of labor power, and that the buyer alone determines the product he wishes to produce, and how. Capitalism, as wage labor, is defined by this structure of rules, some explicit and some tacit, and by a system of sanctioning conformity and deviance from them.

29. Our own critique thus converges here with Jean Baudrillard, *The Mirror of Production* (St. Louis: Telos Press, 1975).

30. Marx and Engels, *Selected Works in Three Volumes* (Moscow: Progress Publishers, 1969-70), Vol. II, p. 206.

5. *Artisans and Intellectuals:*
Socialism and the Revolution of 1848

1. P. H. Noyes, *Organization and Revolution: Working-Class Associations in the German Revolution of 1848-1849* (Princeton: Princeton University Press, 1966), p. 4.

2. For an earlier formulation of parts of this perspective, amplifying certain problems, see A. W. Gouldner, "Reciprocity and Autonomy in Functional Theory," in L. Z. Gross, ed., *Symposium on Sociological Theory* (Evanston, Ill.: Row, Peterson, and Co., 1959), pp. 241-70. For a wider and more recent formulation, see Chapter 1 of *TTM*.

3. N and M-H, p. 76. Cf. the discussion of these societies in Eric J. Hobsbawm, *Primitive Rebels* (New York: Praeger, 1963), pp. 126-74.

4. N and M-H, p. 76.

5. *Ibid.*, p. 77.

6. Frederich Hertz, *The German Public Mind in the Nineteenth Century* (Totowa, N.J.: Rowman and Littlefield, 1975), p. 213.

7. N and M-H, p. 108.

8. Noyes, *Organization and Revolution*, p. 275.

9. Cited in Saul K. Padover, *Karl Marx: An Intimate Biography* (New York: McGraw-Hill, 1978), p. 218.

10. N and M-H, p. 113.

11. Quoted in *ibid.*, p. 114.

12. Hertz, *German Public Mind*, p. 264.

13. Robert Payne, *Marx* (New York: Simon & Schuster, 1968), p. 124.

14. Weitling, *Guaranties of Harmony and Freedom*, 1842.

15. Cited in Padover, *Karl Marx*, p. 173.

16. N and M-H, p. 76.

17. *Ibid.*, p. 77.

18. *Ibid.*, p. 80.

19. *Ibid.*, p. 118.

20. See also P. V. Annenkov, *The Extraordinary Decade: Literary Memoirs*, ed. A. P. Mendel and trans. I. R. Titunik (Ann Arbor: University of Michigan Press, 1968). N and M-H claim that "thirty years later Annenkov could still call up a vivid picture of what the young Marx was like . . . in Brussels in 1846" (p. 118) but the issue is not raised whether that thirty-year interval might have diminished the accuracy of Annenkov's account, if not dulling its "vividness."

21. Of the many accounts which mention Weitling's stylish appearance, not one considers whether, being a tailor himself, he may not have made his own coat.

22. *Future*, p. 28. See Thesis Six, "The New Class as a Speech Community," pp. 28-43, for fuller discussion.

23. Much is made by Marx's adherents of Weitling's fumbling reply, as if this proved its incorrectness. Yet since the time of Solomon Asch's small group

experiments, we have known that an isolated group member, faced with the unanimous opposition of others, will exhibit considerable distress. In short, Weitling's confusion was evidence not of his intellectual inadequacy but of the effectiveness of the ceremony of status degradation Marx's group had staged.

24. Cited in Padover, *Karl Marx*, p. 233.
25. N and M-H, p. 121.
26. Hobsbawm, *Primitive Rebels*, p. 171, footnote.
27. Rudolph Stadelmann, *Social and Political History of the German 1848 Revolution*, trans. J. G. Chastain (Athens: Ohio University Press, 1970), p. 5.
28. Theodore S. Hamerow, "The German Artisan Movement, 1848-49," *Journal of Central European Affairs* 21, no. 2 (July 1961): 136.
29. In Prussia in 1846, "this . . . was an expanding group, having increased in size by some 87 per cent since 1816. . . . This growth in size runs counter to the general picture of decline; indeed, the declining position of the artisans was partly a result of their increased numbers." Noyes, *Organization and Revolution*, pp. 23-24.
30. *Ibid.*, p. 25.
31. *Ibid.*, p. 44.
32. Stadelmann, *German 1848 Revolution*, p. 42, and Barrington Moore, Jr., *Injustice: The Social Bases of Obedience and Revolt* (London: Macmillan, 1978), p. 155.
33. Hamerow, "German Artisan Movement," p. 146.
34. *Ibid.*, p. 138.
35. *Ibid.*, p. 139.
36. *Ibid.*, p. 135.
37. Peter N. Stearns, *1848: The Revolutionary Tide in Europe* (New York: W. W. Norton, 1974), p. 20.
38. Theodore S. Hamerow, *Restoration, Revolution, Reaction: Economics and Politics in Germany, 1815-1871* (Princeton: Princeton University Press, 1958), p. 102.
39. *Ibid.*, pp. 18, 36, 79.
40. Cf. Noyes, *Organization and Revolution*, p. 3.
41. Stearns, *1848*, p. 26.
42. Veit Valentin, *Geschichte der deutschen Revolution 1848-49* (Berlin, 1930-31), Vol. II, p. 557.
43. Lenore O'Boyle, "The Democratic Left in Germany, 1848," *Journal of Modern History* 33, no. 4 (December 1961): 375.
44. Quoted in *ibid.*, p. 377.
45. *Ibid.*
46. See Priscilla Robertson, *Revolutions of 1848: A Social History* (New York: Harper Torchbook, 1960; originally published by Princeton University Press, 1952), p. 49.
47. For these statistics, see Konrad H. Jarausch, "The Sources of Student Unrest, 1815-1848," in Lawrence Stone, ed., *The University in Society* (Princeton: Princeton University Press, 1974), Vol. II, p. 557.
48. Lenore O'Boyle, "The Problem of an Excess of Educated Men in Western Europe, 1800-1850," *Journal of Modern History*, 42, no. 4 (December 1970).

49. Jarausch, "Student Unrest," p. 552.

50. O'Boyle, "Problem," p. 473. O'Boyle also notes Reinhart Koselleck, *Preussen zwischen Reform und Revolution* (Stuttgart, 1967), who also "presents extensive evidence in support of the view that the pressure by educated men for state jobs in Prussia was important." On this see Kosselleck, pp. 438-47.

51. Jarausch, "Student Unrest," pp. 535-36.

52. Lenore O'Boyle, "The Image of the Journalist in France, Germany, and England, 1815-1848," *Comparative Studies in Society and History* 10, no. 3 (April 1968): 290-317.

53. *Ibid.,* p. 300.

54. The *Quarterly Review* is cited in *ibid.,* p. 301.

55. Cited in *ibid.,* p. 306.

56. James J. Sheehan, "Liberalism in Germany," *The Journal of Modern History* 45, no. 4 (December 1973): 590.

57. *Ibid.,* p. 587-88.

58. Hamerow, "German Artisan Movement," p. 141.

59. William H. Sewall, Jr., *Work and Revolution in France: The Language of Labour from the Old Regime to 1848* (Cambridge: Cambridge University Press, 1980), pp. 13, 21, 22, 25.

60. Fritz K. Ringer, "Higher Education in Germany in the Nineteenth Century," *Journal of Contemporary History* 12, no. 3 (1967): 123.

61. KMTR, p. 549.

62. *Ibid.,* p. 546. Bracketed insert by A. W. G.

63. Frank Parkin, *Marxism and Class Theory: A Bourgeois Critique* (New York: Columbia University Press, 1979), p. 44.

64. *Ibid.,* p. 45.

65. As Robert K. Merton has noted.

66. N and M-H, p. 75.

67. Speaking of a later period, Draper is essentially correct in holding that "the advocacy of exclusionism came from that national current in the International which most systematically represented the . . . artisan stratum" (KMTR, p. 655). Some Marxists such as Draper apparently find Weitling's artisan origins a source of comfort; for these allow them to deny that Marx's attack on him was an attack on a "hapless worker," or on a "true proletarian" (*ibid.*). Weitling is then portrayed as the representative of a dying "petty bourgeois" class of artisans rather than, as Marx is alleged to be, a true representative of the proletariat, a class with an historical future. The premise here is, apparently, that only those who have a future are deserving of concern or civil treatment, from which it would seem to follow that the aged and terminally ill are to be turned out onto the streets. I concur entirely that Weitling and his League of the Just were not "proletarians," but then, of course, neither were Marx and Engels.

68. Marx and Engels, *Selected Correspondence, 1846-1895,* trans. Dona Torr (New York: International Publishers, 1942), p. 87.

69. *Ibid.,* p. 123.

70. Payne, *Marx,* pp. 534, 537.

71. Hence sections consisting primarily of students were excluded from membership in the I. W. A., even though there was a rule declaring that "everybody who acknowledges and defends the principles of the I. W. A. is eligible to become a member." KMTR, pp. 562-63.

72. *Ibid.*, p. 548. Draper is highly selective about whose anti-Semitism he condemns. He vigorously defends Marx's anti-Semitism, on the grounds that everyone else was then anti-Semitic, but he condemns the same anti-Semitism when voiced by Marx's *enemies*—especially if directed against Marx.

73. *MEW*, Vol. 19, p. 371.

74. Engels to Laura and Paul Lafargue, in *Frederick Engels, Paul and Laura Lafargue, Correspondence* (Moscow: Foreign Languages Publishing House, 1959), Vol. II, pp. 407 *et seq.*

75. *MEW*, Vol. 22, pp. 69 *et seq.*

76. This section as others in the present chapter relies heavily on and is greatly indebted to N and M-H's work, which remains the best political biography of Marx despite their adulation of their subject and despite the scholarship that has accumulated in the half-century since they wrote. One of the best compendiums of the new researches is the work in progress by Hal Draper against which one should constantly check and compare the earlier work of N and M-H. As will be seen, however, my net conclusion will be that Draper's work is tendentious and deeply flawed by its polemical animus and, importantly, by his failure to maintain chronological clarity, in contrast to the strong narrative line in N and M-H. Nonetheless, wherever Draper has a relevant objection to their work, I shall discuss it in detail.

77. N and M-H, p. 156.

78. *Ibid.*, p. 160.

79. *Ibid.*, p. 161.

80. *Ibid.*, p. 162.

81. Stearns, *1848*, p. 183.

82. N and M-H, p. 163.

83. *Ibid.*, p. 166.

84. *Ibid.*, p. 168. Draper is quite incensed with N and M-H's account of these events. He denounces them, in particular, for stating that "during the first months it [the *Neue Rheinische Zeitung*] avoided anything that might possibly disturb the united front. Not a word was spoken of the antagonism between proletarian and non-proletarian, bourgeois or petty bourgeois democracy." Draper quotes this from N and M-H, p. 167, in *KMTR*, p. 214, footnote, adding that "not a word of this statement is true." Yet Draper *omits* the very next line, in N and M-H, which suggests that they were referring to the *Neue Rheinische Zeitung's* treatment of the *German* scene and *German* working classes. Their very next line reads: "There was not a word about the special interests of the working classes, of the workers' special tasks in the *German* Revolution" (N and M-H, p. 67, italics added by A. W. G.). Set in context of that last sentence, the reference seems to be about Marx's coverage of the German revolution, not about the *Neue Rheinische Zeitung's* coverage in general. It is thus irrelevant to note, as Draper then does, that Marx immediately gave support to the *Paris* rising, and lauded the working classes *there*. Indeed, N and M-H themselves refer twice to that rising and clearly state the *Neue Rheinische Zeitung* supported it *vigorously*: "Strenuously as Marx avoided anything that might have weakened the joint Democratic forces in Germany, he sided just as resolutely with the insurrectionary Paris workers in those days of June" (*ibid.*, p. 168); ". . . articles about the June fighting cost Marx the other half" of his

shareholders (*ibid.*, p. 172). Draper, moreover, acknowledges the correctness of Engel's formulation that the *Neue Rheinische Zeitung*'s was essentially a coalition policy calling for "democracy" and did not inscribe its proletarian character on its banner (*KMTR*, p. 214). Draper acknowledges also that "No doubt Marx would have preferred to take it easy at the beginning on controversial questions." Finally, Draper himself says that the *Neue Rheinische Zeitung* did not present "itself as the organ of a workers' movement, let alone a workers' organization . . . it agitated for the revolution of the Democracy. It did not agitate for communism (or socialism) in Germany but explained, as in connection with the June uprising, that it did not believe that communism was as yet on the order of the day for Germany" (*ibid.*, pp. 218-19), a position altogether compatible with my interpretation that N and M-H had meant their disputed remark to apply primarily only to the *Neue Rheinische Zeitung*'s treatment of the revolution in Germany. Draper's tendentious account has the unfortunate effect of concealing the internal contradictions, tensions, and difficulties in Marx's position, which the latter's own later self-critique, in the March letter of the League's central office, acknowledges when he himself condemns his own earlier discussion of the Communist League. Like other devout Marxists, Draper is bent on seeing Marx's policy as much more smoothly integrated and internally harmonious that it was; N and M-H, while very sympathetic to Marx, simply refuse to paper over the tensions and ambivalences of Marx's policies, and sometimes state plainly that he actually made a mistake! For another account of the *Neue Rheinische Zeitung* policies, see Peter Stearns, who largely agrees with the views of N and M-H, holding that the paper's early success "resulted in large part from Marx's careful concentration on the political issues, particularly during his first weeks as editor" (Stearns, *1848*, p. 182).

85. N and M-H, p. 173. This, of course, was replayed and repaid some years later, during the Russian October Revolution, when the German high command sent funds to support Bolshevik propaganda.

86. *Ibid.*, p. 175.

87. *Ibid.*

88. *Ibid.*, p. 176. The distorted character of Draper's account may also be seen from the fact that he fails to mention that this offer came only after Gottschalk, Moll, and Schapper were being persecuted by the police. Draper, instead, presents it as if it simply exhibited Marx's growing influence over the workers. Thus he writes: "Marx's influence on the Workers Association . . . grew . . . despite the bitter opposition of the Gottschalk clique; later in the year Marx was even elected president of the Workers Association" (*KMTR*, p. 214); but not a word that this happened only *after* the other leaders were jailed or fleeing the police.

89. N and M-H, p. 182.

90. *Ibid.*, p. 186.

91. Quoted in *ibid.*, p. 187.

92. *Ibid.* This situation also is replayed during the course of the Russian Revolution and the Bolshevik position is in part an adaptation to it.

93. *Ibid.*, p. 187. Indeed, as late as 1850, Marx was still asserting that "the real revolutionary movement can begin in England only when the Charter has been realized, just as in France the June battle became possible only when the republic had been won." Quoted in *KMTR* p. 282.

94. N and M-H, p. 187.
95. Quoted in *ibid.*
96. *Ibid.*, p. 189.
97. *Ibid.*, p. 196.
98. All quotations from the Address of the Central Committee are from the translation in Saul K. Padover, *On Revolution, Karl Marx* (New York: McGraw-Hill, 1971).
99. Noyes, *Organization and Revolution*, p. 366.
100. *KMTR*, p. 599.
101. The question then arises, why did the new society receive the support of "two Frenchmen of the Blanquist tendency" (*ibid.*, p. 254) if as Draper also contends "Marx's 1850 vision had *nothing in common* with the Blanquist type putsch" (*ibid.*, p. 244; italics added by A. W. G.).
102. N and M-H, p. 209.
103. *GI*, p. 24.
104. *CM*, p. 16.
105. *Ibid.*, p. 31.
106. N and M-H, p. 210.
107. Cited in *KMTR*, p. 209. Italics added by A. W. G.
108. Saul K. Padover, *Karl Marx*, p. 385. It is Padover's judgment that "Marx and his uncle were not far apart in their views on the desirability of moderate politics. To Marx the achievement of power by the world proletariat was the final consummation of the historic process. But there was no specific timetable. Nor was there any special reason, theoretical or actual, for hurrying the pace through dramatic policies or rash actions." The letter from Lion Philips quoted above is to Marx on Dec. 5, 1864. Although careful to keep his distance from Philips, before his revolutionary comrades, Marx maintained a long relationship with him and his family, went to considerable lengths to send him his writings, and had Ferdinand Lasalle write letters that could be used to impress the banker. Indeed Marx was smitten by Philips's beautiful daughter Antoinette, whom he wooed in a literary way.
109. N and M-H, p. 214.
110. *Ibid.*, p. 216.
111. *KMTR*, p. 78.
112. Quoted in *ibid.*, p. 605.
113. Quoted in *ibid.*, p. 243.
114. Quoted in *ibid.*, p. 245.
115. Quoted in *ibid.*
116. *Ibid.*, pp. 254-55, footnote.
117. Quoted in *ibid.*, p. 605.
118. N and M-H, p. 217.
119. *KMTR*, p. 250. Cf. N and M-H, p. 211: "In June Marx . . . made an intense study of the past decade, and the economic history of England in particular. . . . The more Marx mastered his material, the more plainly did he see the vanity of his [revolutionary] hopes. Europe was not on the verge of a crisis but on the threshold of a new era of prosperity."
120. Marx, *The Class Struggles in France*, quoted in *KMTR*, p. 250.
121. This analysis is developed more fully in my *TTM*, throughout Chapter 5 and especially pp. 145 *et seq.*
122. For the vacillations and ambivalences, see my discussion in *ibid.*

6. *Marx's Final Battle:*
Bakunin and the First International

1. Cf. N and M-H: "In the long years of exile, Marx had consistently declined to associate himself with any sort of political organization" (p. 261). Again, "Bitter experience . . . had convinced him that it was necessary to keep aloof from all intermediary groups, especially organizations of exiles" (p. 267).
2. *Ibid.*, p. 33.
3. Marx and Engels, *Selected Correspondence, 1846-1895,* trans. Dona Torr (New York: International Publishers, 1942), p. 277. Italics in original.
4. Saul K. Padover, *Karl Marx: An Intimate Biography* (New York: McGraw-Hill, 1978), p. 380.
5. Paul Thomas, *Karl Marx and the Anarchists* (London: Routledge and Kegan Paul, 1980), p. 255.
6. Barrington Moore, Jr., *Social Origins of Dictatorship and Democracy: Lord and Peasant in the Making of the Modern World* (Boston: Beacon Press, 1966), p. 505. The full quotation is as follows: ". . . the chief social basis of radicalism has been the peasants and the smaller artisans in the towns. From these facts one may conclude that the wellsprings of human freedom lie not only where Marx saw them, in the aspirations of classes about to take power, but perhaps even more in the dying wail of a class over whom the wave of progress is about to roll. Industrialism as it continues to spread, may in some distant future still those voices forever and make revolutionary radicalism as anachronistic as cuneiform writing." Several demurrers: (1) The radicalism of artisans in large towns such as Paris and London during the first half and middle of the nineteenth century was quite as deep as that of artisans in the small towns to which Moore here limits the matter. (2) Moore's account of the radicalism of the artisans is cryptic and incipiently economistic, leaning primarily on the technological supercession of the smaller artisans. (3) One has reason to be uneasy with such a limited account not because of what it says but because of what it omits. Specifically, it ignores the role of radical professionals (e.g., doctors such as Gottschalk, Che Guevara, and George Habbash) in modernizing countries, as well as of radical journalists and of intellectuals more broadly. Are such professionals and intellectuals so very different from artisans, especially in the nineteenth century? (4) Moreover, intellectuals would not seem to be a dying class "over whom the wave of progress is about to roll." And while intellectuals and professionals may, like artisans, be radicalized when encountering economic deprivations, they are surely not radicalized for these reasons alone.
7. *KMTR,* p. 558.
8. *Ibid.*, pp. 562-63.
9. *MEW,* Vol. 21, pp. 39 *et seq.*
10. John Clark, "Marx, Bakunin and the Problem of Social Transformation," *Telos* (Winter 1979-80): 80.
11. Thomas, *Karl Marx,* p. 252. Thomas's conception of Marx's authoritarianism is that it was simply a response to Bakunin's provocation, a kind of self-fulfilling prophecy in which each made the other what he feared most, thereby confirming his own worst suspicions. Thomas thus writes, "each protagonist acted out the other's nightmare" (p. 253). The difficulty with this would seem plain; Marx's "authoritarianism" was hardly manifested for

the first time in his duel with Bakunin, and hence cannot be explained as due simply to Bakunin's provocation of Marx. The latter's assault on Weitling and his following made that plain enough. At the same time, however, I do not believe that Marx's authoritarianism is simply a trait of character that Marx lugged around unchanged, like a walking stick under his arm, beating stray enemies with it whenever they came within reach. As I stated earlier, Annenkov and Marx's associates on the *Neue Rheinische Zeitung lauded* his dictatorial manner. Thus it was not simply Marx's enemies, or the nature of his character structure, but the admiration and implicit invitation of his admirers, that also reinforced Marx's authoritarianism. A "dictator" is not simply fashioned by his foes, but is also groomed by his friends. The failure to grapple with such obvious considerations produces a one-sidedness in Thomas's work uncomfortably close to apologetics.

12. *Ibid.*, p. 297.
13. N and M-H, pp. 307-8.
14. Ibid., p. 304.
15. Marx and Engels, *Selected Correspondence*, p. 317.
16. N and M-H, p. 289.
17. Quoted in E. H. Carr, *Michael Bakunin* (New York: Vintage, 1961), p. 385.
18. Sam Dolgoff, ed., *Bakunin on Anarchy* (New York: Vintage, 1971), p. 25.
19. Eric J. Hobsbawm, *Revolutionaries* (London: Weidenfeld and Nicolson, 1973), p. 87.
20. Cited in Dolgoff, *Bakunin*, p. 26.
21. G. P. Maximoff, ed., *The Political Philosophy of Bakunin: Scientific Anarchism* (New York: Free Press, 1953), p. 73.
22. *Ibid.*, p. 332.
23. *Ibid.*, p. 74.
24. I must thus reluctantly disagree with Eric Hobsbawm's dismissive conclusion that "anarchism has no significant contribution to socialist theory to make" (p. 87).
25. The link between Bakunin and the Frankfurt School is thus much more direct and intimate than that between it and Marx, whatever that school's self-understanding.
26. Clark, "Marx," p. 93.
27. Maximoff, *Political Philosophy*, p. 249.
28. *Ibid.*, p. 358.
29. From "After the Revolution: Marx Debates Bakunin," in Robert C. Tucker, ed., *The Marx-Engels Reader* (New York: W. W. Norton, 1978), p. 544.
30. *Ibid.*
31. *Ibid.*
32. *Ibid.*, pp. 546-48.
33. Maximoff, *Political Philosophy*, p. 284.
34. *Ibid.*, p. 286.
35. *Ibid.*, p. 288.
36. Arthur Lehning, ed., *Selected Writings of Michael Bakunin* (London: Cape, 1973), p. 266.
37. Maximoff, *Political Philosophy*, p. 328.
38. *Ibid.*, p. 355.

39. *Ibid.*, p. 77.
40. *Ibid.*, p. 78.
41. *Ibid.*, p. 329.
42. John Anthony Scott, *The Defense of Gracchus Babeuf Before the High Court of Vendom* (Amherst: University of Massachusetts Press, 1967), pp. 91, 92.
43. *Ibid.*, p. 55.
44. *Ibid.*, p. 10.
45. *Ibid.*, p. 56.
46. *Ibid.*, e.g., pp. 60 *et seq.*
47. *Ibid.*, pp. 56, 57.
48. Maximoff, *Political Philosophy*, p. 374.
49. N and M-H, p. 281.
50. Maximoff, *Political Philosophy*, p. 169. Frankfurt's convergent theory of domination entailed the use of a similar ontology of human nature—the Freudian.
51. *Ibid.*, p. 64.
52. *Ibid.*
53. *Ibid.*, p. 67.
54. *Ibid.*, p. 148. Cf. p. 103.
55. *Ibid.*, p. 155.
56. *Ibid.*, p. 93.
57. *Ibid.*, p. 96.
58. *Ibid.*, p. 97.
59. *Ibid.*, p. 159.
60. *Ibid.*, p. 164.
61. *Ibid.*, p. 323.
62. *Ibid.*, p. 320.
63. *Ibid.*, p. 155. Bakunin specifies the requisites of a moral society more fully to include birth under hygenic conditions, a rational and integral education inculcating respect for work, reason, equality, and liberty, and a social environment in which persons under full liberty will be as fully equal in fact as in principle or law.
64. For this discussion see Karl Marx, *Critique of the Gotha Program* (New York: International Publishers, 1938), esp. pp. 9 *et seq.*
65. In point of fact, and although Marx and Engels were emphatic in contrasting their own scientific socialism to that of the "utopians," precisely by their emphasis on its industrial requisites, it is frequently unclear whether these requisites for (a) a social revolution that could *seize* power from the dominant class, or for (b) a revolution that could serve as the instrument of a transformation toward socialism—that is, a socialist revolution—or (c) whether these industrial requisites were needed only for the *full* and *final* achievement of a *mature* socialism, but which might not be requisite for a social revolution that only *began* to work toward a socialist society. The ambiguities were rife and emerged fully during the conflict over "socialism in one country" in the USSR. For development, see *TTM*, especially Chapter 8, " 'Economic Determinisms' in Marxism."
66. Thomas, *Karl Marx*, pp. 290-92.
67. Maximoff, *Political Philosophy*, p. 375.
68. *Ibid.*

69. *Ibid.*, p. 378.
70. *Ibid.*
71. *Ibid.*, p. 401.
72. *Ibid.*, p. 204.
73. CM. In the *Manifesto*, Marx places both artisan and peasant together with small merchants and manufacturers, in a middle class who "are, therefore not revolutionary, but conservative. Nay more, they are reactionary, for they try to roll back the wheel of history" (pp. 26-27). Most of the contemporary research on the politics of artisans during Marx's own lifetime and during, for example, the revolutions of 1848 sharply repudiates Marx's judgment on them, and most of the major revolutions of even the twentieth century have relied as much, indeed, far more on the peasantry than on the proletariat. It is Bakunin's carefully formulated judgment on the peasants' revolutionary potential, rather than Marx's runaway rhetoric, that has been substantiated.
74. Maximoff, *Political Philosophy*, p. 401.
75. *Ibid.*, p. 394.
76. CM, pp. 16, 19.
77. Maximoff, *Political Philosophy*, p. 194.
78. *Ibid.*, p. 196. Although lauding the bourgeoisie's vast transformation of productivity, Marx would not have disagreed with this. His theory of "increasing misery" claimed that as wealth accumulated at one pole, misery and poverty accumulated at the other among the workers, while the application of science to industry only increased the reserve army of the unemployed. The main difference, then, was not so much with respect to the implications that technical progress had in the *present*, but (1) rather in Marx's emphasis on the *future* that technical progress permitted. It provided, he held, the foundation for socialism in which the benefits of technical advance would then be enjoyed by the masses, and (2) that Bakunin placed far less stress than had Marx on the importance of economic development.
79. *Ibid.*, p. 204.
80. Tucker, *Marx-Engels Reader*, pp. 543-44.
81. Maximoff, *Political Philosophy*, p. 198.
82. *Ibid.*, p. 301.
83. *Ibid.*, p. 370.
84. *Ibid.*, p. 372.
85. *Ibid.*, p. 369. Italics added by A. W. G.
86. *Ibid.*, p. 300.
87. *Ibid.*, p. 409.
88. *Ibid.*, p. 380.
89. *Ibid.*
90. N and M-H, p. 347.
91. Cited in Raymond Postgate, *The Workers' International* (London: Swarthmore Press, 1926), p. 48.
92. Eric J. Hobsbawm, *Primitive Rebels* (New York: Praeger, 1963), pp. 81-82.
93. *Ibid.*, p. 82.

7. *Marx vs. Bakunin: Paradoxes of Socialist Politics*

1. N and M-H, p. 294.
2. Paul Thomas, *Karl Marx and the Anarchists* (London: Routledge and Kegan Paul, 1980), p. 349.

3. L. B. Namier, *1848: The Revolution of the Intellectuals* (Oxford: Oxford University Press, 1944), p. 9. Italics added by A. W. G.
4. Cited in *ibid.*, p. 10.
5. Cited in *ibid.*, p. 11.
6. G. P. Maximoff, ed., *The Political Philosophy of Bakunin: Scientific Anarchism* (New York: Free Press, 1953), pp. 214, 216.
7. Thomas, *Karl Marx*, p. 344.
8. *MEW*, Vol. 28, p. 189.
9. Carmen Claudin-Urondo, *Lenin and the Cultural Revolution* (Atlantic Highlands, N. J.: Humanities Press, 1977), p. 16.
10. David McLellan, ed., *Karl Marx's Selected Writings* (London: Oxford University Press, 1977), p. 594.
11. Cited in Thomas, *Karl Marx*, p. 299.
12. Max Nomad, *Apostles of Revolution* (Boston: Little, Brown, 1939), p. 62.

8. Marx into Marxist:
The Confrontation of Theoretical Resources

1. For example, see L. Althusser, *Essays in Self-Criticism*, trans. Grahame Lock (London: New Left Books, 1976), p. 64.
2. *Ibid.*, p. 106.
3. *Ibid.*, p. 150.
4. Göran Therborn, *Science, Class, and Society: On the Formation of Sociology and Historical Materialism* (London: New Left Books, 1976), pp. 356-57.
5. Nicholas Lobkowicz, *Theory and Practice* (Notre Dame, Ind.: University of Notre Dame Press, 1967), p. 321. A scintillating book.
6. Karl Marx, *A Contribution to the Critique of Political Economy* (New York: International Publishers, 1970), quoted from the introduction by Maurice Dobb.
7. *Ibid.*, p. 6.
8. Ronald L. Meek, *Social Science and the Ignoble Savage* (Cambridge: Cambridge University Press, 1976), pp. 6, 161, 165-66, 173, 176.
9. *Ibid.*, p. 6.
10. *Ibid.*, p. 161.
11. *Ibid.*, pp. 165-66.
12. *Ibid.*, p. 173.
13. *Ibid.*, p. 176.
14. *Ibid.*, p. 225.
15. Roberto Michels, *First Lectures in Political Sociology* (Minneapolis: University of Minnesota Press, 1949).
16. *Ibid.*
17. G. W. F. Hegel, *Philosophy of Right*, trans. T. M. Knox (Oxford: Oxford University Press, 1967), pp. 129-30.
18. *Ibid.*, pp. 226-27.
19. Friedrich Engels, *Ludwig Feuerbach and the Outcome of Classical German Philosophy* (New York: International Publishers, 1941), pp. 369-70.
20. Marx, *Contribution*, p. 20.
21. *CM*, p. 7.

22. In this respect it is notable how great a change Althusser's accounting for
    the origins of Marxism had later undergone. Where, formerly, Althusser
    had referred primarily to certain mysterious forces, the *coupure*, now he ac-
    counts for the emergence of Marxism in a way much more nearly in terms
    of the sociology of knowledge. In part, this strengthens the consistency of
    Althusser's theory for, according to his anti-humanism, Marx could never
    have been the *maker* of Marxism, since "the real stage directors of history
    are the relations of production." Marx, then, could only have been a *medium*
    through which the impersonal structures of history spoke. A Marxism made
    by Marx was not consistent with Althusser's view that history is a process
    without a subject. It was therefore not consistent to have explained Marxism,
    the "most unprecedented event in history," as a *coupure* made by the man,
    Marx. Be that as it may, Althusser now rejects his former analysis of the
    origins of Marxism, no longer stressing its internal sources, and he now
    views them as grounded in certain external and, in particular, political events
    and processes. For Althusser, the origins of Marxism are now no longer
    found in an autonomous epistemological break, nor is it the product of other
    technical theories such as German philosophy or English political economy;
    the latter is now viewed as only the abstract, theoretical reflection of new
    socioeconomic realities. For Althusser today, Marxism's origin is now to be
    found in the fact that Marx took up a new *political* position, which readied
    him for a new philosophical position, on which basis his scientific discovery
    or "break" was made. Yet there is a basic ambiguity here. On the one hand,
    Althusser accounts for the origins of Marxism by referring to certain "prac-
    tical realities," arguing that "it is the [class] political position that occupies
    the determinant place" (Althusser, p. 158), while, on the other hand,
    grounding his account in the stance that Marx had adopted, that is, in his
    political *commitment* (p. 69). Althusser's present account of the origins of
    Marxism is thus a shambles, relying in the first instance on a mirror epis-
    temology—i.e., Marx simply "mirrored" political reality (but why *him*, rather
    than sixty-five others?)—and, in the second instance, stressing the new
    political stance, presumably at the bottom of the chain of events leading to
    Marxism, and this is essentially a *voluntarism*; for this new stance itself is
    ungrounded, and the political stance is made to *precede* a rational justifica-
    tion in theory, the philosophical shift.
23. George Kneller, *The Art and Science of Creativity* (New York: Holt, Rine-
    hart and Winston, 1965).
24. Arthur Koestler, *The Act of Creation* (London: Hutchinson, 1964), pp.
    119-20.
25. *Ibid.*, p. 182.
26. *Ibid.*, p. 201.
27. *Ibid.*, p. 120.
28. *Ibid.*, p. 177.
29. *Ibid.*, p. 230.
30. *Ibid.*, p. 233.
31. *Ibid.*, p. 257.
32. Jerome Bruner, "The Conditions of Creativity," in H. E. Gruber, ed., *Con-
    temporary Approaches to Creative Thinking* (New York: Atherton Press,
    1962), p. 6.

9. *Enslavement: The Metaphoricality of Marxism*

1. Paul M. Sweezy, "Reply," *Monthly Review* (December 1970), p. 17.
2. Serge Mallet, "Bureaucracy and Technocracy in the Socialist Countries," *Socialist Revolution* (May-June 1970), p. 48.
3. I do not use this term as it was first employed by John Gumperz in "Linguistics and Social Interaction in Two Communities," in J. J. Gumperz and Dell Hymes, eds., *The Ethnography of Communication* (Washington, D. C.: American Anthropological Association, 1964), pp. 137-54. Gumperz—and, for that matter, Joshua Fishman—used the term to refer to an alternation of language varieties. What I am concerned with here, however—and "metaphorical switching" seems the proper term for it—entails the switching of a metaphor from one point of application (or topic) to another, and thus entails a certain continuity in referential meaning.
4. I do not limit the "paleosymbolic" to the pre-linguistic level as does Jürgen Habermas, for reasons that cannot be discussed here. Most basically, our view of the paleosymbolic converges with Basil Bernstein's concept of a "restricted" linguistic code and with Lev Semenovich Vygotsky's concept of "inner speech." For more extended discussion, see the Appendix at the end of this chapter.
5. Cf. the distinctions made by P. Greenfield, L. Reich, R. Olver, and J. Hornsby, in P. Adams, ed., *Language in Thinking* (London: Penguin, 1972), pp. 217 *et seq* and pp. 303 *et seq*. Originally published 1966.
6. Thus K. S. Karel remarks: "To find out if a statesman or intellectual is progressive or reactionary, we must look not so much at his professions of faith as at his attitude toward the United States." K. S. Karel, *Guerrillas in Power: The Course of the Cuban Revolution* (New York: Hill and Wang, 1970), p. 55. Such a functional and concrete rule, of course, runs into trouble when one-time enemies achieve *"détente"*; for according to this rule, one must now conclude that China and the USSR, who have accepted détente with the United States, are reactionary.
7. Karl Marx, *Misère de la philosophie* (Paris: Editions Sociales, 1968), p. 121. Published originally in 1846.
8. Dirk J. Struik, ed., *Birth of the Communist Manifesto* (New York: International Publishers, 1971), p. 165.
9. I am indebted to Catherine Gallagher for calling this to my attention and allowing me to read a first draft of the relevant chapter of her dissertation which attends to "the complex and often contradictory relationship between the spokesmen for the anti-slavery movement and the critics of industrial society. A whole tradition of anti-industrial literature and social criticism appropriated the images, the rhetoric, and the tone of the anti-slavery movement. Simultaneously, however, it inherited arguments and rhetorical strategies associated with the advocates of slavery." The point, of course, is that these early critics of industrialism contrasted the "Yorkshire slavery" which they knew intimately, and which, of course, was altogether different from wage-labor today in Western Europe, with a slavery that they usually did not know at first hand, so that the former might well strike them as more horrendous than the latter.
10. Engels, *Herr Eugen Dühring's Revolution in Science (Anti-Dühring)*, trans. Emile Burn (New York: International Publishers, 1935), p. 216.

11. Karl Marx, *Critique of Hegel's "Philosophy of Right"* (Cambridge: Cambridge University Press, 1970), p. 131. Originally published Paris, 1844.

12. L. Feuerbach, *Sammtliche Werke* (Leipzig: O. Wigand, 1883), Vol. II, p. 253.

13. In the pointed formulation of Nicholas Lobkowicz: "In fact, the whole of Hegel's history is nothing but the growing of the One Truth which Christ has sown, which began to sprout at Pentecost, and matures in man's theological thought. And Hegelianism is the ultimate expansion and fruit of Christian faith; it is faith transfigured into rational thought, faith transfigured into philosophy. . . . Philosophy translates religion's symbolism into rational thought." N. Lobkowicz, *Theory and Practice* (Notre Dame, Ind.: University of Notre Dame Press, 1967), p. 181.

14. Marx, *Critique*, p. 32.

15. *Ibid.*, p. 137. Italics added by A. W. G.

16. And this, of course, is much of what Hegel says about the young *Geist* that does not yet know the world as its own creation and remains alienated from it and itself. Looking backward, Hegel's view was an echo of the Pythagorean–Platonic doctrine of reincarnation, and looking forward, it was part of Nietzsche's doctrine of eternal recurrence.

17. George A. Kelly, *Idealism, Politics, and History: Sources of Hegelian Thought* (Cambridge: Cambridge University Press, 1969).

18. Josiah Royce, *Lectures on Modern Idealism* (New Haven: Yale University Press, 1967), pp. 177-78.

19. Even in his 1844 *Critique of Hegel's "Philosophy of Right,"* Marx insisted that, in bourgeois society, there "is not naturally existing poverty but artificially produced poverty" (p. 142). It is needless poverty, then, poverty imposed by society, not nature, that now becomes the enemy; poverty that is not necessary because the available means of production could overcome it, were they not crippled by the present property system and relationships of production.

20. *CM*, p. 55.

21. The italics here are added by A. W. G. to clarify the point at issue.

22. Joseph O'Malley, Editor's Introduction to Marx, *Critique*, p. xxix.

23. Dick Howard, "On Marx's Critical Theory," *Telos* (Fall 1970): 226, 229.

24. To say, as Mao did repeatedly, that "to rebel is justified" and that "trouble-making is revolution," is to voice the anti-patriarchical resentment of sons and unite it with grievances against public authorities.

25. Jürgen Habermas, "Toward a Theory of Communicative Competence," in Hans P. Dreitzel, ed., *Recent Sociology*, No. 2 (London: Macmillan, 1970), p. 125.

10. *Recovery: The Rationality of Marxism, I*

1. Marx, *Capital*, Vol. III, pp. 770-74.

2. *Ibid.*, Vol. I, pp. 72, 75.

3. Cf. Norman Geras, "Marx and the Critique of Political Economy," in Robin Blackburn, ed., *Ideology in Social Science* (London: Fontana/Collins, 1972).

4. Martin Heidegger, *What Is a Thing?*, trans. W. B. Barton, Jr., and Vera

Deutsch (Chicago: Henry Regnery, 1967), pp. 72 *et seq.* Italics added by A. W. G.

5. George C. Iggers, ed., *An Exposition of the Doctrine of Saint-Simon* (Boston: Beacon Press, 1958), p. 114.
6. *Ibid.,* p. 115.
7. *Ibid.,* p. 118.
8. *Ibid.,* p. 131.
9. *Ibid.,* p. 116.
10. *Ibid.,* p. 118.
11. *Ibid.,* p. 129.
12. *Ibid.,* p. 137.
13. Karl Marx, *Value, Price and Profit,* ed. Eleanor Marx Aveling (New York: International Publishers, 1935), p. 61.
14. Marx, *Capital,* Vol. I, p. 650.

11. *Holism: The Rationality of Marxism, II*

1. *GI,* p. 22.
2. David McLellan, ed., *Karl Marx: Selected Writings* (Oxford: Oxford University Press, 1977), pp. 156-58.
3. For further discussion, see *CC,* pp. 99 *et seq.* For detailed development, see also my "Romanticism and Classicism," in *For Sociology,* pp. 323-68.
4. *CM,* p. 28.
5. *Ibid.,* p. 42.
6. From Joseph O'Malley's splendid introduction to Marx, *Critique of Hegel's "Philosophy of Right"* (Cambridge: Cambridge University Press, 1970), p. lviii.
7. *Ibid.,* p. lii.
8. On the character and importance of contest and struggle in the value system of classical antiquity, see *Enter Plato,* Chapter 2, "The Greek Contest System."
9. *CM,* p. 58. Nietzsche made a similar call to struggle but he had a different gladiator-agent; the manifest mythos of the "overman" is his counterpart to Marx's proletarian. More accurately, Nietzsche's overman does not yet exist (as Marx's proletarian did) and Zarathustra is his pre-figuring outrunner; in effect, Zarathustra is a metaphor focusing directly on the special intellectual who will summon and prepare the overman, in contrast with Marx who enshadows the summoning intellectual and focuses instead on the proletariat that he summons.
10. More fully, "the truth is the whole, but the whole is only the essence perfecting itself through its development." Cf. W. Kaufmann, *Hegel: A Reinterpretation* (Garden City, N. Y.: Anchor Books, 1966).
11. *CM,* p. 35.
12. The indisputably classic source of this remains Max Weber's great essay, "Religious Rejections of the World and Their Directions," in H. Gerth and C. Wright Mills, eds., *From Max Weber* (New York: Oxford University Press, 1946).

12. *Dialectic of Recovery and Holism*

1. For detailed discussion and documentation, see CC, especially Chapter 7, "The Moralistics of Talcott Parsons," and particularly pp. 254 *et seq.*

2. For the formulation of the matter and discussion which clearly sees (even if dubiously explaining) the ambiguities in Weber's position, see Jeffrey C. Alexander's *Theoretical Logic in Sociology* (Berkeley: University of California Press, 1982), esp. Vol. I, Pt. II.

3. At the level of the individual person, it would hardly seem necessary to add that an acceptable doctrine of wholeness cannot maintain, in the manner of the Marquis de Sade, that if anything feels good, it cannot be bad. Nor could it maintain that feeling as such—whatever its character—should never be suppressed. Persons cannot be whole except on the condition that their feelings are accessible to them, and these cannot be accessible unless there are some others to whom—under conditions mutually acceptable—they can confide them. Yet this does not mean that any feeling may be expressed publicly at any time, or that persons are entitled to act upon them, as and when they alone choose. There seems little point in escaping the tyrannical state only to fly into the arms of the tyrannical self.

4. For further discussion, see the Introduction to *Future*, the second volume of my trilogy.

5. For further but still preliminary thoughts on this, see my "Politics of the Mind," in *For Sociology*, pp. 82-128.

Index